JOURNEY TO THE CITY

A COMPANION TO THE MIDDLE EAST GALLERIES AT THE PENN MUSEUM

JOURNEY TO THE CITY

A COMPANION TO THE MIDDLE EAST GALLERIES AT THE PENN MUSEUM

Edited by Steve Tinney
and Karen Sonik

 Penn Museum

UNIVERSITY OF PENNSYLVANIA MUSEUM OF ARCHAEOLOGY AND ANTHROPOLOGY

Distributed for the University of Pennsylvania Museum
of Archaeology and Anthropology by the University
of Pennsylvania Press.

Printed in the United States of America on acid-free paper.

Cataloging-in-Publication Data is on file at the Library
of Congress.

ISBN-13: 978-1-931707-14-5
ISBN-10: 1-931707-14-6
eISBN: 1-931707-17-0

Front Cover (top row, left to right): String of beads (30-12-567),
cuneiform tablet (B10000), painted bowl (33-21-116), and bearded
bull's head and shell plaque from a lyre (B17694A-B).

Front Cover (bottom row, left to right): Gold ostrich egg (B16692),
silver drachma (33-62-31), wine jar (69-12-15), and glazed tile
(2001-15-45).

Half-title Page: Frieze of bulls (B15880).

Title Page: Brick with human footprint (B16460), Queen Puabi's
headdress wreath detail (B17710), and foundation figure (B16216).

Back Cover: Plaque of boy with pipe (L-29-301), portrait tile
(NEP20), string of gold and carnelian beads (30-12-562),
and mosaic panel (NEP58).

Contents

1   **The New Middle East Galleries at the Penn Museum**   **1**
Steve Tinney

2   **The Geography and Agriculture of the Middle East**   **17**
Naomi F. Miller and Katherine M. Moore

2S1: How Old Is It?   23
Naomi F. Miller, with contributions from Renata Holod

2S2: Did the Land Always Look Like This?   27
Naomi F. Miller

2S3: The Material Foundation of the Ancient Near East   37
Naomi F. Miller, with contributions from Renata Holod

3   **The First Cities**   **45**
Holly Pittman

3S1: The Uruk Vase   55
Holly Pittman

3S2: Cylinder Seals in the Ancient Near East   61
Holly Pittman

Dedication

Among the philanthropic partners who supported a line of continued "Penn Firsts" in the Middle East, the Hagop Kevorkian Fund stands alone. Hagop Kevorkian's extraordinary support for an Iranian archaeology program in the 1950s funded the Museum's excavations at the site of Hasanlu led by Robert H. Dyson, Jr., and a visiting lectureship. The Penn Museum recognizes, with deepest gratitude, the profound impact of the Hagop Kevorkian Fund's continued support of all aspects of its Middle East program, and the guidance and counsel of Hagop Kevorkian and Ralph Minasian, Kevorkian Fund president from 1992 to 2017.

Above

Archaeologist Robert H. Dyson, Jr. holds the gold bowl on the day of its discovery at Hasanlu in August 1958.

Donor Acknowledgments

The Penn Museum gratefully acknowledges the support of the following supporters of the creation of the Middle East Galleries, opened April 2018, that this volume is companion to, or to the extended research work in the Middle East that the galleries display.

Naming Donors
Selz Foundation
William B. Dietrich Foundation

Support of Middle East Publications
The Hagop Kevorkian Fund, in honor of Ralph Minasian

Support of the Textile Display
The Coby Foundation

Leadership Support
Anonymous (1)

Meredith Dwyer Burke and Arthur J. Burke, C89, W89

Joanne H. Conrad, C79, PAR12, and William L. Conrad, PAR12

Alice L. George, Ph.D., GGS96

Peter G. Gould, Ph.D., LPS10, and Robin M. Potter, WG80/ PoGo Family Foundation

In memory of Sally Dreyfus Kalish, CW60, Athlete/Scholar

Janet S. Klein, ED51, and Lew Klein, C49

Kowalski Family Foundation

Macquarie Holdings, Inc.

Elizabeth Ray McLean, C78

Andrew Moelis, C10

National Endowment for the Humanities

The Pew Center for Arts & Heritage

Gretchen P. Riley, CW70, PAR00, PAR04, and J. Barton Riley, W70, PAR00, PAR04

John Richard Rockwell, W64, WG66, PAR00

Jeannette and Jonathan Rosen

Kathryn and Sanford M. Sorkin, W67

Jill Topkis Weiss, C89, WG93, PAR19, and Jeffrey L. Weiss, PAR19

Charles K. Williams, II, Ph.D., GR78, HON87

Left
Bearded bull's head
from a lyre (B17694B).

Opposite
Obsidian bowl (35-10-287)
from Tepe Gawra.

Director's Preface

Over millennia, we as humans have gone through a number of fundamental transformations. That from hunter-gatherer to farmer was probably the most dramatic and far-reaching in human history. This is the transformation that the Penn Museum's Middle East Galleries explore: the story of how ancient peoples abandoned ways of life thousands of years old to stay in the same place year-round.

The story of this geographic region and network of ancient civilizations is one that has resonance to all of us. Ten thousand years ago, in the fertile crescent of the Middle East, one of the most transformative points in our human history was set in motion: the domestication of plants and animals prompted the shift from hunting and gathering to farming, establishing the first settled societies. Villages developed, then towns, then the world's first cities. The decision of ancient Mesopotamian peoples to stay in one place dramatically sped up human innovation—writing and mathematics developed for record-keeping, irrigation for farming, construction techniques for more and more buildings, metallurgy and pottery for tools and domestic items. It also introduced many of the issues of human societies that we continue to address today, like social inequality, warfare, and poverty.

This is one of the most pivotal parts of the human story. We often look at the Industrial Revolution as the turning point in human history, when a much earlier, equally important shift happens in the Neolithic Period—which is when the Middle East Galleries begin their story. The next several thousand years, which the Middle East Galleries illuminate in great detail, are essential to understanding our contemporary society—more specifically, to understanding how we became city dwellers. This understanding is particularly relevant as more and more people come to live in cities each year.

The story of how our modern urbanized world can be traced to developments in ancient Mesopotamian societies is one the Penn Museum can tell uniquely well. In fact, the Museum was founded to house artifacts from the first U.S.-led expedition to Nippur (in modern-day Iraq) in 1889. Penn archaeologists went on to excavate an unparalleled constellation of dozens of sites in the region, unearthing objects that illuminate ways of life thousands of years old that still resonate with us today. More than 95% of the artifacts on display in the Middle East Galleries were excavated by Penn archaeologists, which means that we have the unique advantage of displaying these objects in the full context of their excavation records. The Galleries share crucial details about who made and used them, bringing ancient civilizations to life.

Many of these objects are among our finest not just from the region but from anywhere in the world. They are masterpieces of craftsmanship and artistry, like the evocative "Ram in the Thicket" statuette (p. 207), for instance, and delicate obsidian bowl (seen below). Alongside these masterpieces are everyday objects remarkable in their ability to bridge the millennia—to conjure the daily lives of ancient people who lived thousands of year ago. Visitors are greeted at the gallery entrance by a brick containing a single footprint left by a worker in the city of Ur 4,000 years ago (p. ii). One of the world's oldest wine jars (p. 1) is among the first objects encountered after that introduction. Children's toys, receipts of sale, farming implements, sewer pipes, household dishes—all of these are found throughout the Galleries, and in this volume.

We invite our visitors to the Middle East Galleries to make connections with these ancient peoples through their objects showcased right here in the Museum. And we extend that invitation, through this book, to you. I hope that you will enjoy engaging with these fascinating artifacts and their stories as much as I do.

JULIAN SIGGERS, PH.D.
WILLIAMS DIRECTOR

Acknowledgments

In addition to the authors in this volume who served as the curators and content experts for the new Middle East Galleries at the Penn Museum, a number of other people were instrumental in facilitating the exhibition and, more specifically, bringing this companion volume to fruition.

The exhibition project benefited from the overall project management of Dan Rahimi, Executive Director of Galleries, and his full-time, dedicated assistant Laura Iwanyk, Kevorkian Project Coordinator for the Middle East Galleries.

The Penn Museum's collections staff provided access to and processed more than 1,200 objects for the exhibition. These included Katy Blanchard, Fowler/Van Santvoord Keeper of the Near Eastern Collections, Phil Jones, Associate Curator and Keeper of the Babylonian Collections, Lynn Makowsky, DeVries Keeper of the Mediterranean Collections, and Steve Lang, Lyons Keeper of the Asian Collections.

The Museum's Conservation Department, led by Head Conservator Lynn Grant, reviewed all the objects and treated most of them. Tessa de Alarcon and Jessica Byler were the dedicated Middle East Galleries Project Conservators, but they were assisted at times by their colleagues (Julia Lawson, Nina Owczarek, Molly Gleeson, and Alexis North) as well as by a number of part-time assistants (Stephanie Carrato, Erin Fitterer, Marci Jefcoat Burton, Jennifer Mikes, Anna O'Neill, Alyssa Rina, Jonathan Stevens, Celine Wachsmuth, and Tessa Young).

Penn Museum research and collections-based archival and documentation assistance was provided by the Museum Archives, led by Senior Archivist Alex Pezzati, and the Registrar's Office, led by Senior Registrar Xiuqin Zhou with record and database facilitation by Registrar for Records Chrisso Boulis and Database Administrator Danni Peters.

During the gallery installation, the Registrar's Office dedicated significant staff time to install objects. Special Projects Manager Robert Thurlow led the object installation with major contributions from Registrar for Loans Anne Brancati and Associate Registrar Celina Candrella.

In preparation for the companion volume, hundreds of objects were photographed by the Museum's Photo Studio thanks to the work of Photographers Francine Sarin and Jennifer Chiappardi and then catalogued by Assistant Archivist Eric Schnittke.

The initial manuscript for this companion volume was compiled by Deputy Director Steve Tinney, who also coordinated its internal review amongst the authors. The Museum then brought in Karen Sonik, Assistant Professor of Art and Art History at Auburn University, to edit the manuscript in preparation for submission to Penn Museum Publications. One of the authors, Grant Frame, would explicitly like to thank Christa Müller-Kessler and Matthew W. Stolper for their consultation during the writing and editing process.

Upon submission to the Publications Department, the manuscript was further copyedited by Editor Page Selinsky, who also compiled the list of more than 400 images that were requested and began the process of seeking the necessary permissions for those from outside sources. In some instances, artwork was commissioned to be drawn or redrawn from original sources. This work was mostly handled by Museum Illustrator Ardeth Anderson. The design of the volume and additional illustrative work was undertaken by Graphic Designer Matthew Todd. Finally, Jim Mathieu, Head of Collections, Publications, and Digital Media, managed the overall compilation and production of the volume.

My thanks to all who helped bring this project to fruition!

JULIAN SIGGERS, PH.D.
WILLIAMS DIRECTOR

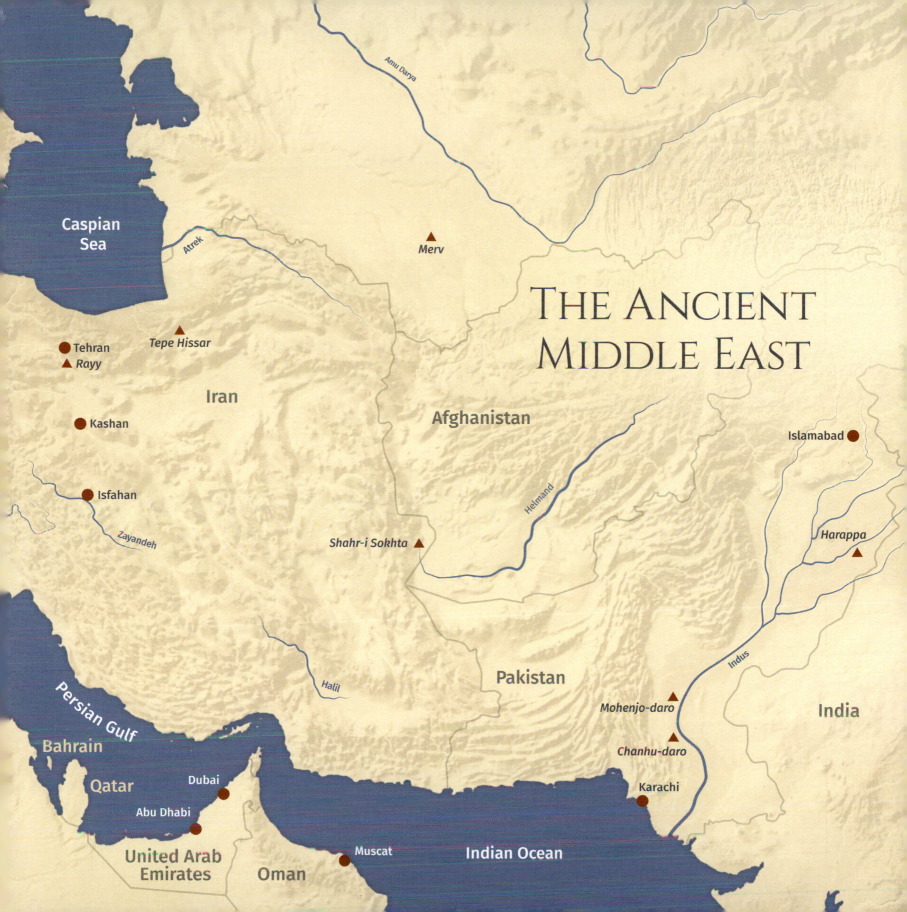

Timeline of Key Periods and Developments

■ Neolithic Period
(ca. 10,000–3000 BCE)

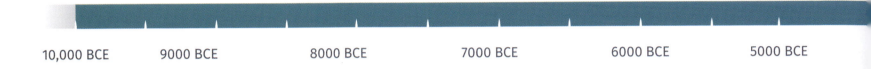

| 10,000 BCE | 9000 BCE | 8000 BCE | 7000 BCE | 6000 BCE | 5000 BCE |

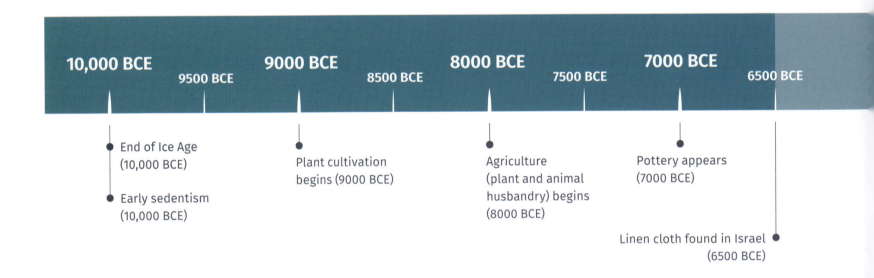

10,000 BCE   9500 BCE   **9000 BCE**   8500 BCE   **8000 BCE**   7500 BCE   **7000 BCE**   6500 BCE

- End of Ice Age (10,000 BCE)
- Early sedentism (10,000 BCE)
- Plant cultivation begins (9000 BCE)
- Agriculture (plant and animal husbandry) begins (8000 BCE)
- Pottery appears (7000 BCE)
- Linen cloth found in Israel (6500 BCE)

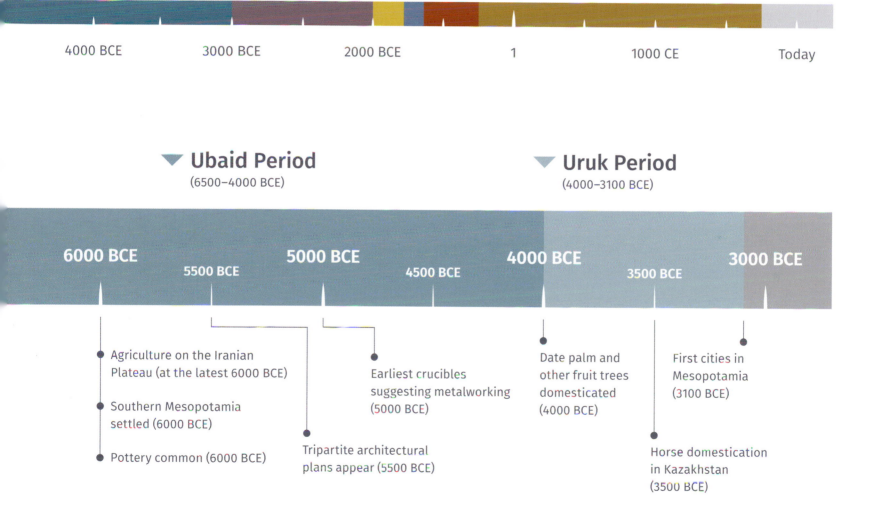

4000 BCE   3000 BCE   2000 BCE   1   1000 CE   Today

▼ Ubaid Period
(6500–4000 BCE)

▼ Uruk Period
(4000–3100 BCE)

6000 BCE   5500 BCE   5000 BCE   4500 BCE   4000 BCE   3500 BCE   3000 BCE

Agriculture on the Iranian
Plateau (at the latest 6000 BCE)

Southern Mesopotamia
settled (6000 BCE)

Pottery common (6000 BCE)

Tripartite architectural
plans appear (5500 BCE)

Earliest crucibles
suggesting metalworking
(5000 BCE)

Date palm and
other fruit trees
domesticated
(4000 BCE)

Horse domestication
in Kazakhstan
(3500 BCE)

First cities in
Mesopotamia
(3100 BCE)

Timeline of Key Periods and Developments

■ Early Bronze Age
(3000–2000 BCE)

10,000 BCE	9000 BCE	8000 BCE	7000 BCE	6000 BCE	5000 BCE

▼ Jemdet Nasr Period
(3100–2900 BCE)

3000 BCE	2900 BCE	2800 BCE	2700 BCE	2600 BCE	2500 BCE

▲ **Early Dynastic Period**
(2900–2334 BCE)

▲ **Early Dynastic III Period**
(2600–2334 BCE)

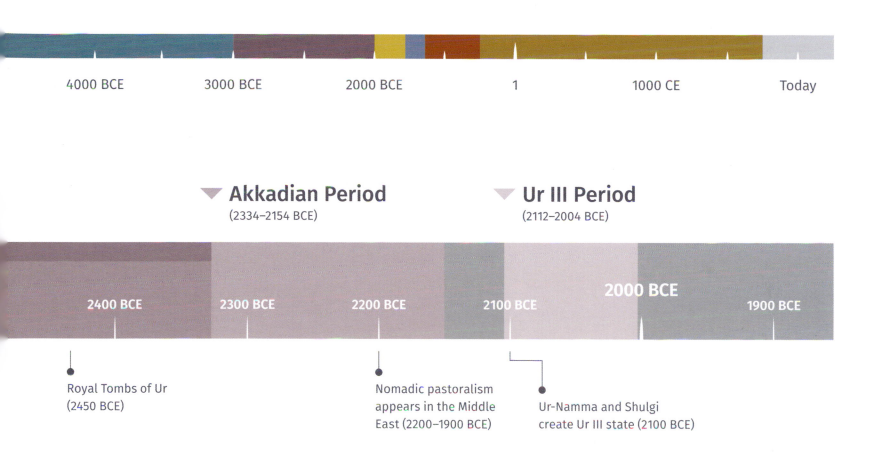

4000 BCE 3000 BCE 2000 BCE 1 1000 CE Today

▼ **Akkadian Period**
(2334–2154 BCE)

▼ **Ur III Period**
(2112–2004 BCE)

2400 BCE 2300 BCE 2200 BCE 2100 BCE **2000 BCE** 1900 BCE

Royal Tombs of Ur
(2450 BCE)

Nomadic pastoralism
appears in the Middle
East (2200–1900 BCE)

Ur-Namma and Shulgi
create Ur III state (2100 BCE)

Timeline of Key Periods and Developments

■ Middle Bronze Age
(2000–1600 BCE)

10,000 BCE   9000 BCE   8000 BCE   7000 BCE   6000 BCE   5000 BCE

▼ Isin-Larsa and Old Babylonian Periods
(2000–1595 BCE)

2000 BCE   1950 BCE   1900 BCE   1850 BCE   1800 BCE

▲ Old Assyrian Period
(1900–1600 BCE)

4000 BCE   3000 BCE   2000 BCE   1   1000 CE   Today

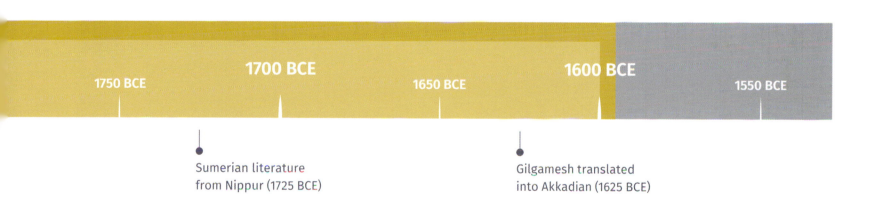

1750 BCE   **1700 BCE**   1650 BCE   **1600 BCE**   1550 BCE

Sumerian literature
from Nippur (1725 BCE)

Gilgamesh translated
into Akkadian (1625 BCE)

Timeline of Key Periods and Developments

Late Bronze Age
(1600–1200 BCE)

10,000 BCE   9000 BCE   8000 BCE   7000 BCE   6000 BCE   5000 BCE

▼ Kassite Period
(1595–1155 BCE)

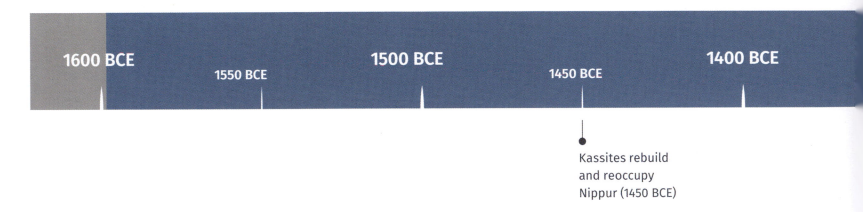

1600 BCE   1550 BCE   **1500 BCE**   1450 BCE   **1400 BCE**

Kassites rebuild
and reoccupy
Nippur (1450 BCE)

4000 BCE   3000 BCE   2000 BCE   1   1000 CE   Today

1350 BCE   **1300 BCE**   1250 BCE   **1200 BCE**   1150 BCE

Resurgence of Babylon
and Assur (1150 BCE)

Timeline of Key Periods and Developments

 **Iron Age**
(1200–500 BCE)

10,000 BCE   9000 BCE   8000 BCE   7000 BCE   6000 BCE   5000 BCE

 **Neo-Assyrian Period**
(911–612 BCE)

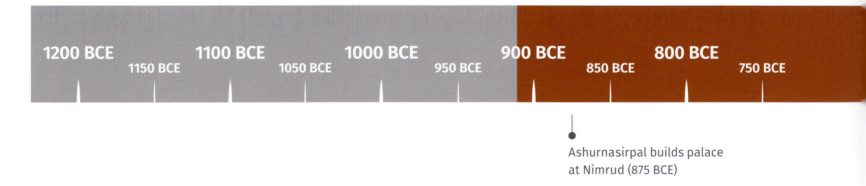

1200 BCE   1150 BCE   **1100 BCE**   1050 BCE   **1000 BCE**   950 BCE   **900 BCE**   850 BCE   **800 BCE**   750 BCE

Ashurnasirpal builds palace
at Nimrud (875 BCE)

4000 BCE 3000 BCE 2000 BCE 1 1000 CE Today

▼ **Neo-Babylonian Period**
(626–539 BCE)

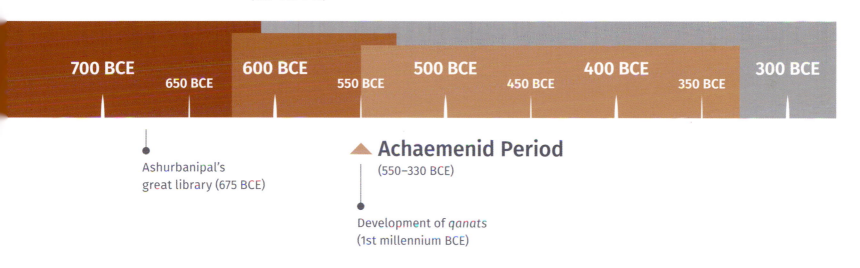

700 BCE 650 BCE 600 BCE 550 BCE 500 BCE 450 BCE 400 BCE 350 BCE 300 BCE

▲ **Achaemenid Period**
(550–330 BCE)

Ashurbanipal's
great library (675 BCE)

Development of *qanats*
(1st millennium BCE)

Timeline of Key Periods and Developments

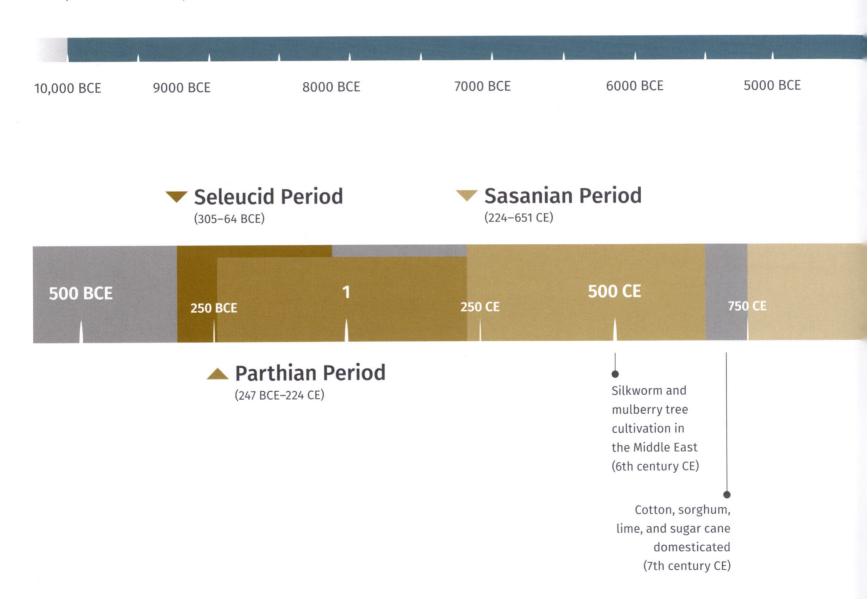

Post Iron Age
(500 BCE–1722 CE)

10,000 BCE   9000 BCE   8000 BCE   7000 BCE   6000 BCE   5000 BCE

Seleucid Period
(305–64 BCE)

Sasanian Period
(224–651 CE)

500 BCE   250 BCE   1   250 CE   500 CE   750 CE

Parthian Period
(247 BCE–224 CE)

Silkworm and mulberry tree cultivation in the Middle East (6th century CE)

Cotton, sorghum, lime, and sugar cane domesticated (7th century CE)

4000 BCE   3000 BCE   2000 BCE   1   1000 CE   Today

▼ **Abbasid Period**
   (750–1258 CE)

1000 CE   1250 CE   **1500 CE**   1750 CE   **Today**

▲ **Safavid Period**
   (1501–1722 CE)

1

The New Middle East Galleries at the Penn Museum

Steve Tinney

Opposite
Found at Hajji Firuz Tepe (Iran), this is one of the oldest wine jars (69-12-15) in the world, dating to ca. 5400–5000 BCE. It contained traces of grape residue and tree resin suggesting a retsina-type wine.

Introduction

The Penn Museum's signature Middle East Galleries, which opened April 21, 2018, are the outcome of a unique development process involving contributions from a large and diverse team of experts and professionals. This companion volume, in addition to highlighting the most remarkable and interesting objects in the Museum's extraordinary Middle East collections, illuminates the primary themes within these galleries and provides a larger context within which to understand them.

The core team involved in shaping the vision for the galleries includes no fewer than ten curators and subject experts in anthropology, archaeology, art history, history, and philology, who specialize in periods spanning the history of the Middle East from its earliest settlement to the breaking up of the Ottoman Empire. Grant Frame, William Hafford, Renata Holod, Philip Jones, Naomi Miller, Holly Pittman, Lauren Ristvet, Brian Spooner, Steve Tinney, and Richard L. Zettler met regularly for over a year to develop a curatorial brief that encapsulated their goals for the galleries. Following the selection of Haley Sharpe Design and Tim Gardom Associates for the project design and interpretation, more than eighteen months of work went into translating the curatorial vision into the galleries now open to the public. This phase of the work involved many of the Penn Museum's own professionals: Jess Bicknell, Katy Blanchard, Tessa de Alarcon Martin, Lynn Grant, Laura Iwanyk, Ellen Owens, and Kate Quinn. It was also ably assisted by current or former Penn students Anastasia Amrheim, Katherine Burge, Julia Chatterjee, and Michael Falcetano, as well as Desirée Annis.

The development of the galleries was anchored in several key points of agreement. The first was that we would build the exhibits around the great strengths of our collections, the magnificent finds discovered during the Museum's many archaeological expeditions to the Middle East, especially to the regions of modern-day Iraq and Iran, from the late 19th century onwards. Expeditions to ancient sites such as Ur, Nippur, Rayy, Gawra, Tepe Hissar, Tureng Tepe, and Hasanlu, amongst others, gave rise to the Museum's collection of more than 70,000 objects from the Middle East (see Appendix: Timeline of Penn Museum Excavations in Iraq and Iran). These objects were assigned to the Museum under the system of *partage*, the division of excavated artifacts between the excavators of a site and the host governments. Importantly, the majority of the Penn Museum's excavations were carried out with careful attention to the contexts within which artifacts were discovered; this enabled archaeologists to situate the objects found within the daily lives of the people who created and used them.

The second point of agreement was that, while the galleries would be organized chronologically, they would also be developed to explore the phenomena of urbanization and urban living. The first cities in the world, after all, arose in the region of present-day Iraq in the late 4th millennium BCE. The process of urbanization, and the establishment

Fig. 1.1 *Opposite*
Shown as mounted in the Middle East Galleries, this tablet (B6164) from Fara (Iraq) is a contract in early cuneiform writing dating to ca. 2600 BCE that concerns the purchase of a house for silver.

of urban lifeways, are the touchstones of these galleries, which begin with the establishment of the earliest agricultural villages in the Middle East around 6000 BCE and continue up to the rise of the great metropolises of the Islamic world. Importantly, the galleries do not end here, but go on to examine urbanization within more recent contexts through a presentation of ethnographic materials dating from the late nineteenth and early twentieth centuries. We end our journey through the galleries in the present, with an exploration of the continuities in urban life from its ancient to its modern contexts, and a consideration of where the Penn Museum itself is situated: contemporary Philadelphia.

In addition to the organizing principles outlined above, five fundamental themes informed the design, and are threaded through the final presentation of the galleries. While we chose not to make these themes explicit in the exhibits, we encourage both visitor and reader to bear them in mind as they read through this volume and explore the exhibits in the galleries. The people in our story **make:** the development of new technologies and processes has the potential to profoundly alter how individuals live and what groups of people working together can achieve. They **settle:** they occupy specific landscapes and environments, which are fundamental to how (and where) communities are established; design buildings, neighborhoods, and public spaces; and develop systems to support their ways of life. They **connect:** trade and conflict, often in search of land and materials, may bring even widely dispersed or very distant groups into contact. They **organize:** recording and sharing information is essential for the assertion of power and support of complex, shared activities. Systems of administration and laws, and the rise of an educated elite to manage and perpetuate these, may extend the reach of a ruler over vast distances and penetrate every level of a society. They **believe:** personal and communal religious and funerary beliefs, a common understanding of power and hierarchy, and shared myths and stories play an essential role in defining individual and group identities.

The Organization of the Companion Volume

Although this volume serves as a companion to the Middle East Galleries, it has been organized with an eye to the reader rather than the gallery visitor. The volume is divided into chapters, each with its own specially designed "spreads" or focused texts that are written from the personal perspectives of the curators and experts who developed the galleries. In addition to showcasing the breadth and depth of the Museum's exceptional collections from the Middle East and testifying to the region's critical contributions to the development of our contemporary global culture, these chapters and spreads are intended to orient the reader to the general Middle Eastern context before diving more richly into the content that informed the galleries. As such, the reader will notice a broader

continued on page 14

Fig. 1.2 *Opposite*
Caught in an eternal worshipful pose, this offering statue (37-15-31) from Khafaje (Iraq) that dates to ca. 2475–2300 BCE is shown on display in the galleries.

Overleaf

Fig. 1.3
Three panoramas of the Middle East Galleries. The first shows Room 1, covering villages to the first cities (center and right), the many different kinds of offerings made in temples (left) and the contrast between lowland Mesopotamia and Highland Iran (center left).

Fig. 1.4
The next shows Room 2, where visitors leave the ceramic and metal crafts of the Highlands behind (background) and encounter an animated journey through Ur that ends with King Shulgi (2094–2047 BCE) making an evening offering to the moon-god, Nanna on top of Ur's Ziggurat.

Fig. 1.5
The third panorama shows the corner across from the animated journey in Room 2. Trade is the focus here, and the widespread origins of raw materials and worked goods in metal and stone that were the key to Ur's riches and power in the 3rd millennium BCE. These riches were used by Ur's elites in peaceful and wartime pursuits.

FIRST GLOBAL TRADING NETWORK

"Enki gave foreign trade to the merchants. He brought the boats..."

Southern Mesopotamia had rich soil and abundant water but few other natural resources. Raw materials and high-quality finished goods were acquired from the neighboring Anatolian and Iranian Plateaus as well as from the Oman Peninsula and Harappan centers in the Indus River valley. Improved land transportation allowed complex trading networks to develop.

Precious stones, metals, exotic goods, and animals travelled thousands of miles to reach Mesopotamian elites at Ur and other cities. People travelled along with commodities, bringing new ideas and technologies.

TRADE ROUTES IN 3RD MILLENNIUM

ANATOLIA AND SYRIA

PERSIAN GULF

CITY ELITES

City elites became increasingly
complex over the course of the third millennium
BCE. Most people continued to farm and herd,
but some expanded their specialized skills,
and new elite groups emerged in the cities.

The king ruled the city, ensuring the welfare of
the people in his role as warrior, priest, and builder
below him was the queen, who had her own estate,
followed by the extended royal family, trusted nobles,
soldiers, priests, and administrators.

THE STANDARD OF UR

FEASTING

FIGHTING

THE TEMPLE:
MOORING POST
OF HEAVEN

perspective presented in the opening chapters of the volume, followed by a shift to more detailed and focused chapters in the latter half of the volume. Throughout the volume, the spreads serve to provide richer detail to those interested in particular topics, without requiring too much digression in the primary chapters.

In Chapter 2, archaeobotanist Naomi F. Miller and zooarchaeologist Katherine M. Moore introduce the physical geography of the Middle East from ancient to medieval times. They also examine the ways in which plant and animal domestication spread across the region and how they both shaped and were shaped by local landscapes in periods preceding and subsequent to urbanization.

In Chapter 3, art historian Holly Pittman, explores the rise of the first cities in Mesopotamia's southern plains. She focuses especially on the numerous subsistence, technological, architectural, administrative, economic, and social developments that accompanied urbanization in the ancient Near East, with an emphasis on the rise of the household as organizing unit.

In Chapter 4, philologist Steve Tinney, with contributions from philologist Philip Jones and archaeologist William B. Hafford, focuses on religion and the gods and discusses the polytheistic religious system of Mesopotamia, with an emphasis on key deities and rituals, the construction of temples and sites of worship, and the great written myths of the region.

In Chapter 5, Holly Pittman, with contributions from William B. Hafford, shifts the view from the cities of Mesopotamia's alluvium, discussed in Chapter 3, to the highland regions of the east that yield the natural resources on which Mesopotamia's cities were dependent. They explore the establishment of overland and maritime trading routes between Mesopotamia and the east up to the turn of the 3rd millennium BCE, and the types of raw materials extracted and finished goods exported from the east.

Looking at the spaces between cities, Chapter 6 by archaeologist Lauren Ristvet examines the role of Nomads in the Middle East. She demonstrates the ways in which nomadic and settled life were intertwined in the ancient Near East, and the symbiotic as well as sometimes adversarial relationships that developed between nomads and city-dwellers in the region.

In Chapters 7 and 8, written by archaeologist William B. Hafford, attention returns to Mesopotamia and to the cities of the 3rd millennium BCE. The Near Eastern city as it developed between 2100 and 500 BCE is the topic of Chapter 7, with a focus on the architecture of daily life from domestic housing and urban layouts to places of burial and worship. Hafford also examines the economic, legal, and administrative life of the city, with a contribution by Philip Jones on education in ancient Mesopotamia.

Chapter 8 begins a closer look at specialized case-studies with an emphasis on life and death in the city of Ur. Hafford discusses the extraordinary Royal Cemetery of Ur, which in the 1920s and 1930s gained worldwide fame for the fabulous nature of

Fig. 1.6 *Opposite*
Gallery case showing beautiful decorative elements from the early Sumerian temple at Tell al-`Ubaid (ca. 2400 BCE).

the burial goods discovered there, as well as for the evidence it yielded for the practice of human sacrifice at the death of deceased rulers of the mid-3rd millennium BCE.

In Chapter 9, archaeologist Lauren Ristvet returns to present a granular approach to life—and death—in Hasanlu, an ordinary town in Iran that was attacked and destroyed by fire. She examines the mystery of Hasanlu's destruction at the end of the 9th century BCE, considering the archaeological and other evidence for the identity of the town's attackers and reconstructing in vivid detail the brutal violence of the last day of Hasanlu. The emphasis in this chapter on a town and its inhabitants rather than on the larger cities that are the primary focus of the volume permits an intimate exploration of lives as they unfolded in one of the other (smaller) types of permanent settlement that dotted the ancient Near East.

In Chapter 10, archaeologists Richard L. Zettler and William B. Hafford, with contributions by philologists Philip Jones and Grant Frame, explore the status of the city of Nippur under imperial rule (1000 BCE to 800 CE): it considers Nippur's place within the Neo-Assyrian, Neo-Babylonian, Achaemenid, Seleucid, Parthian, and Sasanian empires through to its decline in the early Islamic Period and abandonment during the time of the Abbasids (ca. 750 CE).

In Chapter 11, art historian and archaeologist Renata Holod, with contributions by social anthropologist Brian Spooner, and Michael Falcetano, explores the medieval and Early Modern Islamic and Persianate city through the case studies of Rayy and Isfahan, considering the new technologies, global interactions, and new ways of seeing and viewing that developed in the great urban centers of the Islamic world.

In Chapter 12, Lauren Ristvet is joined by the Penn Museum's Interpretive Planning Manager Jessica Bicknell and Merle-Smith Director of Learning Programs Ellen Owens to explore the relationships and continuities between urban centers and ways of life in the ancient world and those familiar to us in the present day.

Finally, in Chapter 13, social anthropologist Brian Spooner offers some reflections on the overarching trajectory of the galleries, the expansion of trade and the growth of globalization.

We hope the readers of these pages and visitors to the Penn Museum alike will relish the diverse approaches to and experiences of the journey to the city evinced in this volume and in the new Middle East Galleries.

Fig. 1.7 *Opposite*
Close-up of the superbly worked and detailed head of the sage-figure (*apkallu*) on the Assyrian relief (29-21-1) from Nimrud (Iraq), dating to ca. 883–859 BCE.

2

THE GEOGRAPHY AND AGRICULTURE OF THE MIDDLE EAST

Naomi F. Miller and Katherine M. Moore

Opposite
This clay tablet from Nippur (B13885)
dates to about 1500 BCE. It illustrates
a canal system that may have been used
for both irrigation and transportation.

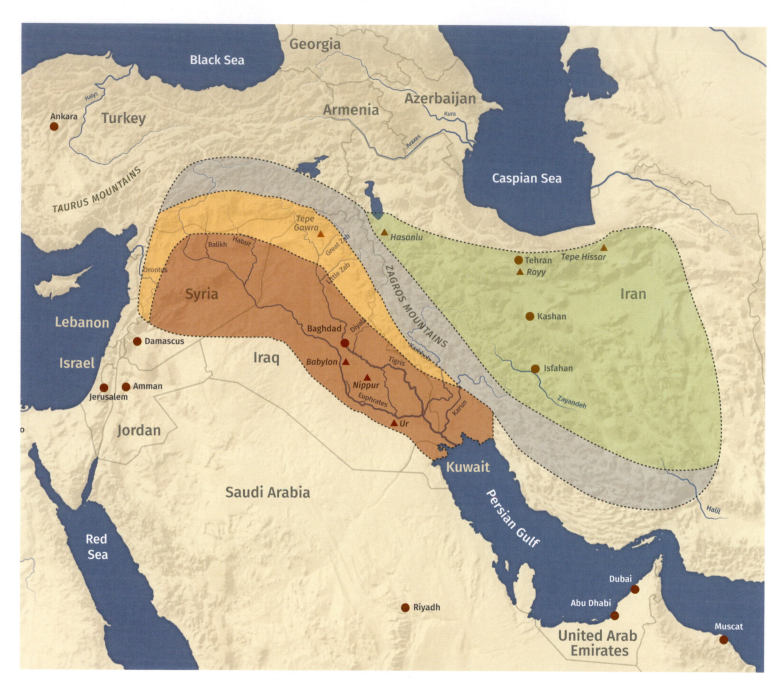

MAP KEY

Lowlands   Piedmont   Mountains   Iranian Plateau

Introduction

The core of the Middle East, the modern term for a region known in ancient and medieval contexts as the Near East, encompasses present-day Iraq, Iran, Syria, and southeastern Turkey. Most of this region experiences a Mediterranean-influenced climate, with cool or cold, wet winters and hot, dry summers. This climate pattern, despite some fluctuation, was established by the end of the Ice Age (10,000 BCE).

In this chapter, the geography and agricultural potential of this region are discussed. The region is divided into four major zones distinguished by long-standing natural and cultural features: (1) a mountainous arc formed by the Taurus and Zagros Mountains; (2) a rolling piedmont zone; (3) the flat lowlands of Mesopotamia; and (4) the Iranian Plateau, which supports both harsh desert and fertile uplands. The maps (Figs. 2.1, 2.2, 2.3) included in this chapter show the relationship between topography, precipitation, and vegetation.

The people of the ancient Near East adapted their lifestyle to existing environmental conditions, but they also changed the landscape in which they lived. By about 10,000 BCE, even before they began to cultivate plants and keep herds, communities in parts of the Near East began to live year-round or nearly year-round in small settlements. These small sedentary communities developed ways of preserving and storing foods from wild plants and animals. While excavating such settlements, archaeologists have found storage pits dug into the ground as well as traces of round stone structures, some residential and some ritual.

There is ongoing debate about the degree to which any period of drought or climate amelioration affected cultural trends and historical events, but agriculture began in about 8000 BCE under conditions favorable for plant cultivation and animal husbandry and became established by about 6000 BCE. Pottery containers made of fired clay first appeared around 7000 BCE and came into common use by about 6000 BCE. Populations grew as agriculture and related technologies became widespread, and human activity played an increasing role in shaping the land. Over millennia, fuel-intensive technologies such as pottery production and metallurgy had an even larger impact on both the vegetation and the land.

Innovations in Agriculture and Animal Husbandry

The area comprising the lowlands of Iraq and the surrounding piedmont of the Taurus-Zagros arc is known as the Fertile Crescent. The piedmont zone, with a natural vegetation cover of grassland and open woodland, saw the earliest experiments in plant cultivation and animal herding (Fig. 2.4). Favored with precipitation exceeding 250 millimeters (10 inches) per year, it is possible to farm here without supplemental irrigation.

Fig. 2.1 *Opposite*
Topographic map showing the four main geographical zones discussed in this chapter: the lowlands, piedmont, mountains, and Iranian Plateau.

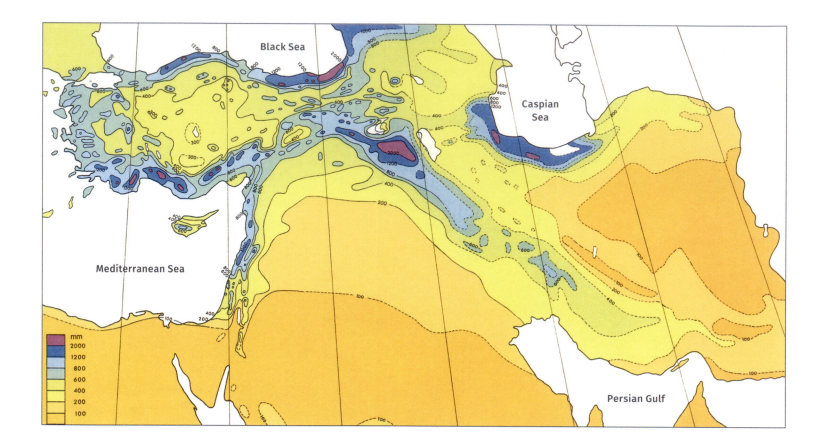

The first farmers began to cultivate locally available plants: wild cereals, like einkorn wheat, emmer wheat, and barley; wild legumes, like lentil, chickpea, pea, and bitter vetch; and wild flax, grown initially for fiber. The ancestors of the earliest domesticated food animals—sheep, goat, cattle, and pig—are native to this part of the world, too. Additionally, dogs had long accompanied the hunting and foraging peoples of the ancient Near East as companions and work animals.

These wild ancestors of the earliest domesticated plants and animals thrived over much of the Near East, especially in the piedmont zone. But not all species occurred in any one place, and it took about a thousand years for the different pieces of the Middle Eastern farming system to come together. Once established in the piedmont zone, agriculture spread to the lowlands of the Tigris and Euphrates River Valleys, the region archaeologists call Mesopotamia.

The first settlers in southern Mesopotamia (ca. 6000 BCE) encountered marshland inhabited by fish and migratory birds at the head of the Persian Gulf, as well as lowland steppe with rich winter pasture located away from the sea (Figs. 2.5, 2.6).

continued on page 25

Fig. 2.2 *Above*
Precipitation map. Rainfall is strongly influenced by elevation. After Zohary 1973: map 5.

Fig. 2.3 *Opposite*
Vegetation map of the Middle East. Forests and woodlands grow in moister regions. The Iranian and Anatolian Plateaus, which lie in the rain shadows of the coastal and Zagros Mountains, are mostly arid. Adapted by N. F. Miller and M. A. Pouls from Zohary 1973: map 7. Redrawn by Ardeth Anderson.

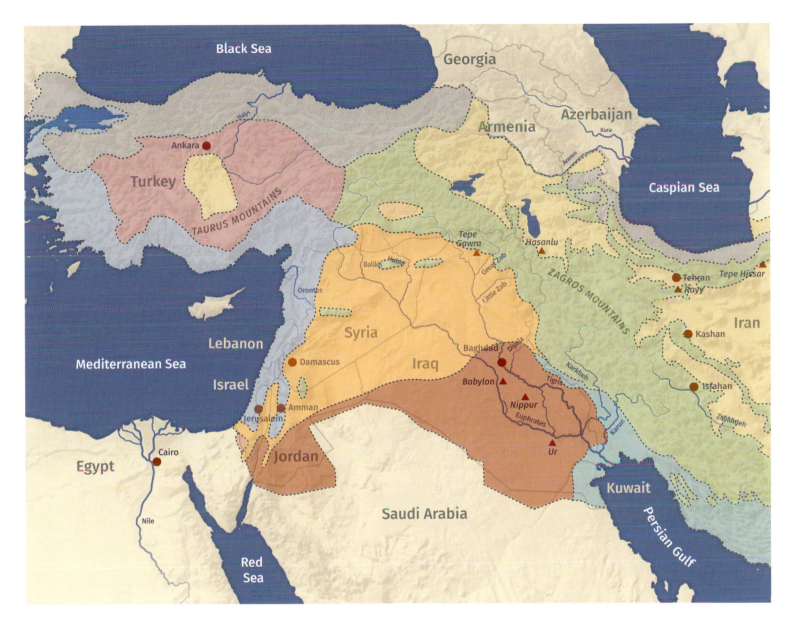

Map Key

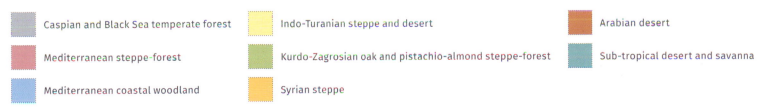

Caspian and Black Sea temperate forest

Mediterranean steppe-forest

Mediterranean coastal woodland

Indo-Turanian steppe and desert

Kurdo-Zagrosian oak and pistachio-almond steppe-forest

Syrian steppe

Arabian desert

Sub-tropical desert and savanna

How Old Is It?

Naomi F. Miller, with contributions from Renata Holod

There are many ways of determining the relative and absolute dates of archaeological sites, deposits, and objects. The techniques described here yield dates of varying degrees of precision.

The Three-Age System

The division of early human history into the Stone, Bronze, and Iron Ages, was proposed in the 19th century by Danish archaeologist Christian Thomsen as a way of organizing European archaeological artifacts for museum display. In excavated deposits, iron tools were found closer to the surface than bronze tools, which were in turn found above stone tools. By inference, the Stone Age was the oldest, followed by the Bronze Age, and the Iron Age was the most recent. Archaeologists no longer use these terms as strict chronological markers. Rather, the Stone, Bronze, and Iron Ages are used as a shorthand to refer to periods roughly defined by a group of related subsistence practices, technologies, and organizational traits, especially as the timing of transition between them varies regionally. For the ancient Near East, the Stone Age is generally associated with societies dependent on wild foods and the first farming societies; the Bronze Age is associated with early literate civilizations and the first expansive political entities of the 3rd and 2nd millennia BCE; and the Iron Age is associated with the later literate civilizations and empires of the 1st millennium BCE.

Relative Dating

Relative dating can determine whether one deposit or object is earlier than another, but by itself does not give a calendar date.

Stratigraphy

Many Middle Eastern archaeological sites are mounds, which were created as people built, tore down, and rebuilt houses, walls, and other structures over hundreds or thousands of years. Later structures that were built over the remains of earlier ones and areas strewn with garbage produce layers of soil and debris, which are called 'strata' by archaeologists. Archaeologists excavate from top (the ground surface and most recent layers) to bottom (the oldest layers and the first to be laid down). Sometimes, pits or graves are cut into older cultural layers. Such features may, therefore, lie below or intrude into the absolute elevation of an earlier surface (Figure 2S1.1). Archaeologists are trained to "read" the layering of the deposits. Mounds are such an important feature of the landscape of the Middle East that the site names in many languages include the word for mound, like the "tel" in Tel Aviv.

Style

Much as we can assign approximate dates to photographs based on clothing styles, archaeologists can trace changes that occur over time in such features as ceramic decoration and even brick size. Combining the analysis of stratigraphy and style creates a powerful tool for correlating dates between sites and regions: the stratigraphic position of an object indicates its age in relation to other objects, and the relative age of different sites (as indicated by the age of the objects found at each) can then also be compared.

Absolute Dating

Absolute dating gives a specific calendar date or date range for an item found in a deposit; archaeologists can infer the date of the deposit from the object within it that bears the most recent date.

Radiocarbon Dating

Charred seeds and wood, which are evidence for ancient vegetation, land use, and food, can be submitted for radiocarbon dating. Dates obtained from organic materials have varying degrees of precision (e.g., 1423 BCE ± 100 years).

Written Records

Long before paper, dated economic transactions and lists of dynasties were impressed on clay tablets in cuneiform writing. Exploits of kings were carved on stone monuments, stone buildings (where stone was available in sufficient quantity for use in construction), and rock cliffs. By themselves, these kinds of records do not provide an absolute chronology, but cross-referencing groups of related records and correlating them with the results of other dating techniques can generate fairly precise chronologies.

Coins

Though not indestructible, coins (especially gold and silver ones) may last a long time in the soil. Dates of coin minting took three forms: a regnal date of a ruler; the date written in Arabic script, a practice that began in the 8th century CE; or a numerical date, which began to appear in the 14th century CE. Even in the absence of a legible date, style and subject matter may also provide a (relative) date range for coins (see Chapter 7S5: Currency).

Clay and Metal Vessels

Sometimes artisans painted, carved, impressed, or incised the date of manufacture onto pottery or metal vessels. In cases where archaeologists understand a historical dating system, it can be translated into our own dating system. We can easily correlate dates from the Jewish, Zoroastrian, Christian, and Islamic calendars; nowadays we use BCE and CE, standing for "Before the Common Era" and "Common Era," rather than BC and AD.

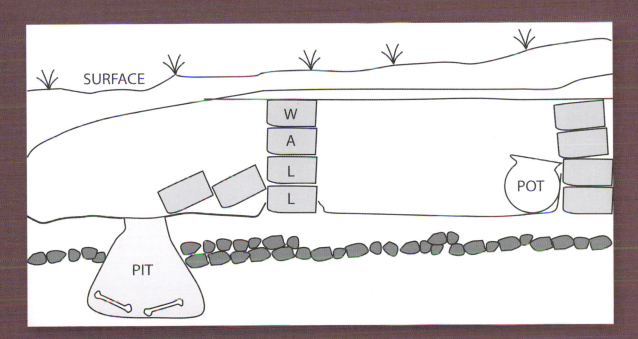

Fig. 2S1.1 *Left*
Schematic cross-section of an excavated building showing two walls and fallen bricks, a later trash pit dug into a floor, and an earlier stone pavement. A clay pot leans against a mudbrick wall. The modern ground surface is indicated with plants.

Wood was scarce, as the only trees grew along the rivers, and stone was almost entirely absent. Thus, the marsh dwellers lived in houses made of reed bundles, while the inhabitants of the drylands (or steppe) built structures of sun-dried mudbrick. Annual rainfall was and still is insufficient for dry farming in this zone, so fields have always been irrigated here. Initially important for irrigation, the Tigris and Euphrates Rivers and their tributaries became important routes of trade, communication, and transport of goods. The climate in this region is warm enough for the date palm, which was domesticated by 4000 BCE.

By 6000 BCE at the latest, agricultural practices spread to the Iranian Plateau (Figs. 2.7, 2.8). This region is characterized by virtually uninhabitable central deserts surrounded by moister uplands that support rain-fed farming or irrigation agriculture. In the 1st millennium BCE, this region saw the development of *qanats*, a kind of irrigation that brings groundwater from higher elevations to fields by means of underground built channels (see Chapter 11S3: Irrigation and the *Qanat*). This region is rich in stone and metal and situated on trade routes between the Mesopotamian lowlands and destinations to the east.

Fig. 2.4 *Above*
Flocks in piedmont steppe. Nowadays, this region is farmed and heavily grazed. In antiquity, this region would have had trees scattered among the pasture and farmland.

The fourth region, the Zagros Mountains, separates the piedmont and Mesopotamia from the upland plateau. The mountain slopes support open woodland of oak in the moister north and pistachio and almond trees to the south (Fig. 2.9). The flat valleys are suitable for dry farming (Fig. 2.10). Some of the peoples of the Zagros Mountains became primarily dependent on herding and moved annually to take advantage of winter pasture in the warm lowlands and summer pasture in the cooler highlands.

Why Farm and Domesticate Animals?

Archaeologists have long grappled with the question of why people began to cultivate plants and herd animals. After all, some ancient Near Easterners had been living successfully in small communities year-round for about a thousand years, subsisting on wild resources. Several factors likely contributed to the shift towards agriculture and animal husbandry. Some plants, like acorn-yielding oak, are very productive but have unpredictable yields from one year to the next even as others, like the wild wheats, can grow as densely in the wild as in a cultivated field and be stored for use over the course of a year. Animals, unlike plants, move around and may become locally scarce due to overhunting or habitat destruction.

Over the long term, it seems that local changes in the plant cover and animals living near settlements combined with ameliorating climate conditions encouraged people to stabilize their food supply by adding cultivation and animal husbandry to their subsistence strategy. Eaten together, cereals and large-seeded legumes (pulses) would have provided energy and protein for the diet; the addition of animals would have provided a ready source of fat, as well as protein; and animal dung would also have helped maintain soil fertility in the fields. Investments in land and animals would have further tied people to one location. For people who were already committed to a settled way of life, and who did not have the option of simply going to the grocery store when times were tough, plant and animal husbandry would have provided a stable food supply. As populations increased, it was no longer possible for them to revert to a hunting and gathering way of life.

Domesticated Plants and Animals

By 6000 BCE, people in much of the ancient Near East had already begun to live year-round in settlements constructed of stone and mudbrick. Their livelihood was based on plant and animal husbandry. Those first cultivated plants and herded animals were the direct descendants of their wild counterparts. As the lives of people, crops, and animals became intertwined, genetic changes created new "domesticated" species.

continued on page 30

Did The Land Always Look Like This?

Naomi F. Miller

Vegetation is largely determined by climate and soil substrate combined with and influenced by other natural and physical factors. Millennia of farming, industry, and urbanization created the landscape of the modern Middle East. Deforestation and the destruction of plant cover by agricultural and urban development make it difficult to know what, in principle, might grow in a place. Therefore, ancient vegetation patterns must be inferred from relict vegetation (that is, plants surviving in out-of-the way pockets) and the reports of plant explorers and botanical researchers, who have been documenting the vegetation for several hundred years.

There are many ways that botanists and archaeologists can trace changes in plant cover over time. Palynologists, who identify and analyze pollen, drill cores through soil layers that have accumulated undisturbed on lake bottoms to extract pollen that blew in from plants growing in the surrounding region. Complementary information can be gleaned from charred seeds and wood excavated from archaeological sites. Unlike pollen grains, which are not visible to the naked eye, these macroremains come from material brought to settlements as food, fodder, fuel, or building material. Climate scientists, too, have developed methods for measuring climate change over time. For example, oxygen isotopes in the Greenland ice cores have been used to trace global temperature changes over several hundred thousand years. Since vegetation is potentially affected by both climate and human activity, it is not

Fig. 2S2.1 *Left*
It is not only the landscape that changes over time. The built environment does, too. Modern satellite images of this Iranian village show that the mudbrick and stone buildings seen in the 1978 photograph have disintegrated over time, just as similar structures did in the ancient past. Some of the forces at work are hinted at by the sugar beet truck and yellow post office box, which connected the village to the wider world.

always clear what caused specific changes in plant cover in particular places. The combined results of these analyses, however, demonstrate widespread human influence on the landscape from the 1st millennium BCE. Localized vegetation changes can also sometimes be traced in earlier periods.

Fig. 2S2.2 *Above*
This village, built at the base of an archaeological mound near the Euphrates River, was made of mudbrick. It is now under the waters behind the Atatürk Dam in southeastern Turkey.

Fig. 2.5 *Opposite*
The first cities of Mesopotamia were situated in the marshlands of southern Iraq.

Fig. 2.6 *Right*
A palm grove in southern Mesopotamia with a traditional mudhif house made of reed bundles.

Fig. 2.7 *Overleaf*
Aerial photograph taken near Rayy in the 1930s by Eric Schmidt showing the close relationship between the Iranian Plateau and the mountains in the distance. Courtesy of the Oriental Institute of the University of Chicago.

The First Crops

The first domesticated plants developed from their native wild relatives. Wild plants have evolved many traits that enable them to spread their seeds without the help of humans: stalks may shatter, barbed appendages may attach ripe seeds to the fur of passing animals, birds may eat berries and then excrete thick-walled indigestible seeds miles away. For plants under cultivation, seeds are selected and dispersed by people. Human seed selection may (intentionally or not) favor certain traits, like reduced toxicity or increased seed size, and plants may no longer need their wild seed dispersal mechanisms.

The first plants cultivated in the ancient Near East were annuals, which die after producing seeds for the next generation. Because annual plants have a short reproductive cycle, they may evolve quickly into genetic domesticates. The first domesticated crops were carbohydrate-rich cereals, protein-rich pulses, and flax.

One of the first changes leading to domestication resulted from cultivation: a size increase of the individual cereal grains. Seeds that are sown, protected from predation and weather, are buried deeper than wild seeds that germinate on or near the ground surface. As a result, cultivated plants need more energy to break through the soil. From the cultivated plant's point of view, then, a larger seed is advantageous. With ongoing cultivation, loss of the wild seed dispersal mechanism makes cultivated cereals dependent on humans: when ripe, domesticated grains are more likely to stay attached to the stalk rather than breaking from the stalk on their own in the manner of wild grains.

The life cycle of the domesticated counterparts of the wild wheats and barley mimics nature. Their seeds are planted in the fall, sprout with the coming of the winter rains, and

continued on page 33

Fig. 2.8 *Left*
Close up view of sparse scrub and
pebbly surface in the Lut Desert of Iran.
© Ninara (flickr)/Kaisu Raasakka.

ripen in the spring. The first domesticated wheats, einkorn and emmer, had wild ancestors
that grew well in relatively moist areas of the Eastern Mediterranean (Israel, Jordan,
Lebanon, Palestine, and western Turkey) and the core of the Middle East (modern-day
Turkey, Syria, Iraq, and Iran). By the time pottery came into use, other wheats, like
durum (macaroni wheat) and bread wheat had already evolved and become more popular
because they were easier to process and cook.

The pulses are large-seeded members of the pea family. First domesticated in
the Middle East, lentil, chickpea, and pea remain popular today. Bitter vetch is now
a minor crop grown primarily as fodder. For the first farmers, who did not yet have
dung-producing domesticated animals, cultivation of the pulses not only improved the
protein content of the diet, but also helped maintain soil fertility through the action
of nitrogen-fixing bacteria living on the roots of the plants. Domestication conferred
another advantage: wild pulse seeds need more protection from insects and unfavorable
conditions for germination, and so have more bitter alkaloids and thicker seed coats
than their domesticated relatives. The bitter taste is removed by boiling or roasting. The
thinner seed coat and reduced toxicity of domesticated seeds would have improved the
flavor with less cooking time. Pulses, whether from wild or domestic plants, are first
found on sites without cooking pots, having been accidentally preserved by charring in
roasting pits.

Another early Near Eastern crop plant was flax, whose stem fibers are used to make
linen cloth. Flax needs a lot of water to grow and is labor intensive to process.

Fig. 2.9 *Right*
Qashqa'i nomads leaving highland summer pastures in the Zagros Mountains. Oak woodland covers the slopes.

The First Domesticated Animals

The process of animal domestication began when people started to confine young animals and animals who did not flee when they approached. Once caught, these tamer animals would have been penned and used for the first attempts at herding. Once humans controlled flocks of animals that could procreate in captivity and keep their young alive in confinement, they could selectively breed animals for desirable physical and behavioral qualities, such as tameness, meat and milk production, and coat quality. The process of sheep, goat, pig, and cattle domestication happened at roughly the same time as ancient Near Eastern populations were becoming dependent on farming.

We know that most early domesticated animals were slightly smaller than their wild ancestors because the bones of early domesticates (sheep, goats, and pigs) are smaller than the bones of their wild counterparts. Archaeologists think that early farmers may have chosen smaller animals because they were easier to handle and needed less food.

These early domesticates would have been kept to supply meat, fat, and skins to early villagers. They would have expanded the food supply of sedentary populations in several ways. For example, pigs are great recyclers, because they can eat many kinds of organic garbage, like vegetable peelings and scrapings and leftover food. Sheep, goats, and cattle are ruminants whose specialized stomachs can digest plants that are too tough for people to digest or of little nutritive value to humans. Ruminants can also graze in pastures that are too dry or too steep ever to be used to farm crops. After hundreds of generations

of selective breeding in captivity, some sheep and goats became tame enough to milk, and some sheep grew a woolly coat that could be sheared for fiber.

The development of both milking and shearing shows how physically and socially close the people of the ancient Near East had gotten to animals. Their meat was an essential food source, and their production of milk allowed people to harvest valuable nutrients for years before slaughtering individual animals for their meat. Artifacts dating to the 6th millennium BCE, including pots for storing and processing dairy products and spinning and weaving implements, are material evidence of this new intertwining of human and animal lives. The arrangement of houses and villages in this period also shows how household organization changed to ensure that animals were safe each night and had access to enough food and water to sustain them.

As the original domesticated species spread across the Middle East, they were taken to places where their wild ancestors had never lived. People had to figure out how to keep their animals alive by identifying what kinds of grass or other food their herds could eat and what time of year it was available; how enough water could be brought to the animals; and how to make sure the herds could survive the driest summers and coldest winters. Each of the original domesticated animals of the Middle East has special characteristics that people took advantage of as complex systems of farming and herding

Fig. 2.10 *Above*
Unirrigated barley field in a fertile Zagros mountain valley.

developed. Goats give the most milk and do the best in extremely dry regions; sheep give richer meat, more fiber, and can live in colder areas; and cattle give more milk and can pull a plow or cart, but can be very expensive to feed and water. Dung from cattle, sheep, and goats is an important fertilizer and can be burned for fuel. Pigs give no milk for people, but they have lots of babies, mature quickly, and can be raised on food scraps and crop waste around individual households.

Dogs had been guard animals and hunting companions long before the domestication of herd animals, and quickly settled into the life of the early villagers. The earliest dog skeletons known from the Near East have been found curled up next to humans in burials as long as 13,000 years ago. Cats were also domesticated, probably when wild cats came to hunt the mice and rats that had moved into these early villages to feed on stores of grain and other foods. These cats were not pets and may not have been very tame, but they became dependent on the environment that humans were creating in this region.

By virtue of controlling and caring for domesticated animals, people's relationship with the world inevitably changed. Nevertheless, wild animals still held an important place in people's lives and thoughts. Deer, onager, and gazelle were still hunted for food, as were wild sheep, goat, and cattle where these could still be found. Fish, birds, and other small animals were important in some times and places for food and specialized products like feathers and fur. Inventions using other animal products, like glues prepared from hides or perfumes from animal musks, do not leave many archaeological traces, but must have developed long before any records of their use. Predatory or fierce animals like lions, wild cattle, and eagles loomed large in the imaginations of many ancient Near Eastern peoples. Cultural and ideological attention to wild animals has persisted into modern times in artistic motifs, religious images, and stories (Fig. 2.11).

Later Developments in Farming and Animal Husbandry

By 6000 BCE, an agricultural complex based on the cultivation of cereals and pulses, as well as sheep, goat, cattle, and pig husbandry, was established from the lowlands of Mesopotamia to the highlands of Iran and beyond. Many people lived year-round in villages, and pottery was in common use.

Food storage and food preservation technologies developed for both plant and animal products not only tided communities over the winter, but also made it worthwhile to generate a surplus of food. The fermentation processes that produced wine from wild grapes at sites like Hajji Firuz Tepe, Iran, made sour grapes potable; people may have discovered how vinegar pickles vegetables. People also learned how to ferment grain for beer. Over the course of the next two millennia, by about 4000 BCE, the domestication of grape and tree fruits, like date, olive, and fig, added nutritional and culinary variety to

continued on page 43

The Material Foundation of the Ancient Near East

Naomi F. Miller, with contributions from Renata Holod

Stone

The first durable material used to make tools was stone.

Cobbles

Cobbles are unmodified stones that are used to break things (other stones, hard nutshells, etc.). Before the invention of pottery, rocks were also heated to high temperatures in open fires; the hot stones were then placed in pits or baskets to roast food or boil water for the preparation of food best cooked by indirect heat.

Chipped Stone

The modification of stones for tools by striking flakes off one stone using another—a practice called knapping—can be traced back to human ancestors who lived at least 2.5 million years ago. Because stone preserves well archaeologically, the increasingly complex technological developments in tool industries are well documented. Sometimes hafted, sometimes not, chipped stone tools have been used to scrape, cut, pierce, and drill.

Most stone tools are made of flint, which is widely available in the Middle East. Sometimes flintknappers used fire to make it easier to control the chipping process. Obsidian (Fig. 2S3.1), a volcanic glass produced when volcanoes erupt, was prized in the ancient Near East for tools and objects. Its geographical distribution is restricted to active, dormant, or dead volcanoes. Each eruption produced obsidian with a unique chemical signature; this signature can be used to track a particular obsidian piece's point of origin and the ancient trade networks through which it passed. Most obsidian found on archaeological sites in the Middle East came from present-day Turkey. Flint was, until relatively recently, used in cigarette lighters, and obsidian blades are so sharp that they have been used in surgery in modern times.

Ground Stone

Some stones, like basalt, are shaped by grinding to create the working surface. Ground stone mortars (grinding slabs) and hand stones or pestles are sometimes found in association with mineral pigments like red ocher. The people of the ancient Near East made bowls, beads, and other objects from fine-grained stone before they began to cultivate plants. By the time they needed grinders to process wild cereal grains, they had only to adapt their existing technology to make them.

Fig. 2S3.1 *Right*
Obsidian core (33-3-163) from which long, thin blades have been removed. It was recovered from Level X (ca. 3800 BCE) at Tepe Gawra (Iraq).

Fig. 2S3.2 *Right*
Unbaked brick is made from a mixture of mud and straw that is placed in a wooden mold and left to dry in the sun. Brick shapes and dimensions are sometimes characteristic of particular cultural periods.

Clay

Clay is one of the most widely available and versatile raw materials. In the ancient Near East, it was used to make small objects including figurines and containers; tools such as spindle whorls; tablets; and buildings. People valued its plasticity, and long before they made pottery to store, cook, and serve food, they understood the principle that fire hardens clay and makes it impermeable to water. Archaeologists value clay because of its extraordinary durability: whether sun-baked or fired, clay artifacts can survive thousands of years of burial. Entire clay objects may break, but their fragments are virtually indestructible. It is thanks to clay, which was used to make buildings, pots, and tablets for writing cuneiform, as well as a wide variety of other things, that we know so much about the economy, society, and literature of the ancient Near East.

Building Material

Clay became the building block for houses and temples in the ancient Near East, especially in wood- and stone-poor regions; most structures in such regions were built with unbaked mudbrick (Fig. 2S3.2). Important buildings, like temples and palaces, were made of more durable baked bricks, some of which were impressed with the name of the ruler who sponsored the work.

Pottery

Potsherds, the remains of fired clay containers of all sorts, are the most common artifacts found on sites in the Middle East. In addition to their practical use in cooking, serving, and storing food, clay ceramics could express the status and cultural affiliation of their users. The archaeological study of potsherds can reveal the function of specific pottery forms or vessels, aspects of social life, date of origin, and

the geographical affiliation of the potters. For example, a narrow-necked bottle would probably have contained liquids, while an open bowl is more likely to have been used for serving food. The fineness of a vessel's manufacture and quality of its design suggest the status of those who used the material. Since shapes and styles of decoration change over time and across space, pottery is very important for dating and correlating sites; the presence of similar or identical pottery shapes and decoration at different sites may provide evidence of trade or other connections among them (Fig. 2S3.3). Technical analyses of the clays used for pottery vessels may reveal the source of the clays, or point to subtle differences in the production techniques used by different potters.

Cuneiform Tablets

From the late 4th millennium BCE, unbaked clay was also formed into tablets of various shapes and sizes (Fig. 2S3.4); these tablets were initially inscribed with pictographic signs, and later with cuneiform writing, to form the first written records. Over the next three thousand years, clay tablets would be used to record economic transactions, political treaties, literary narratives, personal letters, scientific observations, prayers to the gods, and a striking variety of other sorts of information.

Fuel and Pyrotechnology

Well before the Middle East became one of the world's major suppliers of oil, people collected the hydrocarbon bitumen that seeped to the surface in parts of Mesopotamia as an adhesive and to waterproof containers. Other materials such as wood and animal dung were exploited to fuel fires for cooking and heating. The people of the ancient Near East were also familiar with fire's ability to transform inorganic material. The development of fuel-intensive technologies including the heat-treatment of flint, the hardening and waterproofing of clay objects, metallurgy (Fig. 2S3.5), and glass production helped create the world we live in today.

Fig. 2S3.3 *Opposite*
High-quality ceramics like this plate (NEP74) from Kashan (Iran) were produced in late 16th through mid-17th century CE workshops in Iran and Iraq. New glazing techniques created lusterware, which was highly valued and often exported.

Fig. 2S3.4 *Right*
This tablet (B3293) from Nippur (Iraq) is an ancient 'spreadsheet' from ca. 1400 BCE used by a trained scribe to track goods. Each cell contains quantities, but the header row is missing so the function is not clear.

Wood and Charcoal

Wood was the fuel of choice for millennia in forested and lightly wooded areas. In drier regions, small shrubs and animal dung were burned.

The fuel demands of household heating, cooking, and pottery production may have led to some localized loss of woodland resources, but metallurgy added even more stress on the woody vegetation. Bronze, which came into common use in the 3rd millennium BCE, can be produced with wood fuel. Iron smelting, which is even more fuel-intensive, requires charcoal. Charcoal is made when wood is burned in the absence of oxygen. It has a lower moisture content, and its combustible constituents are more concentrated. By weight, therefore, charcoal has a higher fuel value than wood, but producing it uses up a lot of the energy value of the original wood. Deforestation, exacerbated by the expansion of iron metallurgy, became widespread in the 1st millennium BCE.

Fig. 2S3.5 *Above*
Art adorned everyday objects such as furniture. This lion's head sculpture (B17064) was buried along with its owner, Queen Puabi, in the Royal Tombs of Ur (Iraq) ca. 2450 BCE.

Animal Dung

Pre-agricultural peoples of the steppe burned the dung of wild animals, like gazelles, for fuel. Fortunately, the dung of herbivores does not smell bad when burned. In later periods, animal dung (as well as small shrubs) continued to be used for fuel (Fig. 2S3.6). As populations grew and the number of people living in permanent settlements increased, the trees and shrubs in the immediate vicinity of habitations became depleted. Animal dung took up the slack; after animals were domesticated, dung became a handy fuel supplement even in areas of open woodland.

Fiber and Fiber Products

Plant and animal fibers were used to make many items, including cordage, nets, baskets, mats, and cloth. While these organic materials are perishable, traces of fiber artifacts may survive under dry conditions as impressions in soil or other materials and, in the case of reed matting, as phytoliths, visible traces of the silica deposited in the cell walls of reed stems. We can also infer the use of fiber from the tools used for spinning and weaving.

Linen

Linen, made from flax, was the first woven cloth. The earliest surviving example of linen cloth was found in a dry cave site in Israel dating to about 6500 BCE, but flax seeds are relatively common at other sites dating to this period. After sheep wool became available, flax persisted in use as a luxury fiber, especially in Mesopotamia.

Animal Fiber

Goat hair was probably used for making tents and ropes. The first domesticated sheep had hairy coats. Wool became the most common textile in this region after domesticated sheep were bred for woolly fiber.

Silk

Silk production in the ancient Near East and Eastern Mediterranean dates from the 6th century CE, when

Fig. 2S3.6 *Right*
Archaeological mounds are created as mudbrick walls melt and trash piles up in and around abandoned structures. In 1978, people living at the edge of the village of Malyan, Iran, collected their courtyard sweepings, mostly animal dung, to be trucked to the fields as fertilizer. The photograph shows the accumulation of animal dung and ashes over melted mudbrick walls at the edge of the village.

silkworms probably arrived in the region. As silkworms subsist almost entirely on leaves of the mulberry tree, which is native to China, silk production required the import and cultivation of both the silkworm and of the mulberry tree. Depictions of figured silks are shown in late Sasanian reliefs at Taq-i Bustan and in 6th to 8th century CE Soghdian (Central Asian) painting programs at Penjikent and similar sites. Excavations at Rayy, Iran, have found silk cloth remnants datable in between the 10th and 12th centuries CE. Comparable silk remnants have also been preserved in medieval European church treasuries.

Cotton

Cotton does not appear to have been grown in the Middle East until the early Islamic Period. It is mentioned, along with silk, as part of textile production at Rayy and other major centers of the 10th century CE in Persian and Arabic geographical texts in which many different kinds of cloth production are listed, some of mixed cotton and silk, or linen and silk.

Textiles

Textiles have long played an important role in the economy and worldview of the people of the Middle East, as evinced by the images of weavers that appear in pictorial art and the references to textiles in numerous economic texts and literary narratives inscribed on clay tablets and later written on parchment or paper. Woven textiles were a high value, lightweight product that could be traded for other valuable products like metal and fine-grained stone over long distances.

the menu. In Mesopotamia, the date palm became a staple crop for rich and poor alike. After about 6000 BCE, land where rain-fed farming had been marginal or impossible could now be rendered productive through irrigation. Over the following millennia, with the development of trade and communication networks across Eurasia, crops that had been domesticated outside the Near East were introduced. Many of them, like millet, rice, and sesame, could be grown only in the summer under irrigation. By the 7th century CE, a variety of other warm-season crops, such as cotton, sorghum, lime, and sugar cane, were added to the repertoire. It was not until the European Age of Discovery in the 16th century CE that tomato, potato, tobacco, and other crops from the Americas became integrated into Middle Eastern cuisines and lifestyles.

Changes in animal husbandry proceeded alongside developments in farming over the course of millennia. People had long used animal dung as a fuel source to supplement wood, but new animal breeds yielded milk, which could be turned into a variety of storable dairy products with the help of microorganisms like yogurt bacteria and cheese microbes, and wool, which soon dominated textile production. Oxen were harnessed to the plow, which allowed farmers to cultivate more land. Other domesticated animals, such as the donkey, horse, and camel (the one-humped dromedary and the two-humped Bactrian camel) came into the Middle East from elsewhere. The introduction of these animals, able to carry heavy loads across long distances, is associated with increasing long-range trade.

A new mode of life called pastoral nomadism developed, probably in the mid-third and early 2nd millennia BCE, after the time of the first cities. Nomadic groups began to travel with their herds past settled villages, taking advantage of highland pastures in the summer and lowland pastures in the winter. As sedentary people had to limit herd size according to the number of animals they could feed during the dry summer or snowy winter months, their herds were not big enough to consume all the available pasture plants. By fully utilizing seasonally rich pastures, pastoral nomadism could support more animals on the same land.

Smaller animals, like the chicken, became increasingly popular in the 1st millennium BCE. Arriving by the 6th century CE, the silkworm and the mulberry trees on which it feeds are a relatively late, but important, addition to the agricultural systems of the Middle East.

For Further Reading

Miller, Naomi F. 1990. Palm Trees in Paradise: Victorian Views of the Ancient Near Eastern Landscape. *Expedition* 32(2):53–60.

Miller, Naomi F., and Willma Wetterstrom. 2000. The Beginnings of Agriculture: The Ancient Near East and North Africa. In *The Cambridge World History of Food*, eds. K.F. Kiple and K.C. Ornelas, vol. 2, pp. 1123–1139. Cambridge: Cambridge University Press.

Zohary, Michael. 1973. *The Geobotanical Foundations of the Middle East*. Stuttgart: Gustav Fischer Verlag.

Fig. 2.11 *Opposite*
Stag and gazelle pendants (clockwise from top left: B16684.5, B16684.6, B16684.2, and B16684.1) from the diadems of Queen Puabi that were deposited in her lavish burial in the Royal Cemetery of Ur (ca. 2450 BCE). Animals are frequently portrayed in the art of the ancient Near East. Some are clearly food animals, but others may depict specific characters or refer to events in stories.

3

THE FIRST CITIES

Holly Pittman

Opposite
This stone tablet (B10000) from Tello
(ancient Girsu), Iraq, dates to about 2800
BCE. The text concerns land use of various
people and was written on stone because
of the importance of real estate documents.

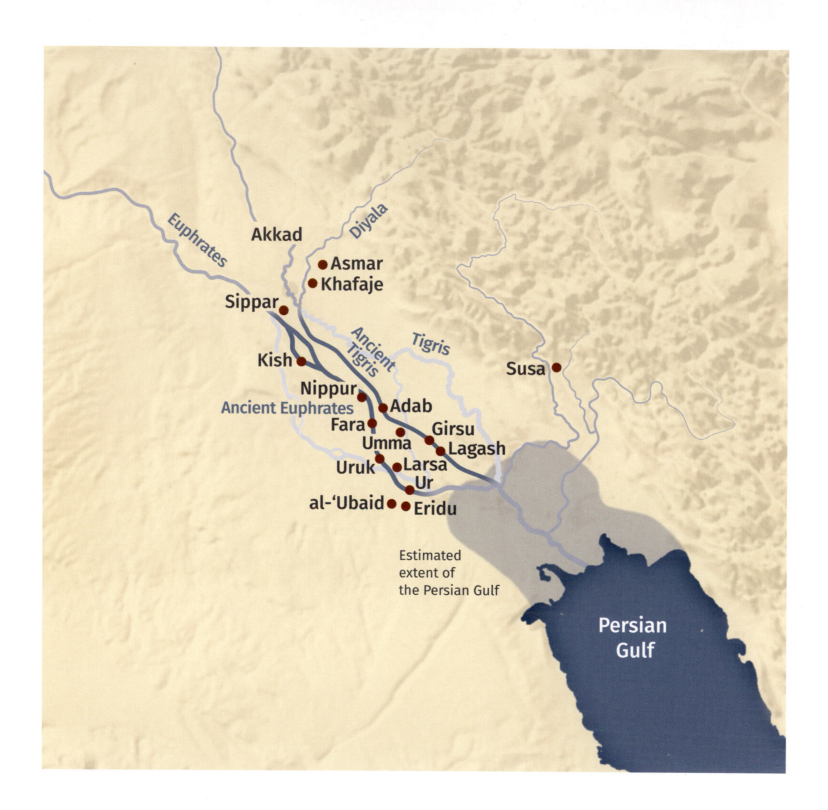

In the Beginning

Early in the 5th millennium BCE ancient Near East, society began to undergo a gradual and irreversible transformation from the egalitarian organization of life in small villages and hamlets to the more stratified and hierarchical organization of larger centers (Fig. 3.1). Although shared, and possessing certain elements in common, the path to urbanization and growing complexity followed in each region was different, depending on the potential of each environment to support ever increasing numbers of people living together in larger villages and towns.

In the rolling landscape of northern Mesopotamia, between the westward reaching Euphrates and the eastern Tigris rivers, the centers of Tell Brak on the Habur and of Hamoukar on the Jaghjagh tributary rivers attracted villagers from smaller sites. Working collectively, these villagers pooled their labor to undertake large-scale agricultural projects that were naturally watered by the abundant annual rainfall.

Further to the south, rainfall became intermittent and less reliable for agriculture. In the upper alluvium south of the modern city of Baghdad, the ancient Euphrates and Tigris almost joined and, unlike their present-day courses, flowed south in parallel and shifting beds. Each river carried vast quantities of water from rainfall and snowmelt off the mountains in the north. This abundant water, when directed through informal irrigation canals, transformed the fertile but dry soil into fields of wheat and barley that were more than twice as productive as those in the north. Despite its tremendous potential, however, this environment was riskier than that of the north and success required both

Fig. 3.1 *Opposite*

Map of the cities of southern Mesopotamia during the third millennium BCE. Each was the home of a tutelary god. Each was politically independent and self-sufficient.

Fig. 3.2 *Right*

Ancient impression (B11158) on clay sealing of a cylinder seal. This impression carries the imagery of a remarkable cylinder seal carved around 2300 BCE. It shows a unique representation of the major pantheon of the Sumerians on the top register. In the bottom register two gods are shown carrying trophies of war on their shoulders in the company of minor deities. This is perhaps the earliest reference to myths of Ninurta defeating enemies of the gods.

Fig. 3.3 *Left*

Modern village in the marshes of southern Iraq. © Nik Wheeler.

the establishment of safeguards and careful planning. In some years, too much water would flow too quickly and wash away all of the crops; in others, abundant harvests produced a surplus that could be shared more widely or saved for a period of want.

As the only source of water available for sustenance, as well as for crops, the rivers were vital to life in the alluvium; the unpredictability of the rivers' courses further encouraged communities to band together in larger groups for mutual support. Nippur, a major center located in the upper alluvium, was one of the sites that grew to great size in the 4th millennium BCE. Nippur, although soon overtaken in size by Uruk in the south, would remain the spiritual center of Mesopotamia for millennia. It was at Nippur that the major gods of the pantheon gathered for their annual rituals and festivities (Fig. 3.2), and it was there that kings would, in later days, come to establish their primacy among the other rulers of the land. The primary temple at Nippur belonged to the city's patron god, Enlil, but other major deities, including Inana, the goddess associated with fecundity and sexual love, also had important temples in the city.

As the Tigris and Euphrates rivers flowed further to the south, their waters mingled in the vast flat delta marshland with the open waters of the Lower Sea, which is now known as the Persian Gulf. In these early days, the mouth of the gulf was located further to the north of where it is today. This marshy environment was entirely different from that of the drier alluvial uplands around Nippur or of the piedmont steppe expanse that stretched between the two rivers in the north. Here, people settled on raised humps of land called turtlebacks (Fig. 3.3), which were separated from each other by watery marshes full of reeds, fish, and fowl.

On the western side of the Euphrates, raised humps were settled in the vicinity of what would later become the city of Uruk (Fig. 3.4); these rapidly grew to constitute an enormous center. In these early days, Uruk was not a single entity. At its heart were two major settlements: Kullaba and Eanna. Separated by natural waterways, which were

Fig. 3.4 *Opposite*

Plan of the sacred precincts at the site of Uruk/Warka around 3000 BCE. The monumental buildings at Uruk were far beyond the scale of any previous public structures. After Roaf 1990:60. Redrawn by Ardeth Anderson.

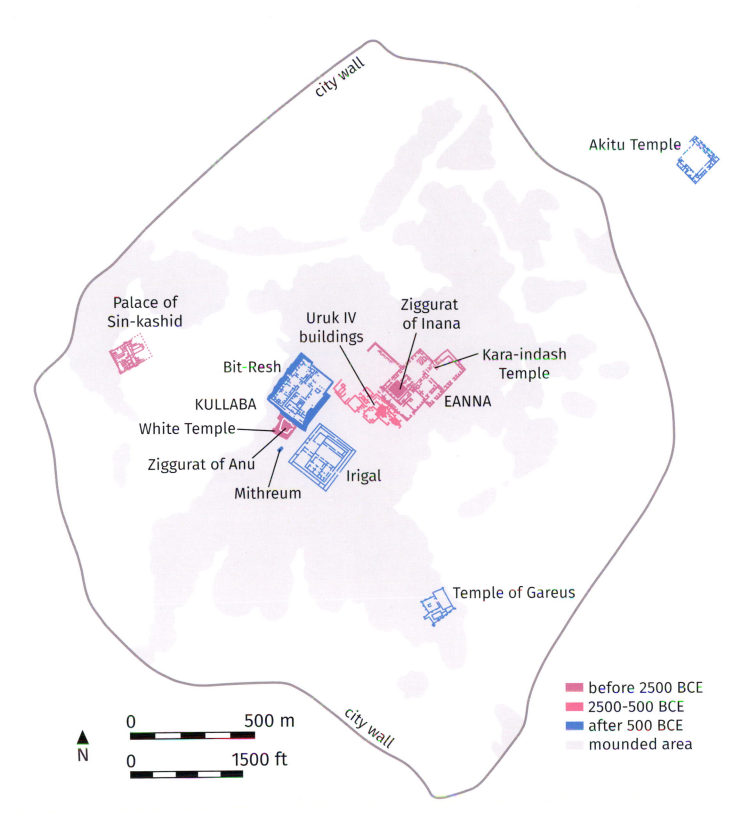

city wall

Akitu Temple

Palace of
Sin-kashid

Ziggurat
of Inana

Uruk IV
buildings

Kara-indash
Temple

Bit-Resh

KULLABA

EANNA

White Temple

Ziggurat of Anu

Irigal

Mithreum

Temple of Gareus

0   500 m

N

0   1500 ft

city wall

before 2500 BCE
2500–500 BCE
after 500 BCE
mounded area

0   10   20 Meters

Building A

Fig. 3.5 *Above*

During the 6th millennium BCE, a new house plan appeared in central Mesopotamia at sites such as Tell Abada. This plan with a tripartite structure around a central court was able to accommodate larger groups. Part (d) of figure 2 from Ur, J. 2014. Households and the Emergence of Cities in Ancient Mesopotamia. *Cambridge Archaeological Journal*, 24(2), 249-268 © The McDonald Institute for Archaeological Research 2014, published by Cambridge University Press.

tended and maintained to become major canals and thoroughfares, these two settlements became the ceremonial and religious hearts of the city, as well as of the region more generally. At its greatest extent in the early centuries of the 3rd millennium BCE, the city of Uruk extended more than four square miles and was home to as many as 150,000 people. It was surrounded by a massive city wall, the building of which was attributed by later legends to the semi-divine king Gilgamesh.

The City Rises

A combination of factors encouraged communities to band together in cooperation. Technological advances in irrigation and farming led to increases in productivity, which in turn led to a reorganization of labor, releasing many workers from the daily chores of food production to focus on other more specialized tasks. Some communities also expanded and were linked to each other through a network of canals. Water transportation was cheap and easy, and this connectivity through waterways encouraged increased specialization and the exchange of commodities between different centers. One center could specialize in products made from reeds, such as mats, boats, and even houses similar to the mudhifs of today. Other centers cultivated date palms in large orchards, while still others specialized in growing apples or other fruits. Communities located close to sources of bitumen, or tar, a sticky black substance effective for waterproofing, harvested this valuable raw material.

For over two thousand years, informal irrigation systems were drawn off the main channels of the rivers, which meandered across the alluvial plain. Gradually, more effective water management expanded the potential of the fertile alluvial soils. These new and larger scale irrigation systems, maintained by the community, increased yields of wheat and barley, and allowed larger orchards to produce date palms, vegetables, and fruits. Large teams of workers became specialized in different types of production. Effective harnessing of this large and specialized labor force required an economic organization capable of redistributing necessary products across all sectors of society.

In addition to the increased productivity of plant crops, exponential growth occurred among the domesticated animals. Herds of cattle were bred for milk and milk products, leather, and their labor for plowing the fields (see Chapter 2: The Geography and Agriculture of the Middle East). Herds of sheep and goats continued to be exploited for their milk and meat but were now also valuable for their wool; this fiber, used for weaving into textiles, became a vital resource, one that would transform the economies of resource poor southern Mesopotamia. In earlier centuries, textiles were woven from flax, a fibrous plant grown in a watery environment that was rendered into thread for linen through labor intensive processing (see Chapter 2S3: The Material Foundation of the Ancient Near East). During the 5th millennium BCE, the so-called fiber revolution unleashed

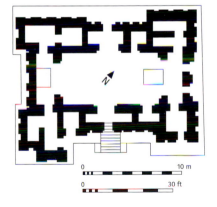

Fig. 3.6 *Above*
Plan of the Ubaid Period temple to the water god Enki in southern Mesopotamia at Eridu. Its tripartite structure with a niched exterior façade served as the model for the house of the god for millennia. After Lloyd and Safar 1947: fig. 3. Redrawn by Ardeth Anderson.

the potential of animal hair, especially that of sheep. Through shearing, spinning, and weaving, animal hair was converted into woven textiles; it would be another five millennia before these would be augmented by cotton and silk. Vast herds, consequently, were selectively bred to improve and diversify the quality and the quantity of their fiber. By the 4th millennium BCE, these herds, comprising thousands of animals each, were being tended by shepherds in the lush pastures of the piedmont regions beyond the river valleys to the east and north. Their wool supplied the factories of the urban centers, where they were transformed into a commodity not only fulfilling local needs but also useful as a valuable exchange good; Mesopotamia's woven textiles were traded to other regions for all of the other types of resources an urban society might require.

Sometime around 5500 BCE, at the beginning of the long road toward the city, a new architectural plan signaled a shift away from communal and collective social organization toward the nuclear family and its autonomous household. This new form of dwelling (Fig. 3.5) was an independent structure with a large rectangular central courtyard flanked on each side by a complex of rooms used for eating, sleeping, and the chores of domestic life. At Tell Abada, bigger and smaller houses of this type were separated by open space for animals and gardens. Far in the south, at the site of Eridu, such a plan evolved over the millennia from a single room structure to a large edifice with niching on the outside. The fact that this structure was rebuilt and expanded on precisely the same spot for more than thirteen levels during a time span of over two thousand years, combined with the discovery of huge quantities of fish bones and the presence of a podium in the main room, indicate that this structural plan (Fig. 3.6) was used from the beginning not only for human domestic dwellings but also for divine dwellings, and specifically for the temple of the god or goddess who dwelt at the center of the city.

The Mesopotamian household in this period was made up not only of the immediate nuclear family but also of relatives of several generations and dependents; it was headed by the elder male, with the support of other respected elders of both genders. Over generations, some households were, either through luck or ingenuity, more successful than others at achieving prosperity and accumulating wealth. Lavish burials discovered at Tepe Gawra in Level X (ca. 4000 BCE) suggest that a local political and economic hierarchy had emerged that gave privilege, wealth, and power to certain families. Either through persuasion or through force, these households assumed positions of leadership within the larger community. They accumulated exotic prestige items, like colorful stones and precious metals that served as visible badges of their success. Over the next five hundred years the trend toward hierarchy and differential access to wealth and power continued unabated. With the emergence of cities, the organizational and political skills of this elite social class became critical to ensuring the success and longevity of the new and truly urban centers. By the beginning of the Uruk Period around 4000 BCE, this new system of powerful households engaged both in cooperation and competition for control of wealth, production, and legitimacy was firmly established throughout the Near East. Archaeological investigation at Uruk in particular provides us with a material record of the kinds of institutions and new technologies for control that were developed to support and maintain this new social order.

Uruk: The First City

The remarkable agricultural productivity of the irrigated fields liberated some inhabitants of the city to engage in other activities. For many, however, these other activities constituted not enjoyable and leisurely pastimes but rather hard and repetitive labor compensated with minimal sustenance and provisions. Two demanding occupations in which many urban inhabitants participated were manual construction—primarily for public buildings—and concentrated craft production—particularly the complex and labor-intensive manufacture of textiles woven from animal fiber. In addition to these labors, activities such as the mundane preparation of foodstuffs for consumption, involving the grinding of wheat and barley into flour, required backbreaking effort.

The archaeological remains at the center of Uruk testify to the enormity of human effort that could now be dedicated to the construction of public monuments far beyond the scale and other requirements of even the wealthiest household. At Eanna, a huge precinct was filled with enormous buildings, including one longer than a football field. The temple's thick mud brick walls rested on foundations of limestone imported from sources some distance to the east. Some of these buildings had a tripartite plan while others were square with enormous exterior niches. Colored stone and, later, also painted terracotta cones were embedded in the exterior walls in patterns that recall the trimmed trunk of a date palm tree (Figs. 3.7, 3.8).

continued on page 59

Fig. 3.8 *Above*
Detail of cone decoration from Uruk (B17981).

The Uruk Vase

Holly Pittman

The most iconic object surviving from the earliest cities of Mesopotamia is the Uruk Vase (ca. 3000 BCE), a tall cylindrical container with slightly flaring sides and a high foot (Figs. 3S1.1, 3S1.2). Carved from a single piece of grey alabaster, this remarkable monument stands a bit more than one meter in height. Its fragments, discovered in the Eanna temple precinct of the goddess Inana at the ancient city of Uruk, were excavated in 1933–1934 by German archaeologists. The object is also known as the Warka Vase, named for the modern village of Warka that is the closest settlement to the ancient site of Uruk.

The vase is encircled with four registers of images that depict the fundamental components of early Sumerian urban society, each building one upon the other. While the imagery does not constitute an explicit narrative or story, it conveys something of the Sumerian worldview at the dawn of history. In particular, it emphasizes the prosperity and abundance that ensue when the king of a city possesses the favor of the gods. Some scholars associate the vase's imagery, and especially its uppermost register, with the Sacred Marriage between the human king of a city (here Uruk) and the goddess Inana, here represented by her human priestess.

At the bottom of the vase are four wavy lines representing the waters of the marshy southern alluvium. From these nurturing waters, plants emerge, depicted in a register of alternating date palm offshoots and flax plants (Figs. 3S1.3, 3S1.4). The date palm and flax were foundational resources

Fig. 3S1.1 *Right*
The Warka Vase (now in the Iraq National Museum in Baghdad) conveys in images the essential structure of early Sumerian society with the god of the city as the single most important resident of the city. © Foto Marburg /Art Resource, NY.

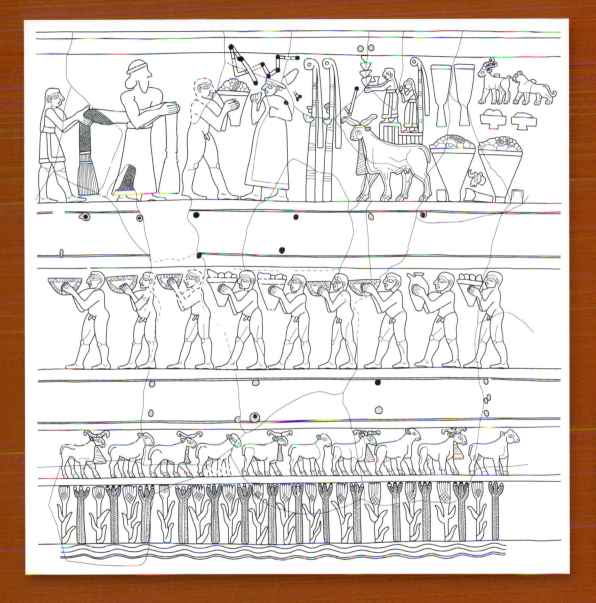

Fig. 3S1.2 *Left*
This line drawing of the registers on the Warka Vase provides a probable reconstruction of the scene on the upper register. Here the priest king is reconstructed as holding a long fabric belt which he will present to the priestess for the goddess. After Suter 2014: fig. 1. Redrawn by Ardeth Anderson.

Fig. 3S1.3 *Below*
On the bottom register of the Warka Vase two plants alternate above water. The plant with the offshoots can clearly be identified as an offshoot of a date palm, pictured here. The other is often interpreted as flax. Together these plants represent the orchard horticulture typical of Sumerian cities.

for Mesopotamia. The offshoot propagated the date palm, assuring abundant harvests, while the flax was the plant from which the goddess Inana wove the wedding sheets for her marriage to the shepherd Dumuzi. This marriage, re-enacted through the Sacred Marriage Ceremony, with the king in the role of Dumuzi, assured the continuation of mankind.

The register immediately above the plants depicts another major element of Mesopotamian prosperity: alternating (domesticated) rams and ewes. These animals, in addition to providing milk and meat, also provided wool, which was transformed by human labor and ingenuity into the textiles that were Mesopotamia's single most important manufactured commodity. Textiles were traded across the ancient Middle East for raw materials and processed goods through to medieval times.

Above the row of animals, separated by a wide band, is a row of nude males carrying baskets, spouted jars, and bowls overflowing with food. This register depicts an endless procession of foodstuffs delivered daily to the divine household shown in the uppermost register. The nudity of the male figures in the procession signals their purity.

The uppermost register depicts the figure of the priest-king, the paramount male figure of the city of Uruk, greeting the priestess of Inana. The priest-king is clad in a distinctive net skirt and accompanied front and back by acolytes bearing offerings of food and textiles. The priestess wears a headdress with two prominent projections and a long plain robe, and gestures to the man in the net skirt with her raised thumb. She stands in front of the gateposts of Inana, which take the form of reed bundles with streamers attached to the upper ring. The form of the reed bundles is identical to that of the proto-cuneiform sign for Inana's name.

Behind the gateposts are depicted a number of cult objects that include, remarkably, two vases identical in form to the Uruk Vase itself. Fruits and baskets full to overflowing with date bunches stand on the floor. In the field above are small stands with loaves of bread or cheese and the head of a bovid.

Fig. 3S1.4 *Right*
Date palms were at the center of Sumerian myth and religion. On the Ur-Namma Stele (B16676), the king pours a libation into the date palm altar that separates him from Nanna, the city god of Ur. Detail from the second register of the Ur-Namma stele.

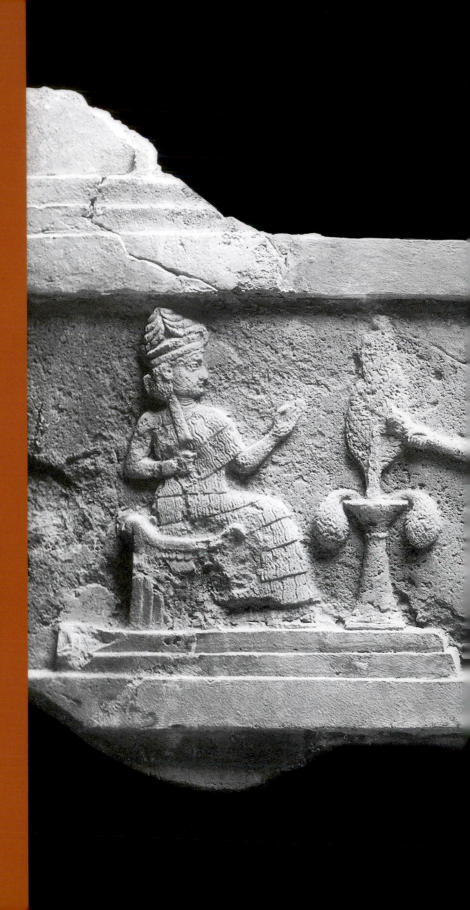

It is unclear whether all of these buildings and open areas were sacred structures, homes to powerful deities. Some may have been residences of elite family units while others may have served as large spaces for communal feasting, ritual activities, and gatherings of leaders and their families. Such activities would have been necessary to maintain and support the collective commitment to this large corporate enterprise. Likely, the structures and open spaces at Eanna served a combination of all of these purposes. At the same time, on Kullaba, the other major settlement mound at Uruk, a smaller structure was built on an artificial platform high above the marshy canals that formed the arteries of the city. This was certainly a temple, perhaps that of the sky god, An (later known in Akkadian as Anu). The White Temple had the tripartite plan typical of the temples known from earlier levels at the nearby site of Eridu.

In addition to architectural remains requiring skilled planners, engineers, and architects, as well as the muscle of manual labor, works of extensive representational art in permanent media like stone and fired clay appear for the first time in the early cities. Drawing directly from contemporary society at Uruk and similar sites, these artworks depict, in clear and legible images, the fundamental elements and principles of organization of pictorial representation in this first urban civilization in southern Mesopotamia. The most important of these works, found in a treasury of the central building complex of Eanna, is known as the Uruk Vase. Made of soft grey local limestone, the vase is decorated with four registers of images in low relief; these are structured so as to depict the most basic elements of community life at the bottom, vegetal life emerging from the waters, and move up through animal and then human actors to culminate in the confrontation depicted in the uppermost register between the king and Inana, the patron goddess of Eanna.

The world symbolically and literally depicted on the Uruk Vase could not run smoothly without highly developed administrative and logistical support. Not only was it necessary to organize and deploy a huge labor force for the construction and maintenance of public works but also there were significant challenges with which to contend when it came to safely moving, storing, processing, and distributing such large quantities of foodstuffs and manufactured commodities as were necessary for long distance trade and exchange. Perhaps most importantly, careful planning for future production and contingencies was necessary to protect against shortages of food and necessary goods or other disasters. To meet these organizational demands, existing administrative tools and technologies were augmented by new and even more powerful ones; these new technologies included writing, which would fundamentally transform human intellectual and organizational potential.

From as early as the 7th millennium BCE, small villages had used clay tokens and stamp seals carved with images to assist in keeping track of goods and services. Tokens having simple shapes may have represented small quantities of important basic commodities in the community, including grain, fruits, and animals. Stone or bone stamp

Fig. 3.9 *Above*
Hollow clay ball with tokens from Susa, ca. 3500 BCE. Before the invention of writing, accounting procedures were accomplished through tokens made from clay in various sizes denoting various quantities of commodities. When a transaction was completed, these tokens were enclosed within a hollow clay ball that was subsequently impressed with cylinder and stamp seals. On occasion, marks recording the tokens inside were impressed on the surface of the clay ball. © RMN-Grand Palais/Art Resource, NY.

seals carved with abstract patterns or figural images, most commonly horned animals, were impressed into moist clay masses used to secure the contents of vessels, baskets, and bags (often by sealing or covering over their openings). At Tepe Gawra thousands of such impressed clay masses were found; while the precise significance of the seal designs is debated, they surely denoted either the commodities' owner(s), identification, origin, or destination. Or perhaps all of these were contained in the image code.

During the Uruk Period (ca. 3500 BCE), the stamp seal was replaced by the cylinder seal, a cylindrical piece of stone or other material carved with imagery running all the way around the curve of the cylinder. Rather than bearing abstract patterns, these seals carried images that were, like those on the Uruk Vase, clearly legible. Often they depicted containers or laborers, or sometimes files of animals in pasturage. Less frequently, they bore representations similar to that on the Uruk Vase, depicting the ruler figure or priest-king with his distinctive headgear and net skirt engaged in various royal duties or actions. Sometimes, the image of a temple is depicted with the divine gateposts, which are symbols of Inana, the goddess of Uruk. These cylinder seals came to be a very important tool in the newly expanded administrative bureaucracy, which was required to keep track of surplus stores of foodstuffs and goods and to protect these from unauthorized pilfering.

Appearing along with the first cylinder seals were other administrative devices that allowed the recording of specific quantities and types of commodities that included, most commonly, grains, animals, and even people. Tokens of different shapes are thought to have signified both an amount and a type of commodity; these tokens were collected and gathered into groups that were sealed into hollow clay balls (Fig. 3.9). The surface of each clay ball was then impressed with a carved cylinder seal, and the shape of the tokens inside the ball was, as a final step, impressed on top of the seal impression. This multi-part document could function as a record of commodities delivered or promised in return for a certain quantity of labor or allow for the transmission and storage of knowledge about an economic transaction or commitment between offices. No longer was it necessary to convey such information by word of mouth: it could now be stored and, later, retrieved without depending on (potentially unreliable) human memory or honesty. This system of tokens, balls, and seal impressions anticipated, though it was independent of, the development of those symbolic marks that quickly led to the singular invention of writing. Writing, unlike tokens and seal imagery, had the potential to record spoken language.

While these developments in the organization and management of labor and goods were underway, a number of industries were also being developed into specialized activities. We know from the texts, for example, that special foods were prepared from dates, apples, and other fruits, perhaps for export but also as gifts from the community to the gods. Perhaps more importantly, textile production was also developed on an industrial scale. Textiles were by far the most important of Mesopotamia's products;

continued on page 67

Cylinder Seals in the Ancient Near East

Holly Pittman

Seals as Administrative Tools

Even before the invention of pottery, small villages in northern Mesopotamia had developed a means of securing foodstuffs or goods that had been placed in containers. A hard object was carved with a particular design; this object could then be pressed into soft clay placed over the opening of a container, leaving an impression of the carved design (Fig 3S2.1). Once the impressed clay dried over the opening of the container, it ensured any tampering with the container's contents would be detected; such tampering would first have to damage or break the impressed clay sealing.

The carved objects used to impress soft clay in this manner are called seals, a term that encompasses a variety of impression-making tools used in administration. In the ancient Near East, the earliest seals were stamps, the carved side of which was pressed into a soft clay matrix. First appearing early in the 6th millennium BCE, stamp seals continued in use throughout the history of the Near East for such purposes as protecting secured items, securing doors and windows, marking written documents, and serving as personal amuletic tokens (Fig 3S2.2). Around 3500 BCE, slightly before the invention of writing, a new type of seal was introduced. Cylindrically shaped, it was carved with a design that covered the surface of the cylinder: the cylinder was then rolled across a soft clay surface to yield a continuous frieze (Fig 3S2.3). This new technology was especially useful when combined with (cuneiform or "wedge-shaped") writing, which was impressed on moist clay tablets using a reed stylus. When rolled across such a (still moist) clay tablet, seals could signify the authenticity of a document and its contents, as well as provide the personal mark of the individual(s) named in the document. This was particularly important for identifying the witnesses to transactions recorded in contracts and deeds.

Fig. 3S2.2 *Left*
Some stamp seals like this one from Gawra (37-16-357) carry the image of a shaman or a priest who dances in the presence of animals. Usually he wears the mask of a horned animal. This individual must have had special status in the town with an ability to communicate with invisible and powerful spirits.

Fig. 3S2.1 *Opposite*
Many of the stamp seals from the Chalcolithic Period from Gawra carry images of horned animals, sometimes surrounded by plant forms and smaller animals. This large round stamp (36-6-306) probably with a domical back has a deer with prominent branching horns. Around it are plants of similar shape.

Cylinder seals remained the dominant seal type in Mesopotamia until the 1st millennium BCE, when stamps were again introduced to impress ink onto parchment that had been inscribed with Aramaic.

The Iconography of Seals

Seals were carved with designs that were meaningful within both the administrative system and their larger cultural contexts. Both the subject and style of their imagery changed over time, as different cultural themes became important. In the Uruk Period around 3200 BCE, for example, much of the imagery carried on seals showed individuals engaged in different types of labor, as well as commodities produced by such individuals. Other seals showed scenes associated with the cult, which could include representations of temple buildings and offerings.

In the Early Dynastic Period (ca. 2900–2334 BCE), seal imagery was dominated by two scene types, the banquet scene and the combat scene, that were repeated with little variation (Fig 3S2.4). The banquet scene shows seated figures, both male and female, participating in a festivity that includes drinking from cups or through long straws from vats of beer. Sometimes there are ancillary figures serving or dancing or playing musical instruments. The combat scene is the other popular scene in this period. Only rarely does this take the form of an actual battle scene. Most often it depicts a cosmic struggle between a nude anthropomorphic or hybrid (bull-man) hero and wild animals, especially lions; the lions are often depicted busily attacking goats or other quadrupeds including, sometimes, human-headed bulls. Appearing on seals for the first time in this period are divine figures, who are often depicted in anthropomorphic form but distinguished from humans by the horned headdresses that they wear. Cult scenes and mythological stories, including images of a divine boat with fantastic creatures, also now appear, and become especially prominent and varied over the course of the Old Akkadian Period (ca. 2334–2154 BCE).

The official seal of the Akkadian court is a combat scene depicting the nude hero grappling with ferocious lions or bulls on either side of an inscription recording the name and title of the seal owner. The majority of the great gods of Mesopotamia (see Chapter 4: Religion and the Gods) are represented on seals during this period, each shown with his or her specific attributes (Fig 3S2.5). The sun god

Fig. 3S2.3 *Left*
Lapis lazuli cylinder seal (B16727) and modern impression from the Royal Cemetery at Ur, associated with the grave of Queen Puabi. The double register seal carries a banquet scene on both registers. In the upper register is an inscription with the name A-BAR-GI.

Fig. 3S2.4 *Right*

Shell cylinder seal (B16747) and modern impression (above) found on the body of a groom in the death pit associated with the burial of Queen Puabi, PG 800. It is carved with a single register combat scene in which a nude hero with upstanding curls is protecting a deer who is attacked by a lion. Crossing the lion is a second lion which attacks a ram. The cylinder is inscribed with the name Lugal-sha-pad-da.

Period, the imagery on seals expanded greatly to include gods recognizable through their attributes. This fine seal shows the Sun God (Utu/Shamash) rising between the mountains in the east. He has rays emerging from his shoulders to associate him with the rays of the sun. He carries a curved sword with which he "cuts" the destiny. To each side of the mountains are "gates of heaven" held by his acolytes. © The Trustees of the British Museum.

Fig. 3S2.6 *Left*

Cylinder seal with Etana Myth (British Museum 89767). Rarely we can associate stories depicted on cylinder seals with myths preserved in the cuneiform literature. This Old Akkadian seal depicts the story of Etana, the shepherd and legendary king of Kish, who rides on the back of an eagle in search of the plant of fertility. As he soars in the sky he surveys the pastoral landscape of southern Mesopotamia below. © The Trustees of the British Museum.

Fig. 3S2.7 *Left*

The presentation or introduction became the most important scene during the Ur III Period. Variously it shows a deity or a king seated receiving the seal owner who is ushered in by a minor female protective deity. These seals frequently carry inscriptions giving the name and the title of the owner. The inscription on this seal (B15592) reads "Lugalushumgal, son of Ursal, the tailor."

Utu/Shamash (the first divine name is in Sumerian; the second is in Akkadian) is shown with the saw he uses to cut his way out of the mountains and rise each morning, as well as to cut the decisions of destiny; the water god Enki/Ea is shown with water and, often, a few fish flowing from his shoulders; and the goddess Inana/Ishtar, associated with sexual love and warfare, is often shown as a warrior with weapons emerging from her shoulders. These divine figures are often shown receiving other deities or human figures in standardized presentation scenes.

In the following Ur III Period (ca. 2112–2004 BCE), seal imagery and function are completely transformed. For the first time, seals are now frequently impressed on cuneiform documents, serving to authenticate or to witness the responsibility of the seal owner to the transaction recorded on the tablet. Most of the Ur III seals, including official as well as private seals, now carry presentation scenes along with the name and the title of the seal owner (Fig. 3S2.7).

City Seals

A particularly interesting type of cylinder seal, the city seal, was used for a period contemporary with the early development of writing in southern Mesopotamia (Fig. 3S2.8). Such seals were carved with the names of cities using pictorial versions of early cuneiform signs. While we cannot read all of the names, those we can belong to cities that were connected by one of the major canals flowing south on the alluvium. The city seal imagery first appears in the Jemdet Nasr Period (ca. 3000 BCE) and continues in use through the early part of the Early Dynastic Period. It is known only through ancient impressions; no actual city seals have yet been found. The largest concentration of city seal impressions was found at Ur in the Seal Impression Strata, a very deep trash area into which the Royal Tombs were built (see Chapter 8: The Royal Cemetery of Ur).

Fig. 3S2.8 *Above*
During a brief period between 2900 and 2700 BCE, a particular type of seal was used to protect goods that were jointly donated to the goddess Inana at Uruk. These seals like this one (33-35-293) are called City Seals because their imagery includes pictorial versions of cuneiform signs for the names of cities.

even into the much later Medieval and Early Modern Periods, luxury textiles remained a principle commodity type of the region. Textual references to the textile industry record huge herds that were accounted for annually, and workers brought in from the east to perform arduous labor; pictorial references include images of textile "factories" which were certainly located at Uruk and other major centers in the south through the millennia. From the 3rd millennium BCE, we know of a major textile production center at Ur and another one in the city-state of Lagash on the other side of the alluvium. These centers produced a full range of textiles from everyday fabrics for workers' garments to superfine fabrics destined for rulers, and from fabrics intended for gift exchange to those intended for the gods.

The textile industry required specialized teams of labor, apparently divided along gender lines, which were divided into supervised groups. The women prepared the fleece, spun it into thread, and rendered the threads into skeins; the men did the actual work at the looms. We know this from depictions on cylinder seals that show various stages of preparation and production (Fig. 3.10), each supervised by a leader shown standing with his or her arms spread to encourage the work. At the end of the work period, the teams of workers were presented to the paymaster by the supervisor, who would inscribe numbers and marks on a tablet (shown as a square) with a stylus.

Uruk Expands

Early urban society, with its core in the southern alluvium of Mesopotamia, expanded northwest in the last centuries of the 4th millennium BCE, following the Euphrates as far as eastern Turkey. The motivations for this expansion were multiple and included the acquisition of raw materials not locally available as well as access to abundant grazing land for the vast herds. A similar expansion, originating at Susa and Chogha Mish in the eastern extension of the alluvium into Khuzestan in southwestern Iran, followed the eastern edge of the Zagros Mountains to settle at important points on the road from the Diyala Valley onto the resource-rich Iranian Plateau. These settlements, which formed outright colonies in some cases and smaller enclaves within local communities in others,

Fig. 3.10 *Left*

This small cylinder seal (31-17-16) from Ur is carved with a scene of spinning fibers in preparation for the weaving of textiles. To judge from the imagery on seals, the work of spinning was done exclusively by women. The women frequently are shown seated on platforms holding various tools. This cylinder seal has the unique depiction of a "machine" used to process the spun thread into a skein. The object with the two handles may be a threader used to combine threads of different colors or textures.

offered direct access to copper mines and sources of hard timber. They were abandoned in approximately 3000 BCE, during the same period in which a major reorganization occurred at Uruk. At this time, the huge buildings that had stood for several centuries as the focal point of the new economic and political order were dismantled, replaced by a vast open area covered with fire pits that suggest a ritual purification of the precinct.

This abrupt and radical destruction seems not to have been caused by the arrival of a new people in the region. Nevertheless, it signals the beginning of a new phase of urban development in Mesopotamia; during the Early Dynastic Period, which spanned much of the 3rd millennium BCE, the urban lifeways known at Uruk in the late 4th millennium BCE would become established at many sites in the alluvium. The material culture, including the technology of writing and record keeping; elite iconography; and the mundane style of pottery, were the same across the sites affected. While there is no indication that this shared material culture corresponded to the political domination of Uruk over the rest of the cities, Uruk continued to be a singularly important and very large center and the cult of its main deity, the goddess Inana, may have taken on regional prominence.

It is from the earliest legible texts that we know that the people of southern Mesopotamia were multilingual and multiethnic from the very beginning. Sumerian was the dominant spoken language in the far south while proto-Akkadian, a Semitic language, was dominant in the northern part of the alluvium. Eblaite, a west Semitic language, was dominant along the Euphrates to the north, while Hurrian was spoken in the northern Tigris region. To the east, on the Iranian highlands, Elamite is the only one of the local languages to be known. The question remains open whether the Sumerian speakers were the original inhabitants of the south, arriving in roughly the 7th millennium BCE, or whether there was a prior population in the region that was absorbed long before the stabilization of writing allowed for the identification of linguistic groups.

City States and the First Dynasties

In the uppermost register of the late 4th millennium BCE Uruk Vase, the figure of a man referred to as the priest-king is represented. Although his functions and his title are not known, he is understood as the most important individual in late Uruk Period society. His appellation, priest-king, is based on the settings in which he is shown acting; these settings are, in later periods, associated with the institutions of both temple and secular rulership, and pertain to warfare, religious and cultic practice, building, and hunting. The priest-king was, in effect, the head of the corporate household that constituted Uruk, fulfilling diverse roles that would only gradually and in later periods be assigned to different institutions. The image of the priest-king seems to represent not any single or specific individual, but rather a stereotype, that of the head executive that would reside in every city. Indeed, it is possible that the disruption in the monumental architecture of the Eanna Precinct at the end of the late Uruk Period marked the end of one form of leadership and established the foundations of the dynastic rulership which was to follow (Fig. 3.1).

By the early centuries of the 3rd millennium BCE, approximately 35 politically and economically independent cities dotted the landscape of southern Mesopotamia; each of these was located along a canal or one of the two main rivers (the Tigris and Euphrates), and so was provided both with water for crops and routes of connection with neighbors. The courses of the rivers on such a flat gradation were not, of course, stable, and major disruptions, especially flooding, could cause the diversion of a watercourse away from one city or towards another. Each city was surrounded by adequate land for farming along the levees. And, within each of the early cities, there was space both for large orchards and pastureland for grazing animals. By the end of the 3rd millennium BCE, the cities had become much more densely populated, with little room for expansive gardens and spacious houses.

Evidence for early connections between cities is provided by tablets found at the site of Jemdet Nasr. In a slightly later context, inscribed tablets were found in a huge trash dump at Ur, along with hundreds of clay sealings used to secure vessels and stores of goods impressed with cylinder seals. Many of these seal impressions carried the names of neighboring cities rendered in a quasi-pictorial script. Although much is still not understood about these images, the cities represented seem to constitute a community or league of urban centers located along one of the major water channels leading to the Persian Gulf. Based on the contents of the tablets, and of other slightly earlier tablets from Jemdet Nasr, it is thought that these cities were linked in some kind of commercial or trading collective. Later in the millennium, a similar community of cities banded together in a political and economic alliance known as the **ki-en-gi** league.

Each city-state comprised an urban center surrounded by an arable hinterland dotted with villages that produced crops and tended flocks. Early in the millennium there was sufficient land between each of these entities that all of their needs could easily be met. Over the centuries, however, as populations grew and cities expanded, the boundaries of the city-states inched closer; this inevitably led to conflict, particularly over water, which was precious in a land with limited rainfall and few perennial springs. The situation was exacerbated by the gradual drying of the climate, which by around 2200 BCE had become a crisis precipitating the collapse of political states.

Each city-state was an independent political entity that shared cultural values with its neighbors. The most important resident of the city was in all cases the city's patron god or goddess, for whose well-being the citizens were collectively responsible. Enlil, associated with wind and air and the head of the Sumerian pantheon in the 3rd millennium BCE, resided at Nippur; the moon god Nanna and his family resided at Ur; and Inana, associated with love and warfare, ruled over Uruk. Each god or goddess, through his or her cult image, lived in the primary temple in the city-state and was supported by a household whose capable administrator was also the ruler of the city-state.

Each city-state, then, had a divine patron and a human ruler. But in these early days political roles and succession had not yet been standardized, and the titles used to refer to the ruler varied from city to city. In some cities, the ruler was given the title **lugal**, which is Sumerian for "big man"; in others, he took the title **en**, which means "priest" in Sumerian. The primary duty of the ruler in this period was to oversee the productivity of the inhabitants of the city in order to provide for the most important resident: the city god who resided in the temple. The ruler was, thus, selected as a competent administrator and organizer, and certainly would have come from among the most successful households in the city.

Periodically, when inter-city conflicts arose that could not be resolved through diplomacy or payment, a city would be required to muster a fighting force from among the able-bodied men of the community. The city's elders then selected the most capable of these assembled warriors as commander, a temporary appointment lasting until the conflict was resolved. We believe that, in the early years of the city-states, the two roles of temple administrator/city ruler and military leader were separate and distinct. But, as inter-city conflict became more common, the military leader accrued loyalty and resources. A special building, highly fortified and divided into private and public zones, functioned as a palace (the **egal** or "great house"). This was separate from the temple complex and household. Toward the end of the Early Dynastic Period (ca. 2300 BCE), which was characterized by the rise of numerous independent city-states across the southern alluvium, the two independent powerful institutions of palace and temple were functionally merged.

During the entire 3rd millennium BCE, the household was the organizing institution of Mesopotamian society. No longer made up simply of members of one's immediate family, the urban household was now a self-sufficient administrative unit. The largest households were those of the temple and the palace; these, in turn, were made up of smaller dependent households that had joined the larger enterprise in expectation of receiving sustenance in exchange for various types of production. Each household owned land, animals, boats, and tools, and had many specialists who produced what was needed from the resources available. Skilled workers, including cooks, barbers, fishermen, farmers, gardeners, craftspeople, and shepherds, as well as their families, were all supported by the household. Merchants and traders functioned to supply raw materials and products not available within any one unit, as well as to redistribute surplus products among households.

The overseer of the household, supported by a cadre of scribes, was responsible for anticipating needs, allocating and reallocating resources, and solving disputes. The records kept by the scribes—accounting documents written in cuneiform—are the primary sources of information that we have about the households: they tell us, sometimes in great detail, about such things as the production quota of certain industries, and the quantity of rations allotted to certain types of workers. Unfortunately, they are completely silent on the topic of much of what we would like to know, simply because there was no reason to commit it to writing. Most of the text archives that have survived to the present come from temples, a circumstance that led early scholars to suggest that the Early Dynastic economy was dominated by a controlling temple bureaucracy. In recent decades, however, this view has shifted significantly. Wealthy households independent of the temple or of the military ruler are now recognized as part of the mixed economy of individual city-states, and households are even thought to have existed outside of the city-state in the countryside.

The household structure, in addition to forming a very productive unit, also served to provide a type of safety net for the weak and vulnerable. As a member of a household, one had a commitment to protect and nurture each member to the degree collectively possible. The institution of the household as the fundamental economic and social unit of society continued down into the 2nd millennium BCE, when changing populations and new patterns of ownership began to support more independent and entrepreneurial economic units.

The Worlds Beyond Sumer and Akkad

Beginning with the Uruk Expansion in the middle of the 4th millennium BCE, the cities of Mesopotamia aggressively sought out those raw materials that were essential to their urban project. Blessed with abundant fertile soil, products of the marshes and gardens, lands for grazing, and a productive labor force, as well as some poor-quality stone and weak timber, the cities had the basics close at hand. But as soon as a hierarchy developed, with an elite class actively looking for ways to distinguish itself, other types of materials were sought out.

Denizens of the river valleys were always aware of the lands beyond their horizons. Silver and cedar trees were to be found in the mountains to the northwest, where the monstrous Huwawa/Humbaba, guardian of the legendary Cedar Forest, waited to battle the hero Gilgamesh and his loyal companion Enkidu. In the east, where the gods lived and the sun rose, treasures beyond all comprehension were to be found. And in the south was paradise, in the gardens of Dilmun in the Lower Sea.

The archaeological record is far more articulate than the texts about the ways in which the wealth of the east made its way to Mesopotamia cities. The early graves at Tepe Gawra, full of gold, lapis lazuli, and agates, testify to the existence of an overland route running west from the lapis lazuli mines of Badakhshan in eastern Afghanistan

across the Zagros Mountains to Mesopotamia. Similar riches, augmented by silver and copper probably coming from the west, are known from the temple caches in Eanna at Uruk. It was in the early centuries of the 3rd millennium BCE, when Mesopotamia's city-states were first establishing their identities, that commercial contacts were made with the east, by water rather than overland routes, in boats that followed the coast of the Arabian shore before reaching the Straits of Hormuz, an easy entry point to the Iranian Plateau. Mesopotamian pottery and seals left behind by traders and explorers at sites on the Iranian Plateau are evidence of attempts to reach the riches of the plateau by water rather than via the long and dangerous overland journey.

The fabulous riches discovered in mid-3rd millennium BCE graves in the Royal Cemetery at Ur (Figs. 3.11, 3.12, 3.13) (see Chapter 8: The Royal Cemetery of Ur) underscore the drive by royal and elite figures to obtain precious exotic and useful materials. While the texts of this period are virtually silent on this topic, the graves of Puabi and her compatriots demonstrate the extraordinary demand for imported luxury materials and goods. There was apparently so much wealth at Ur, materialized in gold, silver, precious stones, alabaster, copper, and chlorite, that it had to be (or at least

Fig. 3.12 *Left*
Many of the deceased attendants in royal graves at Ur wore elaborate chokers around their necks. This example (30-12-706) of alternating triangles of gold and lapis lazuli from Body 7 in PG 1237 demonstrates the style.

could be removed from circulation and) buried to make room for more. The city of Ur was the first docking point for ships arriving from the east heavily laden with luxury and utilitarian goods and materials. The elites of Ur were, thus, the first to make their selections, choosing long carnelian beads made in the Indus Valley, chlorite bowls from the Halil River basin, or agate and lapis lazuli beads made in eastern Iran and imported to Mesopotamia in bulk to adorn the bodies of both the living and the dead.

Less visible in the graves but certainly of greater importance to urban communities were the vast quantities of copper mined and smelted on the Oman Peninsula or the Iranian Plateau before being loaded onto boats in the form of ingots ready to be made into tools and weapons. While most of this copper was alloyed with arsenic to make it more malleable, some tin bronze was also found in the Royal Tombs at Ur. The tin was probably brought from western Iran, where tin sources have recently been located in the mountains easily reached through the Diyala Valley. Mesopotamian craftsmen learned the techniques of working copper from their neighbors on the Iranian Plateau, who had long since attained a high degree of mastery in the craft, and in some cases the Mesopotamians even surpassed their teachers.

The world stretching out to the east fired the imaginations of the Mesopotamians. At the end of the 3rd millennium, the bards and scribes of the Ur III Period (2112-2004 BCE) court composed elaborate legends in which heroic kings of Uruk, the claimed ancestors of the Ur III kings, engaged with their counterparts on the plateau in productive struggle and cultural competition. While these myths, recounted in greater detail in a later chapter (see Chapter 4: Religion and the Gods), cannot be read as historical texts, there is little doubt that they drew their inspiration from the memory of early kings who established their rank, prestige, and legitimacy through the display of the great wealth they amassed for themselves and for the gods.

Fig. 3.13 *Opposite*
Among the fabulous wealth from the Royal Tombs at Ur are vessels made from ostrich egg shells. This one (B16692) from PG 779 is particularly ornate. It is covered with a thick sheet of gold and its rim is decorated in geometric patterns of lapis lazuli and colored limestone, secured in place with bitumen.

For Further Reading

Aruz, Joan, ed., with Ronald Wallenfels. 2003. *Art of the First Cities: The Third Millennium B.C. from the Mediterranean to the Indus*. New York, New Haven: Metropolitan Museum of Art, Yale University Press.

Crawford, Harriet, ed. 2013. *The Sumerian World*. New York: Routledge.

Postgate, J.N. 1992. *Early Mesopotamia: Society and Economy at the Dawn of History*. London: Routledge.

Sallaberger, Walther, and Ingo Schrakamp, eds. 2015. *History and Philology. Associated Regional Chronologies for the Ancient Near East and the Eastern Mediterranean*. Turnhout, Belgium: Brepols.

4

RELIGION AND THE GODS

Steve Tinney

Opposite
Alabaster statuette of a priest (37-15-31)
found alongside many others at Khafaje.

Introduction

Religion and the gods were central to the lives of the ancient Mesopotamian people, and pervade every part of the surviving archaeological, textual, and pictorial records of the region. Scores of temples have been excavated, some located on sites that were in use for thousands of years. At such sites, temples were repeatedly refurbished or rebuilt as they became damaged or deteriorated, sometimes on the same and sometimes on different plans. Ancient artists depicted gods, temples, and rituals in tiny carvings and in monumental sculptures, in stone and clay reliefs, and in vividly colored wall paintings (Figs. 4.1, 4.2). Thousands of gods are known by name from every kind of text, and divine worship, lives, and exploits were recounted in a rich corpus of myths, hymns, incantations, and rituals. The following pages focus first on the gods, then on the mythology which relates their deeds. We then turn to the homes of the gods—the temples—and after that to a description of the intellectual activity which was integrated with the worship of the gods—Mesopotamian scholarship.

While the extant data on religion in Mesopotamia is rich it is also inconsistent: some periods and places are richly documented while others are only scantily so, and still others remain completely unknown. At the same time, we must keep in mind that Mesopotamia was not a religious (or any other sort of) monolith. Instead, its divine realm was both complex and pluralistic, and prevailing belief systems, if sometimes widely held and constant across time and space, were more often local to specific cities, current only during certain dynasties, or even particular to individual ancient scholars. As a result, we generally cannot speak of any single definitive Mesopotamian creation myth or afterlife belief, for example. Belief systems were not absolute and universal: they were local and constantly altered to suit changing political climates.

Gods and Their Cities, Attributes and Families

Each city had a chief or patron deity, who was typically conceptualized as anthropomorphic (human in form) and endowed with a family unit including spouse and children. At Nippur, for example, the chief god was Enlil, his spouse was Ninlil, and their children were Ninurta, Ninhursag, and Nanna. Most gods had particular attributes or associations: Ninurta was a warrior god; Ninhursag was a birth goddess; and Nanna was the moon god.

Most city pantheons, or local groups of gods, were primarily worshipped only in their own cities, but the Nippur gods took on a larger significance. Enlil was the son of An (Anu in Akkadian), the sky god and city god of Uruk, and emerged as a leading force in religious politics in the 3rd millennium BCE. Enlil's city of Nippur, moreover, unlike other cities, never had its own king. Instead, the rulers of other cities such as Akkad, Ur,

Fig. 4.2 *Opposite, Below*
This tablet (B10673) describes the Sumerian myth of the great flood.

and Isin made offerings to Enlil at Nippur; they also supported Enlil's temples in Nippur as a way of demonstrating that they were the rightful rulers of "Sumer and Akkad," an expression that signified the region of southern Mesopotamia as a whole. In this respect, Enlil was the earliest clear example of what we may call a supreme god in Mesopotamia. In the 2nd millennium BCE, Enlil would be superseded in status by the gods Marduk in the south of Mesopotamia and Ashur in the northern state of Assyria.

The god An, Enlil's father, is also mentioned in early texts as one of the most important of the major gods, along with the goddess Ninhursag; An, however, barely figures in the surviving mythological compositions from Mesopotamia. He is, in some creation narratives from the 3rd millennium BCE, one of the original creative forces alongside Ki, "earth," and seems to have been worshipped from the earliest times at Uruk, where writing originated as part of the urban explosion around 3500 BCE. There are no known myths that explain how Enlil overcame An in importance, but this does not rule out the possibility that such compositions once existed or that they may one day be discovered or identified.

The goddess Inana (Ishtar in Akkadian), An's daughter, was the dominant figure at Uruk (Fig. 4.1). It is her temple that is depicted in the uppermost register of the Uruk Vase (see Chapter 3S1: The Uruk Vase). Inana was the goddess of war and carnal love, and was, in various forms, strongly associated with kingship throughout Mesopotamian history. In the Death of Ur-Namma, Inana complains to Enlil that Ur-Namma, the founder of the Ur III Dynasty (ca. 2112–2004 BCE), died in battle because Enlil had sent Inana on an errand, thus leaving the king unprotected. Inana was also the divine spouse of the king from the reign of the Old Akkadian king Naram-Sin (2254-2218 BCE) through to the period of the kings of Isin (ca. 2017–1924 BCE), who succeeded the Ur III Dynasty. This spousal relationship was expressed, amongst other ways, through the Sacred Marriage, a ritual celebrating the marriage of the king and the goddess, which promoted the well-being and prosperity of the state. In a good example of the adaptability of myth, some ancient Mesopotamian traditions made Inana the daughter of Enki (Ea in Akkadian), god of magic and understanding, while others made her a daughter of the moon god, Nanna, and, thus, sister to the sun god Utu (Shamash in Akkadian), who was Nanna's son.

Enki is another of the foundational gods of early Mesopotamia (Fig. 4.1). As the god of wisdom and magic, Enki features in several myths about the creation and organization of the world. Enki is also the god responsible for bringing magic into the world and is the patron of magical experts and their incantations. A friend of humanity, who frustrates the gods' plans to destroy the human race, Enki is the god who, in the flood story, ensures the continuation of humanity and its knowledge through his selection of his most expert worshipper to build an ark and survive the deluge (Fig. 4.2). Enki's city in the 3rd millennium BCE was Eridu but, after Eridu was abandoned in the 18th century

BCE, his cult seems to have relocated to Ur. With the rise of Marduk, the chief god of Babylon, in the 2nd millennium BCE, Enki was recast as Marduk's father and Eridu became the name of a city quarter of Babylon.

Nanna (Sin or Su'en in Akkadian), the moon god and patron of the city of Ur, was also known as Dilimbabbar, "silver scoop" (from the Sumerian **dilim**, "spoon" or "ladle," and **babbar**, "silver"), a reference to the shape of the crescent moon. He was described as having great herds of cows, a notion again inspired by the lunar crescent and perhaps referring to the multitude of the stars in the night sky. One hymn to Nanna, the *Herds of Nanna* (also known as *Nanna F*), asserts: "His fattened cows number 108,000. His young bulls number 126,000. The sparkling-eyed cows number 50,400. The white cows number 126,000."

Mythology

From our discussion of the major gods and their attributes, we may naturally proceed to some consideration of their actions, as expressed in the mythology that is one of our most important sources on the gods. Among the few myths about Enlil is an important early work of Sumerian literature, a large clay cylinder, usually called the Barton Cylinder, which preserves a still mysterious tale about Enlil and Ninhursag, the deity worshipped in the temple erected at the site of Tell al-`Ubaid, ancient Nutur (Fig. 4.3).

continued on page 83

KINGSHIP AND THE GODS

Philip Jones

The political structure of ancient Mesopotamia was very different from that of the modern world. The core unit was the city rather than the nation-state, states were monarchies rather than democracies, and political legitimacy was based on divine favor rather than popular will. Nonetheless, politics and ideas about politics were not static and there were changes in state structures and beliefs over time, just as in contemporary political structures.

Southern Mesopotamia was originally an area of competing city-states. As far back as the late 4th millennium BCE, however, there are indications of larger groupings of cities emerging. Whether these groupings were the result of collaboration or force is not known.

By the early 3rd millennium BCE, the city of Kish in northern Babylonia exercised domination over some of the cities to the south. In fact, the title "King of Kish" lost its geographic specificity and came to imply regional dominance generally, regardless of not only a ruler's home city but also whether he actually controlled the city of Kish itself. Thus, for example, the power of the rulers buried in the Royal Cemetery of Ur (ca. mid-3rd millennium BCE) is reflected both in the magnificence of their burials and in their use of the title "King of Kish" alongside that of "King of Ur."

The city of Nippur, unlike the city of Kish, does not seem to have played an active or direct political role in the struggles of the early city states. There are indications, however, that it functioned as a key religious center in the land, with the rulers of other cities (see Fig. 4S1.1) keen to make offerings there to Enlil, Nippur's patron god and one of the chief deities of the Mesopotamian pantheon.

Where known, all Mesopotamian states were ruled by monarchs, although it is not always clear in the earliest

Fig. 4S1.1 *Above*

The vase B9305+B9601 (also known as CBS 9305+CBS 9601) is inscribed with a text that calls upon Enlil, the god of Nippur, to intercede with the Sky God An to grant Lugalzagesi a prosperous rule over the cities of Sumer. Lugalzagesi was the king of Uruk and hegemon of Sumer in ca. 2350 BCE.

Fig. 4S1.2 *Left*
The tablet fragment B14220 (also known as CBS 14420), probably dating to ca. 1725 BCE, is inscribed with part of the Sumerian King List. Starting with the line, "When kingship came down from the sky," the composition enumerates a succession of kings who supposedly ruled the land in turn from antediluvian times down to the early 2nd millennium BCE. Kings are grouped into dynasties in terms of their home city.

period how strong the principle of hereditary succession was (see Fig. 4S1.2). Early rulers bore a variety of titles, perhaps due to local tradition or variation in the precise type of rulership. A city's chief or patron god was considered its ultimate ruler and, as such, could be addressed with the word for king, **lugal** in Sumerian and *sharrum* in Akkadian. Human rulers could also be termed **lugal**, but they often instead took the title **ensi**, which seems to emphasize the human king's role as steward of the god's city. Royal office was often envisaged as shifting from city to city as An and Enlil granted terrestrial responsibility to the chief god of whichever was the dominant city at any one time; this chief god delegated power to the city's human ruler in turn.

Early Mesopotamia had many gods grouped into a broad family structure. At the head of the pantheon was the sky god An (Anu in Akkadian). Early inscriptions refer to him as the "king of the gods." However, Enlil, the "king of all lands," seems to have played a more active role in the lives of human beings. Divine rule in Mesopotamia might also be imagined as a committee of these two gods plus the god of wisdom, Enki, and the mother goddess, Ninhursag, or indeed as a type of "democratic" assembly of all the gods.

In general, the extant myths from Mesopotamia describe the gods as oscillating between sleeping and eating. Humans were created to labor in place of the gods, and to ensure the gods retained a steady supply of food. A king, consequently, had two crucial tasks: (1) to ensure that there was food to feed the gods when they awoke; and (2) to prevent human disorder from interfering with their sleep.

It begins in the remotest of mythological times, before creation: "In those far-off days, back in those far-off days." The sky god An and earth goddess Ki are then mentioned; we are told they are talking to each other but not what they say. After a break of around 15–20 words, the goddess Ninhursag, oldest sister of the great god Enlil, is introduced. Enlil, in an abrupt turn in the narrative, then has sex with Ninhursag, impregnating her with seven sets of twins. After several breaks in the text, the narrative seems to turn to the alienation of gods from their cities. The text is somewhat fragmentary, but our knowledge of Sumerian literature makes it possible to plausibly read and reconstruct: "s/he made Enki feel bitterness towards the Abzu" (Enki is lord of the Abzu, the subterranean fresh waters); "s/he made Enlil feel bitterness towards Nippur" (Enlil, of course, is the patron god of Nippur), and "s/he made Inana feel bitterness for Kizabalam." The warrior god Ninurta then makes his entrance, clad in lion skins. The text becomes mysterious again: the Tigris and Euphrates are mentioned and various kinds of animals become abundant, possibly indicating a change to a prosperous and happy time effected by some action of the god Ninurta. Ninhursag is described as getting dressed up, putting on eye shadow, and establishing a seat of honor at Kesh. The end of the text is badly broken.

The date of this work cannot be established exactly, but it is probably only a little later than the Ninhursag temple at the site of Tell al-`Ubaid (Fig. 4.4), which dates to approximately 2500 BCE and which was excavated by the British archaeologist Sir Leonard Woolley. Ninhursag, like many Mesopotamian deities, is known by several different names in different myths, some of which probably derive from other local creation or mother goddesses; these names include Nintur, Ninmah, and Belet-Ili. She also features in another creation tale, one very different from that on the Barton Cylinder, known to modern scholars as *Enki and Ninhursag*.

Humans and the Gods

Several surviving myths describe the creation of human beings. In what seems to be a local Nippur tradition, the Sumerian text *Song of the Hoe* relates how Enlil creates humans by placing their form in a brick-mold and planting them so that they grow. In a different Sumerian tradition, known from the narrative *Enki and Ninmah*, an alternate explanation of human origins is presented. This tradition, which finds its way into later Akkadian myths such as *Atra-hasis*, describes humans as created to replace the gods as laborers, and to perform such tasks as dredging the irrigation channels and working in the fields. When *Enki and Ninmah* begins, humans have not yet come into the world, so that "the senior gods oversaw the work, while the minor gods were bearing the toil." As the minor gods start to complain in earnest about their heavy labor, Enki remains sleeping; it falls to his mother, Namma, to wake him and advise him to create humans to bear the toil of the angry gods. The text continues:

> After Enki, the maker of creations had pondered the matter by himself, he said to his mother Namma: "My mother, the creation you proposed will really happen. Impose on him the work of carrying baskets. You should knead clay from the top of the Abzu; the birth-goddesses(?) will nip off the clay and you shall bring the form into existence. Let Ninmah act as your assistant.

The remainder of the composition is marred by some frustrating breaks, but contains a competition between Enki and Ninmah in which Ninmah creates a series of defective human beings and challenges Enki to determine their destinies; Enki wins the competition by successfully identifying a fitting social role for each of Ninmah's creations. Eventually, Enki takes his turn at creating a defective creature and it is left to Ninmah to determine its destiny:

> Umul: its head was afflicted, its…was afflicted, its eyes were afflicted, its neck was afflicted. It could hardly breathe, its ribs were shaky, its lungs were afflicted, its heart was afflicted, its bowels were afflicted. With its hand and its lolling head it could not put bread into its mouth; its spine and head were dislocated. The weak hips and the shaky feet could not carry(?) it on the field—Enki made it in this way.

Ninmah is unable to do anything with this creature, whose name, Umul, means "my day is far." Enki, thus, reveals his extraordinary cleverness and takes his customarily significant role in human history: his creation, Umul, is the first baby. Because Ninmah is another name for Ninhursag, the myths *Enki and Ninmah* and *Enki and Ninhursag* can be read in conjunction with each other. Both narratives provide explanations of the origins of well-known things and places and, between them, contain elements pertaining to cosmic creation and organization; divine creation and organization; and the creation and organization of human beings.

continued on page 88

Enki and Ninhursag

Steve Tinney

The myth *Enki and Ninhursag*, which is only known from tablets dating to the 18th century BCE, opens in the land of Dilmun (modern Bahrain). Here, the god Enki lives with Ninhursag, who is described both as Enki's spouse and as his daughter; this is the first in a series of relationships in the myth that contravene Mesopotamian social norms. Ninhursag complains that the city Enki has given her is failing due to a lack of fresh water, a deficiency that Enki promises to resolve the next day:

> At that moment, by Utu, on that day, when Utu stepped up into heaven, from the jars set up on Ezen's shore, from Nanna's radiant high temple, from the mouth of the waters running underground, fresh waters ran out of the ground for her.
>
> The waters rose up from it into her great basins. Her city drank water aplenty from them. Dilmun drank water aplenty from them. Her pools of salt water indeed became pools of fresh water. Her fields, meadows, and furrows produced grain for her. Her city indeed became a storehouse on the quay for the Land. Dilmun indeed became a storehouse on the quay for the Land. At that moment, by Utu, on that day, thus did (Enki) make it so for her!

The passage above, which is incidental to the main narrative of the text, explains the origin of the freshwater springs, which continued until recently to supply water for Bahrain, and goes on to promise the city's commercial prosperity as a trading center: "May the wide sea yield you its wealth."

As the text continues, Enki copulates with Ninhursag and she gives birth to a vegetation goddess named Ninnisig. Enki, seeing Ninnisig and desiring her, copulates with her as well, and she gives birth to another goddess, whom Enki also impregnates. This pattern continues until Ninhursag intervenes; she collects Enki's semen after he seduces the spider goddess, Uttu, and plants it in a garden that grows a variety of plants. Enki, ever vigilant, espies the plants and consumes them so that he can determine their destinies. Ninhursag is so enraged by this action that she curses Enki, making him sick; the only person who is able to remedy his sickness, moreover, is Ninhursag herself.

The finale of the text is part celebration of Ninhursag's powers and part feast of puns. Ninhursag asks Enki which parts of his body hurt him, and for each body part she gives birth to a god or goddess whose name is a play on the word for the body part. "My brother," she says each time, "what hurts you?" "My mouth (Sumerian **ka**) hurts me," Enki says, and Ninhursag gives birth to Ninkasi, the beer goddess. "My side (Sumerian **zag**) hurts me," he says, and Ninhursag gives birth to the god Enzag. Eight deities are born in this way, the same number as spiders have legs. Ninhursag then determines each of their destinies: Ninkasi will be "the thing that satisfies the heart"; Enzag will be the Lord of Dilmun.

Fig. 4S2.1 *Opposite*
Clay tablet (B4561) preserving the main manuscript of Enki and Ninhursag, from Nippur, ca. 1730 BCE.

In the version of creation contained in the *Sumerian Flood Story* (Fig. 4.2), another part of the picture appears: the origin of earthly kingship. Although the beginning of the text, which probably contained additional creation elements, is missing, when the text becomes legible we read that "after An, Enlil, Enki, and Ninhursag had fashioned the black-headed people (the Sumerians), they also made animals multiply everywhere, and made herds of four-legged animals exist on the plains, as is befitting." After another break, in which the creation of humanity was probably described, the text picks up again:

[Speaker uncertain]: "I will oversee their labor. Let…the builder of the Land, dig a solid foundation."

After the…of kingship had descended from heaven, after the supreme crown and throne of kingship had descended from heaven, the divine rites and the supreme powers were perfected, the bricks of the cities were laid in holy places, their names were announced and their *oversight* was distributed. The first of the cities, Eridu, was given to Nudimmud the leader. The second, Bad-tibira, was given to the Mistress. The third, Larag, was given to Pabilsag. The fourth, Sippar, was given to the hero Utu. The fifth, Shuruppak, was given to Sud.

This description is fascinating, if slightly esoteric. Although the flood tablet was written in the early 2nd millennium BCE, the original set of gods and cities described here belongs to a period hundreds of years earlier, hinting at the long survival of scholarly lore about the history of the gods. Nudimmud is a less well-known name for Enki; the Mistress is Ninhursag; Pabilsag is a god who is later treated as a form of Ninurta, the warrior god; and Sud is the original name of the goddess who becomes Ninlil in the Sumerian myth *Enlil and Sud*.

In the relationship between human beings and the gods, the king assumed the most prominent role. He owed his position to divine support, in exchange for which he was expected to fulfill certain obligations. These included building temples and providing for their economic viability or, in mythological terms, ensuring that people carried out the irrigation and agricultural work necessary to maintain the temples.

The king also took a central role in certain religious rituals, including the Sacred Marriage (see Chapter 3S1: The Uruk Vase), and his purity was maintained and protected by daily ritual bathing and other measures. The complex of support and protection around the king grew over the millennia and, at the time of our best documentation, which comes from the Neo-Assyrian Period (ca. 911–612 BCE), an entire team of scholars surrounded the king, watching for omens that could threaten his safety, carrying out routine rituals to prevent evil from approaching him, and guiding him in his dealings with the gods. In the throne rooms of the Neo-Assyrian kings, the protective environment was also

Fig. 4.5 Opposite

Plaque (32-22-3) showing a "fishman"— a priest wearing a fish cloak during a ritual. The fish cloak is a reference to the myth in which Enki's emissary, Oannes, brings ritual and magical knowledge to humanity in the form of a fish with human head and limbs which emerges from the sea, Enki's domain, with his teachings.

realized in great wall sculptures carved in low relief that depicted divine scholars or genies carrying out rituals in support of the king's well-being and against the approach of evil forces (Fig. 4.5).

The Temple as the House of the God

The mythology we have been discussing was complemented by extensive programs of worship centered around temples. In addition to interacting with each other in the divine realm, the gods were present on earth through their cult statues, which were worshipped in the inner chambers of each temple. The Sumerian for temple, **e₂**, denotes house or household, and the temples functioned and are best understood as the households of the gods.

Archaeological excavations have uncovered hundreds of ancient Mesopotamian temples. In some cases, the temples have very long histories, with the earliest form of the temple, a single small room, dating back to the 5th millennium BCE. Over time, the temples were periodically levelled and rebuilt in the same places, often growing in size and complexity with each rebuilding. Archaeologists are able to identify individual phases in the history of this building and rebuilding from the survival, sometimes only partial, of the wall foundations of temples from different periods. The early single-room shrines were augmented with courtyards and storerooms with surrounding walls. The god's chamber was often doubled, providing space both for the temple's god or goddess and for his or her spouse. The main temple building could be situated on a raised platform; such raised platforms probably inspired the large stepped pyramidal temple towers called ziggurats that were used for worship and rituals in Mesopotamia and that, from the late 3rd millennium BCE, dominated the skyline of cities such as Ur.

A gatehouse guarded entry to the temple, allowing only priests and other temple personnel to pass. Within lay a courtyard that was a hub of activity: temple bakers prepared bread in ovens; temple butchers prepared animals to feed the gods; priests prepared for rituals; and administrators managed storerooms. Around the courtyard, the doors of the storerooms were tied shut with rope, and clay was pressed around the knots and impressed with official seals to protect their integrity (see Chapter 3S2: Cylinder Seals in the Ancient Near East).

Behind the closed doors of the storerooms were the temple's supplies and riches. Serving dishes, jugs, and cups were used to present the meals of the gods. These meals would be shared out among the temple staff after the gods had "eaten." Drums, torches, incense burners, and cedar resin and other aromatics were used for purification in the daily rituals that accompanied the care and feeding of the gods. Although no treasury has survived intact, we know from administrative documents that some temples owned large amounts of metals, jewelry, and gems, and that they tracked their wealth with carefully written inventories.

Fig. 4.6 *Opposite*
Diorite head (B16664) of king Gudea of Lagash wearing the characteristic royal rolled cap.

Beyond the courtyard, within the temple buildings, or up the stairs and across a platform, lay the dwelling of the gods. Already situated in a less accessible part of the complex, the god's private chamber was usually approached by a door in a side wall. In the deepest part of the room, as far from the door as possible, and visible only after entering the room, the statue of the god was set in the flickering gloom on a platform or throne. The statue, created from special woods and richly clothed and decorated, would have been instilled with life by special rituals that brought the divine presence into it. Once it effectively presenced the god, the statue was cared for each day with rites of worship to awaken, dress, and feed it, and, at night, to settle it down to sleep.

This is not to say that the divine statues were exclusively confined to their homes. They could and did leave the temple for parades in their own cities, or even visit rituals taking place in other cities. These rituals could be regularly occurring—associated with the new moon, for example, or the new year—or be held to mark special occasions, such as the building of a new temple. When Gudea, king of Lagash (Fig. 4.6), rebuilt the temple of the city god Ningirsu around 2150 BCE, Ningirsu, needing to be rehoused for the duration of the renovations, went to Enki's city of Eridu until he was able to return to his new home.

The Gudea Cylinders of the late 3rd millennium BCE provide us with our best understanding of the process of temple building, and illuminate several of the narrative elements represented in the carvings of the Ur-Namma Stele. The king of Lagash, Gudea (ca. 2150–2125 BCE), is called to build the temple of the god Ningirsu, patron god of Lagash, by Ningirsu himself. Gudea purifies the site with fire, repeatedly takes omens to ensure that he is doing the right thing and follows all the prescribed rituals with the help of the gods. He creates the first brick, the Brick of Destiny, carrying the clay for the brick himself, molding it, and holding it up for the people of the city to see. This brick is probably the reference point for small stone bricks that have been found, alongside copper statuettes of a figure carrying a basket heaped with clay (Fig. 4.7), buried in foundation deposits under temples. Gudea then carves seven stelae and places them in the temple courtyard. When the building is complete, the king invites Ningirsu to return to it, and prepares a banquet for the gods. His reward is the prosperity of his land.

Archaeological discoveries from a range of different temple sites provide further details. Writing was incorporated into the temple structure in numerous ways: even the individual bricks used for building the temple could be inscribed or stamped with short standard inscriptions such as "For Nanna, Ur-Namma, king of Ur, built his temple and built the wall of Ur." (Fig. 4.8). Such inscriptions were repeated in the foundation deposits, on door sockets, and on various other objects that were either part of the temple or placed within it. The lavishness and meticulous attention to detail that characterized

continued on page 98

Fig. 4.7 *Opposite*
Copper statue (31-17-8) of Rim-Sin from a foundation box in the Enki temple at Ur.

THE UR-NAMMA STELE

William B. Hafford

In 1923–1924, during the second season of the joint Penn and British Museum excavations at Ur, the archaeologist C. Leonard Woolley began finding carved limestone fragments from a royal stele, a type of large, freestanding stone monument (Fig. 4S3.1). These fragments, along with additional pieces of the stele discovered in later seasons, entered the Penn Museum collection and a lengthy process of reconstruction began.

The stele was originally attributed to Ur-Namma (ca. 2112–2095 BCE), the first king of the Ur III Dynasty, by an inscription on the robe of one of the figures. The fragment bearing this inscription was later found to belong to a different monument, but the stele's attribution to the Ur III Period remains consistent both with the findspot of its fragments and with the style of its pictorial representation (Fig. 4S3.2).

Standing nearly 4 meters (13 feet) in height, and weighing well over a ton, the stele would originally have taken the form of an arch-shaped slab. It remains in very fragmentary condition today, but the reconstruction (Fig. 4S3.3) provides a good understanding of the scenes it contained in the five registers carved on each of the two sides. These scenes emphasize the royal responsibilities and authority of the king, his role as a builder of city and society, and his relationships with the divine.

Fig. 4S3.1 *Above Right*
Stele Fragment B16676.14. The pieces of the stele had been scattered and reused in antiquity, some forming pivots for door posts, others used in construction, but many were left scattered. Several pieces were found in the vicinity of a brick base of the Ur III Period, in the courtyard near the entrance to the ziggurat platform. One of these weighed nearly 300 kilograms (660 pounds).

Fig. 4S3.2 *Opposite*
The stele could not be reconstructed in its entirety, as many pieces remain missing. A potential reconstruction drawing, shown here, was completed by Jeanny Vorys Canby in the 1990s. A partial inscription on one side mentions the building of canals, an important duty of the king. The particular Sumerian verb for digging, **ba-al**, used in this inscription is one that primarily appears in texts of Ur-Namma.

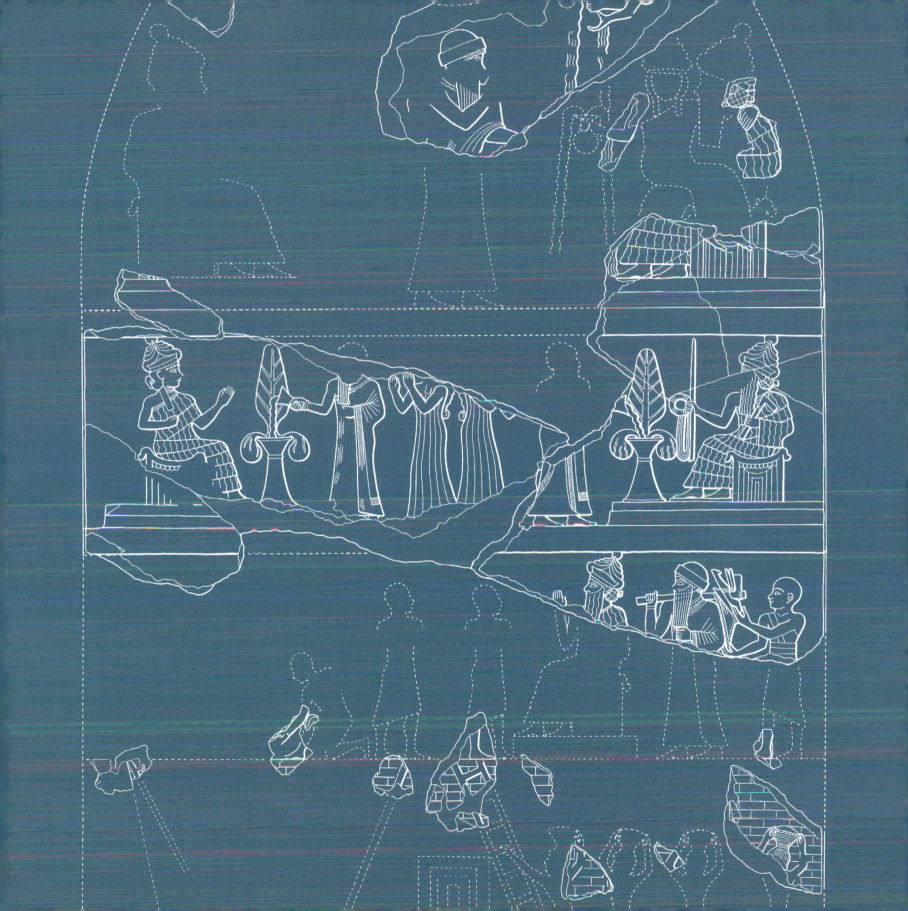

Fig. 4S3.3 *Left*
Laser scans of the pieces completed in the early 2000s allowed for a life-sized reconstruction to be made. The stele depicts the king paying tribute to the gods and overseeing the construction of what may be a temple.

Fig. 4S3.4 *Opposite*
This artist's reconstruction shows the stele as it may have looked standing in place near the entrance to the ziggurat courtyard. Drawn by HSD/John Pearson.

the building program was underscored by the decoration of the temple in friezes of lapis lazuli and shell, by sculptural representations of the gods or the creatures associated with them, and by freestanding stelae which told the story of the rebuilding and other events in narrative images.

Kings dedicated objects such as mace heads and stone bowls and vases to the temple and inscribed them with accounts of their building or military activities. As part of his assertion of dominion over Sumer, the king Lugalzagesi (ca. 2350 BCE) of Uruk deposited dozens of stone vessels and mace heads in Enlil's temple at Nippur; archaeologists discovered these offerings smashed into pieces. Perhaps not coincidentally, we know that Sargon (ca. 2334–2279 BCE), the founder of the Old Akkadian Dynasty, defeated Lugalzagesi and paraded him captive in a neck-stock before the god Enlil. The original Sargon monument, inscribed with this text and erected by Sargon to commemorate his victory in the courtyard of Enlil's temple at Nippur, is lost, but its text is preserved in copies made hundreds of years after the event by scribes who worked in the courtyard and recorded on large clay tablets the texts of all of the stone statues and stelae erected at the site by the kings of Akkad and their immediate successors (Fig. 4.9).

In addition to kings, others also offered various objects to the gods as proof of their devotion, or as part of petitions for a long life for themselves or others, and for the gods' help with health or financial problems. The objects offered included statues and statuettes, stone vessels of various kinds, and models or images of animals.

From Scribe to Scholar: Knowledge and the Gods

The religious practitioners who performed rituals in the temples were often also scholars who were experts in various ancient Mesopotamian knowledge disciplines which reached far beyond the temple proper. Our understanding of their practices is based on tens of thousands of clay tablets: relatively few from the 3rd millennium BCE; significantly more from the 2nd millennium; and a veritable flood of material from the 1st millennium. Several major disciplines may be described.

The *ashipu*, or purification expert, was responsible for a wide range of interactions with the gods. He would have been adept at performing building rituals, which protected the temple from evil forces and ensured its successful completion; directing the magic needed to diagnose illnesses, as well as to heal and protect individuals from harmful forces; and exorcising demons.

The *baru*, or diviner, was responsible for predicting the future and wrote and used thousands of texts, each of which followed a strict form. This form consists of an "If" clause followed by a "then" clause, e.g., "If a raven plaintively cries out on the left of a man, that man will experience sorrow. If it cries out on the right of a man, his enemy will experience sorrow." The same form is also used for laws in collections including those

Fig. 4.8 *Opposite*

Brick (B16461) from Ur-Namma's rebuilding of the Nanna temple at Ur which was stepped on by a dog while it was still drying.

appearing on the Law Stele of Hammurabi (ca. 1792–1750 BCE). The *baru* understood how to carry out the special rituals needed to address the gods before sacrificing a lamb or kid, as well as how to read the messages placed in the organs of the animals by the gods: the liver of the sacrificial animal was called "the tablet of the gods." The study of celestial and astronomical omens formed a special branch of divination whose practitioners were called "scribes of *Enuma Anu Enlil*" ("When An and Enlil"); *Enuma Anu Enlil* constituted a series of omens based on observing the heavens.

The *kalu* or lamentation-priest, for his part, appeased the gods by performing long, repetitive songs detailing the woes caused by divine actions or inattentiveness.

Fig. 4.9 *Above*
Large tablet (B13972) from about 1730 BCE on which a scribe has copied down inscriptions of the kings of Agade from monuments placed by them in the Enlil temple courtyard around 500 years earlier.

These practitioners often worked together: the *baru* might identify a danger in the future, for example, while the *ashipu* carried out a ritual to avert the danger. Rituals began with purification, usually with one or more of the elements of water, incense, fire, and sound. Special magical spells or incantations were used to purify even the materials to be used in the purification procedures, ensuring that the entire process was protected from evil. Ritual actions such as the creation of a protective circle with flour, or the shaping of figurines, were accompanied by the uttering of more incantations. In one of the best-preserved magical series, *Maqlu* ("Burning"), the series includes one tablet of ritual instructions and eight tablets of incantations. The ritual tablet references the incantations by name, telling the *ashipu* to recite particular incantations at particular points in the ceremony. Like many rituals, *Maqlu* is divided into several parts that take place in different locations. The first part is carried out in the evening in the house of a patient who suspects that his or her illness comes from black magic; further rituals take place around the patient's bed; and the finale takes place in the morning in the doorway of the house. Amongst other climactic actions, edible figurines of the evil warlock and witch are fashioned and fed to a pair of dogs, one male and one female, who symbolically devour the authors of the black magic underlying the malady.

We do not know how many people would have had access to this level of worship and ritual. Many of our tablets and series, especially from the 1st millennium BCE, are focused on the king and the royal family, but this is unsurprising given that the bulk of our texts come from the libraries of King Ashurbanipal of Assyria (ca. 668–631 BCE). At the same time, however, non-royal families would certainly have been able to hire experts to carry out healing and funerary rituals, though this kind of activity would have left smaller traces in the written record and, thus, may be underestimated.

With the end of the Assyrian empire and its successor Babylonian empire, the old gods of Mesopotamia began to wane as they became assimilated to the classical deities or restricted in importance to the last lingering outposts of Mesopotamian culture in Uruk and Babylon. As this happened, a different way of thinking about the world of the divine gained currency with monotheistic beliefs taking center stage as the last embers of the cults of An, Inana, Marduk, and Nabu died away.

For Further Reading

Black, Jeremy, and Anthony Green. 1992. *Gods, Demons and Symbols of Ancient Mesopotamia: An Illustrated Dictionary*. Austin: University of Texas Press.

Black, Jeremy, Graham Cunningham, Eleanor Robson, and Gabor Zolyomi (eds.). 2006. *The Literature of Ancient Sumer*. Oxford: Oxford University Press.

Foster, Benjamin R. 1995. *From Distant Days: Myths, Tales, and Poetry of Ancient Mesopotamia*. Potomac, MD: CDL Press.

Podany, Amanda H. 2013. *The Ancient Near East: A Very Short Introduction*. Oxford: Oxford University Press.

5

A View from the Highlands

Holly Pittman

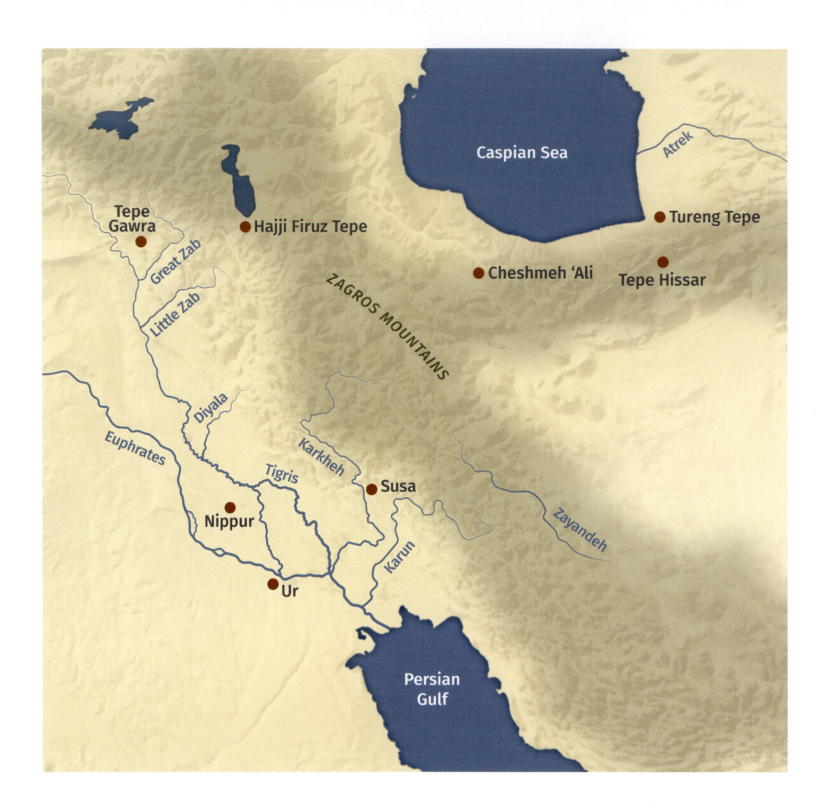

Introduction

The land between the Tigris and the Euphrates rivers, Mesopotamia, was rich in fertile soil, abundant marine life, date palms, and marsh reeds. Spindly trees, and woody date trunks, reeds for matting, bitumen for waterproofing, shells, and soft limestone were all locally available. Wheat and barley grew in the fields, and livestock were pastured in the nearby piedmont lands in the north. And yet, despite all of these resources, the alluvial lowland lacked those raw materials that would become the basis of urban civilization: hardwoods, metals, and colorful stones. These materials were, instead, to be found in the highland regions surrounding the vast Mesopotamian river valley. To the north and west, the Anatolian Plateau was an important source for copper, timber, and silver, particularly during the 2nd and 1st millennia BCE. But it was the east that captured the imagination and the attention of the early Mesopotamians: here, where the sun rose, lay the home of the great gods, and the lands where mythological heroes adventured in the high mountains and vast plains, returning with stories of unimaginably abundant riches. These same riches were sought by rulers to embellish temples—the houses of the gods—as well as their own palaces; to provision soldiers; and to make tools for the fields and workshops.

The region to the east of Mesopotamia's alluvial plains is a vast upland plateau that today constitutes Iran and western Central Asia (Figs. 5.1, 5.2). Unlike Mesopotamia, which is defined by its two major rivers, the Iranian Plateau is an enormous landmass of great diversity and little internal connectivity, possessing instead regional oasis river systems. The Zagros Mountains, running from the northwest to the southeast, are a formidable barrier between the Mesopotamian lowland and the Iranian highland plateau. Ascending more than 4,000 meters (over 14,000 feet) in places (the highest peak is 4,409 m or 14,465 ft), small highland valleys watered by artesian springs and snowmelt streams were home to wild sheep, goats, and bovids. By the 8th millennium BCE, the slow process of animal domestication had begun in small villages, yielding smaller and more docile animals that could be herded in large groups (see Chapter 2: The Geography and Agriculture of the Middle East). At first, such animals were used primarily for their meat, an important source of protein, but soon they were valued also for their milk, used to make cheese and yogurt; their hides and hair, which were made into leather and used for spinning and weaving; and their labor, useful for transportation and for plowing the fields. By the 6th millennium BCE, these domesticated animals, together with the domesticated varieties of wheat and barley that had first developed in the west, had become the fundamental pillars of subsistence in village life.

Beyond the mountain valleys to the east is a highland plain that stretches from the south shore of the Caspian Sea to the Persian Gulf. At its extreme south, this plain is essentially an eastern extension of the Mesopotamian river basin. Through this plain,

Fig. 5.1 *Opposite*
Map of highland regions discussed in this chapter.

Fig. 5.2 *Above*

Landscape view of the Iranian plateau.
© Ninara (flickr)/Kaisu Raasakka.

the Karun and the Karkheh Rivers flow southwest from headwaters in the Zagros until they empty into the Persian Gulf, where they mingle with the water from the Tigris and Euphrates. This region, the site of the modern-day province of Khuzestan in Iran, was the home of Susa, a large and important city founded around 5000 BCE and inhabited until medieval times. From the time of its foundation through to the present day, Susa (now in the region of Ahwaz and Shushtar) has held a uniquely important place in the larger geopolitical landscape, acting as an eastern lowland gateway to the vast Iranian Plateau.

Beyond the central upland plains are the central deserts, the Kavir and the Lut. Together, these deserts form a large and essentially uninhabitable center that is surrounded on the south, east, and north sides by highland valleys that were home to both large and small communities during the Bronze and Iron Ages of the 3rd to the 1st millennium BCE. This part of Iran was densely if intermittently populated, particularly during the 3rd millennium BCE, by self-sustaining communities engaged in agriculture, animal husbandry, and craft production.

Even during the wetter global climate regime of the 4th and 3rd millennia BCE, the primary challenge for productive settlement on the plateau was finding access to reliable sources of water. As in Mesopotamia, rivers met this need. Originating in the mountains surrounding the central deserts, substantial rivers flowed in five different systems. Rather than debouching into the open waters of the Persian Gulf, however, most of these terminated in large marshy inland oases. In what is now Fars province, the Kur River flows through the valley to Lake Bakhtegan; in the region of present-day Kerman, rivers flow north out of the mountains into the great Lut desert; south of the mountains, the Halil River flows in the Jazmurian oasis to be joined by the Bampur River flowing to the west; the Helmand River system in the east originates in the Hindu Kush and flows into the great Helmand salt lake; and, in the north, the same system of oases rivers are found in the regions where today are located Turkmenistan, Uzbekistan, and Azerbaijan. These rivers provided water for crops and for livelihood, and were often augmented by artesian springs from underground sources.

At the very end of the 3rd millennium BCE, a global climate change led to a much drier and colder regime that would persist for centuries. Regions with reliable water sources attracted people away from more arid zones. Much of eastern Iran was profoundly affected by this change, and would not host large populations again until the Persians introduced the *qanat* system of underground irrigation in the middle of the 1st millennium BCE.

Routes and Roads

Moving around the highland plateau was never easy. Wheeled vehicles were rarely used, even for especially for long distance travel, because of the uneven terrain. Pictorial representations suggest that wheeled carts were used exclusively for prestige transport; such usage diverges from that known in southern Mesopotamia, where wheeled vehicles were used by the early Sumerians in warfare. Pack animals, such as donkeys and mules, were the primary beasts of burden, but people also must often have carried loads on their backs or on their heads.

Three overland routes ran between the Mesopotamian lowland and the plateau to the east. In the north, one could follow the Little Zab River up the mountains and wind down the eastern side to reach the Tehran Plain at Isfahan. This route was important in the 5th millennium BCE and was probably the one used for the transport of precious materials such as lapis lazuli and gold that ended their journey in the graves at Tepe Gawra. It was certainly active again in the early 2nd millennium BCE, when it was used by the Old Assyrian traders and their Iranian counterparts, who left evidence of their presence at the sites of Shemshara and Dinkha Tepe. The second and most important route onto the plateau from the lowland was the Great Khorasan or the Royal Road, which led from the lowland at the latitude of Baghdad, up through the Zagros Mountains following the Diyala River, northeast across the mountains, and onto the Iranian Plateau around the

continued on page 111

Sumerian Epic Heroes

Holly Pittman

A series of myths, set in the golden age of Sumer and known to us from the early 2nd millennium BCE, constitute parables of a sort that demonstrate the superiority of the Sumerian urban ways of life over those of other regions. These focus on the heroic kings Enmerkar, Lugalbanda, and Gilgamesh, each of whom, according to legend, ruled Uruk for hundreds of years.

In *Enmerkar and the Lord of Aratta*, *Enmerkar and En-suhgir-ana*, *Lugalbanda and the Mountain Cave*, and the *Return of Lugalbanda*, a contest is described between the cities of Uruk and Aratta, with the former representing Mesopotamia and the latter representing the highland east. Uruk and Aratta vie not only to prove their superiority over the other but also to determine which is the most beloved of the goddess Inana. In a fifth myth, *Gilgamesh and Huwawa*, the contest is based in the west, in the legendary Cedar Forest located in the region of modern-day Lebanon: Gilgamesh, the brave but impetuous king of Uruk, defeats and slays Huwawa, the lonely and isolated but also enormously powerful monster who guards the cedars.

In each case, the Sumerian ruler of Uruk emerges as victor, and as intellectually, physically, culturally, and morally superior to his opponent.

Underlying each of these myths is the dichotomy between the alluvial river valley and the foreign highlands, between civilization as defined either by urban centers, population density, and institutions of culture and rulership (Mesopotamia) or by small population centers (at best) amidst a wealth of raw materials that literally fall out of the mountains and streams (the foreign highlands).

Fig. 5S1.2 *Opposite Page*
This plaque (B15606) was part of the decoration of the temple excavated by Woolley at Tell al-ʿUbaid It carries a scene in low relief of the human-headed bull rising between the branches of a tree at the summit of a mountain. On his back is the lion-headed eagle, known in Mesopotamian mythology as the Anzu bird, the avatar of the warrior god, Ningirsu. Although its precise meaning eludes us, this combination must surely refer to one of the heroic myths in the Lugalbanda cycle.

Fig. 5S1.1 *Right*
This cylinder seal (British Museum 89137) made from a speckled black stone carries a procession of figures on an expedition to the Iranian Plateau. The inscription identifies the owner as Kalki the scribe. He is certainly the figure carrying a small tablet standing behind the central figure with a cap and a mace at his shoulder. Leading the procession is a mountain scout wearing mountain shoes with upturned toes and carrying a bow with a quiver full of arrows. © The Trustees of the British Museum.

In *Enmerkar and the Lord of Aratta*, the best preserved of the myths, the two eponymous protagonists (Enmerkar, the king of Uruk, and the unnamed king of Aratta) compete for the affection of the goddess Inana, who requires a lavishly decorated and opulent temple. Enmerkar demands that the Lord of Aratta supply the lapis lazuli, gold, silver, and strong timbers for this project and the Lord of Aratta refuses, dismayed by the thought that Inana might abandon his own great city for the splendor of Uruk. In the series of three complex challenges designed to resolve the standoff, Enmerkar proves to be the more clever and resourceful opponent. At the same time, a drought hits highland Iran that brings widespread famine. At the moment of crucial resolution, the rains come, Aratta is spared starvation, and the rulers agree to establish a mutually beneficial exchange, understood metaphorically as the "origin of long distance trade."

The story of Lugalbanda, another of the heroic kings of Uruk, spans two related episodes, recounted in *Lugalbanda and the Mountain Cave* and *Lugalbanda's Return*. Enmerkar, Lugalbanda's father, initiates a military campaign against Aratta to gain the highland's riches. On the journey through the rugged and desolate landscape, the commander of the army, Lugalbanda, falls ill and is left behind in a cave while his companions continue without him. He understands, through a dream, that the gods have chosen him for a heroic role. Emerging from the cave, he engages with the monstrous and terrifying guardian of the highlands, the Anzu bird, who controls and protects the east. Anzu grants Lugalbanda the gift of superhuman speed, which enables him to rejoin his comrades in the battle against Aratta. Upon Lugalbanda's miraculous arrival on the battlefield, to the wonder of the companions who had left him for dead, Enmerkar sends him back to Uruk to seek the goddess Inana's help. With his new powers, Lugalbanda makes the journey in one day and, with a magical ritual obtained from Inana, ensures the defeat of Aratta.

Fig. 5S1.3 *Above*
This clay tablet (29-13-209) tells the tale of Gilgamesh and Huwawa (or Humbaba), in which Gilgamesh and Enkidu travel to the Cedar Mountains and kill Huwawa, the rightful guardian of that place. The tablet is written in narrow columns to imitate the text on many stelae because this Gilgamesh story is related to the notion that survival of fame depended on carrying out great deeds and writing them on stone monuments for perpetuity.

In *Gilgamesh and Huwawa*, the hero Gilgamesh, son of Lugalbanda and the most famous of the legendary kings of Uruk, undertakes a journey to the distant Cedar Forest; he is accompanied not only by his companion Enkidu but also by fifty young men (bachelors) from his city. On arriving at the legendary forest, however, Gilgamesh finds it is protected by the monstrous and terrifying but also lonely and isolated guardian Huwawa. Through a combination of bravery and guile, Gilgamesh and Enkidu manage to defeat and slay the monster. This narrative ends somewhat differently from the others; while Gilgamesh is successful in his quest, and presumably in obtaining a valuable raw resource (cedar wood) for Uruk, he also earns the ire of the great god Enlil for slaying Huwawa, who had been fulfilling a divinely appointed and approved role in protecting the Cedar Forest.

Each of the narratives in this group, if variously developed and nuanced, suggests that the superiority of Sumerian civilization justifies the subjugation of the highlands and other regions. Not only do the raw materials from these regions rightly come to Uruk, but so also do the talented craftspeople that are skilled in transforming these materials into objects worthy of the goddess.

Fig. 5S1.4 *Above Left*
Carved on this orange-brown carnelian cylinder seal (British Museum 89763) is the scene of Gilgamesh and his partner Enkidu struggling with the monster Humbaba (earlier Huwawa) who is attempting to escape. To the side a worshipper stands in front of the symbol of the god Marduk and the stylus of the god Nabu. Such scenes of the combat between heroes and monsters are common on 1st millennium seals. © The Trustees of the British Museum.

Fig. 5S1.5 *Above Right*
Huwawa or Humbaba, the mythical protector of the Cedar Forest, was envisioned as a monstrous creature whose wrinkled face resembled the intestines of an animal. Many plaques like this one (B15192) in terracotta were impressed with the "mask" of Huwawa during the early centuries of the 2nd millennium BCE.

modern-day city of Kermanshah. The third possible overland route would have reached Susa in a leg probably still made by boat in the 3rd millennium BCE but subsequently by land, before proceeding southeast toward Fars and Kerman. This is clearly the route which is described in the Sumerian legend *Enmerkar and the Lord of Aratta*.

The other means of reaching the Iranian Plateau, one which also permitted access to the riches of the Omani peninsula, was through maritime travel. Following the coastal edges, boats from Mesopotamia would have found easy passage onto the plateau at the points where the modern ports of Bandar Bushire and Bandar Abbas are located in the Straits of Hormuz. If the Sumerians were great river sailors, it is worth noting that they rarely plied boats all the way to the Indus Valley. Instead, merchants from Mesopotamia would meet Indus or Omani sailors at the entrepôt on Dilmun, contemporary Bahrain. This maritime route was extremely active during the Bronze Age of Exchange of the 3rd millennium, and continued in use until around 1300 BCE.

Natural Resources

The highland zones of the Middle East are rich in raw materials distributed unevenly across the landscape. Initially attracted by their bright colors, curious people soon discovered these materials possessed useful properties when transformed from their natural states. Some of the earliest such materials to be systematically exploited were microcrystalline stones like cherts, which could be flaked to produce sharp cutting edges. The most desirable such material was obsidian, available in the Middle East only in close proximity to two dormant volcanoes, which were located in central and eastern Anatolia respectively. As early as 14,000 BCE, obsidian (in the form of tools) was in use at sites long distances from its points of origin, indicating the existence of informal trading systems to acquire highly desirable and useful materials. Since that early moment, people have sought to acquire ever-greater varieties of such raw materials through direct or indirect acts of trade and exchange.

The Iranian Plateau and its geological extension on the Arabian Peninsula across the Persian Gulf are rich in raw materials useful to people. Lapis lazuli (Fig. 5.3), a beautiful blue stone, is found, like obsidian, in only a very few locations; these include the mines of Badakhshan in northeastern Afghanistan. Turquoise is only slightly more abundant, with known sources located in northeastern Iran near Mashad, in the Sinai near Egypt, and deep in Central Asia. Most of the other colorful and semi-precious stone used in antiquity are found in veins and nodules all over the Iranian Plateau into Central Asia. Agates, chalcedonies, jaspers, and carnelian could be collected as pebbles near riverbanks. The large carnelian beads found in the Royal Cemetery at Ur and in the Indus Valley were probably mined directly from a rich source in the vicinity of modern day Gujarat in India (Fig. 5.4). This region would have been situated at the eastern end

Fig. 5.3 *Above*
The beautiful dark blue stone, lapis lazuli, from distant northeastern Afghanistan was highly prized by Mesopotamians. Because of the uniquely rich find of the Royal Cemetery at Ur we have abundant material evidence for its use. It was imported as a raw material and was made into jewelry, cylinder seals, small vessels, and other luxury objects. This chunk of raw lapis (B17102) was found in the King's Grave (PG 789).

of what became a long-distance network of exchange during the second half of the 3rd millennium BCE.

In addition to colorful stones for jewelry and ornaments, calcites and alabasters, chlorite and steatite, and gabbro and diorite were also highly sought after both locally and abroad. Calcites and chlorites, the most commonly used of the light and dark stones, are found in many locations on the Iranian Plateau in different qualities and quantities. In the 3rd millennium BCE, both types of stone were extensively used by local populations to make vessels, ritual objects, and sculpture; they were also exported to resource-poor Mesopotamian cities. Workshops found in eastern Iran at Shahr-i Sokhta and in south central Iran at Tepe Yahya hint at the burgeoning craft specialization underway across the plateau in the 3rd millennium BCE. Diorite and gabbro, two types of very hard stones, are found on both sides of the Persian Gulf in Iranian Makran and the Omani peninsula. While rarely exploited in Iran in antiquity, both stones were considered highly desirable in Mesopotamia for their hardness and shine and were imported to make monuments celebrating kings and gods.

Metals, perhaps even more than stone, also attracted experimentation due to their transformative properties. Gold, a beautiful and stable but soft metal, was never an industrial material but rather used as a marker of status, luxury, and wealth. It is found in small quantities in many places across the Anatolian and Iranian plateaus and beyond, often as nuggets washed from buried veins. In Iran, gold mines are known from the central Zagros region, the south central region of Kerman, and the northeast around Damghan and Nishapur. Gold mines, some still active today, are also known from Central Asia, in particular from areas close to the sources of lapis lazuli in Afghanistan. Silver and lead, two other important metals for the ancient world, are derived from a single argentiferous ore that is widespread in the Middle East. Early in the 3rd millennium BCE, silver was used by the proto-Elamites in Iran to make sculptures and jewelry. At the same time, silver began to be used extensively in Mesopotamia as the standard of value in economic exchanges (see Chapter 7S5: Currency). By the 2nd millennium BCE, sources for these metals located in Anatolia and Syria overtook those in the east.

More important even than gold and silver for the urban populations of the 3rd millennium BCE Near East were copper and, later, tin (used to alloy the metal into bronze). Already by the 5th millennium BCE, craftspeople in south central Iran had moved beyond simply hammering native copper to mastering the craft of smelting ores to remove impurities. Melting and smelting, importantly, rendered metal liquid, allowing it to be shaped by pouring the molten metal into a mold. Once these basic techniques were grasped, both on the Tehran Plain and in south central Iran near Kerman, the exploitation of copper ores exploded to meet a growing demand for copper and later also bronze tools, weapons, sculptures, and all sorts of other useful objects. Copper ores are conveniently found in the highlands surrounding the Mesopotamian alluvium and so

Fig. 5.4 Above

Carnelian was more readily available than lapis in the landscape to the east of Mesopotamia. Thousands of beads, many already manufactured, were imported and were combined with lapis and gold to make all sorts of items of adornment, like this string (30-12-627) of carnelian and lapis lazuli beads from the Royal Cemetery at Ur.

continued on page 116

Importing Raw Materials and Finished Goods

William B. Hafford

Mesopotamia had few natural resources and had to acquire many materials from afar, particularly stone, wood, and metal. Long before cities arose, the people of this region had already established trade relationships and were adept at acquiring goods that were not locally available. By 3100 BCE, about the time when the first cities were appearing in Mesopotamia, the site of Tarut Island, located

Fig. 5S2.1 *Below*
Mesopotamian cities relied on imports of stone and metal, as well as luxuries, from afar. This map shows the available resources around Mesopotamia and some of the trade routes that were functioning to acquire those resources.

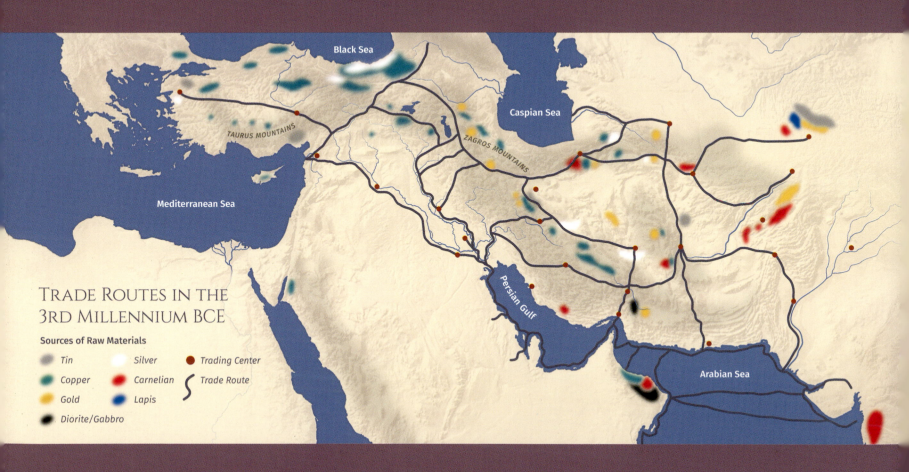

Trade Routes in the 3rd Millennium BCE

Sources of Raw Materials

- Tin
- Copper
- Gold
- Diorite/Gabbro
- Silver
- Carnelian
- Lapis
- Trading Center
- Trade Route

Black Sea

Caspian Sea

Mediterranean Sea

TAURUS MOUNTAINS

ZAGROS MOUNTAINS

Persian Gulf

Arabian Sea

north of Dilmun (modern Bahrain), was already established as a central node in trade with the Gulf region. By the 3rd millennium BCE, not only are seals of the Dilmun type (see Fig. 7S4.1a) found in Mesopotamia but also Mesopotamian artifacts—including a copper bull's head of the type known from musical instruments in the Royal Cemetery at Ur (see Chapter 8S1: The Bull-Headed Lyre of Ur and Its Shell Plaque)—are found on Tarut island.

With the advent of the organizational system of the state, trade relationships could be regularized, systematized, and established over larger distances. Objects and materials came from regions corresponding to modern Iran, Oman, India, Pakistan, and Afghanistan. In return, Mesopotamia sent textiles, perfumed oils, and in some cases grain as well, though this latter was too bulky and perishable to travel very great distances. Trading routes (Fig. 5S2.1) were established both overland and by sea. The sea route was significantly faster and less costly and so the Gulf region, readily accessible by water, became a particularly important destination for traders and merchants.

Copper and diorite that came into Dilmun from Magan (modern Oman) were particularly important in this trade. Products from farther east in Meluhha (modern India) also

Fig. 5S2.2 *Above*
The materials that make up this necklace (B16799) all came from far outside Mesopotamia. Gold from the area that is now modern Iran, lapis lazuli from the mines of modern Afghanistan, and carnelian from the Indus Valley of modern Pakistan and India. The etching on the carnelian in this example is particularly characteristic of the Indus Valley.

Fig. 5S2.3 *Right*
This very large (19 cm or 7.5 inches high and 21 cm or 8.25 inches diameter) stone mace head (B14933) bears an inscription declaring it to be booty taken from Elam (Iran) in the campaigns of the Akkadian king Rimush (2279–2270 BCE).

Fig. 5S2.4 *Left*
Several gold pendants
on this necklace (B16794)
found at Ur are made with
spiral wire in a style that
is so reminiscent of the
jewelry from the region
around Troy in western
Turkey that the necklace
could be an import from
that very distant region.

came to Dilmun for trade. These included carnelian beads as well as lapis lazuli, and gold (Fig. 5S2.2) that had been mined in Afghanistan and shipped down the Indus River.

Items from cities in southeastern Iran, particularly chlorite bowls (see Fig. 5.11), have been found on the small island of Tarut and in Mesopotamia, particularly in temples. These certainly arrived by sea, but some also came via overland routes. Other high value items, such as small amounts of lapis lazuli, gold, alabaster, and carnelian from farther east, may also have been carried overland through sites like Shahr-i Sokhta before finding their way to maritime routes.

When Sargon of Akkad (2334–2279 BCE) took control of Mesopotamia, he decided to bypass the middlemen of Dilmun in his trade with Magan and Meluhha; the two regions are directly referenced in his texts. Control of trade routes in this period was maintained through military means.

If a region failed to engage in trade, the Akkadians would force it to submit, as evidenced by artifacts carried back to Mesopotamia that are inscribed "booty of Magan" (Fig. 5S2.3).

The Akkadians also engaged in trade to the north and west, so that Sargon could boast of ruling an empire stretching from the Lower to the Upper Seas (the Persian Gulf to the Mediterranean). Cedar wood and silver were obtained from Lebanon and Turkey (see Chapter 5S1: Sumerian Epic Heroes), and some of the jewelry in the Royal Cemetery at Ur (see Chapter 8: The Royal Cemetery of Ur) shows stylistic connections with regions as far away as Troy.

With the fall of the Akkadian Empire around 2150 BCE, Mesopotamia's trade routes contracted. When the Ur III kings took control of Mesopotamia around 2100 BCE, however, they re-established extensive trade with the region of the Gulf and Iranian Plateau.

Fig. 5.5 *Above*

Buff pottery painted in dark brown or black paint with bold designs was typical of lowland Khuzestan during the 5th and early 4th millennium BCE. These two impressive vessels on long-term loan from the Louvre—a beaker (L-2018-3-3) and a bowl (L-2018-3-4)—were found in graves at Susa dated to the Susa A Period. The imagery on the bowl appears abstract but can be interpreted as a schematic representation of the landscape surrounding Susa, bordered by the two rivers (Karun and Kharkeh). In the center is a square with a cross which may be a symbol for Susa itself.

could be extracted and smelted into ingots close to their points of origin. The resulting ingots would then be exported and subsequently reprocessed through melting, cleaning, and admixing other compounds to produce a stronger or more fluid metal alloy. Copper from certain regions in Iran was naturally alloyed with arsenic, which has the effect of making the metal more fluid. Lead was another common addition to copper in early periods, and functioned to make the copper softer and less porous. Tin, which rarely co-occurs with copper naturally, was also added to liquid copper to make it stronger; copper-tin alloys were useful for making heavy tools and weapons. Tin bronzes, however, only rarely occur in Mesopotamia during the later 3rd millennium BCE, as the tin had to be imported from small mines in the Zagros and Taurus Mountains. The major tin sources in Afghanistan were not exploited until later in the 2nd millennium BCE, when tin was extracted in large quantities for the Old Assyrian traders.

Early Village Cultures

Self-sufficient village cultures based on rain-fed or irrigation agriculture combined with animal husbandry were well established by the 6th millennium BCE. In the southwest, in the alluvial extension of the Mesopotamian plain into Khuzestan, two important centers at Susa and Chogha Mish followed developmental paths similar to those of contemporaneous centers in southern Mesopotamia. Chogha Mish, a large center on the eastern side of the plain, was surrounded by smaller villages. A large public building excavated at the site was subsequently destroyed by fire and the site and surrounding countryside were abandoned by 4500 BCE. During the same period, the site of Susa was established in the fertile area between the Karun and the Karkheh Rivers. As at Uruk, Susa had two major areas of settlement: these are termed the Acropolis and the Apadana; the name of the latter is derived from its use during the much later Persian Period. Around 4200 BCE, a low platform was built near the center of the Acropolis, against which was situated a huge burial ground with more than two thousand graves. The pottery in these burials was a very high-quality buff ware bearing strong patterns in dark brown paint (Fig. 5.5). Three distinct types of vessel seem to accompany each burial: a large beaker, an open bowl, and a small jar. These vessels carry both figural and abstract designs that seem to reference features in the landscape. Several of the open bowls, for example, carry two bold zigzag patterns with a symbol between them. Given the location of Susa between the two prominent rivers on the plain, this composition may be understood as a schematic map of the position of the site. Similar zigzag patterns on the beakers may also evoke the rivers, with checkerboards indicating the surrounding mountains.

Associated with the period of the burials are an important group of stamp seals carrying images that enliven our understanding of the time. These most often show a

horned quadruped together with vegetation, much like the seals known from Tepe Gawra in northern Mesopotamia. In some cases, male figures with the heads of horned animals are seen mastering snakes. And, in a remarkable series of impressions, human figures depicted with animal horns or tails, and clad in skirts of a range of different patterns, are shown holding up beakers and surrounded by kneeling or standing nude figures holding open bowls. Surely we are seeing here a depiction of the kinds of rituals associated with the burials. One scholar, Frank Hole, has speculated that the burial ground at Susa was in fact a mass graveyard resulting from a deadly episode, perhaps disease or warfare, that brought people from across the plain to Susa, which had been established as a communal ceremonial center. Shortly after the burial event, a high terrace was built close to the low platform, on which have been discovered the remains of what was probably a sacred structure. Subsequently, and throughout antiquity, Susa remained an important center that connected the western Mesopotamian cities to the Iranian highland.

During the 5th millennium BCE, villages and towns dotted the landscape of the Iranian Plateau. Each region was essentially autonomous and subsisted on local

Fig. 5.6 *Above*

Grey ware pottery was produced at Tepe Hissar and Tureng Tepe during the last centuries of the 3rd millennium BCE. The surface of the vessels were highly burnished before firing to give them a high sheen. Some also have geometric patterns polished into the surface. The striking shapes seen here (33-21-853, 32-41-32, 33-41-12) are clearly influenced by contemporary metalwork.

agriculture and animal husbandry, developing craft traditions around available resources. We identify these local cultures on the basis of their pottery, which is usually the most distinctive and ubiquitous type of material culture available to archaeologists. During these early periods, pottery was handmade within individual communities using a variety of techniques: vessels could be built from slabs or from coils, or turned on a slow wheel. Most of the shapes can be associated with the processing, storage, or presentation of food. An important aspect of group cohesion in these small communities was periodic gatherings involving feasting, which served to strengthen social bonds. Depictions of such celebrations on the stamp seals from Susa give form to such important events. The most visible objects at such occasions, apart from probably elaborate clothing and body markings, would have been display pottery, painted with elaborate and significant imagery or patterns, that would signal status and alliances among the community. Pottery, thus, provides archaeologists not only with valuable information about craft production and aesthetic preferences, but also about the range of interactions and kinds of symbolism used by different communities.

To the southeast of Khuzestan is the modern-day province of Fars; this was the homeland of the Elamites from at least the 3rd millennium BCE and, later, of the Achaemenid Persians (550–330 BCE). At the site of Tal-i Bakun in the late 5th millennium BCE, a highly developed community flourished in architectural compounds of attached houses, which diverged in form from the tripartite house of southern Mesopotamia. A brown on buff pottery tradition, related to but different from that known at Susa, was characteristic of this community. Small conical cups rather than larger beakers were common, and were painted with powerful abstract designs. Stamp seals of a variety of shapes were also used at Bakun to control the storage of foodstuffs but these bore distinctive abstract patterns rather than figural images.

To the north, in a zone that extended from the plains east of the Zagros Mountains toward the rolling hills of the Damghan Plain, village culture also flourished, and local communities developed distinctive shapes and decorations to elaborate their pottery. The cups and beakers common in the south were replaced by pedestal goblets and bowls. Some vessels continue to be made from buff ware with black painted designs, but others have a red surface painted with black designs. This difference in color, interestingly, was due to the use not of different clays or slips but rather of different firing temperatures in the kiln. Occasionally, vessels were both buff and red, indicating their positioning in the kiln between the red wares, fired at cooler temperatures, and the buff wares, fired at higher temperatures.

Most of the vessels are painted with geometric patterns that evoke basketwork or vegetation. Some of the most striking examples, however, carry images of mouflon sheep with great sweeping horns, or running leopards. Birds, usually waterfowl and never birds of prey, are another important subject.

Early in the 3rd millennium BCE, the painted pottery cultures of the Iranian Plateau disappeared. In the Tehran Plain and in Fars, large sites were abandoned, apparently replaced by more mobile populations. To the northeast, in the foothills on either side of the Elburz Mountains, the ceramics indicate that the population turned away from the plain to the south and began to engage with the urban centers emerging in the river systems of western Central Asia, particularly along the Atrek River system. At Tepe Hissar, this transition is gradual and is manifested in a switch from red and buff painted pottery to a grey ware tradition that, over the course of five hundred years, becomes ever more elaborate and sophisticated (Fig. 5.6).

Craft Production Centers of the Highland

We have seen that the ceramic and metal craft production industries originated and developed on the Iranian Plateau in the 6th and 5th millennia BCE. Both of these industries are based in the transformation of materials by fire into highly useful and durable forms. In the 3rd millennium BCE, craft production continued to be vital to the lifeway of the villages and centers on the Iranian Plateau. Copper and other metals were extracted from their ores near the mines, and melted or smelted into forms that could easily be transported to centers nearby or far away to be manufactured into desired commodities. Craft production has been closely studied at Tepe Hissar and it has been shown that techniques developed millennia earlier were still in use at the site, suggesting the existence of quite a conservative tradition of metalworking and ceramic production in the region.

The grey ware ceramics from 3rd millennium BCE Tepe Hissar and the related site of Tureng Tepe on the other side of the Elburz are among the most striking of the pottery produced on the plateau until the much later ceramics of the Medieval Period. Grey ware developed its distinctive color from a type of kiln that burns without oxygen; it was fired in what is called a reducing environment. In addition to the specific firing technique they

Fig. 5.7 *Left*

Shapes for vessels were often copied from one material to another. From Tepe Hissar the elongated spout of the silver pouring vessel (33-15-722) was clearly imitated in ceramic (32-41-31). The use of a reducing atmosphere in the ceramic kiln produced the grey surface mimicking the similarly shiny grey surface of the silver vessel.

Fig. 5.8 *Right*
This horned animal head (33-22-177) cut from sheet gold is a simple and powerful image that decorated the burial garment of the individual interred in the grave of the "Priest." Also in the grave was a bronze trident and an abstracted female figurine. These were possibly instruments used in ritual performances.

underwent, grey ware vessels were remarkable for their shapes and decoration, which are unique and transcend anything known from the neighboring regions. Elegant stemmed goblets and bowls are common forms, but it is the jugs with rounded bottoms or raised button bases that are the most striking. These elongated and attenuated shapes are sometimes carinated in a way that suggests imitation of metal (copper or silver) vessels. Jugs with long delicate spouts are represented among both grey ware (ceramic) and silver vessels from Hissar (Fig. 5.7). To enhance the remarkable shapes of these striking ceramic vessels, the potters used a technique of pattern burnishing in which the surface is rubbed to make a shiny (usually herringbone or crosshatched) design.

Around 2300 BCE, Hissar reached its zenith, as has been demonstrated by the excavation of the so-called Burnt Building. This structure, thought to be the residence of a prosperous citizen, contained numerous items of jewelry in precious metals and stones. Some rooms of the dwelling, moreover, seem to have been devoted to craft production while, in another area, a stepped podium with cruciform cutouts led the excavator to identify an altar or some kind of sacred space. In the period following the destruction of the Burnt Building by fire, the site of Hissar diminished in size and seems to have changed character. Dug into the earlier building remains, which had been disturbed by unremarkable simple burials, were six graves or hoards containing extremely rich goods. In addition to containing mouflon head ornaments in gold (Fig. 5.8), mirrors and tridents in copper, and grey ware pottery, the six richest graves also included ritual objects and vessels in alabaster that are very similar to such equipment found to the east at sites in western Central Asia. Although copper, gold, and silver production was certainly practiced at Hissar, there is no trace of alabaster manufacture at the site, and

continued on page 124

THE DEVELOPMENT OF URBAN TECHNOLOGIES

Holly Pittman

Many of the technologies that became fundamental for urban society were discovered and gradually developed in villages on the Iranian Plateau. Like the process of domesticating wild animals, these discoveries occurred in places where raw materials were both abundant and easily accessible. This was true particularly for the technologies that used heat to transform a raw material from one state to another. Among the earliest fired ceramics known from the 7th millennium BCE, for example, are those at the important site of Ozbeki, which is located in the Tehran Plain to the east of the Zagros Mountains. As with most discoveries, the initial observation leading to the innovation of ceramics was probably accidental. A clay object, perhaps a figurine or small air-dried container, may have been set near or accidently dropped into an open fire. When the fire was extinguished, what remained among the ashes was a hard object that would no longer disintegrate when it came into contact with water. The technique for making waterproof and rigid containers, once discovered, rapidly ensured the replacement of early stone vessels—which were much more costly and time consuming to make—with those made of clay. The fire-based technology of pottery production spread quickly across the Middle East and beyond. In fact, the technology was probably discovered independently in multiple places in the region.

Fire-based technologies of course require fuel; clay was abundant, and so were forests that stretched for thousands of miles in all directions across the mountain valleys surrounding the central deserts. Over the millennia, the forests were gradually consumed, leaving the mountain sides

Fig. 5S3.1 *Above*
Copper slag (33-22-343) from Hissar.

essentially barren of anything other than small and scrappy oak and pistachio trees at lower elevations.

Metal is another raw material processed by fire. In the mountains across the Iranian and Anatolian plateaus are rich veins of copper, silver, and lead, as well as pockets of gold. The first experiments with metal involved hammering colorful rock-like nuggets found in streams. Native copper, bright greenish-blue in color, was pounded into shapes for pendants and small pointed tools. When these were exposed to heat, their molecular structure, which had become brittle through the pounding, was reorganized, allowing them to be worked even more. Some of the earliest evidence for copper working comes from the site of Tal-i Iblis to the west of the modern city of Kerman in Iran. Located close to a prominent copper

Fig. 5S3.2 *Left*
This spearhead (33-22-107) is one of the very few tin bronzes found at Tepe Hissar. The overwhelming majority of the hundreds of copper finds contained small amounts of arsenic and lead.

Fig. 5S3.3 *Above*
Copper animal figures (33-15-586 and 33-22-136) from Hissar III.

source, the earliest crucibles for melting the ore and removing impurities were found in a context dating to around 5000 BCE. By the 4th millennium BCE, metalworking had spread across the plateau and into the river valleys to the west, where large urban centers were rapidly forming.

The industrial level production of copper intensified in the 3rd millennium BCE. The ore was in all cases processed close to the point of its extraction. Melting allowed the surrounding impurities to be separated from the metal itself. Different sources had distinct impurities that affected the quality of the metal. Very important as sources of copper ore in antiquity were the Talmessi-Meskani mines in the Anarak district in the central Iranian Plateau. The ores from that region are naturally rich in arsenic as well as other impurities that make the molten ore easier to cast and the finished product strong with a fine finish. Bronze, copper alloyed with tin, was the most common of the copper alloys used from the 2nd millennium BCE onwards. The addition of tin made the copper more brittle but also much harder, and so particularly useful for making a variety of tools and weapons. Tin bronze is rare in the 3rd millennium BCE, particularly on the Iranian Plateau. This suggests that an important tin source in Afghanistan was probably not exploited until the Old Assyrian Period around 1900 BCE, when merchants from Ashur organized the overland trade in tin from the east and transshipped it to Anatolia in exchange for copper.

Tepe Hissar, located to the east of the Caspian Sea in the Damghan Plain, was an early site for the industrial production of arsenical copper; from here, it was certainly transshipped to other points on the plateau and perhaps also to markets in northern Mesopotamia. Huge areas of the site are strewn with slag (Fig. 5S3.1), the byproduct of smelting and purifying the ore. Studies of the industry at Tepe Hissar have shown that two levels of production existed side by side: one, industrial-scale processing, transformed the metal into ingots; the other, undertaken on a smaller and more domestic scale, saw the production of tools, weapons, ornaments, and other objects for local consumption and distribution (Figs. 5S3.2, 5S3.3). A likely source for Hissar's copper industry was nearby at Taknar in modern day Mazandaran province of Iran.

there is no nearby source for the stone. The remarkable alabaster objects (Fig. 5.9) found in the graves could, thus, only have been brought to the site by newcomers arriving from the east; these newcomers represented part of a larger movement of people toward the south and west at the end of the 3rd millennium BCE.

Bronze Age of Exchange

A remarkable millennium of trade and exchange, which brought into contact all of the Middle East from as far west as Troy on the Mediterranean Sea in Turkey to as far east as the Indus Valley in Pakistan, began just after the turn of the 3rd millennium BCE. Although the strongest evidence for this circuit of commercial activity has been found in Mesopotamia, archaeological investigation has shown that it involved the entire (known) world. The period may thus be legitimately characterized as one of globalization, in which independent cultures were brought into direct or indirect contact through the mechanisms of trade, exchange, and, in some cases, the forcible extraction of booty. The process of globalization began around 2900 BCE, with the simultaneous overland expansion of the proto-Elamites out of Khuzestan both toward the north, along the eastern side of the Zagros Mountains, and the southeast following overland and river routes towards Fars and the Halil River Valley, finally arriving at the Helmand River Valley. The mostly overland Elamite cultural expansion was accompanied by a simultaneous expansion through maritime routes by the Mesopotamians living in the ancient city of Ur, which was located on the mouth of the Persian Gulf. The development of maritime routes was vital for the importing of raw materials into Mesopotamia from the Iranian Plateau. Lapis lazuli, gold, and, much more rarely, also turquoise would be combined with agates, carnelian, jaspers, and alabaster; some of these materials came down the Indus to be loaded on Harappan boats while others were collected at large sites in the Halil River Valley and then loaded onto boats at a port site close to modern day Bandar Abbas.

Across the Iranian Plateau in this period, at dozens of sites both large and small, there is evidence for intensive craft production. At Shahr-i Sokhta, tens of thousands of wasters from lapis lazuli bead production are strewn across the site. The discovery of some of the highest quality lapis lazuli in the graveyard at the site indicates a high level of local consumption in addition to production for export. Also found at Shahr-i Sokhta is an area dedicated to the production of alabaster bowls. This cannot have been the only site on the Iranian Plateau to produce such bowls: the hundreds of alabaster vessels found at Mesopotamian sites of this period, as well as the vast numbers recovered from Iranian sites, were clearly made in centralized craft production centers situated near sources of high quality alabaster. At Hissar, during the last period of Bronze Age occupation, large numbers of such alabaster objects were found.

Fig. 5.9 *Opposite*
Objects in alabaster were only found in the richest graves excavated at Tepe Hissar from the end of the 3rd millennium BCE. There is no local source for alabaster and no earlier tradition of its use at the site. In addition to vessels and stands, like the ones shown here (clockwise from top left: 33-15-720, 33-22-186, 33-22-70, 33-15-512), the columns and handled disks are also found in graves to the east in Turkmenistan belonging to the Oxus civilization.

Other important craft products consumed on the Iranian Plateau but also exported to the west are vessels and other objects carved from chlorite, a soft dark stone. While chlorite is abundant in many highland zones, a production site discovered at Tepe Yahya and hundreds of bowls found in looted graves in the Halil River Valley identify other craft centers that produced locally consumed symbolically important objects. Some of these found their way west either as containers for precious ointments or food pastes or carried by Iranian traders and craftspeople. Chlorite vessels have, in fact, also been excavated from the Royal Cemetery at Ur; these were mostly plain (Fig. 5.10), and probably used in the feasts accompanying the extended funerary proceedings, but several examples were carved (Fig. 5.11), carrying figural and geometric patterns identical to those found on vessels recovered from the plateau.

Copper and diorite from the Omani peninsula were among the most highly sought-after commodities delivered to Mesopotamia via the maritime routes. Extensive metal extraction sites are well known in Oman during this period, and cuneiform texts from the end of the 3rd millennium BCE report boats laden with enormous quantities of copper arriving at sites like Ur and Lagash as well as at Susa. These metals were probably brought on boats owned by the seafaring merchants of Meluhha, launched at sites like Sukagen Dor and Lothal on the shore of the Indian Ocean. From the Indus came expertly fashioned carnelian biconical beads, as well as beads etched with white lines. By the reign of Sargon (ca. 2334–2279 BCE), the founder of the Akkadian Dynasty who succeeded in unifying much of Mesopotamia under the rule of kings based in the city of Akkad, we read in the cuneiform texts that boats from Magan and Meluhha docked at the quay of Akkad. At the end of the 3rd millennium BCE, Mesopotamian merchants under the Ur III kings may have bypassed some intermediaries and sailed all of the way to Oman to obtain copper as well as rare and precious goods for their homeland, but Dilmun (the modern island of Bahrain) continued to play a role in trade.

For Further Reading

Alvarez-Mon, Javier, Gian Pietro Basello, and Yasmina Wicks, eds. 2018. *The Elamite World*. New York: Routledge.

Harper, Prudence, Joan Aruz, and Françoise Tallon, eds. 1992. *The Royal City of Susa: Ancient Near Eastern Treasures in the Louvre*. New York: Metropolitan Museum of Art.

Hole, Frank, ed. 1987. *The Archaeology of Western Iran: Settlements and Society from Prehistory to the Islamic Conquest*. Smithsonian Series in Archaeological Inquiry. Washington, DC.

Hole, Frank. 1990. Cemetery or Mass Grave? Reflections on Susa I, pp. 1–14. In *Contribution a l'histoire de l'Iran: Mélanges offerts à Jean Perrot*, edited by Françoise Vallat. Paris: Editions Recherche sur les Civilisations.

Potts, Daniel T., ed. 2013. *The Oxford Handbook of Ancient Iran*. Oxford: Oxford University Press.

Potts, Daniel T. 2015. *The Archaeology of Elam: Formation and Transformation of the Iranian State*. 2nd edition. Cambridge: Cambridge University Press.

Fig. 5.10 *Opposite, Top*

Numerous plain bell-shaped vessels carved from chlorite were found in the tombs at Ur. These were imported, along with the decorated chlorite vessels, from southeastern Iran. They were used in both places as serving vessels. Puabi had more than a dozen of these vessels left from her funerary banquet. The one shown here (30-12-81) came from PG 1068.

Fig. 5.11 *Opposite, Bottom*

Vessels carved from chlorite were imported from southeastern Iran during the Early Dynastic Period. They were manufacture in the Halil River Valley and were brought to Mesopotamia perhaps for their contents. This one (B17168), from the grave of Puabi (PG 800) is one of the finest of its type found in the cemetery. Others, such as the one depicted here (B16226) with images of scorpions, and felines, as well as one with a human figure were also found at Ur.

6

NOMADS

Lauren Ristvet

Introduction

For more than four thousand years, the Middle East has been home to pastoral nomads, people who move seasonally with flocks of animals. Nomadic territory often lies on the margins of the settled zone, in the high mountains or arid steppes, places that are too dry or steep for rain-fed agriculture, but provide grazing for flocks of sheep, goats, cattle, camels, or even horses. In the Middle East, pastoralists (herders rather than farmers) have lived in mountains including those of the Zagros, Taurus, and Caucasus ranges since at least the 3rd millennium BCE. They have dwelt in the vast Eurasian steppe that extends from Hungary to China. And they have traveled the deserts of Arabia, especially after the domestication of the camel at the end of the 2nd millennium BCE. In the past, historians and anthropologists often portrayed nomads as archaic and unchanging. The famous economist Adam Smith believed that nomads represented a stage in social development; he situated them after early hunters but before farmers and merchants. Archaeological evidence, however, indicates that nomadism, far from being a primitive mode of life, is a comparatively recent development made possible by the rise of the city. Moreover, nomads had a symbiotic relationship with the city. As they moved from pasture to pasture, they often brought different goods or ideas from one settled community to another, enabling both trade and the spread of innovation. Nomads were talented riders who domesticated horses and camels, two types of animals coveted by the kings of settled communities for their armies (Fig. 6.1). They were also fierce warriors who spearheaded developments in warfare. Indeed, their military prowess often made nomadic groups a threat to their settled neighbors, whom they fought, raided, and occasionally conquered.

Who were these nomads whose legacy looms so large? How did they live? What was their relationship to the city? We will explore the answers to these fundamental questions by focusing on four very different groups who lived in the mountains or the steppe—the Kassites, the kingdom of Mitanni, the Iron Age people of Luristan, and the Scythians—during the long millennium from about 1500–300 BCE.

Nomadic Lifeways

When discussing nomads, it is useful to distinguish between three words that are often used interchangeably: nomads, pastoralists, and tribes. The word nomad refers to mobility; unlike villagers or city dwellers, nomads have no permanent home. Pastoralist describes a way of life devoted to herding animals rather than farming. And tribe refers to a particular political structure that is more flexible than a state but still maintains allegiance to a leader or chief. The three categories tend to overlap and span a broad spectrum of lifeways. Some nomads, like the Bedouin, move vast distances and spend very short periods in any one camp. Others, like the Lurs, may be semi-sedentary, climbing a

Fig. 6.1 *Opposite*

The Parthians, as represented by this ceramic rider on horseback (B15473), were nomads originally from modern Turkmenistan who conquered much of the Seleucid Empire, establishing a powerful state in Iran in the 3rd century BCE.

mountain range once a year so that they can move between summer and winter pasture. Many nomadic peoples have belonged to tribes, though it is worth noting that people in cities and villages have often also had tribal identities.

In most of the Middle East, the most important herd animals are sheep and goats. Nomads have often supplied settled people with goods from these animals: wool, skin, and dairy products. Pigs and cattle both need more water than is available in the steppe, and pigs cannot walk far. Cattle are sometimes important in some of the better-watered mountainous regions, such as the Caucasus. Donkeys, horses, and camels have also been essential to nomads, permitting relatively rapid long-distance travel. The same animals, of course, served to revolutionize warfare and trade for settled people.

Nomads and Cities

Urban residents have sometimes regarded nomads as deeply foreign, uncivilized, and a threat to their ways of life. But nomads have never been entirely severed from either agricultural or city life. Nomadic groups usually rely on grain for much of their diet and covet other urban goods that they obtain through trading or raiding. Treaties and letters from the Mesopotamian cities of Mari and Shubat-Enlil reveal that, in the 18th century BCE, arable land was interspersed with pastureland and that kingdoms controlled both. Settled peoples and nomads could also belong to the same tribe, a condition that was also true of Safavid Iran in the 16th century CE. Even now some pastoralists bring their sheep and goats to graze on what remains in farmers' fields after the wheat harvest.

In the 1950s, the ethnographer Fredrik Barth lived with the Basseri nomads of southern Iran as they undertook their seasonal migration. He found that the Basseri had a higher birth rate than many neighboring people, but that their numbers remained fairly constant because both the poorest and the richest nomads settled down. When nomads, particularly those who came from small families, lost too many animals to support themselves, they wound up working for wages in villages or towns. Conversely, at a certain point it no longer made sense for the richest nomads to use their wealth to increase their herds; instead they invested the wealth of their flocks into large estates, buying properties in towns and becoming landlords. In the early 2nd millennium BCE, Kassite pastoralists from the Zagros first appear in Babylonian texts as mercenaries or slaves; by the mid-2nd millennium BCE they take over Babylonia and rule it for more than 400 years. This is not an unusual pattern; the same thing happened more than two thousand years later when the Seljuq Turks, who appear in historical records first as servants and then as soldiers, became the rulers of the Seljuq and Ottoman Empires. Some formerly nomadic groups retained a strong separate identity, like the Scythians in Asia or the Mongols who destroyed Rayy in 1220 CE (see Chapter 11: The Medieval and Early Modern Islamic and Persianate City), while others, like the Kassites and the Seljuqs, became strong proponents of an older urban culture.

Mitanni: Enclosed Nomadism

A period of political weakness during the 16th century BCE allowed the Hurrians occupying large swathes of land to the northeast of Mesopotamia to move southward, penetrating deeper into northern Mesopotamia, where they founded numerous small states. Hurrians had been present in this region, particularly in areas near the mountains, since the 3rd millennium BCE and in the mid-2nd millennium BCE they became a major political force. The kingdom of Mitanni emerged in the Habur region of Syria around 1550 BCE, perhaps uniting many of these smaller Hurrian principalities. By the late 15th century BCE, the domain of the Mitannian king stretched from the Mediterranean to the Zagros, and as far north as Lake Van. Configured as a loose confederation of client states rather than a cohesive empire, Mitanni became weakened by internal strife and external pressures in the late 13th century BCE, eventually falling prey to the rising kingdoms of the Hittites in the north and west and the Assyrians in the south and east.

I have argued elsewhere that tribally organized pastoralism first appeared in the Middle East sometime between 2200 and 1900 BCE in northern Mesopotamia, after the collapse of the Akkadian Empire (ca. 2112 BCE) and before the resurgence of kingdoms under the Old Assyrian king Shamshi-Adad (ca. 1813–1781 BCE). In the early 2nd millennium BCE, pastoralists and tribes were an important element of economic, social, and political life in northern Mesopotamia. This area, which relies upon rainfall for farming, is agriculturally marginal and the divide between land suitable for agriculture and land suitable for pasture shifts constantly due to ecological, social, and political changes. To the north and west of northern Mesopotamia, mountain chains and plateaus allow for transhumant pastoralism (the movement of herds between summer and winter pasture), connecting pastoralists to settled populations in Iran, Anatolia, and the South Caucasus. The historian M.B. Rowton referred to this phenomenon as "enclosed nomadism," whereby pastoral nomads live in a territory that contains large numbers of settled peoples. He distinguished such enclosed nomads from the "excluded nomads" of the Central Asian steppe who inhabited a territory with fewer settlements and had very different relationships with townspeople.

What was the relationship between nomads and the kingdom of Mitanni? We have very few textual sources for this enigmatic kingdom. Most of these come from client states on the edges of Mitannian control, which makes it difficult to evaluate the role of tribes or nomads during this period. Archaeological evidence suggests a continued important role for pastoralists and perhaps tribal traditions coming both from the surrounding mountains and from the plains. Beginning in the mid-2nd millennium BCE, people began moving away from high tells and establishing smaller, less dense, and more temporary sites on the valley floor. At the same time, many important cities of the 3rd and early 2nd millennium BCE were abandoned forever. This may indicate an uptick

Fig. 6.2 *Above*
This painted and decorated incense burner (32-20-413) from Tell Billa was probably associated with a settled cult during the Mitanni Period.

continued on page 137

THE ZIWIYE HOARD

Lauren Ristvet

In 1947, a shepherd in the Zagros Mountains of Iran reportedly found a bronze casket filled with objects made of gold (Fig. 6S1.1), silver (Fig. 6S1.2), bronze, ivory, and clay below the ruins of the ancient citadel of Ziwiye. Some of the objects were clearly Assyrian, Urartian, or Scythian (Fig. 6S1.3) imports, while others were locally made. Many were breathtaking, representing some of the finest examples of Iron Age art ever found in Iran. As the objects, which are collectively known as the Ziwiye hoard, made their way onto the antiquities market, museums snapped them up and scholars argued over what they might mean.

Before objects from the Ziwiye hoard appeared on the market, the evidence for Scythians in western Iran was limited. The Greek historian Herodotus wrote that the Scythians ruled Asia for 28 years and letters found in the Assyrian library at Nineveh also describe Scythians in this area. The Assyrian king Esarhaddon (ca. 680–669 BCE) wrote his soothsayers to ask whether he should send his daughter as a royal bride to the king of the Scythians. In separate letters, he asked if there were any signs that the Scythians would invade Assyrian districts on the eastern borders or even the heartland itself. Actual archaeological traces of the Scythians in western Iran, however, remained scarce.

The combination of Scythian, Assyrian, and Urartian objects in the Ziwiye hoard was unique and thought provoking. Were these artworks the trappings of a Scythian royal burial from the 7th century BCE when the Scythians ruled these mountains? If so, they are among the earliest Scythian artifacts known anywhere. Art historians have dated the objects in the hoard to around 700 BCE. Yet the majority of Scythian objects excavated in the region of present-day Ukraine, where Scythian presence is firmly established, date to the 6th century BCE or later, more than a hundred years later. Do the exquisite objects from the hoard hold the secrets to the development of Scythian art and the emergence of these famous raiders (Fig. 6S1.4) who ranged across the Central Asian steppe?

Fig. 6S1.1 *Right*
Gold bracelet with serpent-head terminals (53-31-6), said to be from the Ziwiye hoard, and similar to bracelets worn by Scythians (Sakas) on the Persepolis reliefs.

Fig. 6S1.2 *Above*
Silver rhyton (53-31-1) in the shape of a ram's head,
said to be from the Ziwiye hoard.

Fig. 6S1.3 *Opposite*

Gold leaf (53-31-2A), perhaps originally covering a wooden chest, depicting horned animals and panther heads in the Scythian animal style.

Fig. 6S1.4 *Below*

Sakas (or Scythians) delivering tribute to the Achaemenid Persian King from a relief found at the royal capitol of Persepolis. Courtesy of the Oriental Institute of the University of Chicago.

The Ziwiye hoard raises many questions; unfortunately, it cannot answer them. Since it was not properly excavated, and since there is no secure evidence that all of the objects attributed to the hoard were found together, or even that all of the objects are authentic, the hoard cannot function as proof for any scholarly hypothesis. In the 1940s and 1950s, antiquities dealers claimed that large numbers of artifacts came from Ziwiye. Some of them probably did. But other pieces may have come from elsewhere and a few are almost certainly forgeries. Analysis of gold objects from Ziwiye at the Center for the Analysis of Archaeological Materials (CAAM) lab at the Penn Museum revealed that the gold was quite pure, but it could not show for certain when the objects were made.

In order to investigate these questions, in 1964, the archaeologist Robert H. Dyson, Jr., led a Museum expedition to Ziwiye, clearing a paved stairway that led up to the fortified castle. More recent excavations by Iranian archaeologists have revealed more of the fortress at the site but have not found anything similar to the objects from the hoard. The mystery of Ziwiye continues.

in the importance of pasture as nomadic sites tend to be ephemeral and, thus, leave fewer traces for archaeologists to locate. There is some evidence of far-flung connections, particularly with hilly regions, during this time. Common Style Mitanni cylinder seals are found in the Zagros, elsewhere in Iran, and in the Caucasus. Such seals are also found far to the west, including in Greece and Cyprus, and to the south, in the area of the Persian Gulf.

People in towns subject to Mitanni maintained religious traditions that linked them both to rural and nomadic practices and to the long urban history of the region (Figs. 6.2 and 6.3). A stone sculpture with a roughly modeled face (Fig. 6.4), found at Billa, points to a widespread practice of figural representation among pastoralists in the Near East, the Caucasus, and the Eurasian steppe. The presence of these figures across the area of Mitanni may indicate the continued importance of widespread tribal links.

As was true in the earlier 2nd millennium BCE, northern Mesopotamia was culturally diverse. While many people probably spoke Hurrian, a language related to later Urartian, members of the ruling aristocracy bore Indo-Aryan names and swore by Indo-Aryan gods. Treatises on horse rearing and chariotry likewise employ a number of technical terms that are Indo-Aryan. This has led some scholars, like the archaeologist David Anthony, to speculate that Mitanni was "founded by Old Indic-speaking

Fig. 6.3 *Left*
This is one (31-40-1) of two crouching lions found together with two standing lions from a temple dedicated to the goddess Ishtar at Nuzi.

Fig. 6.4 *Right*
This "Stone Spirit" (92-4-1) is a rough human figure that may have represented an ancestor or a local god. Similar stelae are found throughout the Middle East and Central Asia.

Fig. 6.5 *Left*
This tablet (B3446) is an "ancient spreadsheet," a record of collections at Kassite Nippur.

mercenaries, perhaps charioteers" who came ultimately from Bactria and Margiana, which were located in late 3rd to early 2nd millennium BCE Central Asia. Other people continued to speak and write the Semitic language Akkadian. It is hard to assess the extent to which these languages coincided with what we would understand as ethnicity, given the paucity of sources. But we know that in earlier times, when we find the same mix of languages, that people speaking different languages intermarried. Someone with an Akkadian name could easily have had a father with a Hurrian name and vice versa. Ethnicity, moreover, does not easily coincide with lifeway. It is likely that people speaking all of these languages lived in towns and traveled seasonally with their flocks. As at other times, the lives of nomads, farmers, townspeople, and merchants were tied together in complex ways.

Settling Down: The Kassites

Enclosed nomadism is an important and enduring dynamic for northern Mesopotamia. The Kassites, who came to power in Babylonia in the 2nd and 1st millennia BCE, illustrate another of the long-term dynamics of nomad-urban interaction: how and when nomads choose to settle down. Texts and archaeological evidence document how both the poorest and richest members of a nomadic group can be induced to settle.

Fig. 6.6 *Right*
This tablet map (B10434) shows canals near Kassite Nippur.

The Kassites likely have their origins in the Zagros Mountains of Luristan, where they were originally semi-sedentary like most historical peoples in the region. The Kassites came into northern Babylonia by way of the Diyala region and first appear as a political factor in the mid-18th century BCE, when they attacked and were defeated by the Babylonian king Samsu-iluna (ca. 1750–1712 BCE). They did not appear in the urban centers in northern Babylonia in great numbers but were instead relegated to rural encampments and fortresses. They did, however, participate in the city-organized workforce primarily as agricultural laborers, and they appear in ration lists—rather like the poor Lurs whose herds became too small to support them in the 20th century CE (Fig. 6.5). As they became more integrated into the Babylonian social structure, they were able to own land, act as officials, and excel in horse rearing. The Kassite state emerged shortly after the sack of Babylon by the Hittites around 1595 BCE. It is difficult to pinpoint the exact date as we have very little documentation for this period; much of what we can reconstruct about the Kassite Dynasty comes from the later Babylonian King Lists. By the 14th century BCE, the Kassites controlled the whole of Babylonia and were recognized by their neighbors as a great power.

The Kassite rulers assimilated to the culture of the land they had conquered, building temples to Babylonian deities and collecting and codifying Babylonian literary texts. They became powerful proponents of Babylonian culture and religion. Indeed, there is little evidence that the Kassites living in Babylonia had an essentially different social

continued on page 146

Bronze Age Diplomacy

Lauren Ristvet

The Amarna Archive and the Late Bronze Age World

State correspondence, international diplomacy, and treaties are familiar features of the past few centuries, but have deep roots in the past. An international system began to emerge soon after the development of the earliest states in Mesopotamian and Egypt, and the earliest known treaties date from the mid-3rd millennium BCE. By the Late Bronze Age (ca. 1600–1200 BCE), an interconnected group of kingdoms had expanded to embrace the area from Greece in the west to Iran in the east, and from Egypt in the south to Anatolia in the north. These polities shared certain political, economic, and social conditions. Diplomatic marriages united some powers, while conflicts broke out among their client states. Kings communicated with each other through letters written in Akkadian. Akkadian, a Semitic language used in Mesopotamia, was adopted as a type of diplomatic *lingua franca* during this period. It was written in the cuneiform script on clay tablets that were carried from one kingdom to another.

In 1887, clay tablets bearing cuneiform writing started appearing in antiquities shops in Cairo. The tablets were unusual, not so much because of their appearance but because of where they were being sold. What were cuneiform tablets doing in Egypt? The cuneiform script, invented in Mesopotamia, was eventually adapted to write many of the ancient languages of the Near East: Egyptian, however, was not one of these. Scholars were initially skeptical of the tablets' authenticity, but E.A. Wallis Budge of the British Museum became convinced that they were genuine. After making out the words "to Nibmuariya, the king of Egypt" on one tablet, he realized that they were letters addressed to an Egyptian pharaoh. Archaeologists fanned out, looking for the source of the letters. They found it in Tell el-Amarna, the capital of pharaoh Akhenaten (ca. 1353–1336 BCE), who was known, prior to his fifth regnal year (1349 BCE), as Amenhotep IV. The name Nibmuariya would later be identified as an Akkadian transcription for Nebmaatra, the prenomen of Amenhotep III (ca. 1390–1352 BCE), father of Akhenaten.

The 382 cuneiform tablets ultimately attributed to Amarna during this period are collectively known today as the Amarna archive. The majority of these, some 350 tablets, are letters or lists of diplomatic gifts originally sent with the letters. Nearly all of the letters are written in Akkadian; only one is written in Hurrian, the language of the kingdom of Mitanni, and two in Hittite, the language of the land of Hatti. Alongside the letters were found school texts, including syllabaries, lexical lists, myths and epics, and an Egyptian-Babylonian dictionary (see Chapter 7S6: Education in Ancient Mesopotamia). Egyptian scribes probably used this material to learn Akkadian. The letters can be divided into two main groups. The smaller group (44 letters) was written by the kings of the Great Powers, the states or kingdoms that were equal in status to Egypt (Fig. 6S2.1): Mitanni (in northern Mesopotamia and southeast Anatolia), Assyria (in northern Mesopotamia), Babylonia (in southern Mesopotamia), Hatti

Fig. 6S2.1 *Opposite*
Map of the great powers of the Late Bronze Age in the Middle East and Eastern Mediterranean. Redrawn by Ardeth Anderson.

Map Key

🟨 Mycenaean Greece	🟧 Mitanni
🟫 Arzawa	🟥 Kassite Kingdom (Babylonia)
⬜ Hittite Empire	🟦 Assyria
🟩 New Kingdom Egypt	🟩 Elam

(land of the Hittites in central Anatolia), Arzawa (in western Anatolia), and Alashiya (Cyprus). The larger group is made up of correspondence between the pharaoh—usually Akhenaten though some of the letters date back to the reign of his father, Amenhotep III (ca. 1390–1352)—and Egypt's client states in Syria and Palestine. Other diplomatic archives have been recovered from other sites, including from the Hittite capital of Hattusha, located near Ankara, the present-day capital of Turkey.

The letters between the pharaoh and his clients are full of news, detailing military skirmishes between small kingdoms, complaining about Egyptian officials, and describing concerns regarding trade or tribute. The letters between the kings of the Great Powers are quite different. Ignoring the mundane concerns of warfare and trade, they speak instead of the brotherhood between kings, diplomatic marriages that may unite two powers, and gift exchange. The letters would have been read aloud to the king, and many of them were probably made to look impressive. At the Egyptian court their appearance (clay tablets rather than the papyrus on which ancient Egyptian was written) would immediately have marked them as foreign documents.

The Great Powers of the mid-2nd millennium BCE had much in common. At the center of each power was a highly organized palace sphere, which collected and redistributed

Fig. 6S2.2 *Right, Top*
Nuzi ware, finely made pottery like this cup (32-20-400) from Mitanni cities, occasionally shows elements of an "international style." It may have been used for the gifts that kings exchanged during the Amarna Period.

Fig. 6S2.3 *Right, Bottom*
This Kassite glass bottle (31-43-231) is an example of the type of beautiful *objets d'art* that may have served as a greeting gift.

agricultural commodities and also played an important role in craft production and trade. Records of many of the Great Powers, excluding Egypt, were kept in cuneiform, which was used to write languages and dialects as diverse as Hurrian, Hittite, Assyrian, and Babylonian. Bronze was the metal of choice, and its components, copper and tin, were essential trade materials; some 11 tons (22,000 pounds) of these metals were recovered from a 13th century BCE shipwreck at Ulu Burun, Turkey. Precious objects that may have served as greeting gifts among the great kings combined stylistic elements from several different regional traditions; examples have been found in Egypt, the Levant, and the Aegean, with a few similar objects recovered from Mitanni (Fig. 6S2.2) and Kassite Babylonia (Fig. 6S2.3). These objects emphasize the vibrant international relationships characteristic of the Late Bronze Age Mediterranean and ancient Near East.

This international system came to an abrupt end shortly after 1200 BC (Fig. 6S2.4). Cities were abandoned, and entire Bronze Age kingdoms, like those of the Hittites and the Mycenaeans, went into decline or even disappeared. Historian Robert Drews, who termed this event "the Catastrophe," argues that this was "the worst disaster in ancient history, even more calamitous than the collapse of the western Roman Empire." Even if this is an exaggeration, it is notable that few written records are known from much of the affected area for more than three centuries, including from places that weathered the collapse. The causes of the collapse, too, remain unclear. Egyptian sources blame raiders called the "Sea Peoples" who defeated the Hittites, destroyed cities along the Levantine coast, and threatened Egypt itself. Modern archaeologists have suggested that changes in warfare, earthquake storms, or climate change may be ultimately responsible. Understanding what happened and how affected societies changed or endured, is a major goal of ongoing archaeological research across the Near East.

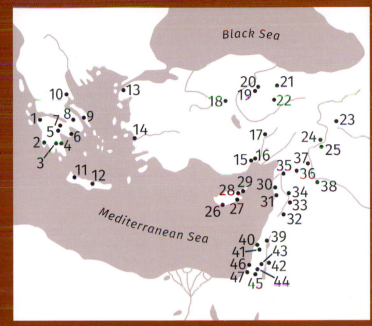

Fig. 6S2.4 *Above*
Map of sites destroyed, ca. 1200 BCE.
After Drews 1993: fig. 1. Redrawn by Ardeth Anderson.

Greece
1. Teichos Dymaion
2. Pylos
3. Nichoria
4. The Menelaion
5. Tiryns
6. Midea
7. Mycenae
8. Thebes
9. Lefkandi
10. Lolkos

Crete
11. Kydonia
12. Knossos*

Anatolia
13. Troy
14. Miletus*
15. Mersin

16. Tarsus
17. Fraktin
18. Karaoglan
19. Hattusas
20. Alaca Höyük
21. Maşat
22. Alishar Höyük
23. Norşuntepe
24. Tille Höyük
25. Lidar Höyük

Cyprus
26. Palaeokastro
27. Kition
28. Sinda
29. Enkomi

Syria
30. Ugarit
31. Tell Sukas

32. Kadesh
33. Qatna
34. Hamath
35. Alalakh
36. Aleppo
37. Carchemish*
38. Emar

Southern Levant
39. Hazor
40. Akko
41. Megiddo
42. Deir 'Alla
43. Bethel
44. Beth Shemesh
45. Lachish
46. Ashdod
47. Ashkelon

* Destruction in the Catastrophe is probable, but not certain.

Fig. 6.7 *Above*
Cheekpiece depicting horses (30-38-11)
—such horse gear was probably buried
with the dead in Luristan.

organization from that of the Babylonians. They might have borne different names and spoken a different language, but in general they seem to have assimilated quickly, giving up their foreign or tribal traditions. Although the level of urbanization and size of the population in Babylonia was lower than it had been in the early 2nd millennium BCE, the Kassite state was able to mobilize labor and resources for various large-scale reconstruction projects (Fig. 6.6), as well as for the foundation of a new capital, Dur-Kurigalzu. The Kassite Dynasty was extraordinarily successful; it stitched together Babylonia into a kingdom and ruled for about four hundred years, an extraordinarily long period of stability. Weakened political authority, an Assyrian invasion, and Elamite raids contributed to its demise in ca. 1155 BCE.

Riders and Raiders

Horses were first domesticated in what is now Kazakhstan around 3500 BCE, and entered the Near East near the end of the 3rd millennium BCE. Originally, horses were harnessed to chariots—the great war vehicles of the 2nd millennium BCE—important for both the Kassites in Babylonia and the Hurrians in Mitanni. By the 1st millennium BCE, however, the development of horseback riding brought highly mobile pastoralists from the Eurasian steppe into contact with the Middle East. These pastoralists, including the Cimmerians and the Scythians, threatened cities and even empires, but also served as cultural intermediaries—carrying Achaemenid Persian motifs, for example, to Siberia. Around the same time, the camel made the nomads of Arabia far more mobile. A thousand years later, the descendants of these nomads would bring Islam to a region stretching from Spain to East Asia, creating in the process the largest empire ever based in the Middle East.

Luristan

Fig. 6.8 *Above*
A horse gear collar (73-5-555) recovered from Hasanlu.

In Mesopotamia during the 1st millennium BCE, horses were highly desired commodities that provided kingdoms with a fighting edge. The Assyrians looked to groups of mounted warriors who lived in the Zagros Mountains to supply them with horses through raiding, trading, or tribute, but they were also wary of the potential of these fighters to threaten nearby provinces. Many of these ancient horsemen lived in Luristan in western Iran—the original homeland of the Kassites—in an area between the powerful settled kingdoms of Assyria and Elam.

Luristan is dominated by three parallel mountain chains that reach heights of 3,000 meters (9,800 feet) above sea level. It is divided into two regions, the Pish-i Kuh to the east and the Pusht-i Kuh to the west. The Assyrians called the people living in the

Pusht-i Kuh "Barnaki" and described them as "a dangerous enemy." The Pish-i Kuh was dominated by Ellipi, a kingdom that survived by playing the Assyrian and Elamite kings off against each other. Almost everything we know about Luristan comes either from excavated cemeteries in Pusht-i Kuh or from bronzes sold on the antiquities market that were probably looted from graves. In Pish-i Kuh, only two settlements have been excavated, Surkh Dum and Baba Jan, both temple complexes. The dearth of settlements speaks to an important aspect of life in Luristan; people in the region have often been semi-sedentary, alternating between farming and pastoralism. This was the case in the early 20th century CE as well, when the first archaeologists arrived.

The excavated bronzes elucidate some important aspects of life in Iron Age Luristan, particularly the importance of riding and fighting within the broader culture. Large quantities of horse gear, particularly bits and cheek pieces, some decorated with animals including horses, attest to the prominence of the horse (Fig. 6.7). These objects date to a similar or slightly later period than the horse gear recovered from Hasanlu (Fig. 6.8) (see Chapter 9: Hasanlu). Alongside horse trappings, people were buried with weapons, including swords (Fig. 6.9), daggers, axes, and maceheads; jewelry; and cultic items (Fig. 6.10). These items were decorated with animal, human, and mythical motifs in a distinctive style. The Luristan material offers insight into the importance of a people the Assyrians feared, traded with, and fought. In Assyrian texts, they appear only as "fierce warriors," but their material culture documents their rich artistic traditions and complex religious ideas.

Scythians

The bronzes from Luristan reveal the importance of horses in the Iranian Zagros, a mountainous environment where most pastoralists probably practiced transhumance. But horses were initially domesticated in the steppe and the great horse-riding nomads of the 1st millennium BCE—the Scythians, the Cimmerians, and the Sarmatians—were most at home there.

The Scythians lived in the grasslands of what are now Ukraine and southern Russia, but related groups controlled the steppe eastward as far as China. The name Scythian, which comes from an Iranian word for archer, is perhaps related to the great importance of mounted archers during this period. In the seventh and 6th centuries BCE, the Scythians appeared in the Near East, where they participated in battles across the entire region. In the early 6th century BCE, they again retreated north, where they established a nomadic empire that stretched across the steppe north of the Black Sea from the Caucasus to the Danube. While the Greek historian Herodotus portrayed them as quintessential barbarians, nomads whose only houses were their wagons, later scholars have called for a

continued on page 152

Fig. 6.9 *Above*
A sword (66-22-36) from Luristan.

Fig. 6.10 *Right*
A disc wand (41-21-5) depicting the
Master of Animals, an important motif
for people in Luristan.

Surkh Dum: Nomads in Archaeology

Lauren Ristvet

Nomads own fewer things than sedentary people, and ephemeral campsites leave fewer traces in the archaeological record than permanent settlements like cities or villages. As a result, much of our archaeological data on mobile peoples comes from their burials, which have often survived better than temporary settlements. In many parts of the Arabian Peninsula, the Caucasus, and the steppe, large earthen or stone tombs have marked nomadic territories. In Iran, graves are less prominent, but often contain elite objects. Given the richness of these burials, it is perhaps unsurprising that many of them have been plundered; only a small number have been excavated by archaeologists. This is especially true in the mountains of Luristan in Iran. Bronze weapons, horse trappings, and decorative arts from the early 1st millennium BCE flooded the market in the early 20th century CE, but almost no excavations were carried out here. It was not until 1938 that the archaeologist Erich Schmidt changed the situation. Schmidt, the head of excavations at Persepolis—the capital of the Achaemenid Persian Empire (in modern-day Iran)—took a break to explore the mountains of Luristan after having mapped them by air the previous year. He spent about three weeks excavating the site of Surkh Dum, which he recognized as "an archaeological bonanza."

Surkh Dum is one of the few settlements that has ever been excavated in Luristan. It provides information about the lives of transhumant pastoralists that complements what we know from excavated and looted graves. A large temple with stone foundations served the local community for centuries. In hoards buried under its floor and in its walls, Schmidt found several collections of locally made pins, bracelets, axes (Fig. 6S3.1), figurines, and pendants (Fig. 6S3.2) alongside imported objects like cylinder seals. Worshippers left these objects—some new and some already antiques—in the temple, perhaps as offerings to a fertility goddess. Each time the temple was refurbished, older groups of offerings were buried under the floors and in the walls, probably as part of a ritual that may have imbued the new temple with the power of the old. Who were the worshippers who gave these gifts to the Surkh Dum sanctuary? A small sounding upslope from the temple complex revealed parts of other buildings separated by a street, suggesting the presence of houses that were occupied either seasonally or year-round. Other worshippers may have been pastoralists who grazed their flocks for part of the year on the mountain slopes surrounding Surkh Dum, perhaps coming together to celebrate important festivals. Surkh Dum may even have been a place of pilgrimage, like so many other religious sites built by nomads.

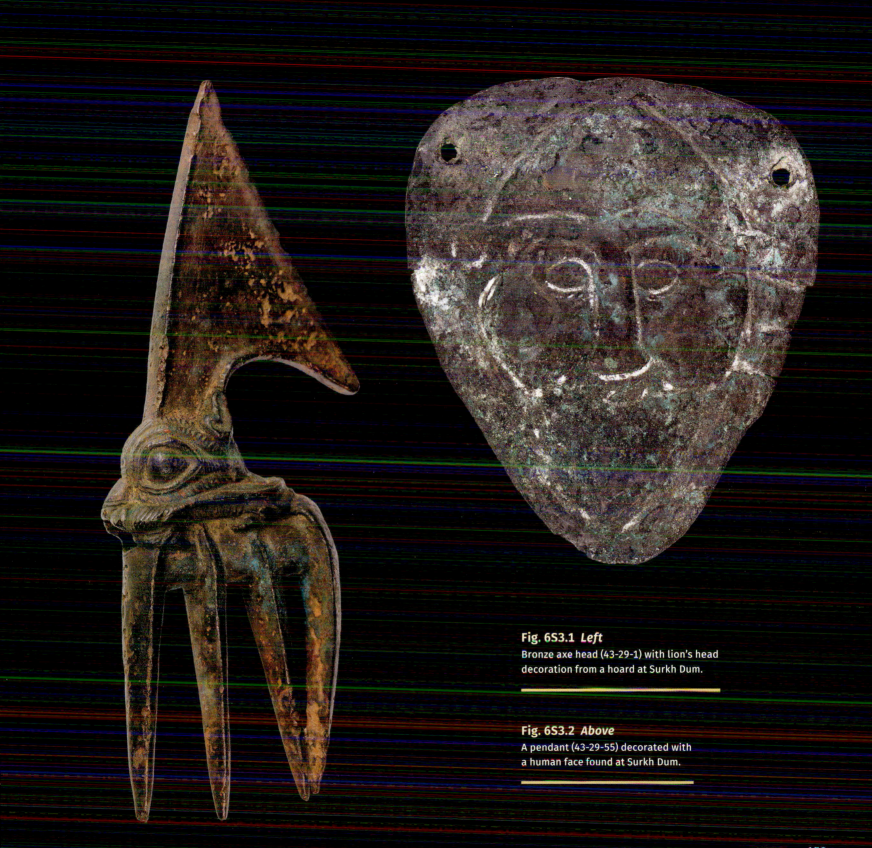

Fig. 6S3.1 *Left*
Bronze axe head (43-29-1) with lion's head decoration from a hoard at Surkh Dum.

Fig. 6S3.2 *Above*
A pendant (43-29-55) decorated with a human face found at Surkh Dum.

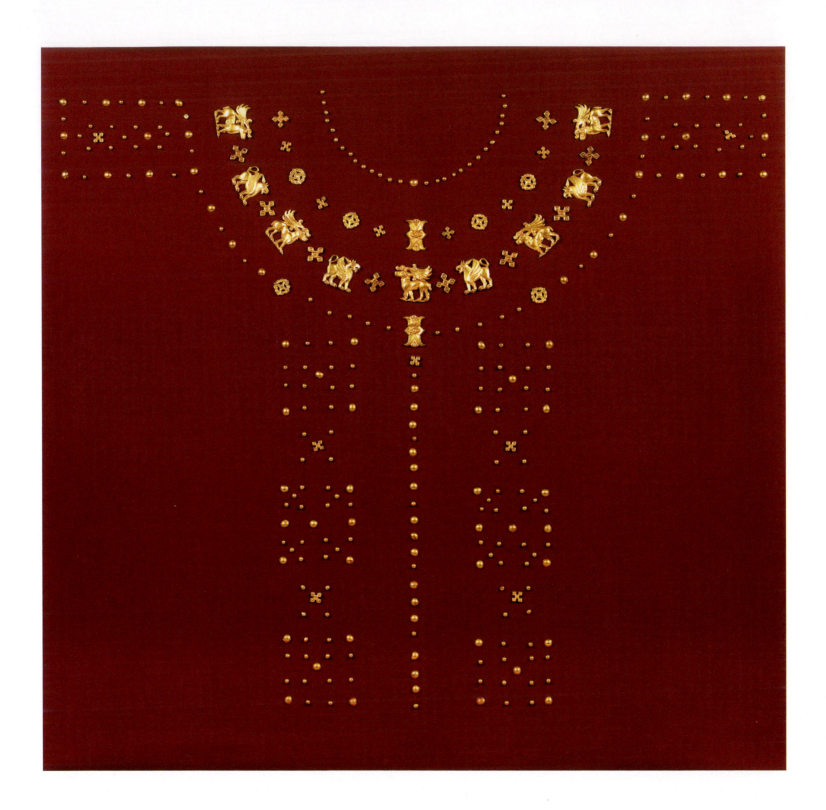

reassessment of the Scythians. These scholars note that it was the Scythians who enabled the creation of the early stages of the famous Silk Road, which connected such far-flung civilizations as Greece, Persia, India, and China. The historian Christopher Beckwith proposes that the emergence of these trade networks sparked the 6th to 4th centuries BCE florescence of philosophy and ethical religious thought in these civilizations. By connecting these regions, the Scythians helped facilitate what has been termed the Axial Age, a critical moment in intellectual development dated to between the 8th and 3rd century BCE.

Like the other peoples considered in this chapter, the Scythians were not pure nomads. The origin myth that Herodotus relates in his account of the Scythians emphasizes that the people were defined by four golden tools relating to their diverse ways of life: a plow, a yoke, a drinking cup, and a sword. Many non-Scythians also lived in their realms. To the north at Bilsk, Ukraine, near the border with the forest-steppe, extensive ruins cover a space of some 40 square kilometers (15 square miles). This might be the city of Gelonus, which probably controlled trade from north to south and where Scythians and others once lived. Greek colonies lay along the Black Sea, at the edge of this great empire. Artisans in these cities created luxury goods for the wealthiest among the Scythians.

Such cities, however, remained the exception rather than the rule in most of Scythian territory. In 513–512 BCE, Darius, the king of the Persian empire, tried to conquer Scythia, marching a huge army to the Danube. The Persian army, however, found it impossible to subdue the Scythians, who had few cities or settlements to defend and so could choose when and where to fight. The Scythian king Idanthyrsus, when Darius requested that he either fight or surrender, responded, "We Scythians have no towns or planted lands.... But if nothing will serve you but fighting straightway, we have the graves of our fathers; come, find these and essay to destroy them; then shall you know whether we will fight."

Idanthyrsus underlines the importance of royal graves, in the form of large burial mounds often called kurgans or kurhans, for the Scythians. Such kurgans, some over 20 meters (66 feet) high, are scattered across the steppe from Ukraine to Siberia. Most of these contain men, but a few belonged to women. The archaeologist Aleksandr Leskov has identified one such royal female burial based not on excavation but on analysis of artifacts and museum archives. He attributes objects in the Penn Museum collection dating from the 5th century BCE to the grave of a Scythian noblewoman from the site of Maikop, Adygea in Russia. The noblewoman was buried wearing an elaborate shroud, which had gold appliques of griffins, stags, crosses, and other elements carefully sewed to the fabric (Fig. 6.11). A full set of elaborate gold jewelry completed her outfit, while other jewelry may have been buried with her. Furniture inlaid with gold ornaments, including a panther head, also accompanied her (Fig. 6.12). Finally, a kylix, a Greek cup used for wine drinking, was found with her; on it are depicted two women playing the lyre (Fig.

Fig. 6.11 *Opposite*
The gold appliqué (30-33-1) from a burial shroud found in a woman's grave at Maikop.

6.13). Burials of other Scythian and later Sarmatian women in the steppe contained armor and weapons as well, perhaps giving rise to the legend of the Amazons.

Conclusion

In the Middle East, nomadic pastoralism in all its diverse forms has been important for at least the past four thousand years. Nomads have traded with permanent settlements, supplying animals and their products and serving as intermediaries in the movement and exchange of a striking variety of other things including metals, luxury items, and even ideas. Pastoralists have often occupied the same places as sedentary farmers, as in Mitanni in northern Mesopotamia. Other nomads have controlled areas just beyond settled lands, particularly in the mountains and the vast Eurasian steppe. Beyond trading and raiding, nomads have been mercenaries, slaves, and kings. This continuity does not mean that the nomadic way of life is monolithic. Rather, the role of nomads, pastoralists, and tribes is historically contingent, as we can see from comparing the Hurrians in Mitanni, the Kassites in Babylonia, the peoples of Luristan, and the Scythians. One of the long-term trends that we can see is increasing interaction with nomadic confederacies facilitating not only the development of trade routes and relationships, but also of ruling empires that brought increasing numbers of people from across Eurasia into contact. The rise of horseback riding greatly increased the range and military might of nomads like the Scythians, and later the Turks and the Mongols, paving the way for the first Silk Road and the later Mongol world system. Until the late 20th century CE, tribes and nomads were omnipresent throughout this area. The true story of the Mesopotamian or Islamic city is not one of urban centers arising in isolation; it is, rather, one inextricably interwoven with the story of the nomads.

For Further Reading

Anthony, David. 2007. *The Horse, the Wheel, and Language. How Bronze Age Riders from the Eurasian Steppes Shaped the Modern World*. Princeton: Princeton University Press.

Barth, F. 1961. *Nomads of South Persia*. Boston: Little, Brown & Company.

Beckwith, C. 2009. *Empires of the Silk Road: A History of Central Eurasia from the Bronze Age to the Present*. Princeton: Princeton University Press.

Cline, Eric. 2014. *1177: The Year Civilization Collapsed*. Princeton: Princeton University Press.

Cribb, Roger. 1991. *Nomads in Archaeology*. Cambridge: Cambridge University Press.

Drews, R. 1993. *The End of the Bronze Age: Changes in Warfare and the Catastrophe ca. 1200 BC*. Princeton: Princeton University Press.

Khazanov, Anatoly. 1994. *Nomads and the Outside World*. Madison: University of Wisconsin Press.

Leskov, A. 2008. *The Maikop Treasure*. Philadelphia: University of Pennsylvania Museum of Archaeology and Anthropology.

Fig. 6.12 *Opposite*
This golden panther (30-33-2A) was probably initially inlaid into wooden furniture.

Fig. 6.13 *Above*
This kylix (30-33-130), a Greek drinking vessel, was imported from a Greek city-state and buried with a noblewoman at Maikop.

7

THE ANCIENT NEAR EASTERN CITY: 2100–500 BCE

William B. Hafford

Opposite

The basic building block of the ancient Near Eastern city was the humble mud brick. This one (B16458) bears an inscription of Ur-Namma, king of Ur around 2100 BCE, saying that he built the ziggurat terrace foundation, called the 'platform clad in terror.'

Defining City

The first cities in human history arose in Mesopotamia, but they did not appear overnight. In fact, the so-called urban revolution unfolded over the course of many centuries. The development of state-level society, and of cities as central places within it, stretched across much of the 4th millennium BCE. The new socio-political structure involved increasing organizational complexity through the creation of hierarchies of power, full-time craftspeople and administrators, regulated metrology, accounting, and written language—all of which remain features of contemporary cities.

By the end of the 3rd millennium BCE, Mesopotamia's cities, defined as large and densely populated settlements within which operational, organizational, and administrative societal functions were performed, were deeply entrenched. Farming continued, but life in cities was more varied than that in villages a thousand years earlier.

Access to water is necessary to the development and sustaining of any human settlement and it is not surprising to find that most of Mesopotamia's cities were located on one of the two major rivers, the Tigris and the Euphrates, or on tributaries or canals running from one of these waterways. Many cities also had at least one interior canal, essentially a constructed waterway running through the middle of town. The only known ancient Mesopotamian city map (Fig. 7.1), dating to the mid-2nd millennium BCE and depicting the city of Nippur, includes representations of both the river alongside the city and a major interior city canal, which was labeled in cuneiform "the canal in the heart of the city."

Canals allowed for navigation, trade, and agriculture, and were vital to civilization in Mesopotamia's floodplain, particularly in the south where rainfall was insufficient to allow for rain-fed agriculture. Waterways were also necessary to carry away waste, and yet the canals were rather slow moving and likely to become polluted. A great deal of energy was, thus, expended in maintaining canals and acquiring water from the river for everyday needs like washing and drinking. While wells have also been found in Mesopotamian cities, they are situated primarily within major public spaces and may not have been sufficient to supply all of the city's needs.

Ancient cuneiform texts reveal that the Mesopotamian city had, in addition to canals and harbors, pits from which mud was extracted to make mudbrick, the basic building block. It also possessed more ornamental and organic features such as gardens and orchards as well as crafting or manufacturing areas. Villages and farmsteads did not disappear, but their organizational structures and daily existence changed as the countryside became urban hinterland and turned its focus to supporting the city.

Power—both secular and religious—was centralized within cities, which housed not only the ruling elite but also the principal gods and goddesses of Mesopotamia. The king himself lived in a particular city, which functioned as his capital, but maintained some

Fig. 7.1 *Opposite*

This map, inscribed on clay and labeled in cuneiform around 1500 BCE, depicts elements of the city of Nippur. It features the Euphrates River, the city walls and its gates, a garden area, a central canal, and the sacred district to the god Enlil. This photo was taken in the field; the artifact itself is now part of the Hilprecht Collection of the Friedrich-Schiller University, Jena, Germany.

sort of presence in most of the cities over which he ruled. Each city also housed a major deity as its patron and protector: thus, the god Enlil, chief of Mesopotamia's divine pantheon in the 3rd millennium BCE, was patron of the city of Nippur; the goddess Inana/Ishtar, associated with love (or lust) and warfare, was patron of Uruk; the sun god Utu/Shamash was patron of Sippar; and the moon god Nanna/Sin was patron of Ur (see Chapter 4S1: Kingship and the Gods). Manufacturing and food distribution, large-scale trade, and juridical oversight were also centered within cities. Towns, villages, and farms, in contrast, were places of decreasing population size and density, as well as decreasing levels of service availability due to the more limited number of professions acting within them.

Cities of Mud

Mesopotamian cities grew by building atop the remains of older versions of themselves. The mudbrick utilized in ancient architecture wore down over time and was often demolished when no longer usable or left to collapse naturally after a period of abandonment (Fig. 7.2). Later inhabitants would then level the debris and build atop it, so that each structure was elevated above the remains of the old. Localized trash disposal also led to a rise in the level of the streets, which were sites for the dumping of broken pottery and other defunct items. In fact, the streets in many ancient Mesopotamian cities rose so high that stairs had to be built from the house floors below to the street level above them: there is evidence for stairs rising as much as 1.3 meters (4 feet) from house to raised street. The cities of Mesopotamia, as a consequence of these building and living practices, rose higher and higher above the surrounding plain with each period of inhabitation. In the modern landscape of the Tigris-Euphrates Valley, tells, the mounds that are the remains of ancient cities, may rise 20 meters (66 feet) or more above the river plain.

Mesopotamian cities were walled; that is, a mudbrick wall, often very thick though probably not extremely high, surrounded the urban area. Some cities, in particular Abu Habba (Sippar) and Tell ed-Der (Sippar Amnanum), had high ramparts around them, apparently built to protect the cities from high Euphrates floods.

In some periods habitation would outgrow the confines of a city's walls, typically when it was at its peak and the population was growing rapidly. In such cases, houses would be built just outside the wall; these new areas, which archaeologists call lower towns, were typically short-lived, and did not change the interior cities.

Housing in ancient cities tended to grow in an aggregate manner, and expansions to existing structures conformed to whatever space was available (Fig. 7.3). Streets, as a result, were often narrow, and frequently terminated in dead ends. But if the cities appeared chaotic in layout, there remained clear elements of order. Specific administrative units,

Fig. 7.2 Opposite and Above
The inscription on this brick (84-26-14) tells of a refurbishment of the *giparu* ordered by the *entu* priestess, Enannatumma, daughter of Isin king, Ishme Dagan. She is the only woman whose name appears on bricks at Ur, or in fact, any city in 2nd millennium BCE Mesopotamia.

for example, existed: these wards or quarters were referred to in Akkadian as *babtu*. Each *babtum* appears to have had its own assembly for deciding legal matters that affected it. This assembly was called *puhrum*, a somewhat flexible term that could refer to anything from a major assembly of the city all the way down to a neighborhood watch. While in medieval and later cities of the Middle East (see Chapter 11: The Medieval and Early Modern Islamic and Persianate City) we often find specific quarters dedicated to groups delineated by kinship, religion, or profession—for example, the foreign merchants' quarter in the early medieval city of Constantinople—the *babtu* of Mesopotamia's early cities seem not to have been defined on the basis of familial or professional relationships. Specific evidence of city wards designated by profession or culture is not known until the 1st millennium BCE; even then, individuals living in such wards did not always conform to the relevant designation. This is not to say there was no clustering of people engaged in similar professions. There is archaeological evidence that Old Babylonian residents near the major temples in Ur, for example, tended to work for the temples, while people living in the only other excavated domestic area farther away from the temples tended to have mercantile associations. Such groupings, however, were neither formal nor particularly consistent.

Early Mesopotamian urban housing areas expanded outward from large public spaces containing major temples and/or palaces that were the focal points of the city.

These public areas were frequently characterized by wider and straighter streets than existed in other parts of the city, allowing for their ceremonial usage by large numbers of people.

The major temple to a city's patron deity was located particularly prominently within that city, usually placed atop a large, elevated platform and visible from afar (see Chapter 4: Religion and the Gods). By the end of the 3rd millennium BCE, such platforms had grown to become ziggurats (stepped towers) in many cities. Just who was allowed into the central area near the ziggurat is not clear but, particularly on festival days, it was likely a busy, crowded space.

Gateways to sacred areas or to cities themselves were seen as places of justice, spaces in which to swear oaths or proclaim innocence in legal proceedings. They may also have been commercial spaces in which goods coming from the hinterland could be bought and sold. The Akkadian term *bab mahirum*, "gate market," is used in some texts and may refer to commercial activities going on at or near the city gate.

Digging into Cities

Mesopotamian cities were so large and were occupied for so long, that controlled excavations cannot hope to uncover them completely. Sir Leonard Woolley, working with as many as 300 diggers over as much as five months of the year for twelve years, uncovered only perhaps 3–5% of Ur. The portions he revealed, moreover, crosscut thousands of years of occupation and, thus, many different versions of the city. But what he and other archaeologists revealed over the past century and more, even if fragmented and incomplete, offers compelling insights into ancient Near Eastern urban life. The discussion below explores the Mesopotamian city and its lifeways primarily through two examples from the south, Ur and Nippur; the Penn Museum played a major role in excavating both cities.

At the end of the 3rd millennium BCE, the city of Ur established hegemony over the other cities of the southern floodplain. This was the period of the Ur III Dynasty (ca. 2112–2004 BCE), the kings of which are well documented in cuneiform texts of the time. According to the Sumerian King List (see Chapter 4S1: Kingship and the Gods), an ancient cuneiform document that records a semi-mythical set of kings leading up to historically attested ones, this was the third time that Ur had risen to become the preeminent city of Mesopotamia. Ur III consequently designates the Third Dynasty of Ur, and it is the only dynasty of Ur that is clearly evident in the archaeological record. Its kings took control after a period of Akkadian rule and they reinstituted many older (pre-Akkadian) practices, including a re-emphasis in writing in Sumerian. For this reason, the Ur III Period is sometimes referred to as the Neo-Sumerian Period. To date, more than 40,000 Ur III tablets have been uncovered. Most of these are economic in nature,

continued on page 165

Ur from Above

William B. Hafford

When seen from above with aerial or satellite photography, some of the broader characteristics of ancient cities become clear. Heavily silted areas of fine soil might represent former water channels while some walls, particularly of major public buildings, are often visible just under or jutting above the soil. Smaller walls can be seen after rains or in traces of salts that leach out of the soil but, as they may belong to almost any occupational period, they may not provide an accurate impression of a city at any one point in its history.

The photo of the sacred district of Ur under excavation in 1926 (Fig. 7S1.1) is a good example of the potential of aerial photography, recognized even at an early period in the history of flight. The walls of excavated major structures are clearly seen, but so are other details such as soil color variations and water run-off patterns. Particularly visible are the massive piles of dirt removed from the excavation areas, piles that are still clear today fanning out across the mound of Ur.

Modern satellite imagery can reveal even more detail. Most of Woolley's excavation areas at Ur, seen as fresh in the 1926 aerial photo, have today filled in with soil wash, but his dirt piles still stand to great heights. Soil variations are often very clear in satellite images and the areas that are labeled as harbors on the map overleaf (Fig. 7S1.2) show up as lighter soil, indicating a fine silt that was likely laid down through water action. Although the soil difference is clear, it could be that some of these areas are associated with drainage into pits that may have initially been associated with mudbrick production. Despite some difficulties in interpretation, aerial and satellite photos are important components of archaeological analysis.

Fig. 7S1.1 *Above*

This image, taken by the Royal Air Force in March of 1926, shows much of the mound of Ur under excavation. The Royal Cemetery had not yet been discovered, but the walls of the public buildings in the temenos area are visible. Massive piles of dirt removed with light gauge rail carts are also clearly seen.

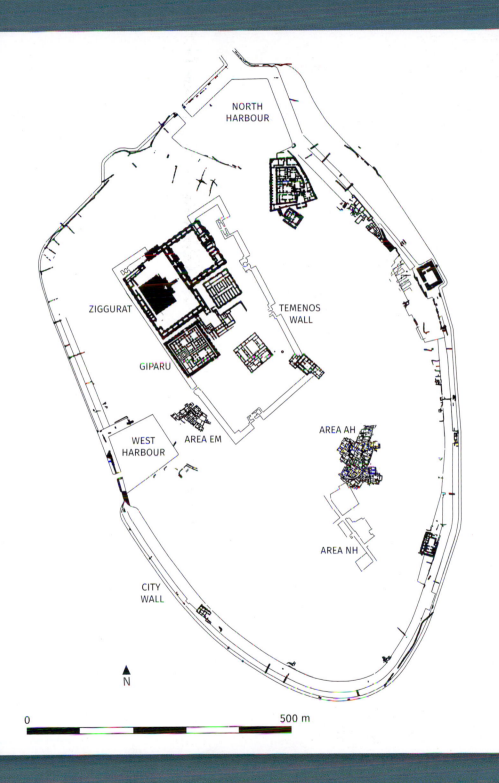

NORTH
HARBOUR

ZIGGURAT

TEMENOS
WALL

GIPARU

AREA EM

WEST
HARBOUR

AREA AH

AREA NH

CITY
WALL

N

0   500 m

Fig. 7S1.2 *Left*
This map shows many of Woolley's excavated areas across Ur, with concentration on Isin-Larsa/Old Babylonian buildings. Note that Woolley does not show a canal through the city, though one may have existed in some periods in the blank area just south of the temenos wall.

recording lists of products and people, for example, or their distribution and costs, and reveal the highly bureaucratic nature of the Ur III state. Other surviving texts take the form of royal inscriptions on buildings and monuments. When a king constructed, expanded, or repaired a major public building, he also typically had his name and a dedication stamped into the mudbricks used for the structure itself. This has left behind a record of royal actions that is very helpful to archaeologists today.

The founder of the Ur III Dynasty, Ur-Namma (ca. 2112–2095 BCE), constructed ziggurats in cities including Eridu, Nippur, and Ur. At the top of each city's ziggurat stood the temple of the city's patron god. At Ur, it was the temple to Nanna, the moon god. Although the upper level of this ziggurat no longer survives and the temple is long gone, the brick stamp of King Ur-Namma is still evident on many of the bricks of the massive lower structure. Ur-Namma also left foundation inscriptions that the Neo-Babylonian king Nabonidus (ca. 556–539 BCE) removed and described more than a thousand years later.

The Ur III Period ziggurat at Ur (Figs. 7.4, 7.5) had three levels, which originally reached an estimated 26 meters (85 feet) in height; approximately 16 meters (52.5 feet) of it still stand today. Its base sat atop a wider raised platform surrounded by storage magazines. Just beyond this platform stood other public buildings that functioned to

Fig. 7.5 Above

The ziggurat as it is presumed to have looked in the Ur III Period just after it was constructed. The top tier and its temple have long since fallen away, as has much of the second tier.

support the cult of Nanna. To the east was a large courtyard and to the south was the temple to Nanna's consort, Ningal. Nearby, the building known as the e_2-gi_6-par_4-ku_3 or *giparu*, housed the *entu* (the high priestess). We know several *entu* by name, all daughters of the reigning king. The tradition of naming a princess to the office of *entu* priestess was not a new one: several hundred years prior to Ur-Namma's reign the Akkadian king Sargon (ca. 2334–2279 BCE), who had taken control of southern Mesopotamia and established the Old Akkadian Dynasty, assigned his daughter, Enheduanna, to the post of *entu* priestess.

A wall dating back to at least the Ur III Period surrounded the sacred space containing the ziggurat and its courtyard, storerooms, and subsidiary temples. This wall, and the overall sacred space it enclosed, was called e_2-kish-nu-gal, typically referred to in contemporary scholarship using the Greek term *temenos*, an enclosed sacred precinct. The raised terrace contained within the *temenos*, on which the ziggurat itself stood, was known as e_2-temen-ni_2-gur_3, literally the "House, Foundation Platform Clad in Terror." Terror here should not be understood in the contemporary pejorative sense but rather as a type of awe. A building within the *temenos* zone known as the e_2-hur-sag, "the house of the mountain," may have been a secular palace. This has been identified as the palace of Shulgi (ca. 2095–2047 BCE), the son of Ur-Namma and second king of the Ur III

continued on page 169

The Importance of the *Entu*-Priestess

William B. Hafford

The *entu*-priestess, one of the most important people at Ur, was in charge of rituals to the chief gods of the city, the moon god Nanna and his consort Ningal. She was also, in some periods at least, the daughter of the king, and may even have taken on the earthly role of Ningal in certain ceremonies.

Already by the late Early Dynastic Period, the *entu* seems to have been an elite figure: the primary burial in the Great Death Pit (ca. 2450 BCE) in the Royal Cemetery (see Chapter 8: The Royal Cemetery of Ur) may have been that of an early *entu*-priestess.

During the dynasty of the Old Akkadian kings, Sargon (2334–2279 BCE), the founder of the dynasty, appointed his daughter Enheduanna as *entu* at Ur. Enheduanna, who is renowned as the first named author in history, wrote and compiled hymns to Inana. In Mesopotamia, her fame persisted for centuries; she was still remembered for her works a thousand years after her lifetime, and compilations of hymns in her name remained in circulation.

A stone disk bearing Enheduanna's name was found at Ur in the *giparu* (Fig. 7S2.1), a building that functioned both as temple to the goddess Ningal and residence of the *entu*-priestess. The disk shows Enheduanna as the tallest and most prominent figure in the scene; she is preceded by a priest who pours a libation and succeeded by two additional male figures.

Later *entu*-priestesses are also known: Enannatumma (ca. 1950 BCE), who lived during the Isin-Larsa Period, is one of the most prominent. A daughter of the king Ishme-Dagan of the Isin Dynasty, she is chiefly known from a statue bearing her name and dedication and from her building inscriptions. Enannatumma instigated the rebuilding of the *giparu* at Ur, and is the only woman known from the city to have had her name stamped onto bricks used for building (Figs. 7S2.2 and 7S2.3).

Fig. 7S2.1 *Above*

Enheduanna disk (B16665). This thick calcite disk was found in two pieces in the *giparu*. It depicts a ritual procession to pour liquid offerings, perhaps in front of the ziggurat. The tallest figure is Enheduanna, Sargon's daughter and *entu*-priestess. Her name and title appear in cuneiform on the back of the disk.

Fig. 7S2.2 *Above*
Enannatumma statue (B16229). This statue was found smashed into many pieces in the *giparu*, just outside the sanctuary of Ningal. It has been restored, including filling in missing pieces by comparing to similar statuary. The inscription is intact, however, and it states that the statue was dedicated by (and likely represents) Enannatumma, Ishme-Dagan's daughter and *entu*-priestess.

Fig. 7S2.3 *Right*
Enannatumma brick (B16543A). The inscription on this brick is a dedication by Enannatumma. It states that she has ordered a rebuilding and expansion of the *giparu*—her home as *entu*-priestess and the main temple of Ningal. She is the only woman whose name appears on bricks at Ur.

Dynasty. While a secular point of control would be needed in the highly centralized and bureaucratic Ur III state, the **e₂-hur-sag** was not particularly large: it was likely a place from which Shulgi oversaw important rituals as part of his royal duties rather than a primary residence or administrative center. The primary palace of the Ur III kings may well exist at Ur outside of the ziggurat area, but it has not yet been located.

Palaces, referred to in Sumerian as **e₂-gal**, literally "big house," were large buildings but not always as well maintained as the temples. In cases in which they have been excavated by archaeologists, as at Eshnunna and Uruk, they have often been eroded down to their foundations. A particularly fine example of an early 2nd millennium BCE palatial building in southern Mesopotamia, despite its heavy erosion, survives from the city of Uruk: this is the palace of the king Sin-kashid (ca. mid-19th century BCE), an enormous structure centered on several massive courtyards that contained many rooms used for diverse purposes. A similar palace exists much farther north at Mari, and it was known as a wondrous residence even in antiquity. Included were a throne room, an audience chamber, many storage rooms or treasuries, workshops, and residential areas. In fact, palaces in the ancient Near East served as households on a large scale (see Chapter 3: The First Cities), containing not only members of the king's family but also servants and craftspeople in royal service. They also served as centers of administration for the city and the state. The king himself (Fig. 7.6), as the link between the human and the divine, ultimately maintained the household of humanity as a reflection of the households of the gods. The latter divine households were established in temples that might contain not only the god and his or her consort (in the form of cult statues and their possessions and treasuries), but also priests and their storage and administrative spaces.

Living in Cities
Private Dwellings and the Urban Population

While there is a large body of archaeological and textual evidence for the public and monumental buildings of the Ur III Period, little is known about private housing during this time. Some Ur III houses were uncovered at Nippur in excavations at the end of the 19th century CE, but most were not well documented. One of these, labeled House J, is associated with more detailed accounts and has been closely studied, but was probably not a typical domestic dwelling. It was quite a large structure and contained evidence (including cuneiform tablets) of not only residential, but also official functions.

House J was a large courtyard house, meaning that it consisted of many roofed rooms enclosing an open central court that helped to circulate air and provide light in a largely windowless building. This type of house was common in 3rd millennium BCE Mesopotamia and is certainly typical of the 2nd millennium BCE. There were, however,

Fig. 7.6 *Above*
The king was something like the head of household for the city and its inhabitants. He was responsible for its well-being and as such, performed rituals to the gods on its behalf. On this plaque (L-29-300) he is shown bringing in a sacrificial lamb.

other types of house in which the courtyard was not completely surrounded or might even be absent (this latter is called a linear house). At Ur, Leonard Woolley uncovered extensive areas containing mixed courtyard and linear houses that dated to the Isin-Larsa and Old Babylonian Periods (ca. 2000–1730 BCE). In some instances, he noted the existence of mudbrick walls, which he attributed to the Ur III Period, directly beneath the Isin-Larsa baked brick walls.

The domestic areas Woolley uncovered at Ur in the 1920s and 1930s constitute the largest expanse of early 2nd millennium BCE private housing ever exposed. In area EM, excavated in 1926, Woolley uncovered twelve complete houses, relatively regularized around a courtyard house plan. Cuneiform tablets recovered from within the houses show that most of the people living here worked for the primary temples at Ur; the area was conveniently located quite near but just outside the *temenos* wall surrounding the main temple zone.

Woolley's area AH, farther to the south and excavated in 1930, was much more extensive, exposing more than fifty contiguous houses. Covering around 7,000 square meters (75,000 square feet), this area offers a good indication of typical house construction and street layout at Ur and provides an idea of just how crowded the city may have felt to its original inhabitants. Even though Ur was no longer the seat of the superordinate king in the early 2nd millennium BCE, the population of the city had grown to perhaps its largest extent. While it is impossible to know the exact number of people inhabiting the city, and even an estimate of the population depends on many variables that cannot be known, the Isin-Larsa to Old Babylonian city of Ur may have housed 20,000–25,000 individuals within its walls, while the overall hinterland may have been able to support up to a total of 85,000.

Estimations of ancient population are highly uncertain, and are typically derived from ethnographic comparisons with an estimate of 100–200 people per occupied hectare (2.5 acres). Some suggest, however, that cities may have had densities of up to 500 per hectare (typically based on comparison to much later cities). Woolley thought some 200,000 people might have occupied the greater region around Ur. More recently, scholars have estimated a likely population range between 17,100 and 27,500 in the early Isin-Larsa Period and between 25,000 and 40,000 in the late Isin-Larsa Period for the entire region around Ur (less than a third of which would have lived in the walled city).

City Plans

The streets of areas EM and AH are narrow and winding, and the houses are closely packed. More regularized streets and house orientation became common only in the 1st millennium BCE. In the 2nd millennium BCE such regularity is primarily apparent

continued on page 173

THIS OLD BABYLONIAN HOUSE

William B. Hafford

Houses in the early 2nd millennium BCE, and, in fact, throughout most of the history of early Mesopotamia, were centered on an unroofed courtyard to admit light and air. Roofed rooms surrounded the courtyard but were relatively narrow since long roofing beams were not easily available. Roofs were high, in order to allow hot air to rise up and keep the lower portions of the house cool. While very few windows have been discovered in excavated houses, even though some walls at Ur are preserved to a height of 2.5 or more meters (8 feet), it is likely that small, narrow windows were placed near the roof to help air circulate.

There has been much debate on whether the typical house was one or two stories tall (Fig. 7S3.1). A two-story house requires walls thick enough to support the second story; domestic structures of 2nd millennium BCE Ur tend to have mud brick walls 60–80 centimeters (24–31.5 inches) thick, but whether this would suffice is not clear. Staircases are present in many houses of the period but these might have led only to the roof, a space that was used for a variety of activities that included sleeping, when the interior of the house was too hot.

Woolley excavated many early 2nd millennium BCE private houses at Ur and believed that most originally had two stories. He identified the ground plan of No. 3 Gay Street in area EM as representing the best example of a standard domestic layout (Fig. 7S3.2). An architect at the site, Algernon Whitburn, drew a reconstruction of the house that followed Woolley's vision, but scholars today tend to agree that most 3rd and 2nd millennium BCE houses had only one story.

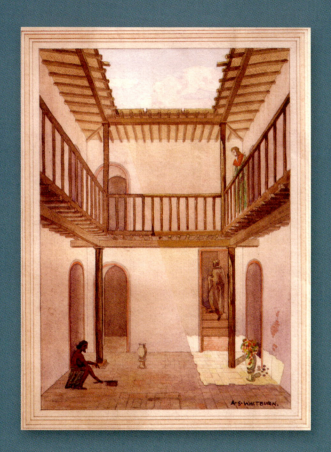

Fig. 7S3.1 *Above*
This watercolor, created by architect A.S. Whitburn, is based on Woolley's reconstruction of No. 3 Gay Street in area EM at Ur. It shows a two-story building with a walkway above the courtyard supported by wooden beams. The evidence for this walkway and a second story in general is very slim. Courtesy of the British Museum.

Fig. 7S2.2 *Opposite*
The ground plan of No. 3 Gay Street. Because it is neatly square in layout with a near perfectly centered courtyard surrounded by smaller rooms, Woolley took it to be the typical Old Babylonian structure. Most houses, however, were less symmetrical in their form.

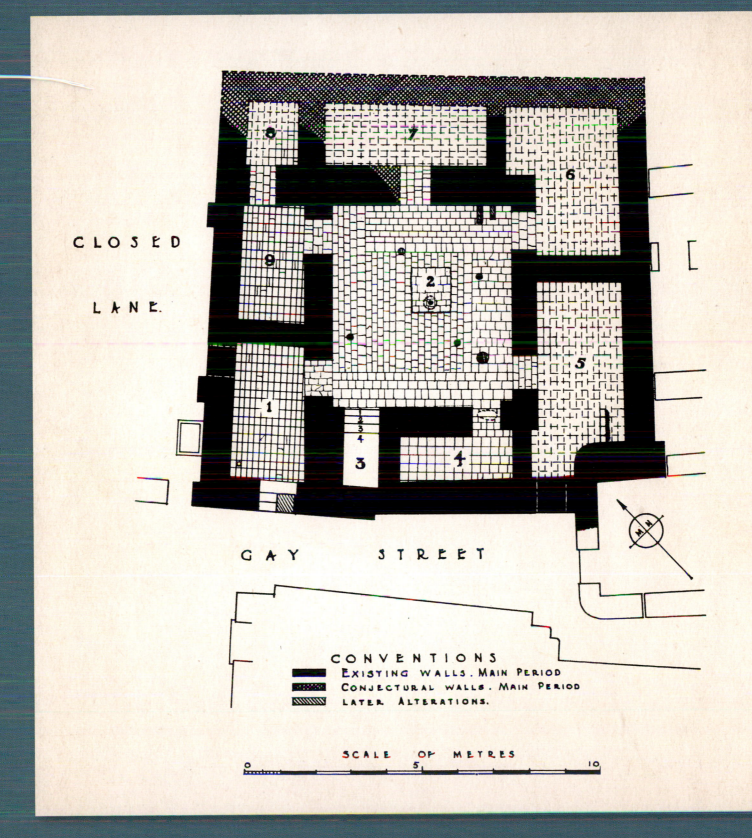

CLOSED

LANE.

8   7   6

9   2   5

1   3   4

GAY   STREET

CONVENTIONS
EXISTING WALLS. MAIN PERIOD
CONJECTURAL WALLS. MAIN PERIOD
LATER ALTERATIONS.

SCALE   OF   METRES
0   5   10

only at small centers carefully planned and constructed in a single building phase for the purposes of state administration. Sites such as Tell Harmal (Shaduppum) and Haradum in the central floodplain show signs of deliberate layout, but these are only about a hectare in size and so do not achieve the necessary population concentration or sociopolitical stratification to be classified as cities (see Chapter 9: Hasanlu). Other 2nd millennium BCE sites such as Dur Samsu-iluna, Kar Tukulti-Ninurta, and Dur-Kurigalzu were also planned, but these were designed as administrative centers or defensive outposts to demonstrate the power of the state. As these centers were situated in areas with insufficient agricultural production to support very concentrated populations, they typically had little in the way of private housing and were maintained only for short periods of time.

The layout of Ur's early 2nd millennium BCE domestic area AH (Fig. 7.7), with its frequent blind alleys and lack of thoroughfares, attests to the unplanned spread of housing typical of early cities: people built where and as they could. This does not mean there was no control over building at all, but it does suggest such control may have been decentralized, with any concerns pertaining to private houses and their construction left to local neighborhoods to resolve. We do not know for certain how large any individual neighborhood might have been, but it is worth noting that at least four local chapels were identified spread somewhat evenly across Area AH. Each chapel may have been the focal point of a neighborhood of ten to twelve houses and several neighborhoods may in turn have constituted a ward or *babtum*.

Shrines and Chapels

Neighborhood shrines, also called wayside chapels, were important for everyday life, as evidenced by the various votive objects discovered within them; such objects were probably dedicated to a local deity by individuals seeking divine protection or favor. Exactly what went on inside such chapels is unknown, though it was probably organizational as well as ritual. Discussion of local issues may have occurred alongside offerings to the local god, who would have been of great importance to the neighborhood's inhabitants. Just as a citizen could not hope to meet a king or member of his court without an introduction, s/he could not hope to enter the presence of a greater deity without the help of a lesser (divine) go-between. This point is attested in visual as well as textual sources: cylinder seals, for example, often show a human figure (presumably the owner of the seal) being led into the presence of a major deity by his or her personal deity (Fig. 7.8).

Many private homes also had personal shrines or chapels. One room of the Mesopotamian house, almost always the most secluded and situated at the back of the dwelling, often contained ritual furnishings including altars and incense chimneys. This room also frequently held the family crypt, typically taking the form of a narrow, vaulted

Fig. 7.7 Opposite
This map, drawn by J. Cruikshank Rose in 1931, shows the domestic area AH with the best-preserved walls and floors of the period ca. 1950–1750 BCE. The name of the owner of a house is sometimes known from tablets or seals found inside. A few of these are highlighted here, along with the nearest local chapel that might have been frequented by that person. Woolley named the streets in a fashion similar to a modern city, assigning house numbers odd on one side and even on the other. Many of the street names appear in the city of Bath, where Woolley lived.

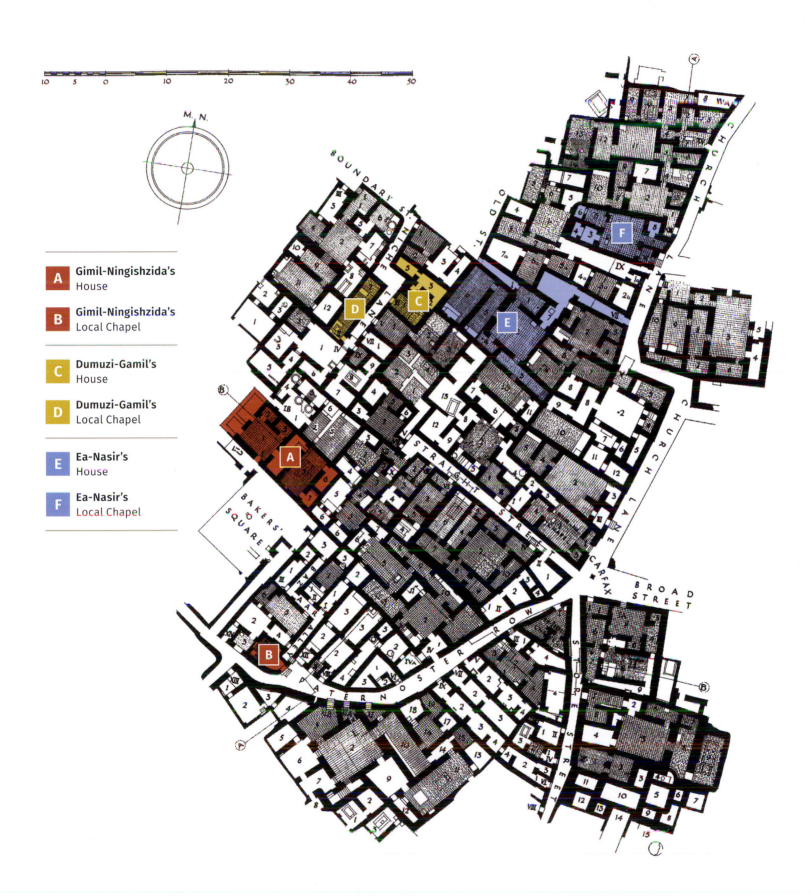

tomb set beneath the floor. The private chapel, then, appears to have been used for the veneration of both the personal god and the ancestors of an individual or family.

The best example of a neighborhood shrine excavated to date is No. 1 Church Lane at Ur, one of the four local chapels identified in area AH (Fig. 7.9). As with the other three buildings designated as chapels in the area, No. 1 Church Lane was clearly not a private house. Its entrance was above street level, reached by three steps, and its doorway was adorned with a large relief plaque (similar to one shown in Figs. 7.10 and 7.14) of a protective spirit. In its courtyard lay a small limestone statue of a goddess; the statue was originally fixed to a plinth but had fallen off of its base. Inside the plinth was another, smaller copper statue. Nearby was the skull of a water buffalo and a limestone slab carved with images of birds and humans. In the cella (the most secluded room in the chapel, sealed off from the courtyard by a reed door), there stood another limestone statue of a goddess on a base, this one showing evidence of breakage and repair with bitumen. Around the statue were many offerings including beads and mace heads. Additional offerings were found in a small storeroom off the courtyard. These included small clay figures and more mace heads, one of which bore a dedicatory inscription to the lesser deity Hendursag; No. 1 Church Lane has consequently also been referred to as the Hendursag Chapel.

Burying the Dead

Intramural burial, the burial of the dead inside the city and even inside occupied houses, was a common practice in the 2nd millennium BCE Mesopotamian city. Woolley initially found it difficult to accept the idea that people would choose to live so close to their dead, preferring to believe that only abandoned houses were used for burial. Eventually, however, he found so many graves directly beneath the floors of Isin-Larsa and Old

Fig. 7.10 *Right*

Plaques like this one (31-43-577) typically adorned the doorjambs into sacred spaces like local (wayside) chapels. This particular plaque was found in the fill above AH House 24 (No. 4 Paternoster Row), directly across from the Bazaar Chapel. See Fig. 7.14 for detail.

G 160

Fig. 7.11 *Opposite*

The pots in this field photograph contain infant burials. They were found just beneath the floor of an Isin/Larsa-Old Babylonian house in Area AH, No. 11 Paternoster Row, room 12.

Fig. 7.12 *Above*

This awl or punch (B17463) was used in leather or woodworking. Its handle (bulbous bit at the bottom) is made of bitumen mixed with small pieces of charred wood, while its shaft is made of copper. X-rays have revealed that the copper shaft (at the top) was originally a garment pin and has been reused as a punch tool.

Babylonian Period homes at Ur that he had to concede that burials were common in occupied homes.

Infant mortality was high in Mesopotamia, and many of the burials that have been discovered within houses are those of infants and children (Fig. 7.11). In one room in area EM at Ur, Woolley found 32 infant burials. When a baby died, it was placed in a clay bowl or pot and buried beneath the floor, usually in a subsidiary room of the private chapel. Adults not buried in the vaulted tomb under the chapel floor were either placed in a simple grave or under a larnax, a specially made clay coffin shaped vaguely like a bathtub. Such graves could be found under the floor of any room in a house but were generally concentrated in and around the private chapel.

Grave goods, artifacts buried with the dead, provide much information about belief in the afterlife and about the status of the deceased. While Mesopotamia has not yielded anything akin to the abundant textual and pictorial accounts of afterlife beliefs known from ancient Egypt, the inclusion of domestic pottery containing traces of food and drink (presumably offerings to the dead) in Mesopotamian burials suggests a belief in some sort of continued existence after death and the journey to the netherworld. Cuneiform texts also document the attention and reverence paid to ancestors, and describe offerings made to them long after their deaths. The dead seem to have needed continual support from the living since food and drink in the netherworld were thought to be spoiled and salty.

In addition to continuing some form of existence in the netherworld, it is possible the dead were thought to continue their professional endeavors: tools and other specialized items are at times found in graves. Larsa Grave 45 in No. 1B Baker's Square at Ur, for example, contained a copper vessel, copper awl (similar to the one shown in Fig. 7.12), copper scale pan, and seventeen stone weights; Woolley suggested, on the basis of these discoveries, that the grave belonged to a coppersmith. The building in which the grave was located also contained two modified furnaces that may have had to do with smelting.

The Economic Life of the City

Grimy crafts such as smelting, which required high heat and generated a great deal of smoke, were fundamental to life in the city, producing tools necessary for other professional and skilled work. Their noise and, in some cases, noxious fumes meant, however, that they were typically conducted outside the city walls and away from domestic dwellings. At Ur, the main location of industrial activity was likely a suburb known as Diqdiqqeh, which was located about 1.6 km (1 mile) to the northeast of the city wall. Diqdiqqeh produced many artifacts related to urban crafting and commerce, including jewelry and figurine molds, test pieces, tools, and weights. Cuneiform tablets recovered from Diqdiqqeh indicate that major canals intersected at the site, so that it

continued on page 183

Trade

William B. Hafford

At the end of the 3rd millennium BCE, renewed trade between Mesopotamia (the Ur III state) and the Persian Gulf region expanded rapidly. The Ur III state had more than 200 ships that operated the trade route; while the ships did not go much beyond Dilmun (modern Bahrain), many of the goods acquired there actually originated in other regions like Magan (the Lower Gulf) and Meluhha (the Indus Valley civilization). Merchants at Ur in this time were, consequently, sometimes referred to as alik Telmun, "men who go to Dilmun."

State control of long-distance trade was quite strong, relying on diplomatic contacts, and possibly some military underpinning, that only the state could provide. Those who imported goods from Dilmun were subject to a ten percent tax on their goods, which typically constituted stone, metals, and luxuries. Textiles continued to be the major export in exchange for these incoming goods. Cuneiform tablets indicate that up to 10,000 women in the area around Ur and 15,000 in the area around Lagash and Girsu worked in the textile industry in the Ur III Period. Such massive effort required substantial organizational control.

In the early 2nd millennium BCE, private trade increased, though merchants still paid taxes or tithes to the state and often worked on behalf of the temple or palace. Trade with the Gulf region remained predominant and Dilmun became an important state with standardized seals (see Chapter 3S2: Cylinder Seals in the Ancient Near East) excavated from many sites (Fig. 7S4.1).

By 1700 BCE, Meluhha had declined and trade in the Gulf diminished precipitously. Mesopotamia had also undergone depopulation or abandonment of many southern sites, including the city of Ur. As political supremacy in Mesopotamia shifted northwards, so too did trade links.

In the late 2nd millennium BCE, trade relationships with regions in the north and west were more common than ever before. During the Kassite Period (ca. 1595–1155 BCE), Babylonia in particular focused on diplomatic and trade relationships with Egypt (Fig. 7S4.2), as indicated by many cuneiform documents found at Amarna, the capital of the Egyptian Pharaoh Akhenaten (ca. 1353–1336 BCE).

Fig. 7S4.1 *Left*
This seal (31-43-75), found at Ur in the domestic area AH, has distinctive carving that is not Mesopotamian in character. It depicts a water carrier flanked by stars in a style that is found in the Gulf region. It is a seal from Dilmun (Bahrain) and attests to the importance of that region in trade with Ur and Mesopotamia in general.

Fig. 7S4.2 *Opposite*
Exotic animals were often represented in reliefs, seals, and figurines, like this monkey (B15724) found at Ur. Monkeys and other exotics were imported from Egypt and other regions, showing the vast trade networks that supplied Mesopotamia.

CURRENCY

William B. Hafford

Taxation, receipts, loan documents, wages, and interest rates were all recorded in Mesopotamia from an early period. In fact, writing in Mesopotamia seems to have been invented in the late 4th millennium BCE primarily for economic reasons: tracking and valuing goods and services was of great importance to early urban inhabitants. But how were these goods and services exchanged?

True barter, the exchange of one item directly for another based on individual need for that item, is a very local occurrence. As societies grow to encompass more people over greater distances, they tend to develop a method of assessing value generally acceptable to all parties. The method is by no means exact and requires negotiation (another meaning of the word barter), but there is a conceptual go-between beyond individual need in the minds of the people involved. When it takes physical form, the go-between is called currency, value manifest in a particular commodity. Eventually it can develop into a more standardized and guaranteed form, marked with symbols of the authority guaranteeing it. At that point, it becomes coinage.

Through most of Mesopotamia's history, the primary currency was silver by weight. Standardized weights for measuring silver in hand balance scales came in a variety of shapes but the most common were stone ovoids similar in form to an olive or date pit (Fig. 7S5.1). The next most common

shape was that of a duck with its head resting on its back (Fig. 7S5.2). Such objects were very common in the 2nd millennium BCE, and have been recovered from private, public, and funerary contexts. In the southern floodplain, such weights were standardized to the 8.4 gram (0.3 ounces) shekel; in the north, 9.4 grams (0.33 ounces) was typical, while in Dilmun (Bahrain) and the Indus Valley, 13.6 grams (0.48 ounces) was the standard unit.

Silver was not the only currency in Mesopotamia. Its high value meant that common workers rarely dealt in it. But there were established exchange rates between silver and grain. One shekel of silver (8.4 grams [0.3 ounces]) was equivalent to 1 GUR of grain (300 liters [8.5 bushels]); workers were typically paid in this larger volume and less durable commodity. Their pay was thus around 10 liters of grain a day, from which could be made the family's daily bread. Both silver and grain could be loaned out at interest, but rates varied. The Law Stele of Hammurabi states that interest on loaned silver was twenty percent; on grain it was thirty-three percent.

Silver was often fashioned into thick spiral wires, sometimes worn in the hair or perhaps tied to a belt. Such wire could easily be clipped for weighing and, thus, for payment. Excavations have uncovered hoards of valuable silver currency in the form of cut spirals, small ingots, and broken jewelry that were hidden away and never recovered by their owners (Fig. 7S5.3).

Fig. 7S5.1 *Left*
This standardized weight (B17101) found in a domestic area at Ur shows the typical ovoid shape used throughout Mesopotamia. It is marked with 7 vertical lines showing that it is meant to weigh 7 shekels. At 58.7 grams total weight, each shekel in this case is 8.386 grams.

Fig. 7S5.3 *Right*

These 52 pieces of silver (38-10-82) constitute the Penn Museum share of 102 pieces found in a jar buried beneath the floor of an Early Dynastic III house at Khafaje (the remaining 50 pieces and the jar went to Baghdad). Made up of thin cut pieces, bent and cut ingots, beads, and spiral wire, it is a currency hoard hidden away because of its value. The unbroken spiral pieces weigh around one shekel each (~8.4 grams).

Fig. 7S5.2 *Left*

This tiny (1.8 cm long) duck weight (B6210), found at Nippur, demonstrates the skill of Mesopotamian workmanship and precision in weighing. It is carved of banded agate with a white band forming the duck's head, and it weighs 2.1 grams, making it 1/4 of a standard Mesopotamian 8.4 gram shekel.

Fig. 7.13 *Left*
The inscription on this weight (B12468) states that it is one half of a true mina (approximately one pound), but the fact that it has been defaced (a large dent struck directly across the inscription) shows that a controlling authority found it to be wanting and ensured it would not be used.

may also have served as a harbor or business district, as well as a locus, at least during the Ur III Period, for private economic activities. Diqdiqqeh may also have been the site of a kind of watchtower capable of spotting incoming ships and caravans.

Crafting in general, particularly during the Ur III Period, was heavily controlled by the state, likely because it required the sort of organizational capacity that only (or primarily) the state could muster at the time. Private craftspeople probably existed as well, perhaps employed on occasion by the state, but it is only in the Old Babylonian Period by ca. 1900 BCE that there is significant evidence of merchants and craftspeople working in a private capacity.

Trade was vital to the functioning of the city. Southern Mesopotamia lacked many basic resources, including hard stone and the types of wood suitable for building, and so relied on imports of these from other regions. Much of this trade was carried out with mountainous regions to the east and the plateau beyond (modern Iran), but exotic and luxury materials such as lapis lazuli, gold, and carnelian were also imported from places as far away as Afghanistan. Much of southern Mesopotamia's long-distance trade was conducted by water, with boats traveling to and from the Indus Valley through the Persian Gulf. At this time the head of the Gulf was nearer to Ur than it is today and this placed the city in a good position to manage the luxury trade during the third and into the early 2nd millennium BCE—this favorable geographical position is one of the reasons for Ur's importance and large size during this period.

Weights and measures for the evaluation of goods became an essential part of trade and were standardized. King Shulgi's name is found on several large weights dedicated in the temple of Ningal; these may have functioned as standards to show the importance of a specific and regular weight measurement. The weight of a shekel, which represented about a month's wages for a laborer when measured out in silver, was 8.4 grams, and this remained the standard weight in southern Mesopotamia for more than a thousand years. There is also evidence from Nippur of weights being checked for accuracy and defaced if they did not meet the standard (Fig. 7.13). The Law Stele of Hammurabi (which dates to his reign 1792–1750 BCE), perhaps the best known royal inscription extant from Mesopotamia, also sets out punishments for using false weights, and lists interest rates on silver and grain.

The calculation of interest rates and recording of economic transactions required skills in mathematics and writing, and, therefore, an education system. Vocational apprenticeships in various crafts were common in Mesopotamia and some of them lasted many years, but higher education in writing and mathematics are also documented. Just how widespread such education was cannot be directly determined, but writing certainly played a fundamental role in urban life.

Evidence of schooling comes from both Nippur and Ur, which have yielded thousands of cuneiform tablets dating to the late third and early 2nd millennia BCE. Some of these are clearly practice tablets written by students training to become scribes: typically characterized by a distinctive circular or lentil form, these are covered in crudely formed and repetitive writing. Other tablets have been identified as belonging to later phases in the scribal training curriculum, which progressed from teaching students to shape the clay tablets on which they would write, on to mastering the cuneiform signs that were to be impressed into the surface of these tablets using a reed stylus, and finally to copying out various types of compositions including lexical lists, mathematical problems, and famous literary texts.

Reoccupying Cities

Hammurabi (ca. 1792–1750 BCE), king of the city of Babylon and the most famous ruler of the Old Babylonian Dynasty, gained control of Mesopotamia at the beginning of the 18th century BCE. His rule followed the lengthy struggle for supremacy between the cities of Isin and Larsa, for which the Isin-Larsa Period is named, and clashes between Larsa and Babylon continued even after the establishment of the Old Babylonians kings as supreme rulers of Mesopotamia. The king Rim-Sin II of Larsa (ca. 1742–1738 BCE), for example, led a coalition of southern city-states including Ur and Uruk in a rebellion against Samsu-iluna (ca. 1750–1712 BCE), Hammurabi's son and successor as king of Babylon.

Samsu-iluna put down the rebellion with an iron hand and is described as destroying the walls of Ur, Uruk, and Larsa in his eleventh regnal year (ca. 1738 BCE). Indeed, excavations at Ur have demonstrated that occupation fell off drastically at this point: some squatter occupation may have continued but the city was, for the most part, abandoned.

continued on page 190

Education in Ancient Mesopotamia

Philip Jones

Education in ancient Mesopotamia was very different from that in the modern world. The great majority of the people of Mesopotamia would have followed in the footsteps of their parents and most education would, therefore, have been obtained "on the job." Schools as we understand them did not exist and, with one extremely important exception, the vast majority of training has left virtually no trace in the archaeological or textual record. The one exception is scribal education.

Mesopotamia was one of the earliest literate societies and, over the course of three thousand years, generated an enormous corpus of written material. Texts were written in both the Sumerian and Akkadian languages using the same cuneiform writing system. Levels of literacy among the general population were always relatively low throughout Mesopotamian history. Scribes, thus, controlled an important strategic resource—the ability to read and write—that cemented their social status and supplemented the income from their own landholdings and businesses. In particular, scribes provided crucial managerial services for the two great economic centers of every Mesopotamian city: the palace and the temples.

The nature of the training necessary to become a scribe—the repetitive practicing of cuneiform writing exercises on clay tablets—has resulted in the survival of a huge corpus of school tablets, discarded but virtually indestructible in the dry climate of Iraq, that encompasses almost the entire three thousand-year-plus span of cuneiform. The discarded student exercises of the early 2nd millennium BCE Old Babylonian Period represent an especially important group of documents

Fig. 7S6.1 *Left*
The new student would begin by practicing the correct way to impress wedges into a damp clay tablet (B6043) using a reed stylus.

Fig. 7S6.2 *Opposite*
Students learning standardized lists of words and phrases used tablets like this one (B14156) to practice their assignments. On the left, a teacher would write a master copy of the exercise; on the right, a student would repeatedly copy out and erase the exercise until he had mastered it. The right side of this tablet is erased and ready for another attempt at copying; repeated erasures have also left it noticeably thinner than the left side. On the back of this type of tablet, students wrote out (from memory) passages learned earlier in their training. By studying the subjects that appear on the front and back of such tablets, we gain insight into the order in which material was learned.

within this larger corpus: they constitute one of the world's few bodies of literature to predate the more familiar biblical and Classical texts of the first millennium BCE.

The Old Babylonian Scribal Curriculum

New scribal students would first practice the correct way to impress wedges into the clay (Fig. 7S6.1). Then they would begin the laborious process of learning to construct and use cuneiform signs. This involved writing out a series of standardized lists and literary compositions in a roughly set order (Figs. 7S6.2, 7S6.3). The texts included in the curriculum included lists of signs, words and phrases, metrological units, mathematical problems, legal formulae, and proverbs.

This initial phase of the education would allow a scribe to practice preparing most of the documents that he would be called upon to write in his professional life: managerial lists, legal contracts, and letters in Akkadian. It may be that some scribes never bothered to continue beyond this phase.

However, in order to also be able to write in Sumerian, a scribe would have to complete the next phase of instruction, which involved memorizing and writing out Sumerian literary compositions (7S6.4).

By the Old Babylonian Period, Sumerian had almost certainly died out as a spoken language. However, just as children in early modern Europe had to learn Latin, the scribal training of the Old Babylonian Period still focused on learning the dead Sumerian language rather than the living Akkadian. The compositions incorporated into scribal education included Sumerian myths, legends, historical poems, and hymns (Fig. 7S6.5). Among these were a series of short tales about Gilgamesh, a legendary king of Uruk and eponymous hero of the famous (and later in date) Akkadian Epic of Gilgamesh. The Sumerian Gilgamesh narratives incorporated into the scribal education curriculum include Gilgamesh and Huwawa, in which the heroes Gilgamesh and Enkidu travel to the legendary Cedar Forest, where they confront and ultimately slay the forest's monstrous guardian Huwawa (see Chapter 5S1: Sumerian Epic Heroes); this narrative is closely related to an episode in the later Akkadian Epic of Gilgamesh.

Fig. 7S6.3 *Opposite, Top Left*
This round tablet (B7866), known as a lentil to modern scholars, was used in scribal schooling. Typically, the teacher wrote out a brief quote on the lentil, often from a lexical list, which was then copied on the same tablet by a student. This tablet contains a quote from the first literary text in the scribal curriculum, a hymn to the king Lipit-Ishtar (ca. 1934–1924 BCE) of the city of Isin. The lines read: "(The goddess) Nisaba, the woman sparkling with joy." The small amount of text written by the student on these tablets suggests lentils functioned less as teaching tools than as commemorations, perhaps of a student's length of attendance at a school.

Fig. 7S6.4 *Opposite, Bottom Left*
This small rectangular single column tablet (B7051) is known as an imgidda in Sumerian. Tablets like this would be used for a student's first attempts at writing out compositions from memory rather than by referring to a teacher's copy. The text is usually a short excerpt from a lexical list or literary narrative; this particular tablet bears a short humorous composition about school life. Other tablets of this type bear short excerpts.

Fig. 7S6.5 *Opposite, Right*
Large multi-column tablets such as this one (B7847+29-15-472) were used by students to write out entire lexical lists or literary compositions, perhaps to demonstrate their successful memorization of the pertinent composition. Written on this tablet is a hymn to the goddess Inana, a composition that was (purportedly) composed by the *entu*-priestess Enheduanna (ca. 2300 BCE), daughter of the Old Akkdian king Sargon (see Chapter 7S2: The Importance of the *Entu*-Priestess).

In fact, most of the cities of the south were heavily depopulated around this time, though some smaller centers of occupation did continue in the area. Even Nippur, in the more central part of the floodplain, was affected by the conflict between Samsu-iluna and the cities of the south and was mostly abandoned by Samsu-iluna's thirtieth regnal year (ca. 1719 BCE).

Sometime after 1500 BCE, during the period of the Kassite Dynasty in Babylon (ca. 1595–1155 BCE), southern Mesopotamia underwent significant revitalization. The Kassite ruler Kurigalzu I (ca. early 14th century BCE) rebuilt Babylonia and undertook an extensive program of reoccupation and repair at Ur in the late 15th or early 14th centuries BCE. He made some changes to the structure of the public buildings, including moving some of the major temples, but for the most part he rebuilt and maintained the old cultic structure. This practice of maintaining traditional southern Mesopotamian religious structures and practices was undertaken in other cities as well. While specifically Kassite deities were installed in Babylon, and while Kurigalzu I set up new temples at old cities like Uruk as well as at new cities like Dur-Kurigalzu, the Kassite Dynasty also established and emphasized its legitimacy by maintaining traditional Babylonian religious centers and rebuilding their old temples.

Domestic structures in the Kassite Period are not well attested but appear to have followed the lines of the earlier Old Babylonian Period, taking the form of close-set buildings on winding streets. Only 21 houses of Kassite date are definitively known from excavated sites across Babylonia. While Woolley reported many potential Kassite houses at Ur, these were, unfortunately, neither well preserved nor well excavated; only two can be confirmed as belonging to the Kassite Period and these followed the courtyard house plan known from earlier in the 2nd millennium BCE.

A similar situation exists at Nippur, where many public buildings show evidence of Kassite rebuilding, but domestic dwellings of the Kassite Period remain more elusive. From Nippur, however, there is evidence of planned rebuilding in the form of the only ancient city map known from Mesopotamia (Fig. 7.1). This map shows the outline of Nippur's walls and city gates, as well as canals, the river, and a few major spaces within the city. It directly labels the sacred district (the **Ekur**, temple of Enlil), at least seven city gates, a garden area within the walls, and a canal running through the city. This map, which was likely a plan for rebuilding the city after its long abandonment, is largely accurate, matching the excavated remains of Nippur, particularly in the shape of the city wall.

After the Kassite Period there was a second period of depopulation at the site of Nippur (following that which occurred during the reign of Samsu-iluna in the 18th century BCE). There is little evidence of habitation from approximately 1225 to 750 BCE in the city, and Ur's population may also have decreased at this time, though it picked up again sometime in the 8th or 7th century BCE. The pattern of maintaining or rebuilding old cultic centers also returned in the mid-1st millennium BCE, probably

Fig. 7.14 *Opposite*

Detail of plaque (31-43-577) shown in Fig. 7.10. The goddess depicted holds a flowing vase associated with abundance.

because it provided legitimacy to new dynastic rulers; by upholding entrenched traditions, a new king could ensure the support of people who had lived in the area and observed those traditions all their lives. During the Neo-Babylonian Period (ca. 626–539 BCE), Ur and other southern centers saw renewed efforts at revamping the old temples, particularly under the kings Nebuchadnezzar II (ca. 604–562 BCE) and Nabonidus (ca. 556–539 BCE). The foundation cylinders (similar to the one depicted in Fig. 7.15) that Nabonidus placed inside the ziggurat at Ur tell the story of how he discovered and read the much earlier Ur III Period foundation inscriptions. These explained that Ur-Namma, founder of the Ur III Dynasty, had begun the original ziggurat, and that his son Shulgi had completed it. Nabonidus then honored the ancient kings by restoring and improving the ziggurat: while the old structure had been three levels high, the Neo-Babylonian version may have had as many as seven levels. The new ziggurat incorporated layers of color rising from black to red and then to white; a trim of blue tiles appeared at its top.

City planning appears to have become much more deliberate and regular in the re-envisioned cities of the mid-1st millennium BCE. Streets, even those running through residential areas, tended to be wider and straighter with more regular intersections. The wealthy Merkes quarter in Babylon during the reign of Nebuchadnezzar II, for example, was extensively excavated in the early 20th century CE to reveal a large domestic zone where streets ran in relatively straight lines and crossed at near right angles.

Houses of the mid-1st millennium BCE also tended to be larger than those of the 2nd millennium BCE, and many evince a peculiar saw-tooth facade. At Ur, Neo-Babylonian houses lie very near the surface and are, thus, heavily eroded by thousands of years of exposure. Nonetheless, Woolley mapped the remaining foundations of seven such houses in a domestic area he called NH (Fig. 7.16).

Woolley also excavated a very large (approximately 5,000 square meters [54,000 square feet]) Neo-Babylonian building, which he called the Palace of Bel-Shalti-Nannar, near the temenos at Ur and found it possessed many of the characteristics of the Merkes quarter buildings at Babylon. Though the building is unlikely ever to have been a palace, it may have had some administrative functions; it is very large in scale and built on an extended double courtyard house plan. Because it was heavily eroded, few artifacts were recovered from within it that might have clarified its function. Woolley suggested it served as the residence of Nabonidus' daughter, whose name is now read En-nigaldi-Nanna. She was appointed *entu*-priestess of the moon god, maintaining a tradition already quite ancient by Nabonidus' time and contributing to the legitimation of Nabonidus' kingship.

The Neo-Babylonians kept the temple to Ningal on the ziggurat platform at Ur where the Kassites had moved it, but rearranged and merged the *dublalmah*, a monumental gate onto the ziggurat terrace and a law court or place of judgment, with the *giparu*, which

Fig. 7.15 *Opposite*
This foundation cylinder (L-652-1) describes the feats of the Neo-Babylonian king Nebuchadnezzar II. Much of the late reworking of Ur (1st millennium BCE) is attributed to this king and one of his successors, Nabonidus.

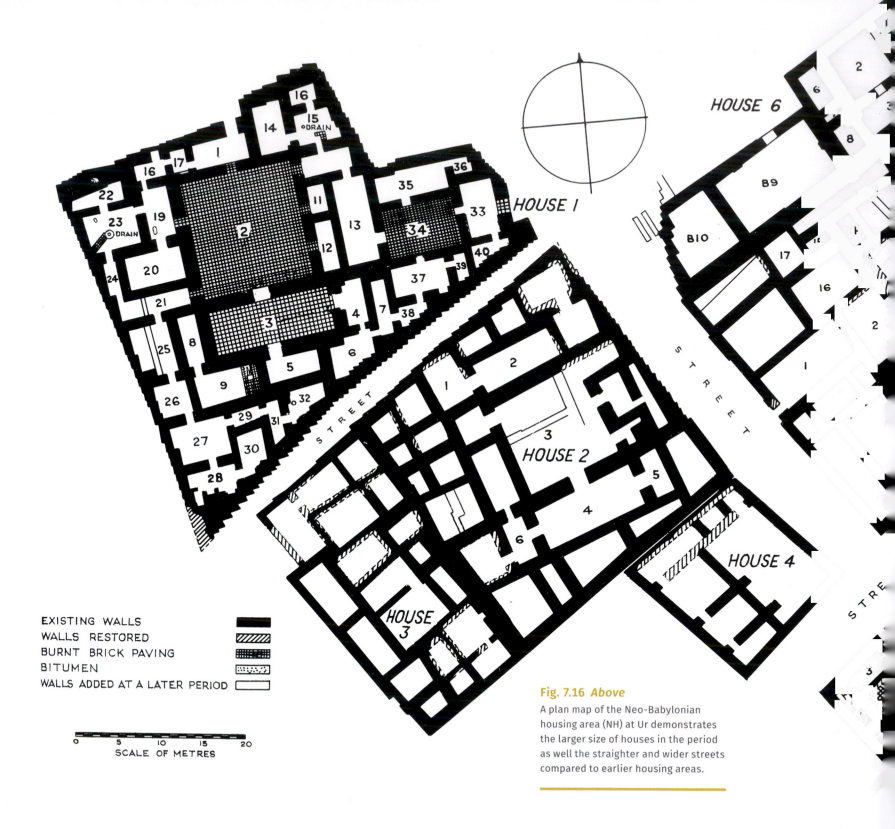

EXISTING WALLS
WALLS RESTORED
BURNT BRICK PAVING
BITUMEN
WALLS ADDED AT A LATER PERIOD

0   5   10   15   20
SCALE OF METRES

Fig. 7.16 *Above*
A plan map of the Neo-Babylonian housing area (NH) at Ur demonstrates the larger size of houses in the period as well the straighter and wider streets compared to earlier housing areas.

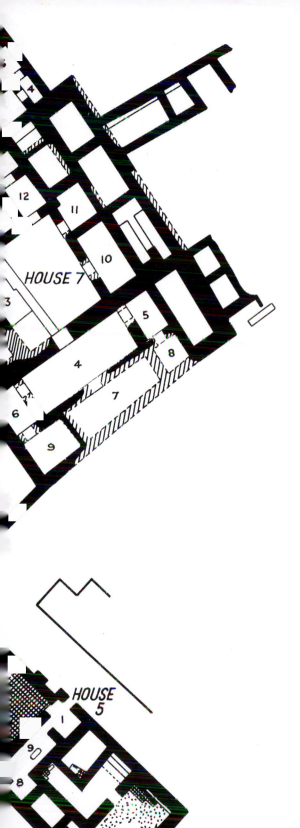

had housed the *entu*-priestess in earlier times. They also surrounded the *temenos* zone with a wider and more regularized wall, which enclosed a much larger area than before, and rebuilt what had been a temple storehouse, the **ga$_2$-nun-mah**. They appear to have misinterpreted the ancient purpose of this building as they transformed it into a temple proper with the name **e$_2$-nun-mah**.

In spite of the obvious changes Nebuchadnezzar and Nabonidus made to Ur, the overall character of the site remained rooted in the ancient past. This traditional stability was characteristic of all major southern Mesopotamian cities, which functioned as the political anchors for kings spanning a period of more than a thousand years. Yet, as the world grew still wider and more interconnected, and as empires grew stronger and more expansive, southern Mesopotamia lost much of its political and religious significance. The cities of the region would remain important but the nature of their roles would begin to change.

For Further Reading

Hilprecht, H. V., Benzinger, I., Hommel, Fritz, Jensen, Peter Christian Albrecht, and Georg Steindorff. 1903.
 Explorations in Bible Lands during the 19th century. Philadelphia: A.J. Holman.
Roux, Georges. 1964. *Ancient Iraq*. London: George Allen & Unwin, Ltd.
Woolley, C. Leonard. 1929. *Ur of the Chaldees: A Record of Seven Years of Excavation*. London: E. Benn Limited.
Wright, Henry. 1981. "The Southern Margins of Sumer: Archaeological Survey of the Area of Eridu and Ur," pp.
 295-345 in R. McC. Adams, *Heartland of Cities: Surveys of Ancient Settlement and Land Use on the Central
 Floodplain of the Euphrates*, Chicago: University of Chicago Press.

8

THE ROYAL CEMETERY OF UR

William B. Hafford

Opposite

View of the Goat in a Tree (30-12-702) on display in the new Middle East Galleries at the Penn Museum. Likely a stand for a small offering or incense bowl, this highly detailed sculptural furnishing from the "Great Death Pit" in the Royal Cemetery reflects the high standard of artistic development in the Early Dynastic Period.

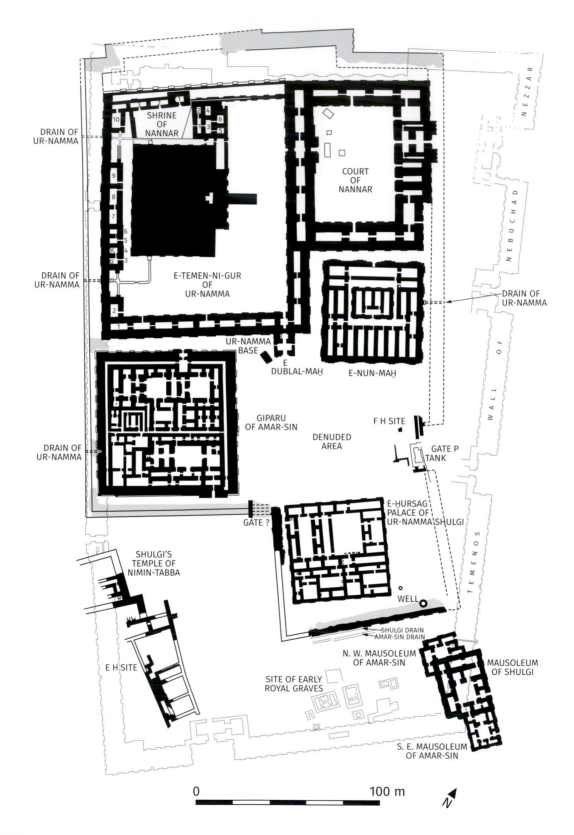

DRAIN OF
UR-NAMMA

SHRINE
OF
NANNAR

10

COURT
OF
NANNAR

DRAIN OF
UR-NAMMA

9

8

7

6
5
4
3

E-TEMEN-NI-GUR
OF
UR-NAMMA

2

1

DRAIN OF
UR-NAMMA

UR-NAMMA
BASE

E
DUBLAL-MAH

E-NUN-MAH

NEZZAR

WALL   OF   NEBUCHAD

GIPARU
OF AMAR-SIN

DENUDED
AREA

F H SITE

GATE P
TANK

DRAIN OF
UR-NAMMA

SHULGI'S
TEMPLE OF
NIMIN-TABBA

GATE ?

E-HURSAG
PALACE OF
UR-NAMMA SHULGI

TEMENOS

E H SITE

WELL

SHULGI DRAIN
AMAR-SIN DRAIN

N. W. MAUSOLEUM
OF AMAR-SIN

MAUSOLEUM
OF SHULGI

SITE OF EARLY
ROYAL GRAVES

S. E. MAUSOLEUM
OF AMAR-SIN

0   100 m

N

Introduction

The famous Royal Cemetery of Ur is only one part of a large and very deep burial ground in the middle of the ancient city. The site's initial excavators divided this burial ground, known in archaeological parlance as Area PG, into three primary layers or periods of burial that might be considered discrete cemeteries within it, with the latest burials situated closest to the surface. These vertical distinctions help us to understand the complicated sequence of burials and will be referred to in this discussion—even if they are not as clear as Sir Leonard Woolley, director of the joint Penn Museum and British Museum archaeological expedition at Ur from 1922–1934, believed. In actuality, the burial ground was in nearly continuous use for a thousand years, from a little before 3100 to just after 2100 BCE, making its division into discrete cemeteries a difficult and problematic prospect (Fig. 8.1).

The uppermost and most recent layer of burials in Area PG date to the Akkadian (ca. 2334–2154 BCE) and partly into the subsequent Ur III (ca. 2112–2004 BCE) Periods; we will consequently call this layer the Akkadian Cemetery. Graves of this upper cemetery were typically found between 2 and 5 meters (6.5 and 16 feet) below the modern ground surface.

The burials of the middle layer, typically found between 5 and 11 meters (16 and 36 feet) below the surface of the mound, mostly belonged to the Early Dynastic III (ED III) Period (ca. 2600–2334 BCE). It is this layer that is identified as the Royal Cemetery, since all of the sixteen graves designated as royal were found in this vertical zone.

The deepest and oldest graves in the burial ground, located some 11 to 18 meters (36 and 59 feet) below the surface, date from the end of the Late Uruk through the Early Dynastic I (ED I) Period (ca. 3100–2600 BCE). Within this span is a short, transitional period sometimes termed Jemdet Nasr, so that we can call these burials, as Woolley did, the Jemdet Nasr Cemetery.

Overall, more than 2,000 graves were uncovered in Area PG at Ur, located at varying depths below the surface and spanning a thousand years of history. Because the middle or ED III Period cemetery, the so-called Royal Cemetery, has garnered the most attention and remains the most mysterious, much of this chapter will be dedicated to it.

Some 750 graves were excavated in the Royal Cemetery, but only 16 of these included the type of extravagant display of precious objects and human sacrifice that led to their designation as royal. There is good reason to examine these tombs carefully, for such extravagant display is well beyond that found in any other excavated grave or other site of this period (ca. 2450 BCE) in Mesopotamia. Yet, not a single one of these 16 graves can be definitively associated with historically attested kings and queens of Ur. If the occupants of these tombs were royalty, then what was their dynasty, and why is it not attested in the textual records extant from Mesopotamia? If they were not royalty, how

Fig. 8.1 *Opposite*

The Royal Cemetery (Area PG) is seen at the bottom right of this plan map of the sacred zone of the city of Ur. It lies to the south of the Ur III temenos wall and was crossed over by the later, Neo-Babylonian temenos wall.

were they able to amass such wealth as was buried with them and such dedication as is attested by the human sacrifices that accompany them? Furthermore, why were so many other and much less elaborate burials found in and around these 16 extraordinary tombs, often cutting through and destroying parts of them? Finally, what was the process and ritual involved in the burial of the individuals found in the so-called royal tombs and what was the nature of the belief system behind it?

We do not know the precise answers to these questions, though theories abound. Indeed, much about the Royal Cemetery remains a mystery and the subject of ongoing research. In order to attempt an understanding of this remarkable archaeological area and the artifacts it has yielded, we must first look to the history of excavation at Ur, which began almost a century ago.

Excavating Area PG and the Royal Cemetery

In 1922, C. Leonard Woolley's first excavation trench at the ancient Mesopotamian city of Ur uncovered traces of what would later gain worldwide fame as the Royal Cemetery. This trench, Trial Trench A, revealed scattered artifacts such as gold and lapis lazuli jewelry that could have been high-end burial goods. As no clearly defined walls or graves were discovered, however, Woolley's team did not pursue further excavations at Trial Trench A immediately but concentrated instead on Trial Trench B, which had exposed major architecture in the sacred zone near the ziggurat. In later years, Woolley claimed also to have intentionally avoided further excavations in the vicinity of Trial Trench A until his workers had gained more experience digging at the site.

It was only in 1926, then, that Woolley would return to excavate the area. Upon digging four additional trial trenches and discovering hundreds of graves, many of which contained impressive small finds, he ultimately expanded his excavations to an area of nearly 4,000 square meters (43,000 square feet). He assigned sequential numbers to the graves he found, preceded by the letters PG. These letters, which appear in the earliest field notes to stand for Pre-dynastic or Prehistoric Grave, later came to denote Private Grave (since none of the excavated graves actually belonged to prehistoric periods) and were then applied to the entire area of the cemetery as Area PG. The discovery within this cemetery of a handful of private graves containing very rich grave goods, which were heralded worldwide as rivaling those from Tutankhamun's tomb in Egypt found only a few years earlier (Fig. 8.2), has sometimes led to the mistaken popular appellation of the entire Area PG as the Royal Cemetery of Ur.

Woolley and his team worked in Area PG for five years, uncovering more than 300 graves per season (Fig. 8.3). Eventually, the number of graves exceeded 2,000. One grave would often encroach on or obliterate another and evidence of looted and scattered graves was commonplace; Woolley estimated that the original number of graves in area

Fig. 8.2 *Opposite*
Newspapers picked up stories of the Ur excavations, particularly after the discovery of the Royal Cemetery. Queen Puabi (her name then read Shubad) was a favorite source of speculation. She was often compared with 'flappers' of the day.

Grim Tragedy of Wicked Queen Shubad's 100 Poisoned Slaves

Science at Last Reveals How the Greatest Suicide Pact in History Was Carried Out at the Tomb of the Beautiful Oriental Ruler Who Died 5500 Years Ago

One of the most beautiful golden cups found amongst the treasures of Queen Shubad's buried poisoned slaves

The picture by Henry Semiradsky, depicting the cremation ceremonies at a great Slav chieftain in ... wives ... women, slaves and slaves were poisoned at the foot of the pyre in the belief that they would accompany him into the next world

---

Science Unearths the "Flapper" of 6,000 Years Ago

Rouged Her Cheeks Red and Her Eyes Green, Used the Lipstick, Bobbed Her Hair and Danced at the Jazz Parties at the Temple in the Patriarch *Abraham's* Ancient City of *Ur* and

Here Is How She and Her Fellow Flappers Danced and Sang When a Slave Was Sacrificed to the Moon God. Drawing from the London Illustrated News, by A. Forestier, the Noted English Illustrator, from Material and Information Supplied by Director C. L. Woolley of the Joint Expedition of the British Museum and Pennsylvania Museum to Mesopotamia

Here Is the Way She Dressed When She Was Introduced to the High Priest of the Moon God, Who Looked Her Over to See if She Was Pretty Enough for the Jazzy Temple Dance Parties.

This Is One of Her Love Letters of Baked Clay.

Sunday   ST. LOUIS POST-DISPATCH   Magazine

A PRINCESS of 3000 B.C.

A PRINCESS OF 3000 ... The restoration above is from the British ...

What Science Has Discovered About the Personal Adornment of Chaldean Ladies.

1208

Fig. 8.3 *Above*

Leonard and Katharine Woolley are seen
here digging with a few local workmen in
the "Great Death Pit," PG 1237. Many of
the flattened skeletons can be seen at the
bottom of the picture, while the Woolleys
are digging amongst the collapsed lyres.

PG may have been two or three times greater than he actually counted. Some graves, moreover, contained multiple burials while others contained bones that had completely deteriorated; the total number of people buried here is, thus, impossible to calculate, though it certainly ranges in the thousands.

The cemetery sat to the southeast of the sacred temple zone that included the ziggurat of Ur. Much later, the Neo-Babylonian king Nebuchadnezzar II (ca. 634–562 BCE) extended the sacred zone and built a new wall surrounding it. The southeast corner of this new wall ran directly over the top of the cemetery, which had been long out of use by that point. Woolley dug down below the Neo-Babylonian wall, through ancient dumping layers, and into the cemetery. He then dug several test pits that were deeper still to reveal evidence of a much earlier cemetery beneath. In some pits he reached a depth of nearly 20 meters (65.5 feet) below the modern ground surface.

Because the cemetery had been covered over by heavily eroded debris and refuse, Woolley's Trial Trench A had uncovered little evidence of the graves. As he expanded the trench, however, he found that most had been cut into an earlier rubbish dump that had formed an irregular and sloping surface. The rubbish formed a complex set of layers sloping down toward what was possibly a marshy area or canal just outside the earliest city. After excavating the Akkadian and ED III graves, Woolley extended the area to the south in order to explore the deepest, Jemdet Nasr, cemetery.

The different layers of dirt in Area PG yielded characteristic artifacts that helped to date them. Many contained administrative artifacts, such as archaic tablets and seal impressions, that were particularly diagnostic of their time periods. Especially in the southwestern portion of the cemetery, Woolley encountered layer upon layer of these administrative artifacts; he dubbed these layers the Seal Impression Strata (Fig. 8.4). The study of these and their contents has helped to refine our understanding of early 3rd millennium BCE administration at Ur. The archaic texts from these layers are among the earliest known from Mesopotamia, and the sealings come from doors, jars, and other commodities sealed for protection or identification. They were likely dumped in Area PG from an early temple of Nanna or other important building that once existed near this space.

Since the graves in Area PG were cut into sloping ground and to varying depths below this sloping surface, the elevation of one burial relative to another offered little insight into their dates. However, since later burials commonly overlay, cut through, or otherwise disturbed earlier ones, Woolley was able to gather data from groups of superimposed burials to create a developmental sequence of artifacts such as pottery, stone and metal vessels, and metal tools and weapons. By comparing the objects recovered from a grave to this developmental sequence, any single burial could be assigned a relative date with respect to the other burials discovered. This allowed Woolley to differentiate what he initially reported as two cemeteries, the later Akkadian and the earlier Royal (ED III). The oldest Jemdet Nasr graves had not yet been excavated at this point; in fact, Woolley's

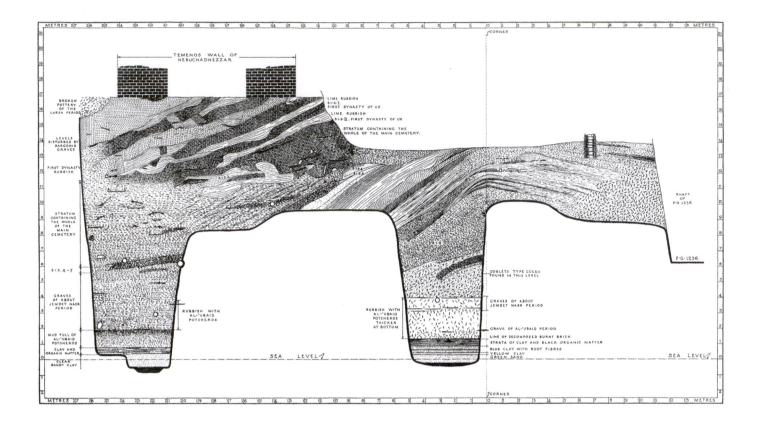

Within the figure:
TEMENOS WALL OF NEBUCHADNEZZAR

BROKEN POTTERY OF THE LARSA PERIOD

LEVELS DISTURBED BY SARGONID GRAVES

FIRST DYNASTY RUBBISH

STRATUM CONTAINING THE WHOLE OF THE MAIN CEMETERY

S·I·S·4-5

GRAVES OF ABOUT JEMDET NASR PERIOD

MUD FULL OF AL-'UBAID POTSHERDS

CLAY AND ORGANIC MATTER

CLEAN SANDY CLAY

RUBBISH WITH AL-'UBAID POTSHERDS

SEA LEVEL

CORNER

LIME RUBBISH S·I·S·I. FIRST DYNASTY OF UR
LIME RUBBISH S·I·S·II. FIRST DYNASTY OF UR
STRATUM CONTAINING THE WHOLE OF THE MAIN CEMETERY.

RUBBISH WITH AL-'UBAID POTSHERDS THICKER AT BOTTOM

GOBLETS TYPE CCCXII FOUND IN THIS LEVEL

GRAVES OF ABOUT JEMDET NASR PERIOD

GRAVE OF AL-'UBAID PERIOD.
LINE OF DECOMPOSED BURNT BRICK
STRATA OF CLAY AND BLACK ORGANIC MATTER
BLUE CLAY WITH ROOT FIBRES
YELLOW CLAY
GREEN SAND

SHAFT OF PG·1236

P·G·1236.

SEA LEVEL

CORNER

1934 publication entitled *The Royal Cemetery* covered only the ED III and Akkadian Period graves. He was convinced that there was a break between these two cemeteries, marked by a division in the Seal Impression Strata, but the division is not particularly clear and even Woolley recognized the existence of a few graves intermediate in date between the two cemeteries.

Woolley's methodology in dating the burials in Area PG at Ur was seemingly solid, but a number of questions remain, and many studies have continued to examine the stratigraphy and relative dating of the burial ground's thousands of graves. These studies generally suggest the more or less continuous practice of burying the dead in Area PG in the centuries between the Early Dynastic III through the Akkadian Periods, and probably also into the Ur III Period.

Burial Patterns

Although a few graves in Area PG held tremendous wealth, particularly the sixteen royal graves in the Royal (ED III) Cemetery, the burial ground overall suggests an

Fig. 8.4 *Above*
Stratigraphic profile drawing of the west side of area PG, including deep test pits Y and Z. Note the steep slope of the upper layers of soil. Many of these are Seal Impression Strata (layers containing archaic seal impressions) and it appears the material in them was thrown downhill from a built-up area to the north (right side of the drawing). This would have been an administrative area, possibly associated with an early temple.

overwhelming preference for simple inhumations with few grave goods. The body, wrapped in reed matting or placed in a wooden, wickerwork, or clay coffin, was set at the bottom of a rectangular pit averaging 1.50 x 0.70 meters (5 x 2 feet). The graves were almost always oriented with the corners at or near the cardinal points. With a few (royal) exceptions, the body was always placed on its side, either left or right; the head could be at either end of the pit. In the Royal (ED III) and subsequent Akkadian Cemeteries, the legs were slightly flexed and the arms bent at the elbow so that the hands were at about the level of the mouth. Woolley deemed this the position of sleep and differentiated it from the fetal position of bodies buried in the Jemdet Nasr Cemetery. The deceased—clothed or perhaps wrapped in a shroud, and often with his or her personal ornaments—typically held a cup or drinking vessel of metal, stone, or clay. A jar or bowl was almost always nearby, probably indicative of the need for the dead to be supplied with food and drink in the afterlife. In some burials, the pit was larger than needed for the body alone; in these cases, it was common to find utilitarian goods, such as other bowls, jars, weapons, and tools, included in the grave. Such functional objects were probably associated with the profession or duties of the deceased in life; the quantity and quality of these goods further reflected the wealth and social status of the dead. It is worth noting that, although gods, goddesses, and temples played a large role in Mesopotamian life, no clear representations of deities—apart from those appearing in scenes on cylinder seals—were found in the graves.

Of more than 2,000 graves excavated in Area PG, Woolley designated only sixteen as royal and all of them were found in the middle zone (ED III Period) of graves dating to around 2450 BCE. Woolley believed, though he found no actual material traces of this in his excavations, that the royal tombs were marked on the surface by chapels or other monuments where the dead kings and queens might be honored, and which constituted the nucleus around which the cemetery grew. In Woolley's reconstruction, a double row of royal chapels ran from southwest to northeast across the cemetery. The people of Ur, elite and common alike, wanted to be buried near their revered rulers and, from the beginning, smaller graves encroached on the royal burial grounds. At first these more humble burials were clustered near the tombs of the kings and queens; gradually, they moved outwards. Eventually, as space ran out, they began cutting into the fill of older pits and even into each other; many of the graves Woolley uncovered had, indeed, been partially or largely destroyed by later grave digging and intentional grave robbing.

The deepest and oldest burials, those of the Jemdet Nasr Cemetery, were also densely packed and often cut into one another. The overall pattern of simple inhumation, with the body on its side and hands holding a cup near the face, was the norm for this early cemetery, just as it was for the later. Here, however, the bodies were contracted in a near fetal position, with heels nearly touching the pelvis and knees at times near the chin. These burials were far from grandiose; most of the goods they contained were clay or

continued on page 209

THE BULL-HEADED LYRE OF UR AND ITS SHELL PLAQUE

William B. Hafford

In the death pit of PG 789, the so-called King's Grave at Ur (see Chapter 8S3: Lovers among the Ruins?), Woolley discovered a most interesting artifact. At first it was unclear what the artifact was—he encountered only the upper portion of a wooden frame, which appeared as discolored soil since the wood had deteriorated thousands of years before. When he came upon the inlaid sound box and gold bull's head attachment farther down, however, he realized that it had once been an intricate lyre (Fig. 8S1.1). It was the first of several lyres that would be found in the Royal Cemetery.

The bull's head was made of hammered gold over a wooden core and had a beard made of lapis lazuli. The bearded bull was a symbol of strength and power, one that represented both the sun god and the king himself.

Under the bull's head the sound box was inlaid with an extensive shell panel that seems to tell a story relating to the Sumerian netherworld (Fig. 8S1.2). The panel is divided into four registers tapering slightly from top to bottom. The uppermost register shows a bearded hero wrestling with two human-headed bulls, also bearded. This register may

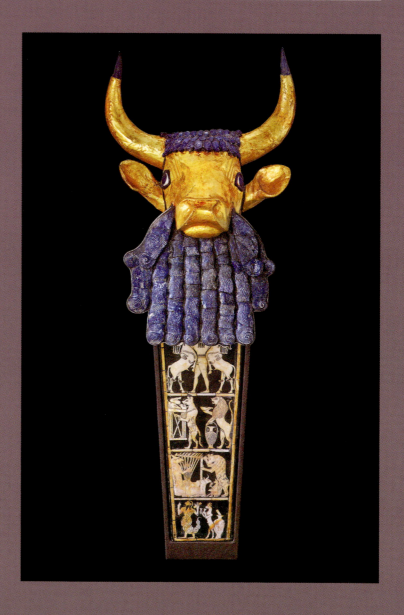

Fig. 8S1.1 *Right*

The golden bull's head (B17694B) with lapis lazuli beard, along with the shell plaque (B17694A) beneath it, originally adorned the front of a wooden lyre. The decayed and crushed remains were found in PG 789, the so-called "king's grave." The bearded bull may have represented the god Shamash, as well as the might of the king, and large lyres like this one were said to have the deep sound of a braying bull.

represent the might of the king. The two middle registers probably indicate the topsy-turvy nature of the underworld: animals, acting like humans, participate in a funerary banquet. Above, a jackal with a dagger on its belt carries food offerings and a lion carries vessels of liquid offerings; both animals walk upright. Below, an equid playing a lyre is accompanied by a small dog with a rattle while a bear dances. The lyre in this third register has a bull's head attachment, a visual reference to the lyre on which the plaque itself appears.

The fourth and lowermost register contains a scorpion-man, perhaps a netherworld guardian, holding an unidentified object in each of his raised hands; to his left, an anthropomorphized antelope or gazelle holds two cups, which have been compared to those held by the attendants in the Great Death Pit (see Chapter 8S5: The Great Death Pit: Reconstructing a Funeral Feast). The image of the scorpion-man—a motif scene in the Epic of Gilgamesh—may have been transmitted from the mountainous regions to the east; the distant mountains were thought in some periods to house the entrance to the netherworld itself.

The imagery in shell inlay on the lyre may thus represent the death of a hero or king and his subsequent journey through the funerary feast into the mixed-up world of the afterlife, where he will finally meet with the guardian of the netherworld.

Fig. 8S1.2 *Left*
The shell plaque (B17694A) seems to tell the mythical story of the journey into the afterlife. It depicts a struggle between hero and animals in the uppermost register and animals conducting a funerary feast in the turned-around world of death. Finally, it depicts the scorpion-man, who was thought to guard the entrance to the netherworld.

The Goat in a Tree or The "Ram in the Thicket"

William B. Hafford

The Goat in a Tree, once renowned as the "Ram in the Thicket," (Fig. 8S2.1) is one of the most iconic artworks extant from southern Mesopotamia. Made of shell, lapis lazuli, and gold over a perishable wood and bitumen core, the piece had collapsed long before Woolley excavated it (Fig. 8S2.2) and another similar one from the Great Death Pit in 1929. Both required extensive conservation and restoration.

In popular circles, the sculpture came to be called the "Ram in the Thicket," a name drawn from a Biblical narrative (Gen 22:13) in which Abraham spied a ram caught in a thicket and ultimately sacrificed it in place of his son Isaac. But the subject of the work is clearly a goat rather than a ram and it is not caught but rather feeding on the leaves high up in the tree—a typical sight in the scraggly brush of Mesopotamia. The eight-petal flowers in the tree may represent the goddess Inana and the overall motif may represent the repeating cycle of life that she and her consort Dumuzi came to personify.

A central support running through the body of the goat and out its back indicates it was originally part of some type of small furnishing rather than a freestanding sculpture. It may have been a stand or support for a dish or bowl used for small offerings or perhaps for incense (Fig. 8S2.3).

Fig. 8S2.1 *Right*
This sculptural furnishing was found along with another very similar one (now in the British Museum) in the west corner of the Great Death Pit (PG 1237) near Body 61, the likely owner of the grave. Often called "The Ram in the Thicket" (30-12-702), it actually depicts a goat in a tree.

Fig. 8S2.2 *Below*
Fig. 8S2.2 *Below*
The "ram" as originally found, crushed nearly flat on its back. It required much conservation; Woolley's original reconstruction placed the central stem of the tree too deeply into the base, throwing off the angle of the branches. A much more recent reconstruction corrected the tree, resulting in an additional correction of the goat's forelegs in relation to its body.

Fig. 8S2.3 *Below*
The use of zoomorphic stands in Mesopotamia in the Early Dynastic Period is indicated in the enlarged image detail below, from this cylinder seal (VA 3878) from the collection of the Vorderasiatisches Museum in Berlin. The "ram" may once have held a small tray for incense or offerings.
© bpk Bildagentur/Vorderasiatisches Museum, Staatliche Museen, Berlin, Germany/Olaf M. Tessmer/Art Resource, NY.

stone jars and bowls with little in the way of personal ornamentation. Still, some of these early graves were better appointed than others, probably signaling the existence of economic stratification already by this early period (ca. 3000 BCE). The differential expression of wealth in the graves increased greatly in the Royal (ED III) Cemetery.

The Royal Tombs

Quite in contrast to the simple burials found throughout Area PG, the sixteen largest graves discovered in the Royal (ED III) Cemetery were particularly notable in terms of the precious materials found in them, the peculiarities of their structures, and the evidence they contained of ritual performance. Woolley called these graves royal tombs, assuming they contained the deceased kings and queens of Ur. In support of this interpretation, he found cylinder seals inscribed with the Sumerian titles **lugal** (king) and **eresh** (queen) associated with several of the tombs.

Woolley's designation of any particular burial as royal was based on the following three criteria:

(1) Ritual: The grave had to show evidence of major ceremony, with human sacrifice representing a clear element of such. Evidence of other ritual observances, such as libation and extensive offerings, should also be present.

(2) Architectural: The grave had to contain one or more built chambers in brick or stone, typically with a vaulted or domed roof. The primary chamber would have contained the royal body. Other chambers or spaces, such as the death pit (an open pit beyond the primary chamber) or the shaft above the grave, would contain sacrificial victims, presumably attendants of the dead king or queen.

(3) Material: Lavish furnishings had to be present; even where plundered, traces of such would typically remain. The wealthiest artifacts would be found with the royal corpse inside the primary chamber, though attendants would likely also be heavily ornamented. Ornate objects would be found throughout the grave; these might include musical instruments, wheeled vehicles, weapons, furniture, game boards, jewelry, and cylinder seals.

The sixteen tombs meeting Woolley's three criteria for designation as royal have the PG numbers 337, 580, 777, 779, 789, 800, 1050, 1054, 1157, 1232, 1236, 1237, 1332, 1618, 1631, and 1648. In many cases, later analysts replace the letters PG with RT to show more clearly that these are Royal Tombs rather than simply Private Graves. These tombs, despite the seemingly concrete nature of Woolley's criteria, demonstrate significant variation in construction and layout; they are by no means a homogeneous group and Woolley had to, at times, explain away the absence of one of his criteria when identifying a burial as royal. Tombs PG 580, 1232, 1237, and 1337, for example, have no built chamber; Woolley suggested that later plundering was responsible for obliterating the chamber in these cases. Other variations in construction are notable. PG 789 and 800B had vaulted tomb chambers and the former at least had an extensive death pit. PG 777, 779, and 1236 consisted of multi-roomed chambers that occupied the entire pit. PG 1050 and 1054 were large, single-chamber tombs set at the bottom of a deep shaft, both apparently with minor chambers in the shaft fill that contained subsidiary burials. In the southern end of the cemetery, PG 1618, 1631, and 1648 may represent yet another distinct tomb type; these take the form of small, single-chamber tombs set at the bottom of small pits.

In one case, Woolley may have conflated parts of two tombs into a single royal one: he associated the chamber of PG 800B with a death pit some 2.5 meters (8 feet) above its floor. Having discovered the built chamber of PG 800B, a queen's tomb, while excavating the neighboring PG 789, he interpreted the proximity of the two tombs as suggesting a close relationship between their occupants. Unfortunately, Woolley's romantic story of the queen who outlived her husband (presumably buried in PG 789) but so loved him that she demanded to be buried next to him when she died (thus placing her burial chamber much lower than the sacrifices attendant upon her, which were situated in the death pit above), has little basis in fact. There were no identifiable remains in the chamber of PG 789, which Woolley called the King's Grave. The intact chamber of PG 800B, in contrast, contained the skeleton of Queen Puabi (whose name was originally read and widely publicized as Shub-Ad). She was identified by an inscribed cylinder seal complete with name and title found on her body; there is, however, no discernible evidence linking her tomb to the death pit (labeled PG 800) located 2.5 meters (8 feet) above. This leaves open the question of where the death pit actually associated with PG 800B may be located, if one ever existed.

How, then, is the death pit situated above PG 800B to be understood, if it does not belong to PG 800B? No other chamber was found that might be associated with this death pit, but this does not preclude its belonging to a separate tomb altogether. Woolley certainly excavated royal tombs that lacked accompanying built chambers (e.g., PG 580, 1232, 1237, and 1337), and this death pit may belong among their number.

The royal tombs, in addition to containing the bodies of deceased kings and queens, also contained the bodies of what have been identified as retainers or attendants, often found in the so-called death pits. Some of the tombs contain numerous such bodies; others only very few: for example, PG 789 contained 63 additional bodies, the majority of which were women; PG 1237, which Woolley dubbed the Great Death Pit, contained 74, again mostly women; PG 1050 had 40 bodies below its floor; PG 800B had three in the chamber with the queen and 21 in the death pit Woolley associated with it; and still other royal burials, such as 1618 and 1648, contained fewer than five additional bodies. Unfortunately, this variation in the number of accompanying bodies in the royal graves remains as puzzling today as it was when Woolley first uncovered the cemetery nearly a hundred years ago.

continued on page 215

Lovers among the Ruins?

William B. Hafford

When Woolley uncovered the tomb chamber and death pit PG 789, he found an immediately adjacent chamber, which he numbered PG 800B. He suggested, on the basis of their proximity, that the owners of PG 789 and PG 800B represented a loving royal couple that had wanted to be buried together. The king, according to Woolley's reconstruction, died first and was buried in PG 789; his queen, identified as Puabi, held an elaborate burial ceremony and created a death pit outside his tomb filled with 63 attendants who would accompany him in the afterlife. Years later, when Puabi herself died, she was buried in the adjacent tomb chamber PG 800B. Puabi's own funerary ceremony (Fig 8S3.1) was then enacted in a space

above the tombs of the two lovers (it is actually above tomb PG 789), and the remains of the ceremony were preserved in the death pit labeled PG 800.

Woolley's reconstruction attempted to make sense of the complicated and somewhat puzzling archaeological evidence for PG 789 and PG 800B, particularly the presence of a death pit (labeled PG 800) significantly above rather than on the same level as the tomb chamber, PG 800B. But it also ignores some important points.

The first is that PG 800B was actually set some 40 centimeters (15 inches) lower than the adjacent PG 789 (Fig 8S3.2). It is possible, consequently, that PG 800B rather

Fig. 8S3.1 *Left*
Artist's reconstruction of the PG 789 death pit as it may have looked just before the attendants were sacrificed. Created by the Anglo-French artist Amédée Forestier in 1928 for the *Illustrated London News*, it followed Woolley's advice from the excavated evidence closely. © Illustrated London News Ltd/Mary Evans.

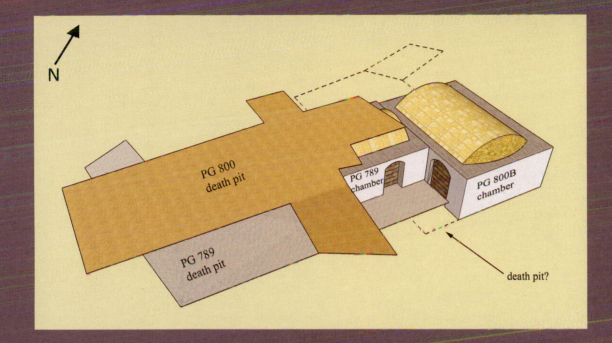

N

PG 800
death pit

PG 789
chamber

PG 800B
chamber

PG 789
death pit

death pit?

Fig. 8S3.2 *Left*

This model shows the positioning of PG 800 and PG 800B in relation to PG 789. The death pit Woolley associated with PG 800B (PG 800) is situated above PG 789 and seems to have little connection with PG 800B, the chamber that is located 40cm lower than PG 789. A death pit might exist at the lower level of PG 800B (dashed line in the model) but Woolley did not dig beneath PG 789 to find out.

than PG 789 is the earlier tomb, and that its death pit is not PG 800 but was actually situated below what would later become the floor of PG 789. Woolley never excavated below this floor and so would not have come across traces of this possible death pit. The second is that PG 800B is described as having no door. Woolley suggested that its occupant, Queen Puabi, was placed in from above, even though this maneuver would have been exceedingly difficult to perform in a vaulted tomb. Yet, Woolley's original notes suggest the presence of a sealed door at the southern end of the tomb's southwest wall. The only clear space on the tomb's floor was between this possible doorway and Puabi's body; heavy deposits of grave goods were found everywhere else. This, then, was probably the path used to place both the body and the grave goods in PG 800B.

When all of the above evidence is considered, alternate visions of the relationships between tombs PG 789 and PG

800B, and between tomb chamber PG 800B and death pit PG 800, emerge than those proposed by Woolley. It is likely that the burial of Puabi in tomb PG 800B was the earlier, followed at a later date by the burial of the unknown occupant of tomb PG 789 (this tomb had been looted before its excavation). As for the death pit PG 800, located more than 2 meters (6.5 feet) above the floor of tomb PG 800B, this almost certainly belonged to a separate and later tomb altogether, one either built without a tomb chamber or with a tomb chamber that was later destroyed. Woolley's poignant story of the loving couple that occupied tombs PG 789 and PG 800B is intriguing and perhaps still possible, but only if it was the occupant of PG 789 who wished to be buried near Puabi who had already been placed in PG 800B.

Queen Puabi

William B. Hafford

The occupant of PG 800B, the tomb chamber originally and probably erroneously associated with Death Pit PG 800 (see previous "Lovers among the Ruins?"), was Puabi, a queen of Ur around 2450 BCE (Fig. 8S4.1). We know her name, which means something like "word of my father" in Akkadian, because it was inscribed on a cylinder seal she wore on her body. The title, eresh, which means queen, was also inscribed on the seal. It was unusual for a cylinder seal to be inscribed with only a female name and title; the fact that Puabi's husband or father are not named on the seal suggests she may have ruled in her own right.

The massive wealth found in Puabi's tomb further bespeaks her power and prestige. Her grave goods included thousands of beads; silver, gold, and exquisite stone vessels; and, perhaps most impressive of all, a headdress of gold and imported stones that weighed some 2.21 kilograms (4.85 pounds). The main headdress (Fig. 8S4.2) was formed of four wreaths of sheet gold cut into the form of poplar and willow leaves; it was elaborated with beads and pendants of gold, lapis lazuli, and carnelian. Tiers of gold ribbon, measuring some 12 meters (39 feet) in total length, layered her hair; her hair was also supported in the back by a large golden comb topped with seven rosettes.

Fig. 8S4.1 *Right*
The arrangement of Puabi's jewelry as she likely wore it in death. Her body was found covered in beads and her skull surrounded by a gold headdress. More than 80 strands of beads make up her cloak and the headdress weighs around five pounds (or a little more than 2 kilograms).

Fig. 8S4.2 *Left*
Puabi's headdress as found; note the gold comb and wreaths at the top of the image. Note also the cylinder seal and garment pins at the left, as well as the many beads visible in the soil. It is easy to see why the exact arrangement has been difficult to recreate, resulting in many different displays through the years.

While Puabi's was the only royal tomb in the cemetery at Ur to escape ancient looters, part of its vaulted roof had collapsed and it was difficult to know precisely how her jewelry was originally arrayed on her body. Shortly after the excavation, Katharine Woolley (wife of archaeologist Leonard Woolley) made a plaster head on which she arranged the headdress; this arrangement, however, was influenced by contemporary fashions of the 1920s (Fig. 8S4.3). In 1929, after the jewelry came to the Penn Museum, Curator Léon Legrain made a new reconstruction—though this had its own biases. He eschewed the large wig reconstructed by Katharine Woolley in favor of a hairstyle more in keeping with that known from figurines recovered from Sumer. The circumstances in which the headdress itself was excavated, however, seem to indicate Katharine Woolley was correct to envision the jewelry's placement on a large hairdo, probably a prearranged wig.

Puabi's headdress and beaded cloak have gone through many reconstructions during their time at the Penn Museum and are today displayed in a manner as close to the original (as indicated by the excavation records) as possible. While many details are still unclear—we do not know, for example, whether the many beads found above and below Puabi's body really made up a cloak, and we do not know whether the gold rings at her waist constituted a separate belt or were attached to the upper belt—the great beauty of Puabi's accoutrement, and her role as a powerful woman of Ur, are undeniable.

Fig. 8S4.3 *Right*
Katharine Woolley's original reconstruction of Puabi's jewelry in a colorized image that appeared in *Ur Excavations* volume II and in the *Illustrated London News*. The diameter of the headdress as found was around 30 cm (roughly one foot), the basis for the width of the hairdo shown in this model. © Illustrated London News Ltd/Mary Evans.

Human sacrifice, whether voluntary or involuntary on the part of the accompanying retainers, and the burial of the sacrificed retainers with the deceased ED III Period kings and queens of Ur was, for Woolley, an integral element of Ur's royal tombs. Unfortunately, written explanations or even clear archaeological evidence for the precise process of elite burial and the motivation(s) for human sacrifice are not known; Woolley was, thus, left to (re-)construct these by analyzing aspects of the various royal tombs he had excavated at Ur. In particular, he interpreted the well-organized rows of retainers' bodies in PG 1237, the so-called Great Death Pit, as indicating the peaceful (and self-sacrificing) nature of the retainers' deaths. He suggested the retainers had drunk a soporific drug and then lain down to the long sleep of death without disturbing their elaborate jewelry and headdresses. In support of this interpretation, he cited the presence of a small cup that was found with each body, though he admitted in a footnote that not all bodies were actually associated with such a cup; moreover, Woolley had actually found cups with most of the dead buried throughout the cemetery and had not taken those to indicate self-sacrifice.

A possibility that Woolley either failed to consider, or dismissed as unlikely, was that the retainers had been killed elsewhere, their bodies preserved or desiccated to some extent, and then dressed in their finery and deliberately arranged in the death pits. This is a complicated reconstruction, but it accounts for the well-ordered rows of dead retainers discovered with all accoutrements in place. Recent analysis of the few bones saved from Woolley's excavations also supports this alternate reconstruction: many of the bones, including those analyzed from PG 1648 and PG 1237, show evidence of having been heated to temperatures of 150–250 degrees Celsius (302–482 degrees Fahrenheit). Such heating may have occurred as part of a deliberate process designed to preserve the bodies. Computed tomography (CT) scan analysis has also revealed that at least two of the skulls of death pit individuals, one recovered from PG 1237 and the other from PG 789, had perimortem fractures resulting from blunt force trauma (Fig. 8.5): such fractures suggest the deceased may have been killed by a blow to the back of the head. This would naturally have preceded the heating of the body and arrangement of the headgear.

That the royal tombs contained the bodies of wealthy and powerful people, possibly kings and queens, along with associated individuals of lesser status is not in doubt; the circumstances surrounding the deaths of the lower status individuals, and the reasons for the inclusion of their bodies in the royal tombs, however, remain in question. Some scholars understand these additional bodies as displays of power by potentially deified kings. Others suggest a connection to temple and religious observance, and reference the myths of a dying fertility god who must be resurrected for the continued growth of crops, or suggest some relationship to a rite peculiar to Ur and its patron god Nanna.

It is also possible that some of the graves, perhaps those without chambers, are the burials of high religious officials. In PG 1237 (the Great Death Pit), for example, Body

Fig. 8.5 *Opposite*
This CT scan of a soldier found at the entrance to the PG 789 death pit shows the underside of the crushed skull. The ear-flaps of the copper helmet can be seen as well as the holes for sewing in the leather lining. More importantly, the damage to the skull beneath the helmet is clear as a dark hole with radiating fractures. This puncture wound was likely the cause of death, inflicted before the helmet was placed on the head. Furthermore, the helmet appears to be placed on the head backwards, with the wider opening at the back of the skull.

61 (her name is unknown) has been identified as that of a woman who was potentially both a princess and a high priestess. She was buried among the retainers in the death pit rather than in a separate chamber; while the cups associated with other bodies were clay or stone, however, hers was silver. Moreover, she wore far more jewelry than any other person in the death pit. In fact, her jewelry was comparable only to that of Puabi in PG 800B, who was clearly designated a queen on her cylinder seal.

The other bodies in the Great Death Pit were arranged in such a way as to imitate a banquet or funerary feast, a ceremony often seen on cylinder seals, including on a seal belonging to Puabi. Such funerary feasts included the playing of music, dining, drinking, and dancing, all of which are indicated in the PG 1237 finds. Furthermore, a cylinder seal found on Body 7 in the Great Death Pit itself also depicts a banquet—perhaps the very one the bodies were arranged to reenact—and bears an inscription reading "child of the gipar" (Fig. 8.6).

The *gipar* or *giparu* was the official abode of the *entu*-priestess, the high priestess of Ur (see Chapter 7S2: The Importance of the *Entu*-Priestess). She maintained the cult of the moon god Nanna and his consort Ningal, the chief deities of Ur, and was one of the most important people in the city. Typically, she was also the daughter of the reigning king, a circumstance that would have bolstered her power and status. It is possible that the cylinder seal found on Body 7 in the Great Death Pit actually depicts the individual we call Body 61—the woman at the center of the retainer's attention, the one with the silver cup and the stunningly elaborate jewelry—as *entu*-priestess and as the person to whom the tomb actually belongs. She may well be the first recognizable *entu*-priestess at Ur, predating other famous *entu* whose names we do know, such as Enheduanna (ca. 2300 BCE) of the Akkadian Period, and Enannatumma (ca. 1950 BCE) of the Isin-Larsa Period. If this interpretation is correct, the elaborate burial in PG 1237 may signify the importance of Body 61 in her roles both as priestess and as princess.

The wealth displayed in the royal tombs implies a powerful group was in control of Ur at a very early period. Moreover, the types of displays evident in these tombs, particularly the human sacrifices, are not known from any other place or time period in Mesopotamia. It is tempting to connect these graves with an early dynasty of kings ruling at Ur noted on the Sumerian King List, but the few names found in the royal tombs of the Royal (ED III) Cemetery do not match those on the list. It appears that the royal tombs predate the kings on the list. How such wealth could be gathered and expended on lavish burials by a group otherwise so ill attested in the textual and archaeological records of the Near East remains a major question for historians.

One scholarly suggestion has been that, while temple elites held political power in the preceding Jemdet Nasr Period and into the earlier part of the Early Dynastic Period, a more secular elite was gaining dominance by the later part of the Early Dynastic Period. At this critical juncture, rulers may have been powerful enough to accumulate great

Fig. 8.6 *Above and Opposite*
This cylinder seal (30-12-2) was found in the Great Death Pit, on Body 7 near the lyres. It shows a banquet scene, with music, dancing, and feasting, that is very much like the one that the dead in the pit were laid out to reenact. Its inscription can be read "Child of the Gipar" and may indicate that the primary burial, Body 61, was an *entu*-priestess.

continued on page 222

The Great Death Pit: Reconstructing a Funeral Feast

William B. Hafford

In PG 1237, more famously known as the Great Death Pit, 74 bodies were arranged as if in attendance at a Sumerian funerary banquet (Fig. 8S5.1). Rows of women in elaborate jewelry and headdresses stretch from one side of the pit, where at least three lyres were found, to the other, where two statuettes in the form of gold and lapis lazuli goats (see Chapter 8S2: The Goat in a Tree or the "Ram in the Thicket") stood near Body 61, the most highly adorned woman in the group. A little apart from the women were a row of six men who guarded the ceremony into eternity.

Body 61, which was draped in very rich jewelry, may represent the female owner of the grave. When she died, her body was probably preserved, wrapped, and adorned, and then honored with a funerary ceremony. The acts of eating and drinking were accompanied by music, played on harps and rattles or clappers, as well as by dancing. Afterwards, those in attendance at the banquet either drank poison, as Woolley suggested, or were killed with a pickaxe , as more recent studies of the skeletons from the pit have indicated. Then they too were preserved, adorned, and arrayed for the afterlife.

While much of what was in the grave had disintegrated with time, parts of lyres, cups, other vessels, and personal adornments were recovered. The Penn Museum, with the help of artist John Pearson, decided to reconstruct how a funerary banquet might have looked in life, before it reached its fatal end (Fig. 8S5.2). First, the skeletons and instruments were righted and placed in the order in which they were found; then flesh was put back on the bones. Bodies that had held a jar or jug in the grave were shown as standing; those holding cups and adorned with more elaborate jewelry were shown seated and drinking. The attendees at the banquet were, in effect, depicted toasting the honoree, Body 61, who held a silver cup to her mouth.

To reconstruct details of clothing and furnishings that might have been present but that had deteriorated, Penn Museum curators and professionals examined figures depicted on clay plaques and models contemporary with PG 1237. It was also not clear where the ceremony was held, but this was possibly in the pit itself, which may have been decorated for the occasion. We added to the reconstruction a few potted plants, evidence for which is seen in some reliefs from Mesopotamia; reed mats on the floor; and a kind of sidebar   with food offerings, the presence of which was suggested by inlaid poles found in the south corner of the pit.

This process of reconstructing PG 1237 was a long one: images were drafted, considered and reconsidered by scholars, and then redrafted. The picture emerging from this process is by no means a definitive recreation of the original funerary banquet as it occurred some 4,500 years ago, but it is a *potential* version of the event (Fig. 8S5.3). It humanizes the participants in the banquet, the bodies of whom were excavated in PG 1237 by Woolley, and offers us new ways of exploring ritual life in the period of the Royal Cemetery at Ur.

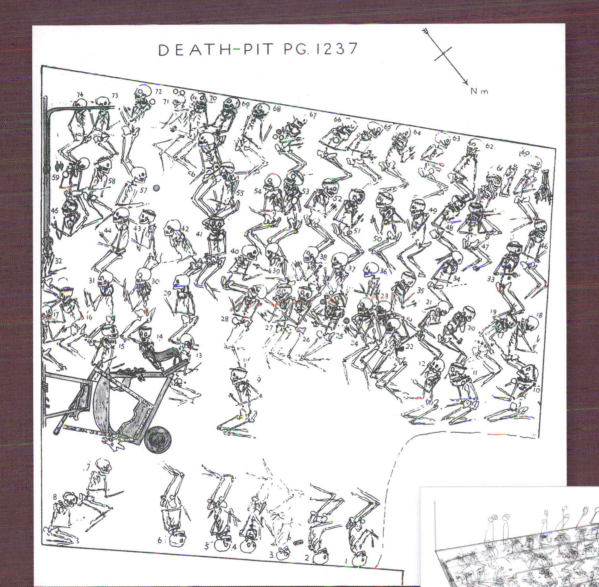

DEATH-PIT PG. 1237

N m

Fig. 8S5.2 *Below*
To recreate the people standing, the artist has imagined the space in three dimensions and here is beginning to plot out the rows of seated and standing figures. Drawn by HSD/John Pearson.

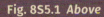

Fig. 8S5.1 *Above*
Leonard Woolley's published plan map of the Great Death Pit (PG 1237) as found. Body 61, the most highly adorned woman in the grave, is in the upper right of the image near the ram furnishings while the lyres are in the lower left. A total of 74 people were buried in this one grave pit, arranged as if in a funerary banquet.

Fig. 8S5.3 *Above*

The final version of the recreated banquet in the Great Death Pit, by artist John Pearson. Each of the numbered bodies is in the place indicated by Woolley's plan map, and each has been shown wearing or using artifacts found on or near them. Drawn by HSD/John Pearson.

wealth during their reigns but kingship as an institution was not sufficiently strong and regularized to maintain itself. Rituals would have been needed to maintain the authority of the king during periods of succession and the ritual destruction of great wealth—human, animal, and material—may have brought the survivors and heirs of individual rulers the recognition necessary to maintain their elite social status. This suggestion, while compelling, remains speculative.

A Later Royal Tomb?

At the eastern edge of Area PG stand the remains of a most impressive structure. Made largely of baked brick, it has survived the ravages of time better than many other structures in the ancient city. Some of its walls are as much as 3 meters (10 feet) thick and it is nearly 40 meters (131 feet) long. Its central building is made with bricks stamped with the name of the Ur III king Shulgi (ca. 2095–2047 BCE), but added onto the center are two annexes built with bricks of his son, Amar-Sin (ca. 2046–2038 BCE). Partly because of its clear association with these two rulers, the combined building is generally called the Mausoleum of the Ur III kings (Fig. 8.7). Beneath the building are vaults that may once have housed royal remains, though they were found looted and almost completely empty. A few scattered bones led Woolley to suggest that an outer chamber held retainers or attendants while the inner held the king himself, in reflection of the much earlier practice of human sacrifice noted in the Royal Cemetery proper. But if the multiple chambers

THIRD DYNASTY CONDUIT

Fig. 8.8 *Below*

In this general plan of Area PG the many small graves infringing on each other and on the larger "royal" tombs are readily apparent. It appears as a huge number of chaotically placed graves, but there were even more—at least 500 of the graves dug in the Trial Trenches were never mapped and do not appear on this plan. Redrawn by Ardeth Anderson.

NEO BABYLONIAN TEMENOS WALL

0   50 m

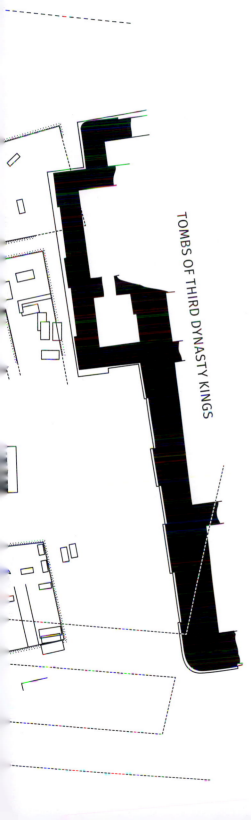

TOMBS OF THIRD DYNASTY KINGS

beneath both the main building and the annexes could indeed have been used in this way, there is not enough evidence to prove it.

The building above the vaults had also been looted, perhaps by the Elamites when they sacked Ur around 2000 BCE. While its layout was that of a standard courtyard house, the remaining furnishings and artifacts indicate that it had ritual functions. Altars and gold leaf decoration found within it probably reflect high-level cult activities associated with honoring the dead kings. The building's sheer size and the stamped bricks used to construct it also underscore its role as public architecture rather than private. Other burials of Ur III date also occur in the so-called Akkadian Cemetery, although Woolley did not recognize them as such; most of these late burials gather near the Ur III Mausoleum. It seems, then, that this portion of the cemetery was still in use around 2100 BCE, even though burial of the dead beneath private house floors was becoming the standard burial practice at this time. Woolley suggested that the courtyard house layout of the Mausoleum reflected something of the contemporary changes in burial custom on a monumental and royal scale, with the king effectively being buried beneath a monumental and ritual house.

Non-Royal Graves of the Royal and Akkadian Cemeteries

While the sixteen ED III Period royal graves in Area PG have taken pride of place in publications on the burial grounds, these are vastly outnumbered by the non-royal burials occurring throughout all periods of Area PG. The general pattern of these non-royal burials has already been established, but a few specifics will help to illuminate the cemetery as a whole and emphasize the similarities and differences among the non-royal graves across the vast chronological and spatial territory they occupy (Fig. 8.8).

Most of the non-royal graves in Area PG were humble, with no additional offerings or only a few items of clay or stone. Some, however, were far better appointed, reflecting disparities in socioeconomic status that only increased with developing urbanization. PG 1609, found 5.8 meters (19 feet) below the surface and contemporary with the massive royal graves of the ED III Period, is an example of a relatively common burial type that nonetheless had markers suggesting the deceased had some minor status. The body of a man lay beneath an oval, clay coffin called a larnax. In his hands was a small calcite bowl and nearby was a copper dagger. He wore a modest necklace made up of a central carnelian bead with two lapis beads on either side. Also buried with him was a seashell cut into a lamp and a set of 17 very small stone weights.

A second larnax grave, PG 1608, sat only 20 centimeters (8 inches) away. It was the grave of a woman and Woolley suggested that she was related to, and perhaps even the wife of, the man in PG 1609. She wore a three-strand necklace of small gold and lapis lazuli beads, a pair of spiral gold earrings, and a copper cloak pin. She also had a calcite

bowl and cup, but they were located at her feet along with a set of cockleshells containing cosmetic pigments.

These two graves, PG 1608 and PG 1609, would appear to represent a relatively well-to-do couple, perhaps a merchant and his wife if the balance weights can be taken as indicative of a profession. Unfortunately, such graves are so heavily overshadowed by the mysterious grandeur of the royal tombs that they go virtually unnoticed and often remain understudied.

More often mentioned in scholarly and other literature are those graves containing evidence of extreme wealth but not the bodies of sacrificed retainers, an omission that precludes their designation as royal according to Woolley's criteria. The best example of such a splendidly equipped burial is PG 755, a large grave of the ED III Period. It contained a wooden coffin and many spectacular offerings that are only paralleled in the royal tombs. Some of the grave goods also had explicit royal connections, including several metal vessels bearing the names of the ruler Meskalamdug and Queen Ninbanda. The tomb has come to be known as that of Meskalamdug, though there are conflicting attestations of the name in the Royal Cemetery. The young man buried in PG 755, an apparent warrior prince whose name may have been Meskalamdug, since the name appears on items in his grave. He is not, however, the king of the same name whose artifacts appear scattered elsewhere in the cemetery, though it is possible he was related to that king. If he died prior to being crowned, this might explain the absence of the sacrificed retainers that seem to have accompanied full royal burials.

The coffin in PG 755 was marked by rows of upright spears at both its head and foot. The bones inside it were those of a robust young man who wore a silver-plated belt from which hung a gold dagger and a whetstone made of lapis lazuli. An electrum helmet made in the form of an elaborate wig (Fig. 8.9), a form sometimes associated with Early Dynastic kings, was set near the man's skull. Two electrum axes, a gold lamp, a gold bowl, and many beads were also found near his body. Outside his coffin were many more offerings including copper, clay and stone vessels, as well as daggers or short swords, axes, and arrowheads. The overall impression is not solely of wealth but also of military might.

The type of grave containing a wooden coffin marked by upright spears continued in use into the later period of the Akkadian Cemetery, as evinced by PG 1422. In this grave, dating some 250 years after Meskalamdug, we find a wooden coffin surrounded by offerings of metal and clay vessels. Inside the coffin were the bones of a sturdy young man with weapons and jewelry. Although not as richly adorned as Meskalamdug of PG 755, he had a silver axe and copper dagger, as well as six bracelets and a great many beads of agate and other semi-precious stones. He had no helmet but on his head were six hammered gold fillets or diadems. The man, likely a warrior as indicated by the weapons on and near his body, was clearly wealthy and important, though he lacked the royal or near royal accoutrements of Meskalamdug.

Fig. 8.9 *Opposite*

PG 755 was an Early Dynastic III (ca. 2450 BCE) burial of an apparent warrior prince who may have been called Meskalamdug, as the name appears on objects outside his coffin. He was buried with many offerings including this electrum helmet decorated to look like an elaborate hairstyle. The photograph is of a copy of the helmet (29-22-2) in the Penn Museum. The original is in the Iraq National Museum in Baghdad.

continued on page 230

AN AKKADIAN WARRIOR'S GRAVE

William B. Hafford

The most elaborate of the graves in the uppermost (Akkadian) cemetery was PG 1422. Artifacts within date it to the late Akkadian Period or early Ur III Period and the burial inside is likely that of a warrior (Figs. 8S6.1 and 8S6.2). Placed on one side of the pit was a wooden coffin topped with a gabled lid. At the head of the coffin stood six spears with their tips pointing upwards. The spears collapsed as their wooden shafts deteriorated and only three of the spear points were recovered; one of these, however, was found above the coffin lid. This suggests the spears may originally have marked the grave above ground level.

Inside the coffin were offerings surrounding and covering the bones of a man who lay on his right side facing west. These offerings included smaller clay jars and cups, a silver box, a copper dagger, and copper and silver axes. The man also wore a great deal of jewelry including six fillets, or diadems, of thin hammered gold on his head; gold earrings; at least four necklaces of agate, gold, and carnelian beads (Fig. 8S6.3); and six bracelets. The rest of the pit was strewn with additional grave goods (Fig. 8S6.4) including two entire sheep or goats, many clay pots, a copper cauldron, and a

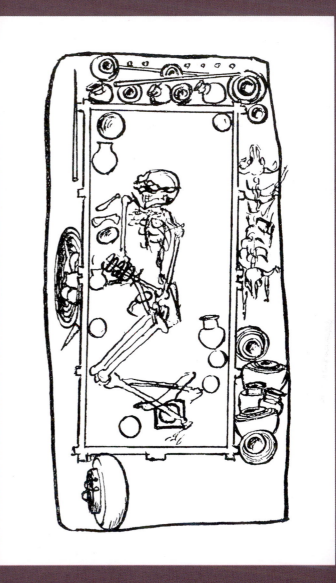

Fig. 8S6.1 *Right*
Leonard Woolley's published plan map of the grave PG 1422. The six circles at the top center represent the six spear shafts that rose at the head of the coffin. Two axe blades are seen at the left of the body inside the coffin. These elements seem to identify the man as a warrior.

Fig. 8S6.3 *Below*

Along with the weapons buried with the man in PG 1422 were many impressive pieces of jewelry. Here are shown a very long necklace (30-12-567) of banded agate and gold beads and one of the six gold diadems or fillets (30-12-600) he wore on his forehead.

Fig. 8S6.2 *Above*

Field photograph of PG 1422. The bones of the warrior's arms can be seen in the center right along with the single bracelet on the right wrist and five bracelets on the left. The leg bones can be seen near the top and the impression of the wooden coffin stands out against the soil all around.

mass of corroded copper cups and bowls on a large copper tray. The cauldron buried with the warrior in PG 1422 may suggest he had a number of dependents or led a large band of soldiers.

The earlier grave PG 755, dated to the Early Dynastic III Period, has several features in common with PG 1422. It also takes the form of a large pit containing a wooden coffin and twelve spears (six erected at both its head and foot), as well as offerings including weapons and jewelry. It is possible that this type of burial was specifically designated for warriors and used into later periods.

Fig. 8S6.4 *Above*

The man buried in PG 1422 carried two lapis lazuli cylinder seals with gold caps. One of the seals (30-12-38 shown here) had at one point borne an inscription but it had been scraped away, probably indicating it was an older seal that was reused by the deceased.

Fig. 8.10 *Right*

Field photograph of the model bitumen boat loaded with jars found in PG 627, an Akkadian Period grave. Such boats may have been symbolically carrying food and drink along with the deceased into the netherworld.

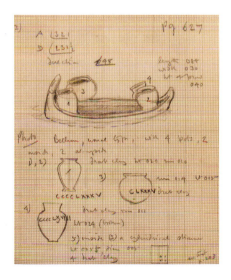

Fig. 8.11 *Above*

Drawing of the model boat with jars and notes recorded on the PG627 field card. Courtesy of the British Museum.

Woolley dated approximately 450 graves from Area PG to the Akkadian Period, though he detailed only six in his primary publication. There was little to distinguish between the common burials of this later Akkadian Period and those of the (slightly) earlier ED III Period, since the morphology of the graves and the position of the bodies remained nearly identical. The general depth of the graves from the modern ground surface, too, while it helped to generally distinguish the different cemeteries from each other, was not absolute; individual graves were cut into the sloping ground to varying individual depths, and so could not be dated exclusively on the basis of their depth. It is only close examination of the grave goods themselves that suggests a few possible differences between the ED III and Akkadian Period graves. Akkadian Period grave goods, like those in PG 1422, were more likely to include agate beads, probably due to a particular supply route exploited during this period. They were also more likely to include a bitumen boat in the grave shaft (Figs. 8.10 and 8.11). The boat held a few clay vessels and may have been conceptually intended to supply food to the dead, though Woolley suggested it was placed to distract evil spirits away from the grave.

PG 958, located in the Akkadian Cemetery, is a good example of a burial containing relatively modest, but still very interesting and informative grave goods. Located only 1.2 meters (4 feet) below the modern ground surface, it may actually date to the Ur III Period. It contained no coffin; the body was instead placed in a simple rectangular trench. Around the head and shoulders were six pottery vessels, mostly jars, and near the chest was a group of objects that had likely been contained in a woven bag. Evidence of the cloth bag remained impressed on a corroded copper disk that may have been sewn onto it. The contents of the bag included various pieces of stone, including small bits of lapis lazuli with one piece half formed into a bead. There were also pieces of a copper drill bit. The grave was almost certainly that of a bead-maker and these were the raw materials and tools of his trade.

The Jemdet Nasr Cemetery

In 1934, his last season at Ur, Woolley had already excavated and published the Akkadian and Royal (ED III) Cemeteries. He had cleared away some 11 meters (37 feet) of soil depth over nearly 4,000 square meters (43,000 square feet) in Area PG, and had also found evidence of deeper and older graves in small test pits cut beneath the lowest uncovered levels. He now wanted to understand the full extent of the use of the burial grounds. Because it appeared that the concentration of early burials was mainly to the south, he opened an extension to the southern edge of Area PG that is known as Pit X or Area PJ (Fig. 8.12).

Because the trench was so deep, its walls had to be sloped to keep them from collapsing; as a result, Woolley's pit, which measured 1000 square meters (11,000 square feet) on the surface, had dwindled to only 440 square meters (4,700 square feet) in size by the time the concentration of the Jemdet Nasr Cemetery was reached, some 17 meters (56 feet) below ground level. Even within this greatly diminished trench, however, Woolley recovered more than 200 graves of the period. Most of the bodies found had been wrapped in matting; alternatively, matting was used to line the grave shaft itself. In only one case was there evidence of a coffin, situated in the area to the southwest where the larger and somewhat better appointed graves were located.

The Jemdet Nasr skeletons often had their hands near their faces, as was the norm in the later cemeteries. Small cups made of lead were relatively common, but these were typically placed over the mouth of a clay jar. The bodies were more contracted than those of the later Royal (ED III) and Akkadian Cemeteries and their burial goods, apart from pottery, were typically sparse. Woolley referred to the position of the Jemdet Nasr skeletons as the fetal position, and that of the ED III and Akkadian Period skeletons the sleeping position, but did not speculate on what this distinction might have meant for the people to whom these burials belonged. A change in burial custom may signify a change in belief system, but the change here is not extreme and does not seem to reflect major differences in religious or existential thinking. Woolley also found changes in grave goods over the centuries of burials in the Jemdet Nasr Cemetery, with clay vessels being most common in the earliest and stone vessels becoming more common in the latest. Such changes might reflect the expansion of trade networks in the Early Dynastic I Period, and the consequent greater availability of objects such as stone vessels.

Fig. 8.12 *Opposite*
Pit X as seen in early 1934. Only a few weeks after work had begun, Woolley and his 170 workers had removed more than 13,000 cubic meters (ca. 17,000 cubic yards) of earth to reach the "Jemdet Nasr" Cemetery.

It is worth noting, with respect to the dating of the graves incorporated into the Jemdet Nasr Cemetery at Ur, that many of its graves date into the ED I Period, continuing essentially up to the beginning of the Royal (ED III) Cemetery at around 2600 BCE. This was an important time for the formation of cities and the founding of dynastic kings.

None of the Jemdet Nasr graves appear to be royal, but they do show variation in wealth of grave goods. For example, the body in Jemdet Nasr Grave (JNG) 363 was buried with seven clay vessels, one stone vessel, a lead tumbler and a copper mirror; the body in JNG 215 had only a shell and three clay vessels. The body in JNG 191 wore a necklace of shell and carnelian ring beads and had five stone and three clay vessels, while the occupant of JNG 97 had seven clay vessels and a pierced clay disk.

Conclusion

Area PG, the great burial ground at Ur containing the famous ED III royal graves, and many other graves besides, was in use as a cemetery from as early as the late Uruk Period (3100 BCE or a little before) to the beginning of the Ur III Period (2100 BCE or a little after). It contained more than 2,000 documented graves ranging in form and burial goods from simple to elaborate and, in the 16 royal graves recovered from the ED III phase of the burial ground especially, yielded some of the most spectacular objects known from southern Mesopotamia. The tremendous wealth accumulated in the royal graves highlights the socioeconomic power and reach of the kings and queens buried at Ur; the grave goods are remarkable not only for their stunning artistry but also for their incorporation of a wide variety of exotic materials which could only have been obtained through sophisticated trade networks and relationships (Fig. 8.13). Ur's situation with respect to the Persian Gulf trade was likely one of the reasons it rose to prominence in this early period (see Chapter 5S2: Importing Raw Materials and Finished Goods). The city was, thus, able to sustain an elite that could demand such impressive burial ritual and accoutrements—and that could, in death, remove so significant an amount of wealth from circulation.

Fig. 8.13 *Opposite*
A few of the extraordinary artifacts discovered in PG 800 at Ur: (top) decorated cosmetic box lid (B16744A); (center) gold cosmetic dish made in the shape of a cockle shell (B16710); (bottom) gold tweezers and fingernail cleaner (B16714).

For Further Reading

Woolley, C. Leonard. 1929. *Ur of the Chaldees: A Record of Seven Years of Excavation*. London: E. Benn Limited.

Zettler, Richard L., and Lee Horne, eds. 1998. *Treasures of the Royal Tombs of Ur*. Philadelphia: University of Pennsylvania Museum of Archaeology and Anthropology.

9

HASANLU

Lauren Ristvet

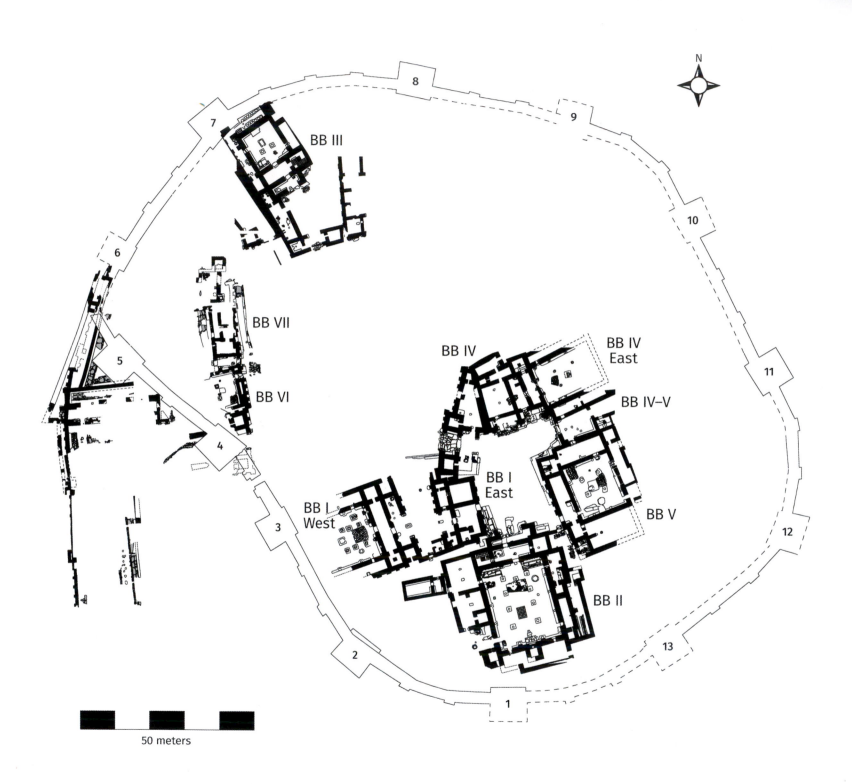

BB III

BB VII

BB VI

BB IV

BB IV
East

BB IV–V

BB I
East

BB V

BB I
West

BB II

N

7

8

9

10

11

6

5

4

3

2

1

12

13

50 meters

The Last Day of Hasanlu: An Archaeological Mystery

The invading army appeared at the foot of Hasanlu's citadel on a dry, hot day in late summer (Fig. 9.1). For weeks, the town's occupants had heard rumors of their depredations elsewhere. On this, the last day of Hasanlu, it is not clear whether the invaders entered the city after defeating Hasanlu's chariots and infantry on the broad Ushnu-Solduz plain, or whether they attacked the city while a large part of Hasanlu's fighting force was away on some other military campaign.

What we do know is that foreign soldiers swarmed the city, scaling the high hill, fighting their way through the internal gateways, plundering the temples, elite residences, stables, and palaces. The townsfolk—the men, women, children, and infants who remained there—huddled on the citadel, many of them taking refuge in a monumental temple. Perhaps they hoped that the gods would protect them. This hope would prove futile. In the open areas of the citadel, the clanging of sword on sword rang out, as did the sickening crunch of stone on bone and the singing of arrowheads, which formed a counterpoint to the screams and moans of the wounded (Fig. 9.2).

The fire began in the northwest of the citadel, near where the marauding army first appeared. Perhaps a solider set it deliberately, or perhaps it was accidental, the result of a lamp knocked onto a floor in the commotion. The tall, columned buildings at Hasanlu were made of non-flammable mudbrick on stone foundations; the timber used for columns, doorjambs, rafters, and roofing, however, as well as the reed mats that covered the floors, caught fire in an instant.

The strong summer winds fanned the flames. These spread rapidly south and east until they engulfed the temple, where so many of Hasanlu's residents had gathered. Raiders surged into the building, desperate to strip the temple's treasury, which was filled with precious imports and delicate furniture, while residents fought to save their gods.

Fig. 9.1 *Opposite*
Plan of the excavated area of the Hasanlu Citadel, Period IVB Destruction Level with Period III Citadel Wall. After Kimberly Leaman Insua's 2009 plan. Redrawn by Ardeth Anderson.

Fig. 9.2 *Right*
Arrowheads (73-5-90) fused together from the force of the fire.

Fig. 9.3 *Left*
Skeleton wearing lion pin in Hasanlu's Burned Building II.

The smell of the blood seeping from the wounds of the dying infused the dark rooms. A thundering roar heralded the splintering of the roof boards and the weakening of the columns. In an instant, the ceiling collapsed, plunging the people on the second floor to their deaths, and trapping and crushing everyone gathered on the floor below. As the fire raged, attackers probably bound some of the survivors, tying their hands with rope and leading them away as slaves. A day or two later, as the ashes cooled, the last stragglers among the invaders returned to paw through the rubble for treasure. They executed some of the weakest and most troublesome of the prisoners, staving in their heads with maces. And then they left, loading their horses and donkeys with gold and wine jugs, and driving their stolen herds and slaves behind them. The hill lay silent. Only the cries of scavengers could be heard, vultures and wild dogs drawn by the reek of the charred and rotting flesh of the more than 285 corpses that lay in the ruins (Fig. 9.3).

The events of the last day at Hasanlu have emerged with remarkable clarity. Unlike many Iron Age cities, no written records belonging to Hasanlu's administrators were found and we do not know the city's ancient name for certain. Nonetheless, extensive archaeological analysis and comparative historical research has allowed us to piece together the overall scenario above, even if specific details are subject to change as further research on the remains is completed. This reconstruction takes into account evidence gathered during excavation, contemporary written records about military campaigns, analysis of the skeletal remains, and even meteorological conditions in northwest Iran. But questions remain. Determining precisely when Hasanlu's last day fell is harder. Although most evidence points to around 800 BCE, some researchers think the massacre occurred as late as 714 BCE. Identifying the perpetrators of the attack is harder still, and demands that we consider some of the reasons behind Hasanlu's destruction. Who were the people of Hasanlu? How did they live? And why did so many perish on that fateful day?

The Victims
The People of Hasanlu

The high mound of Hasanlu rises 25 meters (82 feet) above a fertile plain south of Lake Urmia, the largest lake in the Middle East. By the Late Bronze Age, this citadel encompassed more than three hectares (seven acres) and housed the predecessors of the elite buildings that the invaders would encounter. The citadel was probably fortified, although perhaps not strongly. Surrounding the high mound is a lower mound or lower town, 8 meters (26 feet) high and covering an area of 30 hectares (75 acres) or more. On that dusty day when the citadel of Hasanlu burned, the lower town probably included a cemetery, industrial areas, and perhaps dispersed houses. In the Iron Age, Hasanlu was probably a medium-sized town; several larger cities are known, some even from the region.

One of the great mysteries of Hasanlu is where its occupants actually lived. Many of the people who died on the citadel had gathered there because of the military threat posed to the town; typically, only the town's wealthiest residents and their servants dwelled on the citadel. While some artisans and farmers probably lived in modest houses in the lower town, such as the Artisan's House (see p. 241), excavation has revealed little evidence for such occupation. Others probably lived primarily in scattered farmsteads on the plain— one has been found on a hillside—or with their flocks in temporary camps. Even if they did not actually live in the citadel or even the lower town, these latter two groups may nevertheless represent a large percentage of the people who died on Hasanlu's last day, as well as of those who were buried in its cemetery in more peaceful times.

Nearly a hundred graves belonging to the period just prior to Hasanlu's destruction have been excavated. The skeletons provide evidence of important aspects of people's lives, including any violence they might have encountered, their nutritional status, and their overall health. Both men and women were buried with personal goods that seem to have been important to their individual identities, and perhaps also to the rituals performed at their deaths. Many burials, particularly of men, contained no more than two objects, but a few richer burials give us an idea of social values and hierarchies. Elite men were buried with metal belts, swords, maceheads, and spears. Other men were buried with arrows. Such men were probably considered or functioned as warriors in life. Elite women, interestingly, also embraced warrior accoutrements and status. Although they were not buried with traditional weapons, armor and long pins that could be deadly if used to attack were included in the richest female graves. Many of the objects from the burials indicate close connections to other people living in northwest Iran and the South Caucasus.

Houses and Workshops in the Lower Town: The Case of the Artisan's House

Material recovered from what has been dubbed the Artisan's House, a dwelling from the lower town, helps round out this picture of how people lived. Life at the Artisan's House ended in a violent conflagration, perhaps part of the same fire that decimated the citadel. Here it killed at least one person, three dogs, and a colt kept outside the house. The small building probably housed a family that specialized in bronzeworking. Smashed vessels found in rooms on both the first and second floors may have held water or foodstuffs for the family's meals. Another room probably served as a workshop and contained objects related to metalworking, including a pottery vessel that once held molten metal and a variety of specialized tools. More metalwork may have been conducted outside of the house, where a bronze ingot, other tools, and molds for axes, ingots, and jewelry were also found. The large quantities of goods excavated in the graves in the cemetery and on the citadel indicate that potters, glaziers, blacksmiths, furniture makers, and others also operated in the town and may have lived in similar houses (Fig. 9.4). Much of the pottery and metalwork has parallels to nearby regions, particularly northwest Iran, the Caspian, and the South Caucasus.

Life on the Citadel

Excavations on the citadel reveal a different side of life at Hasanlu, showing us how the rulers lived and how people worshipped. We know the most about Burned Building II, the large temple reconstructed in the opening section of this chapter; more than 1,500 objects were recovered from this site, probably because the fire reached this building before much of it could be looted, or there was little looting at the site. In the normal course of things, people empty out houses before abandoning them, removing valuable and useful objects. The fire here preserved both the precious and the everyday, allowing us to reconstruct how the temple was furnished and how it was used.

In plan, Burned Building II resembles other northern Mesopotamian temples. A long outer sanctuary led to a small inner sanctuary, both of which were lined with storerooms filled with pottery. Three plain stone stelae, well known from Late Bronze Age temples in Syria, were erected at its entrance (Fig. 9.5). The outer sanctuary contained two rows

Fig. 9.4 *Above*
A typical Hasanlu spouted bowl (60-20-71A) and tripod stand (60-20-71B) found together during excavation.

Fig. 9.5 *Above*
Burned Building II during excavation.

of columns flanking an offering table and a platform in front of the entrance to the inner sanctuary. A pair of large inlaid eyes found alongside a group of six skeletons probably belonged to a divine statue (Fig. 9.6). The excavators Robert Dyson, Jr., and Mary Voigt argue that the skeletons were likely those of attendants who were attempting to carry the god to safety when the building collapsed in flame. Two other eye inlays were found elsewhere, perhaps belonging to another cult figure. Remains of a drum made of bone plaques were scattered in the outer sanctuary; the boom of this drum would have accompanied many rituals. In front of the entrance to the inner sanctuary, two wooden thrones were discovered, along with a lamp (Fig. 9.7). The god may have sat here in normal times. Red deer skulls and antlers found at the north end of Burned Building II's columned hall also probably represented the god. Deer seem to have been royal or divine animals at Hasanlu.

continued on page 245

Ironworking

Lauren Ristvet

At some point in the latter half of the 2nd millennium BCE, blacksmiths mastered the art of working iron. This event was so momentous that scholars named an entire era after it: the Iron Age (ca. 1200–500 BCE). Work by the archaeologist Vincent Pigott, who analyzed the almost 2,000 iron artifacts excavated from Hasanlu, has transformed our understanding of how and why iron became the material of choice for tools and weapons.

Originally, iron was a relatively rare metal, a by-product of the copper smelting process. Smiths made jewelry and luxury goods from iron, treating it as they did silver, gold, and bronze. These early iron objects were valuable and include an eleventh century BCE sword (Fig. 9S1.1) from Luristan in western Iran (see Chapter 6: Nomads) that was probably made for a burial rather than for battle. Analysis has shown that this sword was not welded; instead, it was made of eight to fifteen pieces of iron that were riveted together, perhaps by bronzesmiths who did not fully understand iron's unique characteristics but were brilliant improvisers. This sword is one of the earliest decorated iron weapons known from Iran, or anywhere in the ancient world. Early ironsmiths also experimented with bimetallism, producing objects like Hasanlu's iconic lion pins, which combined bronze and iron (see Fig. 9.9).

By about 900 BCE, blacksmiths began smelting and forging iron to produce weapons and tools. Iron did not supersede bronze entirely, however. Hasanlu's artisans continued to use bronze for jewelry, horse gear, architectural decoration (see Fig. 9.15), household objects, and some weapons. After 800 BCE, iron was increasingly used for tools and weapons (Fig. 9S1.2), while bronze remained important for more decorative uses.

At first, scholars did not question why iron replaced bronze. They assumed that it was less costly and militarily superior. Iron is widely available across Western Asia, unlike the components of bronze, copper and tin; iron would, thus, have been easier to obtain. Similarly, steel, which is an alloy of iron, is between two and five times harder than bronze, making steel weapons stronger and far more effective in battle; iron weapons were assumed to have something of the same properties. Analysis of iron weapons at Hasanlu, however, shows that they were no harder than those made of bronze. Working iron is more difficult than bronze, requiring five production steps rather than two, which adds to the cost of manufacture. What, then, was the reason for the shift? Vincent Pigott argues that blacksmiths began producing iron in imitation of the Assyrian empire, which was an early adopter of the material. Since iron is only cost-effective if mass-produced, Hasanlu's decision to keep up with the Assyrian Empire had major social consequences. Among other things, it meant that iron remained the metal of choice in Iran long after the citadel at Hasanlu burned down.

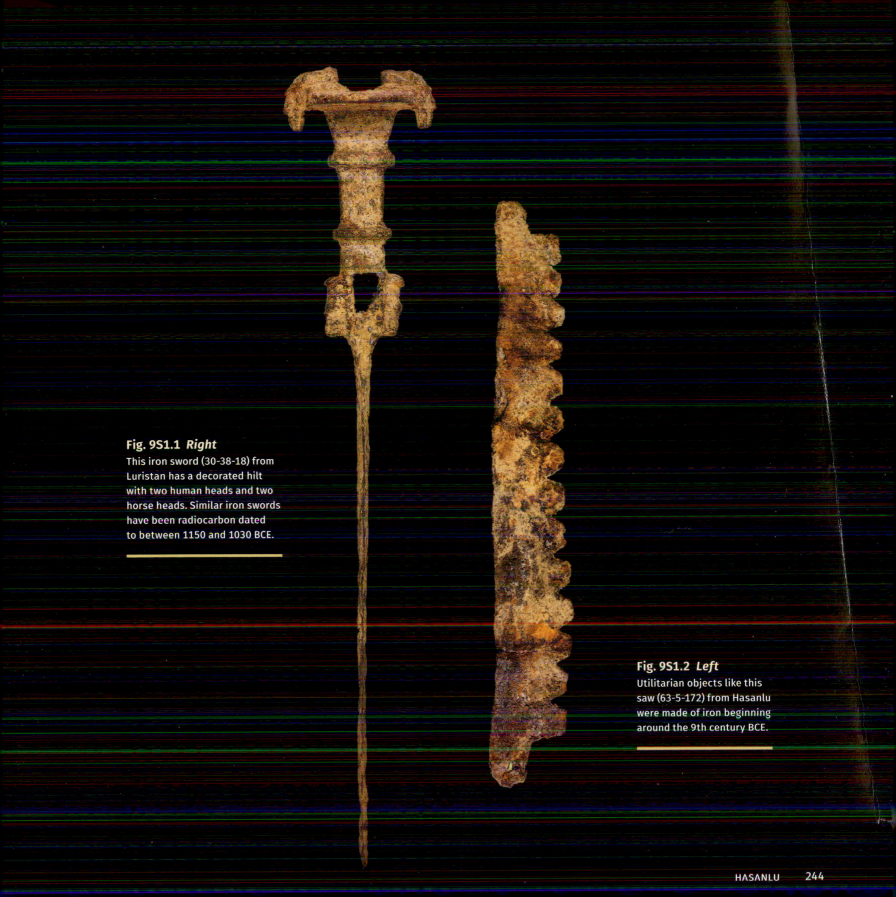

Fig. 9S1.1 *Right*
This iron sword (30-38-18) from
Luristan has a decorated hilt
with two human heads and two
horse heads. Similar iron swords
have been radiocarbon dated
to between 1150 and 1030 BCE.

Fig. 9S1.2 *Left*
Utilitarian objects like this
saw (63-5-172) from Hasanlu
were made of iron beginning
around the 9th century BCE.

Fig. 9.6 *Far Left*
Inlaid eyes (65-31-339 and 61-5-205), possibly from a cultic statue.

Fig. 9.7 *Left*
This wooden throne foot (65-31-611) may have belonged to the chair where the deity sat.

The bodies of 55 adults and young children lay jumbled together at the northern end of the outer sanctuary of Burned Building II. Some of the crushed skeletons wore jewelry and were probably female. Others wore helmets and carried weapons, including types not found in the graves, which may indicate they were enemy soldiers. About half of the victims wore lion pins (Fig. 9.8), large and costly dress pins made from both iron and bronze in the form of recumbent lions. Unique to Hasanlu, these pins probably indicated high rank, military power, and local identity.

The storerooms lining the outer sanctuary contained ritual furnishings and other objects, including large quantities of pots and tens of thousands of stone beads and necklaces (Fig. 9.9) Most of the objects recovered from Burned Building II, however, had been stored on the second floor. This was the location of the temple's treasury, which contained a variety of precious objects, heirlooms, and valuable imports. It yielded large quantities of glazed wall tiles, ivory inlaid furniture, imported ivory boxes, glass, metal vessels, wood and ivory statuettes (Fig. 9.10), and weapons. Some of the objects were locally made, while others had been imported from Assyria, North Syria, or elsewhere in Iran. Some of the imports, notably, were centuries old (Fig. 9.11). A few, inscribed with names of kings from neighboring kingdoms such as Assyria, Babylonia, and Susa, may have arrived as diplomatic gifts, part of an age-old custom of kings presenting precious objects to temples belonging to their allies. Another treasury identified at Hasanlu was located on the top-level of Burned Building I-West, which may have been the palace. Precious objects stored here include the Hasanlu Gold Bowl (Fig. 9.12), Silver Beaker, a bronze tetrapod stand (Fig. 9.13) and other ceramic, stone, and metal containers.

Fig. 9.8 *Above*
The cast bronze head of a garment pin (56-20-1) depicting a recumbent lion. The shaft of the pin was made from iron.

Fig. 9.9 *Above*
Thousands of beads like these (65-31-728)
were found in BBII and the nearby "Bead House."

Imports and Emulation

The objects stored in the treasuries at Hasanlu visually and materially demonstrate the town's incorporation into a wider international sphere. Letters from Assyria state that most kingdoms in the northern Zagros were ruled by elite families or tribes. They used diplomacy and trade to carve out a space for themselves in a complicated and sometimes treacherous political landscape. Ambassadors from Assyria were permanently installed in the courts of certain states in western Iran to ensure the loyalty of these states. The Assyrian ambassadors were also responsible for ensuring the smooth transport into Assyria of various goods, especially horses (see Chapter 6: Nomads); were involved in espionage; and sought to influence the decision-making of the local rulers. The presence of fine imports at even small Iranian sites such as Hasanlu emphasizes how essential gift-giving was to diplomacy. Objects could be re-gifted, sometimes several times, so

Fig. 9.10 *Above Left*
This burned ivory lion (65-31-353), carved in the round, is an example of an exquisite statue made by an artisan at Hasanlu.

Fig. 9.11 *Above Right*
This unique glass goblet (65-31-403) was made in Kassite Babylonia. It may have come to Hasanlu as a diplomatic gift. Dark green portions of the goblet are modern restorations.

Fig. 9.12 Above Left
Archaeologist Robert H. Dyson, Jr. holding the Hasanlu Gold Bowl.

Fig. 9.13 Above Right
This cast copper stand (59-4-116) for two vessels is decorated with men and animals in the "local style" made at Hasanlu.

that they might even circle back to their places of origin. Diplomatic gifts were probably retained primarily for their economic value and political symbolism.

Many of the precious locally made objects in the treasuries at Hasanlu are also related to the types of imports described above. Hasanlu's elites emulated Assyrian and Urartian courtly arts, seeking to appropriate something of those empires' power and status. Elites and artisans knew of foreign art from diplomatic gifts and visits, and Hasanlu's artists copied motifs from Assyria, Urartu, or Syria, probably from cylinder seals or imported ivories, rendering these in a variety of different media. Among the nearly 70,000 attendees invited to celebrate the construction of the palace of Ashurnasirpal II (ca. 883–859 BCE) at the city of Nimrud (ancient Kalhu) were representatives of various Zagros states, possibly even Hasanlu. These attendees would have seen the finest of Assyrian court arts, a sight which perhaps inspired many of the objects subsequently produced at Hasanlu in a local style but still demonstrating a foreign influence. In other cases, the

Fig. 9.14 *Left*
A metal plaque (63-5-177) depicting a fortified town that may have resembled Hasanlu.

combined use of both ivory and bone inlay, as well as some of the metalwork (Fig. 9.14), suggests Urartian influence. Hasanlu's artists may also have drawn upon the rich historic traditions of northwest Iran, rendering motifs known particularly from the Late Bronze Age (from which period many of the heirlooms date). The Gold Bowl, for example, could have been made in the last part of the 2nd millennium BCE or the early 1st millennium BCE. The scenes that decorate it probably illustrate Hurrian myths, perhaps suggesting ties between Hasanlu and Hurrian speakers or others (like Urartian speakers?) whom they influenced.

The elites of Hasanlu, importantly, did not merely adopt Assyrian or Urartian visual conventions, but rather adapted these to create their own unique style. Artisans borrowed popular Assyrian themes like hunts, mythic combats, and royal processions to decorate metalwork, seals, and ivory, but put their own stamp on these themes, exaggerating facial features, substituting local boots for sandals, preferring squat figures, and adding more abstract decoration (Fig. 9.15). They also used different techniques from those of artisans of other regions, such as carving ivory in relief in addition to incising it. Trade, diplomacy, and even the seasonal movement of pastoralists meant that the people who lived at Hasanlu were intimately tied to a larger world.

continued on page 253

Fig. 9.15 *Opposite*
The carved ivory head (65-31-355) of a woman found at Hasanlu.

ASSYRIA

Lauren Ristvet

Beginning in the 1st millennium BCE, a new political configuration arose in the ancient Near East: the empire. This would define the Near East and, indeed, much of the rest of the world for the following three millennia. Including several territories or peoples under a single sovereign authority, empires are by definition large and diverse. Assyria, the earliest undisputed empire in the region, expanded from the city state of Ashur in northern Iraq until it ultimately encompassed much of the region between Egypt in the west to the Zagros Mountains in the east, and from Southern Anatolia in the north to Babylonia in the south.

Although Ashur had been an important city-state since the 3rd millennium BCE, it only emerged as an imperial center after the fall of Mitanni, a Hurrian-speaking state spanning much of southeast Anatolia and northern Iraq and Syria, around 1350 BCE. The king of Ashur, Ashur-uballit I (ca. 1365–1330 BCE), quickly took over much of Mitanni's territory in northern Iraq and even wrote letters to the powerful Egyptian pharaoh as a ruler of equal rank. Assyria had arrived on the international scene. From 1300–1200 BCE, under a series of forceful kings including Adad-nirari I (ca. 1307–1275 BCE), Shalmaneser I (ca. 1274–1245 BCE), and Tukulti-Ninurta I (ca. 1244–1208 BCE), Assyria conquered the land between the Zagros

Fig. 9S2.1 *Right*
This Assyrian relief (29-21-1) from the palace of King Ashurnasirpal II (883–859 BCE) at Kalhu (Nimrud) depicts a winged genie (*apkallu*) engaged in a ritual.

Mountains and the Euphrates. Subsequently, except for a brief flash of light during the reign of Tiglath-pileser I (ca. 1114–1076 BCE), much of the history of Assyria is murky until about 900 BCE. It is clear that, during this time, the fledgling empire withdrew to its core around the Tigris River. Assyria was not alone in experiencing such a decline. This period saw the fall or contraction of many of the other great kingdoms of the Late Bronze Age (ca. 1600–1200 BCE), including the Hittite Empire, Kassite Babylonia, Mycenaean Greece, and Egypt (see Chapter 6S2: Bronze Age Diplomacy).

Beginning just after 900 BCE, Assyrian kings, particularly Ashurnasirpal II (ca. 883–859 BCE) (Fig. 9S2.1) and Shalmaneser III (ca. 858–824 BCE), reestablished the empire and undertook military campaigns to the north, west, and east. Although Assyria did not annex territories outside of its borders, it did establish client states whose rulers paid tribute to the Assyrian kings. Its powerful armies made it a formidable presence from the Mediterranean to the Zagros for a hundred years. Following another century of retrenchment, the final century and a half of Assyrian rule saw the establishment of a vast state that spanned the Middle East from the Southern Levant to Western Iran. The Assyrian king Esarhaddon (ca. 680–669 BCE) even managed to conquer Egypt in the early 7th century. Soon after Assyria reached its apogee, however, it fell to a coalition of Medes and Babylonians, formerly subject people who united to throw off Assyria's yoke and destroy its capital, Nineveh, in 612 BCE.

In their own minds, the Assyrians represented civilization itself, the hallmarks of which included the construction of temples, the foundation of cities, and the extension of agriculture. Through the power of the god Ashur, they subdued the dangerous lands beyond Assyria,

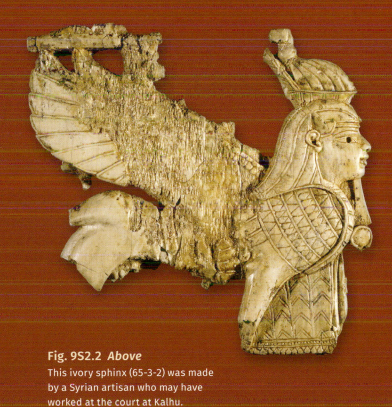

Fig. 9S2.2 *Above*
This ivory sphinx (65-3-2) was made by a Syrian artisan who may have worked at the court at Kalhu.

which were populated with nomads, rebels, witches, and demons. This periphery, however, also supplied raw materials and manpower to the empire. Assyrian kings hunted exotic animals (and captured them for royal menageries) and acquired ivory (Fig. 9S2.2), stones, precious metals, and rare woods as booty or through taxes and tribute. They also, beginning with the reign of Tiglath-pileser III (ca. 745–727 BCE), deported large numbers of conquered peoples from their homelands; this broke down local identities and prevented rebellions against the empire. Imperial control, however, was not as absolute and pervasive as it was portrayed by the Assyrian kings. The empire overall constituted a network of outposts or nodes that were connected by routes of communication along which people and goods traveled.

The Suspects

It is to this larger world that we must now turn. Our discussion of cultural affiliation, imports, and diplomacy already points to two of the prime suspects in Hasanlu's destruction and to their motivations: Urartu and Assyria. In the 9th and 8th centuries BCE, Hasanlu was located at the crossroads of trade routes through the Zagros Mountains; these led to Assyria in the west, Urartu in the north, and Elam in the south. As Urartu and Assyria expanded in the early 1st millennium BCE, they both campaigned in northwestern Iran. The site of Hasanlu, predictably, was caught in the crossfire. Urartu and Assyria were not the only possible aggressors against Hasanlu, however. Before Urartu consolidated its territory, numerous small kingdoms vied for power in the mountains of Anatolia, Iran, and the Caucasus. Military campaigns led by the rulers of these kingdoms were annual affairs, occurring in the summer during the lull in the agricultural season.

Urartu, Menua, and Empire Building

The first suspect, Urartu, was identified by the excavators of Hasanlu as the most likely destroyer of Hasanlu. In the late 9th century BCE, Urartian kings campaigned widely in northwestern Iran, Armenia, and southeastern Turkey, pushing the borders of the empire ever outward. Ishpuini (ca. 828–810 BCE) and his son Menua (ca. 810–786 BCE) campaigned both separately and together (they ruled jointly for a time) in Armenia, Naxcivan, and northwest Iran, winning battles and building fortresses. In an inscription at Karagunduz, Turkey, they describe a campaign they undertook in northwest Iran, where they wreaked destruction and secured a huge booty. This account lavishes particular detail on the city of Meshta, which Mirjo Salvini, the foremost scholar of the Urartian language, believes was probably Hasanlu. Radiocarbon dates on grain and carbonized grapes stored in a kitchen of one of the elite houses on Hasanlu's citadel indicate that the attack probably occurred in the late 9th century, according well with a date of 800 or 810 BCE and linking it to these rulers. The archaeologist Michael Danti proposes this reconstruction based on a new study of the material accompanying the skeletons found with the Gold Bowl. He argues that weaponry indicates an origin in the north, probably in Urartu. In this case, several spiked maces (Fig. 9.16), unusual in other contexts at Hasanlu, might be the 9th century BCE equivalent of a smoking gun. Other weapons found on the citadel also have close links to examples known from the South Caucasus.

According to this scenario, Urartian soldiers rushed into the valley in the summer of 810 BCE, overcoming the local armies that were arrayed against them and decimating Hasanlu. Later, they constructed fortresses around the valley at Qalatgah, Tashtepe, Agrab, and, finally, at Hasanlu itself, consolidating their control over the area west

continued on page 258

Fig. 9.16 *Above*
A spiked mace head (59-4-175)
found at Hasanlu that may have
come from the South Caucasus.

Urartu

Lauren Ristvet

Assyria's greatest rival was Urartu, an empire that controlled the highland region where present-day Turkey, Iran, and Armenia meet. In the 2nd millennium BCE, this area was home to large numbers of fortress-states engaged in constant warfare. In the 9th century BCE, Assyrian military campaigns to the region probably encouraged these states to unite. By the latter part of the 8th century BCE, the Urartian king Sarduri I, (ca. 830 BCE) had established his capital at Tushpa (present-day Van, Turkey) and written his first royal inscription—in Assyrian. Later inscriptions were written in Urartian, a language related to Hurrian and perhaps also to languages spoken today in the Northern Caucasus of Russia. Urartian is difficult to read and the history of Urartu has more holes in it than that of Assyria. The dates of the kings' reigns are only known when they line up with events known to us from Assyria.

Located just to the north and east of Assyria, the landscape of Urartu is starkly different from the rolling plains characterizing the landscape of the former. Mountain ranges, including the Caucasus, bisect the area, creating small, isolated valleys; high volcanoes, like the perennially snow-covered Ararat, rise from basaltic plains; and the two largest lakes in the Middle East, Van and Urmia, border this area. From fall to spring, much of this territory is covered with snow and the mountain passes are blocked.

Large fortresses, situated atop hills adjacent to fertile land, were the administrative nodes of Urartu. Fortresses across Urartu look quite similar in plan, as do the pottery and luxury goods, such as metalwork and ivory, found within them. This region has always been culturally diverse;

Fig. 9S3.1 *Above*
Fragment (65-36-7) of a storage vessel with Urartian stamp seal impressions.

today, it is home to people speaking over 50 languages. This diversity was probably only greater in the past. The distinctive Urartian style of specific material goods, as well as the use of a common administrative language, may have helped to unite this fractious region (Fig. 9S3.1). Haldi, a warrior god whose temple was located near Urartu's border with Assyria, became the chief god of the royal family and army. Religion also played an important ideological and unifying role.

Urartu expanded from its heartland on the shores of Lake Van in the late 9th and early 8th centuries BCE, during a period of relative Assyrian weakness. Assyrian kings avoided direct contact with Urartu for decades, though wars broke out over the shifting alliances of vassals and were fought on territories between the two kingdoms in southeastern Turkey and northwestern Iran (Fig. 9S3.2). In 743 BCE, the Assyrian king Tiglath-pileser III (ca. 745–727 BCE) defeated a coalition led by the Urartian king Sarduri II (ca. 754–735 BCE) at Arpad in Syria; he subsequently pursued Sarduri II back to his capital, Tushpa.

Although the Assyrians were ultimately unable to penetrate the city, Assyrian interests were reasserted, and over the following years, many client kingdoms became provinces ruled by Assyrian governors. In 716, Rusa I of Urartu installed a figurehead ruler on the throne of Mannea, an area of western Iran south of Hasanlu that had been under Assyrian influence and was an important supplier of horses to the Assyrian army. The Assyrian king Sargon II (ca. 721–705 BCE) first replaced the Mannean king and then fought the Urartians near Lake Urmia before sacking the important temple of Haldi in Musasir. In a letter to the god Ashur, the chief god of Assyria, Sargon claimed this was a monumental victory. He exaggerated. The Urartian capital emerged mostly unscathed from its encounter with the Assyrians and was eventually restored to the Urartian sphere of influence. Assyria and Urartu established a wary détente. Invasions by the Scythians and the Medes subsequently served to fracture Urartu, and the remains of the kingdom were overtaken by the Medes in the early 6th century BCE.

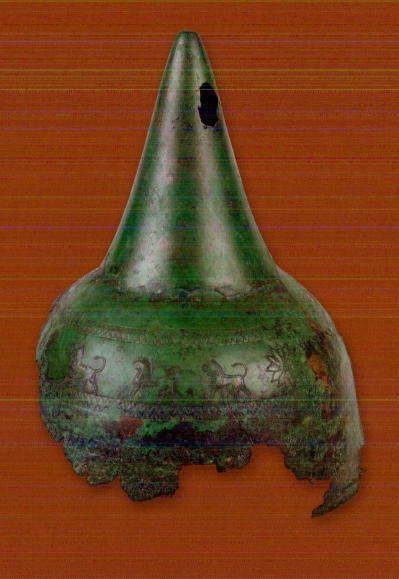

Fig. 9S3.2 *Above*
Urartian helmet (67-39-21), decorated with an incised frieze of animals and other symbols.

of Lake Urmia. King Menua left an inscription at Tashtepe, 40 km (25 miles) east of Hasanlu, indicating that he ruled the entire Ushnu-Solduz Valley by the early years of the 8th century BCE.

The Urartian kings Ishpuini and Menua make attractive villains, but the evidence remains equivocal. The spiked maceheads found with the bodies at Hasanlu, for example, are indeed known from the South Caucasus, but from an area that was never incorporated into Urartu. The same is true for most of the other weaponry. This discrepancy might be because most of the Urartian material known dates from more than a century after Hasanlu's destruction. In the late 9th century, as Urartu was consolidating, its soldiers may have wielded weaponry quite different from the standard 8th century and later weaponry that is known to contemporary scholars. Or this discrepancy may be due to the possibility that there were no Urartian soldiers in Hasanlu that day.

Assyrian Campaigns near Urmia

The inconsistencies in the reconstruction identifying the Urartians as the aggressors at Hasanlu have led some archaeologists to propose that Hasanlu's citadel fell instead to the Assyrian army. While radiocarbon dating points to a destruction date of approximately 800 BCE for Hasanlu, this technique cannot determine the exact calendar year in which the destruction occurred. It is possible, although not likely, that Hasanlu's destruction happened during the 8th century, as the archaeologist Peter Magee argues. A slightly different theory, but one also involving the Assyrians, has been proposed by Inna Medvedskaya of the Russian Academy of Sciences. She notes that Hasanlu's violent destruction does not fit in with the overall scenario of what happened when Urartu took over northwest Iran. Once the Urartians had conquered the valley, they invested in it heavily, building fortresses, canals, and gardens. They did not leave ruined hills behind. When the Assyrians campaigned in the region in 714 BCE, seeking to counter Urartu's further expansion, they would have encountered a land full of people; unlike the Urartians, however, they would have had no interest in maintaining the city. According to Medveskaya's reconstruction, then, Hasanlu underwent two phases of destruction. In the first, it was burned by the Urartians, but later it was rebuilt, adopting many Urartian features in the architecture of its public buildings, and flourished for a time. In the second phase, a result of Assyrian attack in 714 BCE, Hasanlu underwent its final destruction and subsequent abandonment. The Assyrian incursion and destruction forced Urartu to retract to the northern part of the lake, allowing for further Assyrian expansion to the south, in the areas of Ellipi and the Medes.

While there is no clear material evidence at Hasanlu for an Assyrian role in the destruction, pointed helmets, resembling those worn by Assyrian soldiers in palace reliefs

Fig. 9.17 *Left*
A helmet (61-5-352) found at Hasanlu of a type probably worn by both Urartian and Assyrian soldiers.

depicting warfare, have been found at the site (Fig. 9.17); some scholars have pointed out, however, that these could have been worn by Urartian soldiers. Medvedskaya has also argued that there are Urartian features in Hasanlu's architecture that could only have occurred in the 8th century following the area's conquest. It is worth noting that, at some time (probably several decades) after the second phase of destruction at Hasanlu, masons built a typical Urartian fortification wall; the second phase of destruction at Hasanlu was, thus, likely not as permanent as has sometimes been suggested. Finally, the vast majority of the radiocarbon dates for Hasanlu's second destruction level exclude the possibility of an 8th century attack, whether by Assyrians or anyone else, and also make an earlier 9th century attack unlikely.

Northern Attackers

The final possible perpetrators of the destruction at Hasanlu have perhaps the least support in the archaeological community. But as the mystery writer Agatha Christie, who spent years excavating at the Assyrian capital of Nimrud with her archaeologist husband Max Mallowan, might remind us, the least likely suspect is often the murderer. It is noteworthy that, despite having recovered the bodies of enemy soldiers and large numbers of their weapons from Hasanlu, and despite the fact that Assyrian and Urartian weaponry are better known than those of other groups and so might be more readily identifiable by archaeologists, we actually have no definitive proof that soldiers from either empire were present at Hasanlu's destruction. Instead, a recent study of all the weaponry at Hasanlu by the archaeometallurgists Christopher Thornton and Vincent Pigott shows that most of it comes from the Caucasus—particularly Azerbaijan and Georgia—and the Caspian rim. These regions remained outside of both Urartian and Assyrian control. Recent excavations have revealed that, before the rise of Urartu, the area of eastern Anatolia, the South Caucasus, and northwest Iran was characterized by several common cultural features but was politically fragmented. Violence was a persistent feature of the political landscape as the numerous kingdoms occupying that vast territory sought to expand or defend their holdings. This feature may have persisted even with the rise of the empires. Hasanlu could have fallen victim to a northeastern neighbor who, like its better-known Urartian and Assyrian counterparts, was seeking the wealth of the Gadar River (or Ushnu-Solduz) Valley. Such a scenario may be less interesting than an attack by either Assyria or Urartu, but it fits the archaeological evidence better.

Solving the Mystery

It has been more than forty years since the excavations at Hasanlu ended, but research on the town and the circumstances of its destruction continues. We know more now than we did ten years ago about the lives of the victims of Hasanlu, following a study of the skeletons. Individual objects like the Hasanlu Gold Bowl, which has received a great deal of attention since its discovery sixty years ago, have also benefited from reanalysis. Still, there is more work to be done to help confirm the specific date of the destruction at Hasanlu and to provide better information on both the victims and the perpetrators of that destruction. Will we ever solve the mystery of who attacked Hasanlu and why? Slow analysis of the existing remains, as well as further excavation of other sites of this time period in Iran, offers the hope of new information that may someday allow us to definitively identify the perpetrators of Hasanlu's destruction.

For Further Reading

Burney, Charles, and David Lang. 2001. *The Peoples of the Hills: Ancient Ararat and Caucasus*. Phoenix Press.

Danti, Michael. 2014. Hasanlu (Iran) Gold Bowl in Context: All that Glitters. *Antiquity* 88(341):791–804.

Dyson, Robert, Jr., and Mary Voigt, eds. 1989. East of Assyria: The Highland Settlement of Hasanlu. *Expedition* 31(2–3).

Dyson, Robert, Jr., and Mary Voigt. 2003. A Temple at Hasanlu. In *Yeki Bud, Yeki Nabud: Essays in Honor of William M. Sumner*, ed. Naomi F. Miller and Kamyar Abadi, pp. 219–236. Los Angeles: UCLA.

Frahm, Eckart, ed. 2017. *A Companion to Assyria*. Hoboken, NJ: Wiley Blackwell.

Magee, Peter, 2008. Deconstructing the Destruction of Hasanlu: Archaeology, Imperialism, and the Chronology of the Iranian Iron Age. *Iranica Antiqua* XLIII:89–106.

Medvedskaya, Inna, 1988. Who Destroyed Hasanlu IV? *Iran* 26:1–15.

Piotrovsky, Boris. 1969. *The Ancient Civilization of Urartu*. Spokane, WA: Cowles Book Co.

Radner, Karen. 2015. *Assyria: A Very Short Introduction*. Oxford: Oxford University Press.

Salvini, Mirjo. 2011. An Overview of Urartian History. In *Urartu: Transformations in the East*, ed. K. Koroglu and E. Konyar, pp. 74–101. Istanbul: YKY.

Selinsky, Page. 2009. Death, a Necessary end: Perspectives on Paleodemography and Aging from Hasanlu, Iran. PhD diss. University of Pennsylvania, Department of Anthropology, Philadelphia.

Thornton, Christopher, and Vincent Pigott. 2011. Blade Type Weaponry of Hasanlu Period IVB. In *People and Crafts at Hasanlu, Iran*, ed. M. De Schauensee, pp. 135–182. Philadelphia: University of Pennsylvania Museum of Archaeology and Anthropology.

10

THE CITY UNDER EMPIRE: NIPPUR FROM 1000 BCE–800 CE

Richard L. Zettler and William B. Hafford

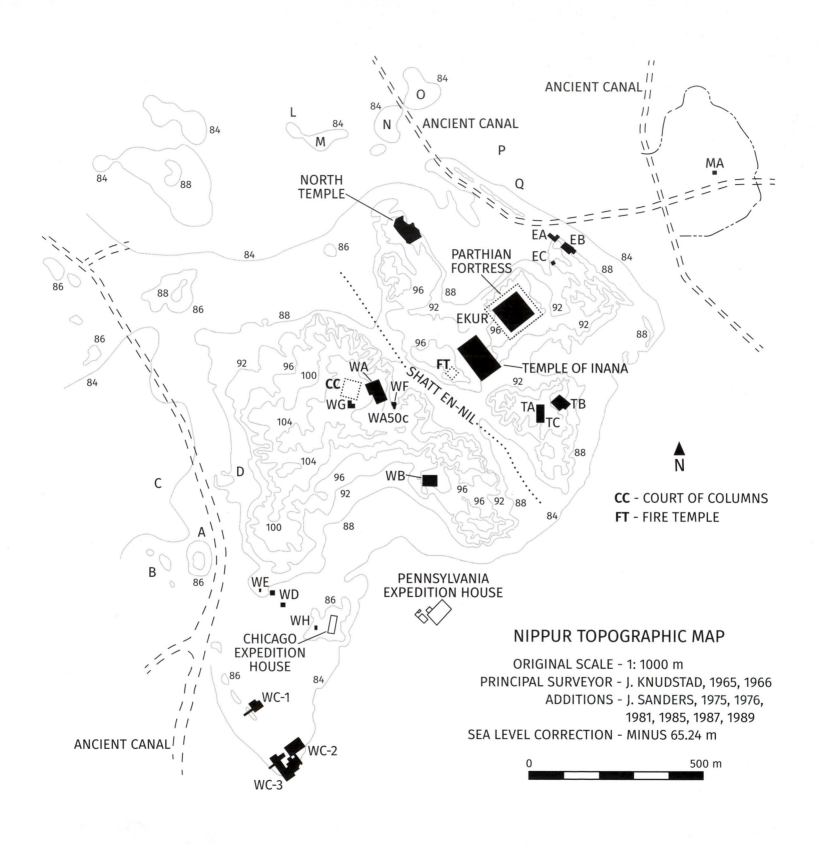

ANCIENT CANAL

84

O

L

84

N

84

ANCIENT CANAL

84

M

P

ANCIENT CANAL

Q

MA

84

NORTH TEMPLE

EA

EB

EC

84

84

88

PARTHIAN FORTRESS

96

88

92

92

EKUR

96

92

88

96

TEMPLE OF INANA

84

86

86

86

88

86

86

86

84

88

88

96

92

96

100

WA

CC

WF

WG

WA50c

FT

92

TA

TB

TC

SHATT EN-NIL

104

92

88

104

D

96

WB

96

92

N

C

100

88

96

92

88

CC - COURT OF COLUMNS

FT - FIRE TEMPLE

84

A

B

86

WE

WD

86

PENNSYLVANIA EXPEDITION HOUSE

WH

CHICAGO EXPEDITION HOUSE

NIPPUR TOPOGRAPHIC MAP

ORIGINAL SCALE - 1: 1000 m

PRINCIPAL SURVEYOR - J. KNUDSTAD, 1965, 1966

ADDITIONS - J. SANDERS, 1975, 1976, 1981, 1985, 1987, 1989

SEA LEVEL CORRECTION - MINUS 65.24 m

86

84

WC-1

ANCIENT CANAL

WC-2

0   500 m

WC-3

Introduction

As centuries passed and cities continued to fulfill their functions in support of state societies, organization, specialization, and population tended to grow—and so did the boundaries of the state. Expansion led to increased conflict at borders. Smaller states began to be absorbed into super-states, or, as they are better known, empires.

While the fundamental concept and functions of the city remained, some cities, such as Babylon, grew into particularly large centers for the administration of expanding empires. The hierarchy of place itself became more complex and varied, with farmland villages and smaller cities performing their functions in the hinterlands of what were developing into increasingly large cities and newly emergent mega-centers. Some cities near the edge of empire took on the role of gateway trading posts or caravan through-points and customs stations. Others served primarily as military strongholds intended to protect borders; the edges of empire, however, were fundamentally unstable. They might push outward, fragment, or even retract.

With the possible exception of Babylon, cities in southern Mesopotamia were no longer as central as they had been in the 3rd and 2nd millennia BCE. Nevertheless, urban populations generally expanded over the next two thousand years and various cities (at various times) gained a degree of imperial significance; they were especially important for their location on key trade routes linking east and west as the various empires of the 1st millennium BCE, and, later, 1st millennium CE, expanded. The cities came first under the control of the Neo-Assyrian (ca. 911–612 BCE), Neo-Babylonian (ca. 626–539 BCE), and Achaemenid Persian (ca. 550–330 BCE) empires. They were subsequently conquered by Alexander the Great (ca. 330 BCE) and, then, incorporated into the Seleucid Empire (ca. 305–63 BCE) that emerged following his death in 323 BCE. They later came under Parthian (ca. 247 BCE–224 CE) and Sasanian (ca. 224–651 CE) control from the east before eventually falling to the Muslim conquest in the aftermath of the Battle of Qadisiyah (636 CE).

Initially, the cities of southern Mesopotamia may have retained an archaic appeal that caused the great imperial powers to pay respect to old traditions, rebuilding and renewing many of the ancient temples and maintaining, adapting, or appropriating older cultural markers. At other times, however, the cities were largely ignored and were either depopulated or became centers of rebellion against distant imperial administrations.

This chapter will take as its case study the southern Mesopotamian city of Nippur between approximately 1000 BCE and 800 CE (Fig. 10.1). Nippur was important as an agricultural center and local market town, and its location in the center of the floodplain gave it a pivotal role both in trade and relations between northern and southern Mesopotamia. It was also one of only a few southern cities to survive the rise and fall of all of the empires that ruled southern Mesopotamia between the 1st millennium BCE

Fig. 10.1 *Opposite*

This topographic map of Nippur shows the location of the buildings first revealed by the Penn Museum excavations 1889–1900 as well as the areas excavated in the Post-World War II period (1960s–1980s). The Penn Museum and the University of Chicago conducted three seasons as a joint project before Penn withdrew. Nippur's eastern and western mounds are separated by the dried bed of a branch of the Euphrates River or a canal that is called the Shatt en-Nil. Map redrawn by Ardeth Anderson based on map courtesy of McGuire Gibson, Oriental Institute, University of Chicago.

and the 1st millennium CE. Extensive excavations by the Penn Museum at the site of the city have, consequently, provided a unique window into urban life as it unfolded across those many centuries.

Frontier Struggles: Nippur 911–539 BCE

As the seat of Enlil, chief god of the Sumerian pantheon, Nippur was an extremely important city in 3rd and 2nd millennium BCE southern Mesopotamia (see Chapter 4: Religion and the Gods). Though it was home to no particular dynasty, and though no king ruled directly from Nippur, all the kings of southern Mesopotamia paid homage to Enlil. They tended Nippur's temples and some rulers may even have been invested with their symbols of office there.

By 1200 BCE, Nippur had already lost much of its religious centrality. Other gods, particularly Babylon's god Marduk, gained primacy, and Babylon itself was the preeminent urban center of the south. From this point onwards, Nippur was among the many cities situated near the edge of emergent and growing empires, the heartlands of which were far from the southern Mesopotamian plains.

Successive emperors increased their domains and governed Nippur from afar. During the roughly 1,800 years covered in this chapter, Nippur fell under the sovereignty of seven major empires; it was also involved in at least two revolts or periods of turmoil, becoming associated with loosely autonomous states in these periods. Because of its size and location on important trade routes, the city maintained a certain amount of prominence, but its role within the larger structure of empire varied.

Near the end of the 2nd millennium BCE, the main Euphrates River flow moved down a western channel away from Nippur and the city's population fell drastically. Thus, from about 1225 to 755 BCE, Nippur's population remained relatively low and the city functioned largely as a religious and market center for pastoral tribes that had infiltrated the area in the early 1st millennium BCE. Its location on the edge of the major Chaldean and Aramean tribal territories of the south, combined with the return of waters down the central channel of the Euphrates around the turn of the 8th century BCE, allowed for population increase and caused the Neo-Assyrian kings, whose capital cities lay in northern Mesopotamia, in the vicinity of modern-day Mosul, to take interest. Archives of the governor of Nippur in the year 755 BCE show that the city was a growing center, one that would be important in Assyria's attempts to dominate the south.

The southern Mesopotamian floodplain was at this time a patchwork of semi-autonomous regions of shifting alliances; a similar configuration had been characteristic of the region in times past and would recur several times in the future. Nippur found itself in a unique position between the old cities of the north, the prosperous Chaldean tribes of the central Euphrates in the west, and the pastoral Arameans around the lower

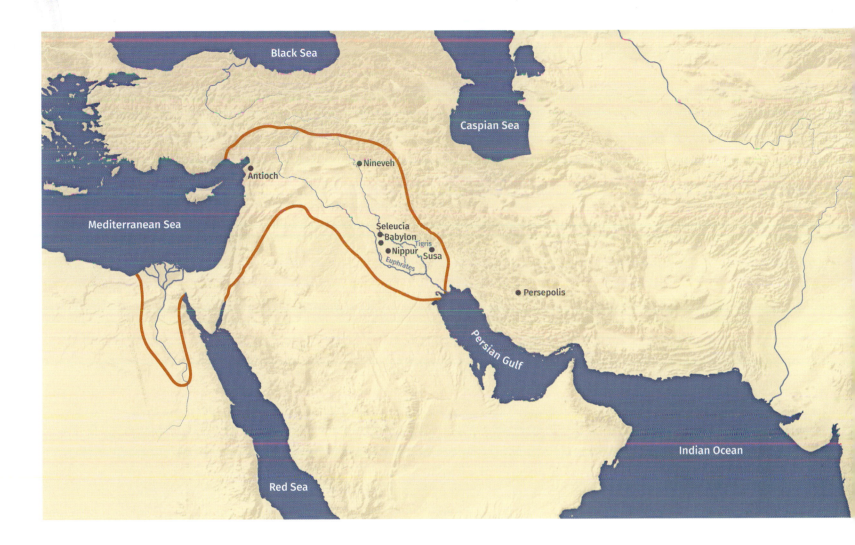

Black Sea

Caspian Sea

Nineveh

Antioch

Mediterranean Sea

Seleucia
Babylon
Tigris
Nippur
Euphrates
Susa

Persepolis

Persian Gulf

Indian Ocean

Red Sea

Fig. 10.2 *Above*

Approximate boundaries of the Neo-
Assyrian Empire under Ashurbanipal
(688–627 BCE).

Tigris to the southeast. The city was still remembered as a traditional cult center and, with the return of water, it once again became a significant producer of grain and wool. Furthermore, it had always been an important marketplace where producers, merchants, and consumers from many different cultures could meet.

For all of these reasons, Nippur was a desirable place to control and, in the years of the 8th and 7th centuries BCE, it fell sometimes under the control of the Assyrian Empire to the far north and, at other times, the Chaldean-led resistance. The Assyrian king Ashurbanipal (ca. 668–631 BCE) finally established stable sovereignty over Nippur in 651 BCE (Fig. 10.2).

Ashurbanipal reconstructed many of the long-neglected buildings at Nippur and left his inscriptions on numerous bricks. He restored the Ekur, Enlil's temple, and completed

continued on page 269

MARDUK, KING OF THE GODS

Philip Jones

Southern Mesopotamia was traditionally characterized by a disconnect between the centers of political power and the centers of religious power. Rulership or political hegemony was conceived as rotating in turn among a number of competing cities; this conceptualization is evident in a composition known as the Sumerian King List, which recorded the transfer of kingship from one city and dynasty to another from the era before the flood down to the early 2nd millennium BCE (see Chapter 4S1:s Kingship and the Gods).

From the time of Hammurabi onwards, however, Babylon became the permanent focus of political unity, in theory if not always in fact. At first, this had little effect on religious belief, as Hammurabi was happy to acknowledge the old divine order. Eventually, however, this political dominance began to turn into a religious one as well, particularly as the city of Nippur suffered a precipitous, albeit temporary, population decline in the mid-2nd millennium BCE. Subsequent to this decline, the ideological status previously accorded to Nippur and Enlil was transferred to Babylon and its patron god, Marduk (Fig. 10S1.1).

Marduk, importantly, was not just another version of Enlil; he was instead a different type of supreme god altogether. The famous myth, *Enuma elish*, better known as the *Babylonian Epic of Creation*, tells of how the first gods were formed from the mingling of two primordial bodies of water, the female Tiamat and the male Apsu. Soon, however, the gods grew numerous and noisy, disturbing the sleep of Apsu, and he plotted to destroy them. Apsu's plans were thwarted by the god Ea, who slew Apsu and made his home among the waters of his vanquished opponent. Tiamat, enraged at the slaying of her mate, created an army of terrifying monsters to wreak vengeance against her children, the gods. When the gods, faced with this army, proved too afraid to act, Ea's son Marduk offered to act as their champion against Tiamat, on the condition that the gods would acknowledge him as king on the success of his endeavor. After a momentous battle, Marduk slew Tiamat and created Heaven and Earth from her dismembered corpse. He then undertook a wholesale organization of the cosmos, of a type and scale that had never been attributed to Enlil. His fellow gods celebrated him by according him fifty names, which marked the sublimation of their powers into his person.

Enuma elish came to be read out annually at the most important festival of the year, the *akitu*—or New Year's festival—at Babylon. The composition, in addition to explaining Marduk's ascension to the kingship of the gods, also tasked him with the responsibility of feeding his fellow gods, a task that had previously been undertaken by the king. With Marduk acting as a royal god laying down a primordial blueprint for earthly life, there was no need for a divine king; Babylonian kings, consequently, became purely human figures.

Fig. 10S1.1 *Opposite*
The symbol of Marduk, the spade, on a boundary stone (*narû*) of Nebuchadnezzar I (29-20-1).

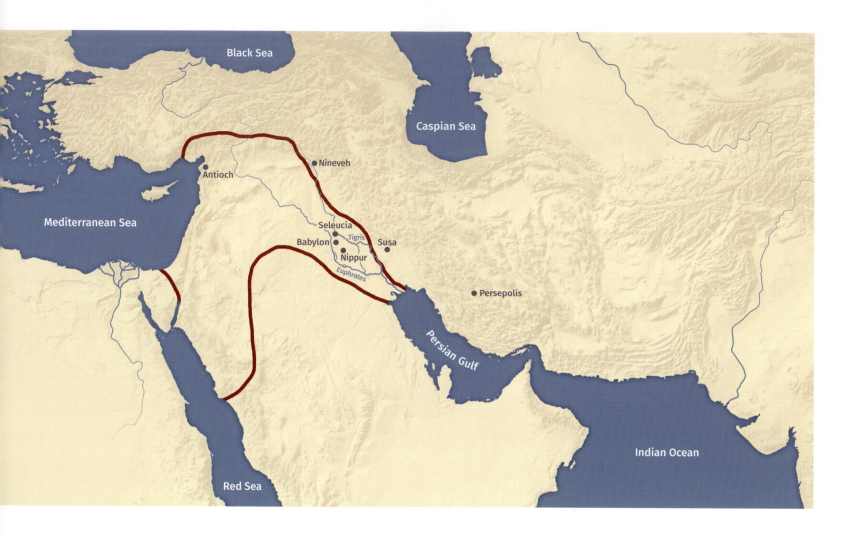

Black Sea

Caspian Sea

Mediterranean Sea

Antioch

Nineveh

Seleucia

Tigris

Babylon

Susa

Nippur

Euphrates

Persepolis

Persian Gulf

Indian Ocean

Red Sea

the work of his predecessor, the king Esarhaddon (ca. 680–669 BCE), on the temple of Inana, located just southwest of the Ekur. He also fortified the southern corner of the city and made Nippur a military outpost in Assyria's attempts to subdue the rest of the south. But stable Assyrian control would not last long.

The first ruler of the Neo-Babylonian dynasty, Nabopolassar (ca. 626–605 BCE), a self-proclaimed "son of a nobody," began his career as a high-ranking official of the Assyrian king, but eventually expelled the Assyrians from southern Mesopotamia, which was now known by the regional name Babylonia, in the late 7th century BCE. He took control of Nippur around 615 BCE. He then supported the armies of the Medes, a people based in northwest Iran, in their ongoing confrontation and destruction of the Assyrians and ultimately extended his control all the way to the Arabian oases and the border of Egypt (Fig. 10.3).

Fig. 10.3 *Above*
Approximate boundaries of the Neo-Babylonian Empire under Nebuchadnezzar II (605–562 BCE).

Though preoccupied with military activities, Nabopolassar expended considerable resources on Babylon. A bullet-shaped clay cylinder (Fig. 10.4), purchased in 1890 during the second expedition to Nippur, records an account of his reconstruction of the temple tower (ziggurat) of Marduk, the Etemenanki, the "house (temple), foundation platform of heaven and earth."

Nabopolassar's son and successor, Nebuchadnezzar II (ca. 604–562 BCE), is unquestionably the best known of the Neo-Babylonian kings. He continued and expanded his father's building program, and the city of Babylon that is described by the Greek historian Herodotus in his mid-5th century BCE *Histories*—the one that tourists see today, with its famous Ishtar Gate and central processional way—is largely his work. Like his father, Nebuchadnezzar also campaigned extensively in the west. The Hebrew Bible recounts his campaigns against Jerusalem in ca. 598/597 BCE, when Nebuchadnezzar conquered the city and deported the king (Jeconiah), his court, other prominent persons, and a large part of the population to Babylon. Nebuchadnezzar returned again a decade later following the revolt of Judah in 589 BCE, and laid siege to Jerusalem. The siege occasioned famine, and Nebuchadnezzar eventually captured and looted the city, dismantling its walls and setting fire to the royal palace and the temple.

Nippur functioned as a regional capital in the Neo-Babylonian Period, much as it had in the Neo-Assyrian Period. The kings of Babylon make no claims to have rebuilt or repaired Nippur's temples—perhaps in keeping with a deliberate effort to elevate Marduk and Babylon over Enlil and Nippur—and only houses, with their pottery, small finds, and occasional cuneiform tablets, attest to the city's occupation in the 7th and 6th centuries BCE.

Despite the lack of royal building activities, Nippur flourished as a participant in long-distance commerce under the Neo-Babylonian kings. Incense burners imitating those from South Arabia attest to the success of the newly domesticated camel in forming caravan trains across previously untraveled deserts, permitting the import of aromatics and other luxuries from afar. The city of Nippur in this period developed characteristics that would define it for centuries to come. Its position on the tribal frontier and on important trade routes would solidify it as a melting pot of peoples and ideas.

Economic Powerhouse: Nippur 539–330 BCE

The Achaemenid Persians, based in what is today Iran, ended Babylonian hegemony over Mesopotamia in 539 BCE when Cyrus II, known as Cyrus the Great, marched into Babylon. He took the title "King of Babylon and of the Lands" but changed little in the way of laws, allowing life in Mesopotamia to continue under the Achaemenid Empire much as it had in the preceding centuries. This may have changed after 486 BCE when Mesopotamian revolts led Xerxes (485–465 BCE) to place new controls on the region.

continued on page 273

Fig. 10.4 *Above*

Hollow, bullet-shaped clay cylinder (B9090) from Babylon recording the restoration of the temple tower Etemenanki by Nabopolassar (626–605 BCE), founder of the Neo-Babylonian dynasty. Etemenanki, "House (Temple), Foundation Platform of Heaven and the Netherworld," was the ziggurat, or temple tower, of the god Marduk in Babylon.

Expanding Neo-Babylonian Trade Relationships

William B. Hafford

With the expansion of empires came frequent military raids and acquired booty, but the influx of goods from such actions could not sustain a growing region. A longer-term solution arose from the expansion of trade networks, connections into a hinterland at the edges of growing imperial borders and across it to other states and empires.

Trade was vital to cities from their very beginnings. The opening of new routes through new technologies or stronger organizational capabilities, such as had occurred at the end of the 3rd millennium BCE (see Chapter 7S4: Trade), meant exposure to new materials and ideas along with increased prosperity for many inhabitants in the cities and across the network.

In the early 1st millennium BCE, new land routes opened across previously inaccessible deserts through the domestication of the dromedary (one-hump camel).

The two-humped Bactrian camel had been domesticated earlier (mid-3rd millennium BCE) in Central Asia, but was rarely seen in Mesopotamia, and the dromedary was more suited to the southern deserts (Fig. 10S2.1).

Not only could dromedaries traverse deserts successfully, but they could also carry far more than most other transport beasts. The standard donkey load was 90 kilograms (198 pounds), but the camel load more than doubled this to nearly 200 kilos (440 pounds).

Using camels, traders pushed well across the Syrian and Arabian deserts to reach new ports of call. The discovery of square incense burners in Neo-Babylonian contexts at Nippur attests to the existence of these far-flung trade networks. Some of the burners are made of clay in imitation of the South Arabian style. Others are made of stone and are inscribed with South Arabian script, showing that they originated in the area of modern-day Oman or Yemen. Along with these burners undoubtedly came frankincense and other exotic aromatics. In fact, inscriptions on stone burners (Fig. 10S2.2) often mention such sweet-smelling ingredients—a kind of incense recipe of the day.

Fig. 10S2.1 *Left*
This dromedary (one-hump camel) figurine (31-43-336), found at Ur and dating to around 650 BCE, is an indication of the domestication and importance of the dromedary in southern Mesopotamia.

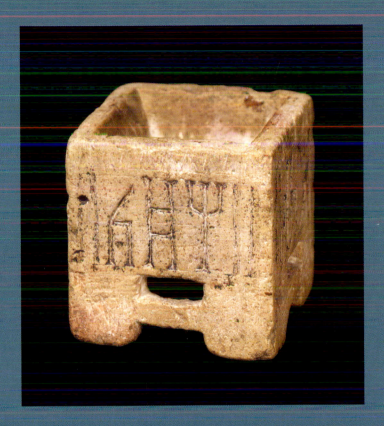

Fig. 10S2.2 *Above*
Limestone incense burner (30-47-31) made in
South Arabia (ca. 400–200 BCE). Deeply incised
South Arabian script is a key element of the
decoration, forming the word for an aromatic
plant on each face.

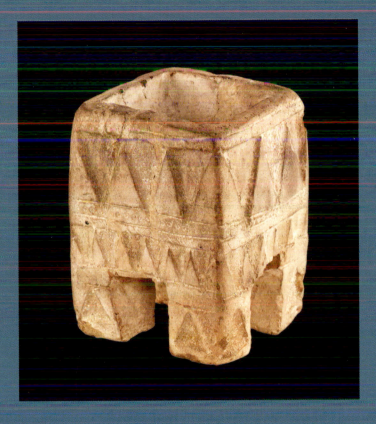

Fig. 10S2.3 *Above*
Clay incense burner (B15520) made in Mesopotamia.
The square shape and geometric decoration are
clear imitations of a South Arabian style showing
connections with that region. Soot and charring on
the interior shows its use in burning incense.

The importance of the trade network across the Arabian
Peninsula in the 1st millennium BCE (Fig. 10S2.3) is further
indicated by the fact that the Neo-Babylonian king Nabonidus
set up a royal residence in the Arabian city of Tema from
551–541 BCE. Some scholars suggest this represented a self-
imposed exile on the part of the king, but others hold that
the residence was established to secure an increasingly
important trade network.

In the early 1st millennium CE, competition for important
desert trade networks becomes clear with the success of
the major oasis city, Palmyra (Tadmor). The strength of
oasis cities, with power founded on their position on trade
networks, led to new dynamics including the weakening of
Parthian control of trade in that period. Such shifts in trade
balance may have played a role in the end of the Parthian
Empire itself.

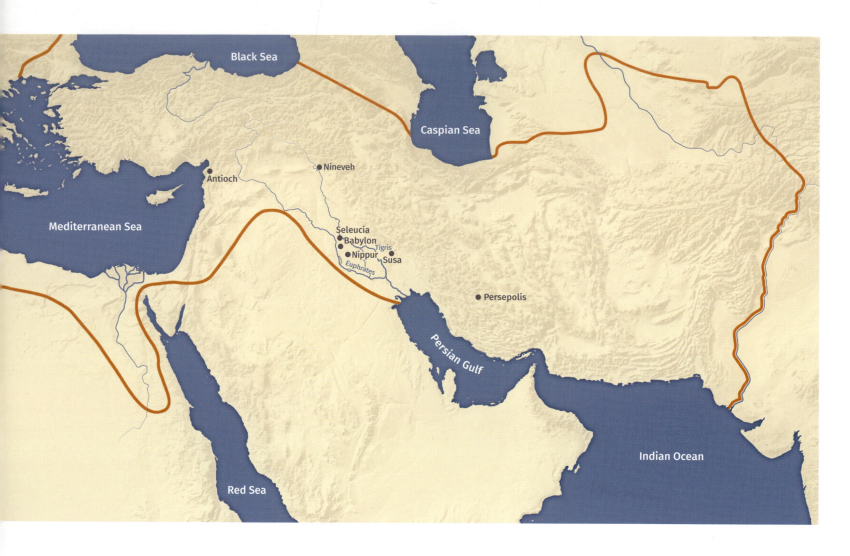

Black Sea

Caspian Sea

Nineveh

Antioch

Mediterranean Sea

Seleucia
Babylon
Tigris
Nippur
Euphrates
Susa

Persepolis

Persian Gulf

Red Sea

Indian Ocean

From this point on, the Persian ruler's title became solely "King of the Lands," reflecting the loss of Mesopotamia's prior status and autonomy in Persian political matters. It remained a wealthy region as a whole, particularly in crops and manufactured goods, but it was now more directly ruled by governors placed in its cities by the Achaemenid kings. The Persians, with their principal capital at Persepolis, near Shiraz in southwestern Iran, extended their empire farther than any previous imperial power (Fig. 10.5). The Achaemenid Empire ran from Turkey, Libya, and Egypt in the west to Pakistan and Uzbekistan in the east. It crosscut cultures and religions, an aspect reflected in many of its cities, Nippur not least among them. Artifacts from Nippur dating to this period include multilingual texts and objects from far-flung regions. A large alabastron (Fig. 10.6), purchased in London in 1888, at the time of the first expedition to Nippur, reflects the

Fig. 10.5 *Above*
Approximate boundaries of the Achaemenid Persian Empire at its height.

Fig. 10.6 *Right*

Alabaster jar (B10), said to be from Babylon, with the name of the Achaemenid Persian king Xerxes I (486–465 BCE) in four languages: Old Persian, Elamite and Akkadian in the cuneiform script and Egyptian in the hieroglyphic script. The inscription reads "Xerxes, the Great King."

Fig. 10.7 *Above*

Terracotta figurine (B9454) of the Egyptian bow-legged dwarf god Bes, a protective deity, especially associated with the protection of children and women in childbirth.

multicultural character of the Achaemenid Empire. It bears a quadrilingual inscription in Old Persian, Elamite, Babylonian Akkadian, and Egyptian hieroglyphs reading "Xerxes, the Great King." Artifacts from Egypt—a land Cyrus's son and successor, Cambyses, conquered in 525 BCE—such as the terracotta depicting the Egyptian deity Bes (Fig. 10.7), protector of women and children, appear at Nippur for the first time.

Yet, perhaps the most intriguing evidence for conditions in and around Nippur— and the region of Babylonia more generally—at the height of the Achaemenid Persian Empire in the second half of the 5th century BCE comes from an archive of cuneiform tablets recording the business activities of one Murashu family, which was essentially organized as a firm involved in land management. The tablets were found on Nippur's west mound, near Area WA (Fig. 10.1), in late May and early June 1893, at the beginning of the third archaeological expedition to the site.

When the Macedonian king Alexander III, commonly known as Alexander the Great (ca. 336–323 BCE), marched through Mesopotamia defeating the Persians, its cities acknowledged him as the new emperor; his reign, however, was short-lived. He died in Babylon in 323 BCE and the vast empire he had united through his conquests fragmented

continued on page 278

The Murashu Family

Grant Frame

In 1893, approximately 875 clay tablets and fragments were found at Nippur that describe the business activities of the sons and grandsons of one Murashu ("Wildcat") (Fig. 10S3.1). Dating between 454 and 404 BCE, during the reigns of the Persian kings Artaxerxes I, Darius II, and Artaxerxes II, the tablets were recovered from a single room of one house and are collectively known today as the Murashu archive. They deal mostly with agricultural contracting (e.g., land leases and receipts for rents and taxes paid) and the issuing of short-term loans secured by liens on land. Individuals who had been granted land by the state in return for the performance of military and/or labor service often leased the land to the Murashu family, which guaranteed the payment of taxes on the land and the performance of the required military and/or labor duties. Clients of such agricultural contracting included members of the middle class as well as high Persian officials and members of the royal family.

The archive provides insight into the Murashu family's business procedures, accounts, and assets. It serviced properties that on the whole belonged to others, functioning as a third-party manager, repository, and distributor of wealth. The family used six major and sixty minor canals as principal arteries of communication and administration to service more than 180 outlying settlements.

Approximately 95 of the tablets in the archive bear short notes in Aramaic in addition to the main text in Akkadian (Figs. 10S3.2 and 10S3.3). About one-third of the people mentioned in the tablets from the Murashu archive bear not Babylonian names, but rather Aramaic or other West Semitic (including Judaic), Iranian, or Anatolian names, indicating the mixed nature of the population in the Nippur area. Some of the individuals referenced in the Murashu tablets have names that include forms of the divine name Yahweh (e.g., Yahu-laqim and Yahu-natan), indicating their descent from the Judeans exiled to Babylonia by Nebuchadnezzar II (ca. 604–562 BCE) (Fig. 10S3.4).

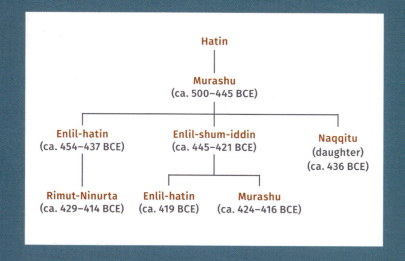

Fig. 10S3.1 *Above*

Murashu Family Tree (following Matthew W. Stolper). Four generations of the Murashu family are known, although the archive only attests to the activities of the last two generations. Note that the names of three members of the family include the divine name Enlil, who was the patron deity of Nippur as well as one of the most important gods of ancient Mesopotamia.

Fig. 10S3.2 *Right*

Some legal and administrative documents from ca. 725–400 BCE bear brief notes or summaries written in Aramaic, likely intended to aid in the retrieval of stored documents by individuals more familiar with the Aramaic script and language than with the cuneiform script and Akkadian language. The Aramaic notation on tablet B5503 states: "Document concerning the fields of the carpenters that Hiduri son of Habṣir gave to Ribat son of Bel-erib for rent." (The tablet is shown here with the Aramaic text right side up.)

Fig. 10S3.3 *Left*

Land could be assigned by the king to individuals on condition that they performed certain, normally military, duties. Here on tablet B5372 land assigned to makers of parchment or leather scrolls is placed under the control of Rimut-Ninurta of the Murashu family, who guaranteed the payment of the taxes and other obligations due for the land.

Fig. 10S3.4 *Right*

Composed in or after the 33rd year of the Persian king Artaxerxes I (432 BCE), tablet B13089 states that four people with Judean names (Mattan-Yama son of Amusheh, Shelimmu son of Yahu-laqim, Aqbi-Yama son of Bana-Yama, and Yahu-zabaddu son of Tubha) offer to supply Enlil-shum-iddin of the Murashu family with workers for one month to repay the debt they owe him. "Yahu" and "Yama" in the names represent the pronunciation of the name of the Hebrew god Yahweh. These were probably descendants of Judeans deported to Babylonia in the time of Nebuchadnezzar II.

Fig. 10S3.5 *Left*

Two stamp seal impressions are found the edge of tablet B5231; they confirm the presence of the two individuals as witnesses to the transaction recorded on the tablet. The short inscriptions on the edge tell us that they are the seals of Enlil-iddin and Ardiya. The impression at the top depicts a Persian hero (king), wearing a long pleated robe and a crown. He is grasping a rampant winged lion by the top of its head with his left hand and holding a dagger pointed diagonally upward towards the lion's abdomen in his right hand.

Fig. 10S3.6 *Right*

According to tablet B5267, in the first year of the Persian king Darius II (423 BCE), a law case was brought against Enlil-shum-iddin of the Murashu family by the official Bagadata, who claimed that Enlil-shum-iddin's servants had stolen silver, gold, cattle, and sheep belonging to him. Enlil-shum-iddin denied this, but gave him barley, wine, oxen, wool, and some other commodities to settle the dispute.

into territories ultimately taken over by his three principal generals, Antigonus, Seleucus, and Ptolemy. Legend has it that Alexander's last words were that his kingdom should go "to the strongest"; each of his generals seemingly recognized that description only in himself.

Return to Struggle: Nippur 305 BCE–224 CE

Despite the fragmentation of Alexander's empire, the three empires founded by his generals were significant in size. Seleucus I Nicator (305–281 BCE) took control of the largest and easternmost portion of the empire (Fig. 10.8), which stretched from the middle of Turkey to the edge of India. Initially, Babylon was Seleucus' primary city, but he subsequently enlarged a settlement farther north, near the confluence of the Diyala and Tigris Rivers, as a new capital. He called it Seleucia (also called Seleucia-on-the-Tigris to distinguish it from other cities called Seleucia), and it became the Seleucid capital. This marked a general shift to the Tigris from the Euphrates as the major waterway in Mesopotamia—for travel, commerce, and irrigation—and further reflects the shift of power to the north and east.

Southern Mesopotamia was at least partly neglected by the emperor. Though Nippur shows evidence of significant early Seleucid habitation—particularly in the number of coins dating to the 3rd and early 2nd centuries BCE found on the surface all over the site—it and the southern region fell gradually into turmoil. Various semi-autonomous polities began to spring up in the south in the last century BCE, and they incited revolts against the larger empire. A few copper coins of these semi-autonomous kingdoms have been found at Nippur, but there is little other evidence of late Seleucid occupation revealed by excavations in the city.

The Parthians, whose homeland was in northeastern Iran, took control of Mesopotamia around 141 BCE during the reign of Mithridates I (ca. 171–138 BCE). They founded a new capital, Ctesiphon, on the east bank of the Tigris River, opposite Seleucia, in the 1st century BCE (Fig. 10.9). Parthian control and interest in southern Mesopotamia fluctuated markedly in the first two hundred years under Parthian rule, and Nippur appears to have been sparsely populated from around 150 BCE to 50 CE. At roughly this time, Parthia was engaged in struggles with an expanding Rome and evidence suggests that the clashes depleted their treasuries; they reduced the silver content of their coinage substantially in the years 138–123 BCE.

Bolstered by apparent Parthian weakness, other kingdoms moved in on Parthian territory. Chief among these was the small but ambitious kingdom of Characene. With its capital Charax Spasinou, modern Naysan (also known as Jabal Khayaber), near the head of the Persian Gulf, Characene was well poised to take control of southern Mesopotamia. Around 137 BCE, the first king of Characene, Hyspaosines, joined forces with another

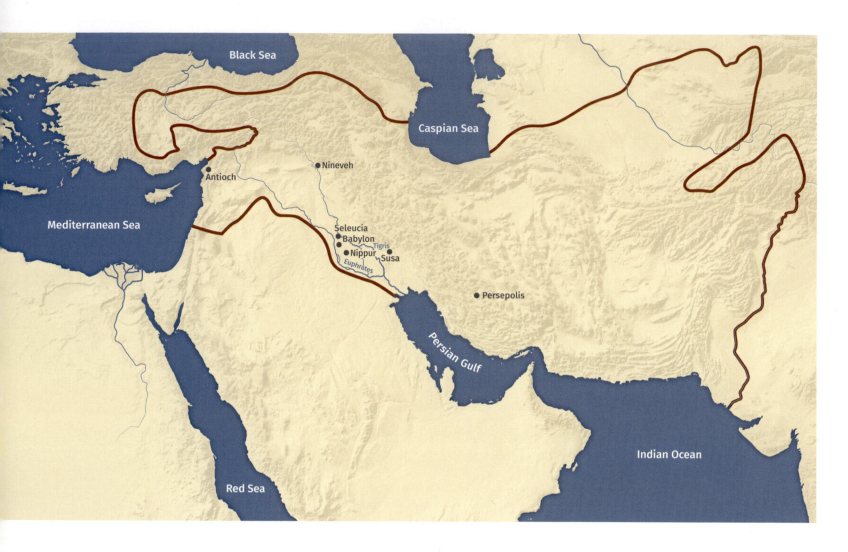

Fig. 10.8 *Above*
Approximate boundaries of the
Seleucid Empire at its greatest
extent in the early 3rd century BCE.

semi-autonomous kingdom, Elymais, and led an army into southern Mesopotamia. After this he likely held nominal control over Nippur, though there is little physical evidence for this.

Eventually the Parthian emperor Vologases I (ca. 51–78 CE) began to consolidate his control; he was particularly keen to gain unrestricted access to the Persian Gulf trade. Nippur became part of his "southern strategy" aimed at keeping Characene in check. Vologases ordered a massive fortress to be constructed at Nippur with the aim of making it a way-station and guard post that would house troops to stave off Characene's advances. Building the fortress at the highest part of the city, around the ziggurat on which had stood the venerable temple to Enlil, was a massive undertaking. The task included the digging of foundations as much as 5 meters (16 feet) deep to secure outer walls 3 to 5 meters (10 to 16 feet) thick.

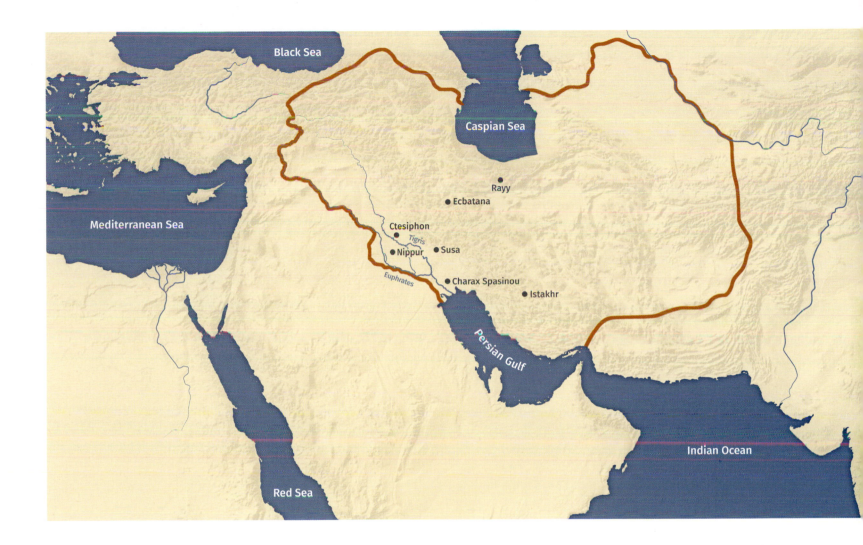

Black Sea

Caspian Sea

Mediterranean Sea

Rayy
• Ecbatana

Ctesiphon
Tigris
• Nippur • Susa
Euphrates
• Charax Spasinou
• Istakhr

Persian Gulf

Red Sea

Indian Ocean

Fig. 10.9 *Above*

Approximate boundaries of the Parthian Empire at its greatest extent in the time of Mithridates I (ca. 171–138 BCE.)

Because the Parthian building work at Nippur was so extensive and relatively late in Nippur's history, its remains covered much of the upper mounds; thus, finds from this period dominated the earliest excavations. In fact, many of the first artifacts uncovered at Nippur in the first season of excavation in 1889 were Parthian.

Evidence from the Parthian Period was uncovered at Nippur, not only in Penn's excavations in the late 19th century, but also in excavations conducted in the 1950s and 1960s. Three buildings in particular, the temple of Inana, the Court of Columns, and the Fortress, tell the story of the Parthians and their syncretistic approach to cities and life within them. They maintained some of the old traditions, rebuilding the temple of the goddess Inana that dated back to early 3rd millennium BCE. Next, they adapted architectural styles from other cultures, a practice particularly visible in the so-called

Court of Columns, a building so manifestly Greek in its influence that the excavators initially claimed it to be Mycenaean. Finally, they introduced Iranian traditions, including Persian-style halls known as *iwans*, in a late phase of their fortress.

These distinct architectural traditions, taken in combination with the finds recovered from within them, reflect the grand cultural mix in Nippur in the late Parthian era. Perhaps most recognizable are bone and clay figurines, some of the traditional Mesopotamian type, others more classically (Greek) influenced, and still others strongly Parthian in character. These latter are often of the horse and rider type (Fig. 10.10a–b), probably reflecting the Parthian warriors' proficiency with archery from horseback. There are equally varied pottery, stone, and metalworking traditions in evidence across the site as well.

A Symbol of Strength

The Parthian fortress was constructed around Nippur's ziggurat, the stepped temple tower originally built at the end of the third millennium BCE, probably over a still older temple platform. High ground is always important for military purposes, and what had been a religious edifice 2000 years prior now became a symbol of power and a lookout at the center of the fortification. The fortress was built and functioned in three phases over roughly a hundred years. Each phase expanded the scope and presence of the Parthian military in the southwestern extent of their empire, sending a message of strength to nearby kingdoms and securing trade networks into Parthia.

Though it was begun some thirteen years before his death, Vologases I did not survive to see the phase I fortress completed. The pressure he applied to Characene succeeded, however, and by 73 CE he may have established a Parthian governor in Charax itself. Vologases I died in 78 CE but construction on the Nippur fortress continued under his successor, Pacorus II (ca. 78–105 CE). A coin of this emperor was found on a floor of the first building phase, helping to date the later portion of that building phase around the year 83 CE (Fig. 10.11).

In the initial phase of construction (Figs. 10.12), the Parthian builders plastered over the decaying core of the ziggurat and constructed a massive terrace around it. They then enclosed the area with thick walls built atop the standing brickwork of Ekur's earlier enclosure. The walls had buttresses and circular towers at their corners. Evidence of temporary reed structures, probably houses for builders or other personnel, was found in the southern corner of the fortress.

In the second phase, begun around 90 CE, the builders reinforced the already substantial Phase I enclosure wall (Figs. 10.12). They encased the eroded core of the ziggurat's second and third stages in mudbrick and added rectangular projections to each

continued on page 285

Fig. 10.10 *Above*
Parthian terracotta figurines (B2625B and B15474) depicting a horse and rider wearing a hood (*bashlyk*). The bodies of the horse and rider were hand formed, while the face was pressed in a mold for added detail.

Fig. 10.11 *Above*

Silver coin (33-62-37) of the Parthian king Pacorus II (78–105 CE). The obverse shows the head of the king with a short beard due to his relative youth, facing left. The reverse shows a figure seated before a fire altar, turning a bow to light the sacred fire, and an inscription.

COINS IN THE NEAR EAST

William B. Hafford

While coins are first found in western Turkey in the late 7th century BCE, they did not become widespread in the ancient Near East until the Achaemenid Persian Empire starting in the late 6th century BCE. For at least two thousand years prior to the introduction of coins, the people of the ancient Near East used silver by weight to assess value; even after they became widespread, most coins continued to be weighed, much as circulating silver had been in earlier periods.

Early Persian coins have an image on one side, often that of the ruling king or emperor, and an impression of the punch that was used to force the metal into the engraved die on the other (Fig. 10S4.1). Coin makers rapidly moved to engrave the punch as well so that an image could be placed on both sides of the coin with each strike. The images appearing on coins tended to become more elaborate over time, and coins were subsequently used to spread messages pertaining to imperial power and religion (Fig. 10S4.2).

Fig. 10S4.1 *Left*
Gold daric (29-126-517) of the Persian Empire, showing Darius II (424–405 BCE) carrying a spear on the obverse and a deep punch mark on the reverse. This type of coin was often called an 'archer' (*toxótai* in Greek) because the king holds a bow along with his spear. The shape of this particular example, however, means the bow held out to the right of the king is not visible.

Fig. 10S4.2 *Left*
Silver drachma (33-62-2) showing Alexander the Great wearing a lion headdress, likening him to the hero Hercules after his defeat of the Nemean Lion. The reverse depicts Zeus with an eagle on his outstretched arm and bears Alexander's name in Greek. The coin was struck posthumously in Lampsacus, Turkey, ca. 310 BCE.

Coins are common finds in archaeological layers dating after their introduction and they greatly assist in dating the contexts in which they are found. They also provide an indication of the authority in control at a site and an impression of the site's density of inhabitation: small coins are often lost, and so the more stray coins of a period that are discovered, the greater the likely population. For example, many early Seleucid coins have been found scattered across Nippur, suggesting a large Seleucid population in the earlier part of the Seleucid Period (ca. 305–150 BCE); by the later Seleucid Period (ca. 150–64 BCE), when smaller semi-autonomous states were rising up around southern Mesopotamia, very few coins are known from the site (Fig. 10S4.3).

Fig. 10S4.3 *Above*
Silver drachma (33-62-9) showing Kamnaskires III and Anzaze. They reigned over the semi-autonomous state of Elymais from 82–76 BCE. Coins like this were found at Nippur in this time of struggle between minor states and the Parthian Empire.

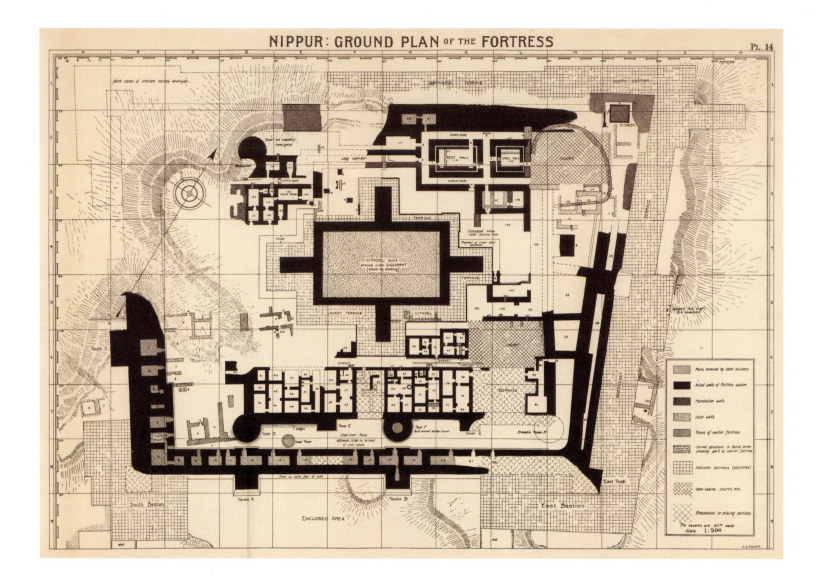

Fig. 10.12 *Above*
Ground plan of the Parthian Fortress at Nippur. Clarence S. Fisher, one of the architects who worked at Nippur in 1899–1900, plotted the three phases of the fortress's construction on a single plan (Clarence Fisher, *Excavations at Nippur* 1905: pl. 14).

side of the ziggurat to buttress the new tower. A well dug from the top of the northeast buttress implies substantial activity atop the new tower.

A string of small structures (Fig. 10.13) on the southeastern side of the enclosure probably functioned as apartments for personnel associated with the fortress. They were divided by a street with a drainage channel down its center from a second row of houses or storerooms closer to the ziggurat to the northwest. Most of the houses were small two- or three-room structures but one had six rooms, perhaps reflecting the importance of the individual who inhabited it. These humble buildings produced some of the most informative artifacts for Parthian life at Nippur.

Nº 56.

Fig. 10.13 *Above*

General view of one of the houses on the southeast side of the Parthian fortress in Phase II. The house includes the rooms numbered 73–80 on Fisher's plan of the fortress.

In 116 CE, the Roman Emperor Trajan clashed with Parthia but there is no evidence that Nippur was directly affected. Trajan did not succeed in his incursions and, afterwards, the silver content of Parthian coinage improved, reflecting a period of peace and increased trade. With growing Parthian strength and confidence came more grandiose plans for the Nippur fortress in Phase III, begun somewhere around 120 CE. In the third phase of construction (Fig. 10.12), the builders expanded the fortress and ziggurat to a greater extent than ever before. They created an enlarged terrace by razing some of the old buildings and filling in beyond them. They then constructed a massive new outer enclosure wall (Fig. 10.14), with interior rooms accessed from the fortress, at

Fig. 10.14 *Left*
Parthian fortress looking from the top of the old ziggurat to the southeast. The massive mudbrick wall in the background is the outer enclosure wall of the latest phase of fortress construction. The wall was set in a wide foundation trench. The doorways at the top of the wall led into small interior rooms.

the edge of the terrace. The new wall, set in wide foundation trenches, enclosed an area twice as large as the Phase II fortress.

Most of the apartments in the southern portion of the fortress continued in use but to the north of the old ziggurat two monumental halls were constructed whose use and layout are not completely clear due to heavy erosion. They consist of large open spaces surrounded by thick double walls; one contained evidence of a hearth. An outer corridor joins both halls, surrounded by a third outer wall. These may have been gathering places for ceremonies. One was likely to have been a larger courtyard shown on the ground plan of the Parthian Fortress published by Clarence Fisher, one of two architects who worked at Nippur in 1899–1900. Edward Keall, an archaeologist at the University of Toronto and Royal Ontario Museum, has closely examined the evidence and reconstructs a court with four small annexes, or *iwans*, used as special reception areas. Such a structure has a close parallel in the north Mesopotamian city of Ashur under Parthian rule and reflects a classic Iranian monumental hall design.

The three fortress phases described above were not completely discrete; rather, one phase morphed into the next and construction was almost continuous. The extant evidence implies that no phase was truly complete before the next began. Yet, around 165 CE, the attention dedicated to the fortress began to fade. Parthia had once again

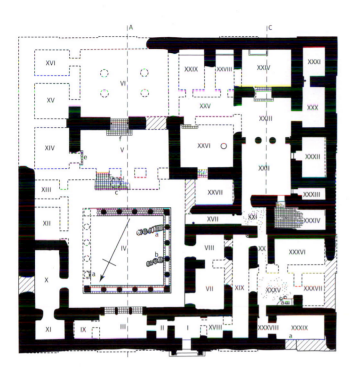

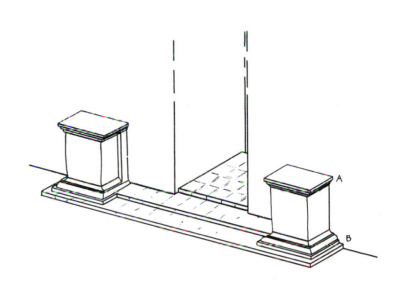

Fig. 10.15 *Above*

Plan of the Parthian building with a peristyle courtyard or "Court of Columns," with excavated walls (or portions of walls) shown in solid black and reconstructed walls hatched or dotted. After Fisher 1904: plate XIV. Redrawn by Ardeth Anderson.

Fig. 10.16 *Above Right*

Reconstruction of the main entrance in the northwest wall of the Parthian building with a peristyle court. The doorway was flanked by pedestals with molded bases and crowns.

run into political and financial strife, primarily due to Palmyra's success in the caravan trade surpassing its own territories' ability to compete. Vologases IV (ca. 147–191 CE) attempted to rectify the situation with military action around 162 CE. He failed. A Roman counterattack led by the general Avidius Cassius in 165 CE led to the destruction of Seleucia-on-the-Tigris and the burning of the palace at Ctesiphon. Vologases sued for peace, ceding much of northern Mesopotamia to Rome. Parthian silver coinage fell to an all-time low in terms of actual silver content as the economy all but collapsed.

This tremendous defeat signaled the beginning of the end for Parthia and the scaling back and eventual abandonment of the fortress at Nippur. In fact, the site literally became a graveyard; excavators found late Parthian clay coffins cutting into and through various parts of the fortress plan.

Influence from Afar

The layout of the structure that the early excavators termed the Court of Columns, located on Nippur's west mound, between Area WA and Area WG (Fig. 10.1), shows clear Greek influence. The building measures 50 by 50 meters (164 by 164 feet) (Fig.

Fig. 10.17 *Left*

Courtyard IV of the Parthian building with a peristyle courtyard from the southeast.

10.15), and the outer walls on three sides are decorated with shallow pilasters. The main entrance in the northwest wall is ca. 1.7 meters (5.5 feet) wide and flanked by pedestals with molded bases and crowns (Fig. 10.16). It leads through a series of small rooms into a peristyle courtyard (IV) whose columns would have supported a roof with the center open to the sky (Fig. 10.17). The columns stood 4 meters (13 feet) high, tapering from the base to the top that supported clay capitals in the Greek Doric style. Still more Greek in design is the inclusion of a suite of rooms with a megaron plan in the southern corner of the building. It consists of a wide rectangular hall (XXII–XXIII) with two central columns between rectangular engaged piers. The hall leads up a single step into another room (XXIV) of apparent importance. Such constructions often appear in Greek temples and palaces from as early as the Mycenaean Period in the late 2nd millennium BCE.

The original excavators thought they might have discovered a Mycenaean building, but most archaeologists have dated the structure to the Seleucid era (ca. 305–63 BCE). More recently, McGuire Gibson, who directed the University of Chicago's excavations at Nippur from 1972–1989, argued convincingly that the Parthians built the Court of Columns at roughly the same time as the first phase of the fortress. Gibson discovered the foundation trench for the building, cutting into older Seleucid levels or strata, in excavations nearby in the late 1980s, and he noted that the extensive foundation walls for the villa were cantilevered inward like the foundations of other Parthian buildings at Nippur. The Seleucids were still active in the early Parthian Period and semi-autonomous states related to or allied with them functioned at this time on the Parthian borders. At times, they incited revolts in southern Mesopotamia, being particularly successful around 90–55 BCE. A few coins of these semi-independent kingdoms have been found at Nippur and Greek influence here should not come as a surprise. Furthermore, the Parthians themselves adapted many designs and technologies from other cultures, so even though the building does not appear to have been directly created by Greek peoples, it is still not completely out of place.

The exact function of the Court of Columns complex is not known, but it was clearly important. It has been described as a palace and this may not be far from the truth. The megaron hall, placed as it is in a relatively secluded corner of the building, might even be seen as a throne room. Its isolation, however, led Fisher to interpret it as the women's quarters.

Whatever the function of the court of columns, the building fell out of use fairly quickly, perhaps during the period of the second fortress phase. Its columns were found collapsed in long strings of clay brick drums and its walls worn down, covered by layers of soil. Some 5 meters (16 feet) of fill lay atop it and many graves of the later Parthian Period were cut into the fill.

Survival of Old Traditions

Many of the coffins found above the Court of Columns and elsewhere were decorated with molded figures of nude females, arguably representing the goddess Nanai, identified with the old Sumerian goddess Inana. Confirmation of the goddess's ongoing importance in the Parthian era is shown by the rebuilding of the temple dedicated to her at roughly the same time as the first phase of construction on the fortress began.

By the early 1st century CE, the old temple, located just southwest of the ziggurat, was largely in ruins. The Assyrian king Assurbanipal sponsored the last known repairs in the 7th century BCE; though the temple is mentioned in a Neo-Babylonian text, no physical evidence of the building in that time period survives. The Parthians were faced with the difficult task of repairing or completely rebuilding a decaying structure, and they undertook the latter with zeal. They leveled the mounded ruins on the site of the old temple and dug down deeply into the earlier remains, wiping out all but the front wall of temple buildings dating to the 2nd and 1st millennia BCE and leveling most of the temple constructed by the Ur III king Shulgi in the late 3rd millennium BCE to its foundations. The Parthians then laid out a massive rectangular retaining wall on the site,

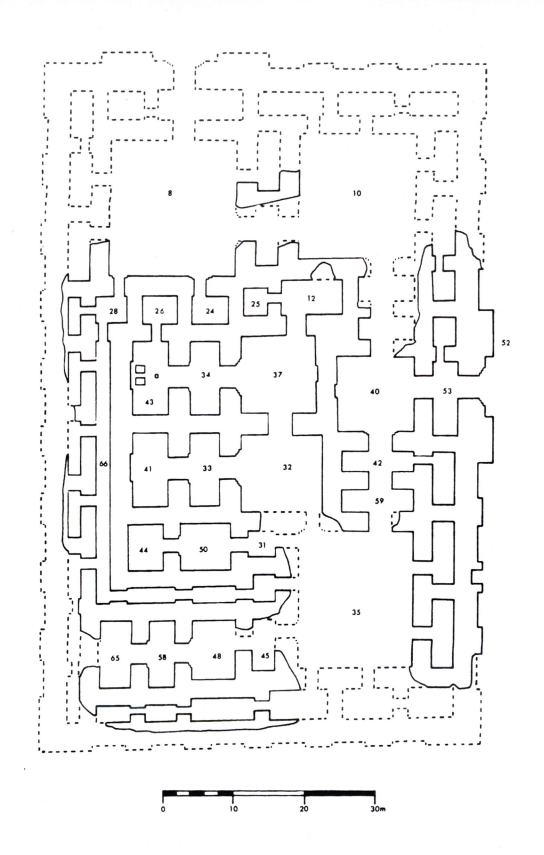

Fig. 10.18 *Opposite Page*

Plan of the Parthian rebuilding of the temple of Inana.

Fig. 10.19 *Above*

Archaeological remains of the Parthian Inana temple, seen from the east-northeast. Courtesy of McGuire Gibson, Oriental Institute, University of Chicago.

which they packed with 2–3 meters (6.5–10 feet) of debris from the old temples they had cut away, both from that site and from other sites nearby. Their foundation platform created a stable footing for their new temple.

The building was apparently in use for a long period of time, with as many as seven floors accumulating in most rooms to a depth of 3 meters (10 feet). Along with these changes in floor level, there were accompanying minor restructurings or repairs to the building, but the overall ground plan remained stable throughout, demonstrating consistent usage.

The building was enormous, measuring 70 by 100 meters (230 by 328 feet) (Figs. 10.18 and 10.19) and included a series of courtyards and rooms leading to two nearly identical sanctuary complexes laid side by side. The double sanctuaries were in keeping with a longstanding architectural peculiarity of much earlier versions of the temple. A series of elongated halls that surrounded the sanctuaries is highly reminiscent of elements of traditional Neo-Babylonian temples at Babylon.

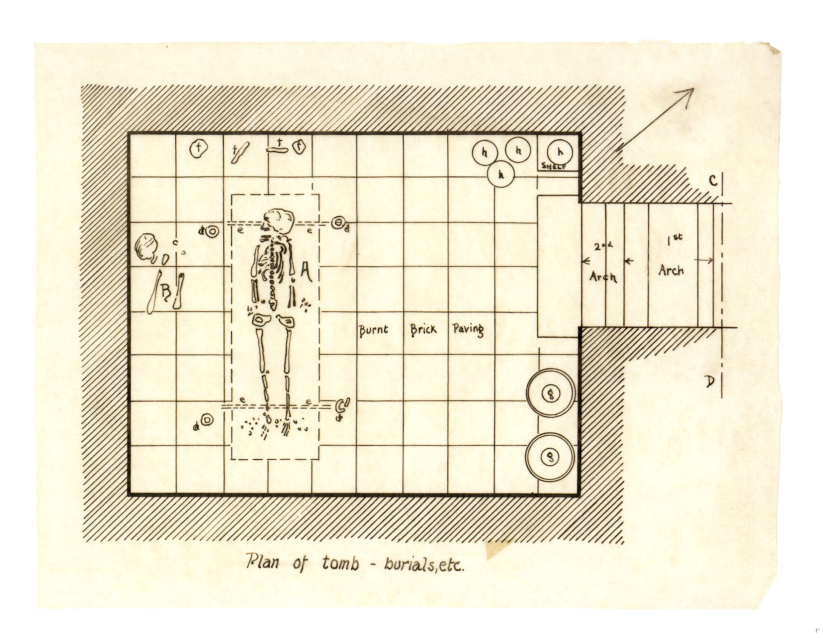

Plan of tomb - burials, etc.

Fig. 10.20 *Above*
Plan of the vaulted tomb chamber below Room 6 in the outer enclosure wall of the Parthian fortress Phase III.

Parthian Burial Customs

The inhabitants of the southern floodplain during the Parthian era buried their dead in a variety of ways, possibly reflecting the diverse beliefs of the peoples in the Parthian Empire (and within empires generally) who lived side-by-side in its urban centers. The burials range from pot burials to vaulted chamber tombs, with many other types between.

Perhaps the richest grave discovered at Nippur was a vaulted tomb chamber made of baked brick located beneath a floor in one of the rooms in the outer enclosure wall of the Phase III fortress (Fig. 10.20). A flight of steps provided access down to the grave's entrance.

Within the tomb chamber were the skeletons of two males, both apparently of high rank, located side by side on the brick floor. Both skeletons had been damaged by plaster falling from the roof of the chamber but the one nearest the entrance was apparently somewhat protected by the wooden coffin in which it was buried and, so, was somewhat better preserved. The wood of the coffin had decomposed, leaving nails and metal fittings on the floor.

A square sheet of hammered gold, roughly the size of the face, and a scalloped gold headband were found near each of the two skulls. The skeletons had two barrel-shaped gold beads found near the waist, perhaps originally placed on cinctures, or belts with tassels. One was found with a total of 48 small gold buttons and twelve larger rosettes, originally attached as decorative elements to his garment, and gold shoe buckles at his feet. The buckles were decorated with lions' heads in high relief enameled with turquoise and set with rubies. A small gold ring and a gold coin were also found in the chamber. The gold coin, found near the head of the more intact skeleton, was from the time of the Roman Emperor Tiberius (14–37 CE) and was much older than the burial, perhaps a family heirloom. The chamber also included four pottery bowls on a small shelf and two large jars on the floor near the east corner.

Despite occasional finds like these, grave goods were not common in the Parthian Period, at least not on the bodies themselves. Some goods, especially pottery, were often found near the bodies or outside the coffin, when one was present. The most common type of coffin—characteristic of Nippur in the Parthian era—is the so-called slipper coffin, named for its peculiar shape, with a wide opening at the head narrowing towards the feet, which generally resembles a giant slipper (Fig. 10.21). Measuring up to 2 meters (6.5 feet) in length and weighing as much as 100 kilograms (or 220 pounds), these coffins were made of clay, decorated with various designs, and sometimes glazed a dark green color.

Figural decoration on slipper coffins most often occurs in panels separated by rope patterns. While the raised clay rope motif may be indicative of actual ropes used to secure or move coffins, the particular imagery within the panels may be more an expression of personal or familial belief. Many slipper coffins at the city of Uruk (located near

Fig. 10.21 *Left and Below*
Green glazed slipper coffin (B9220) with molded relief decoration featuring four nude females set in rectangular panels formed by rope-like bands. The females have elongated necks; the left arm bent with the hand on the abdomen and the right arm straight at the side with the hand on the hip. The rectangular head of the molding around the opening is decorated with stamped concentric circles in two corner panels formed by rope-like bands.

121.

Samawah, ca. 120 km [74.5 miles] south of Nippur) display Parthian warriors impressed into the clay with a stamp, but most at Nippur depict molded nude women (Fig. 10.21). Apart from a large opening at the head, many slipper coffins also have a small opening at the foot. This may have facilitated firing the coffin, allowing heat to run more completely through the coffin's length for a more even result. It may also have facilitated the positioning of the body inside. The typical position of the deceased was flat on his or her back with hands at the sides or crossed over the pelvis or stomach. The legs were usually crossed at the ankle and, in three known cases at Nippur, rope remains were preserved around the leg bones (Fig. 10.22). The rope seems to have been tied around the legs of the corpse and then threaded through the hole at the foot of the clay coffin. The body could then be pulled inside. Not all slipper coffins, however, have a hole at the foot and in these cases the rope method could not have been used.

After the body was placed, the opening at the head was covered with a specially made oval lid or simply covered over with pottery sherds or mudbricks. It was also common to

IV. N. 81

Fig. 10.23 *Left*
Slipper coffins near the Shatt en-Nil
arranged parallel to one another and
stacked at right angles as if they had
originally been placed beneath the
floor of a square or rectangular room.

place a large jar over the opening. This jar sometimes contained the bones of yet another, probably related, burial. The different methods of covering and decorating the coffins may be indicative of their owners' social status or wealth.

Most slipper coffins contained a single body, probably wrapped in a shroud, as is indicated by trace preservation of cloth on the head, hips, legs, and feet. Some 53 (roughly ten percent) of the coffins found at Nippur, however, contained the remains of two or more individuals. The coffins are so narrow that inserting one body would be problematic enough; two would be a tight squeeze indeed. When more than two bodies are found in a coffin, this almost certainly indicates reuse of the coffin. The bones of one of the bodies in such cases are gathered near the large opening rather than being articulated as a whole, and sometimes only the skull of the earlier body is present.

Although commonly found at Nippur, it remains unclear whether Parthian burials were solely located beneath building floors or also placed in specifically designated

Fig. 10.24 *Above*
Group of six slipper coffins discovered over the western rooms of the Parthian building with a peristyle court, April 7, 1900.

Fig. 10.25 *Above*
Approximate boundaries of the core region controlled by the Sasanian Empire during the 3rd century CE.

cemeteries. There are indications of intramural burial, as coffins have been found beneath or alongside walls. Even when no walls are apparent, coffins are often found parallel to one another or stacked at right angles in squares, as if they were originally placed beneath the floor of a square or rectangular room (Fig. 10.23).

The most densely packed and often best-preserved group of Parthian graves was discovered above the remains of the Court of Columns (Fig. 10.24). This building had gone out of use probably in the middle of the Parthian occupation of Nippur and the area may have become a designated burial ground with no buildings. Some 5 meters (16 feet) of fill with numerous intrusive burials covered the floors of the Court of Columns. The burials included numerous slipper coffins, brick-built chamber tombs, and even a chamber tomb with a slipper coffin inside it.

An Imperial Breadbasket: Nippur 224–651 CE

As Parthia's might faded in the late 1st and early 2nd centuries CE, a client kingdom centered at Istakhr in Fars Province, southwestern Iran, rose to prominence and rebelled against the Parthian King of Kings. Named for its ruling dynasty, the House of Sasan

Fig. 10.26 *Right*

Six incantation bowls in situ under the floor of a house on Nippur's west mound, near the Parthian building with a peristyle courtyard, the so-called Court of Columns, March 20, 1900.

became the Sasanian Empire (Fig. 10.25) from the reign of the king Ardashir I (ca. 224–241 CE).

The Sasanians occupied Ctesiphon, the Parthian capital, but the only remaining Sasanian construction there is the Taq-i Kisra (or Iwan of Khusrau), a monumental vault or archway. The Sasanians invested heavily in Mesopotamia, rebuilding old cites and founding new ones like Veh Ardishir, which they situated south of abandoned Seleucia and across the Tigris River from Ctesiphon. They also constructed a new, highly sophisticated, and interconnected canal network, completing the shift to systemic dependence on the Tigris rather than the Euphrates River for travel and irrigation. The new network required a high order of management and upkeep, but the Tigris had the benefit of being navigable much farther up the plain than the Euphrates.

Average population had been steadily increasing across Mesopotamia for millennia prior to its peak in the early Sasanian Period. The survey work conducted by Robert McCormick Adams suggested as much as a nine-fold increase in the number of urban sites (defined as larger than 10 hectares [25 acres] in size) during the Parthian Period and into the Sasanian Period. With increased irrigation supplementing an already extensive crop yield, Mesopotamia became a breadbasket for the expanding Sasanian Empire—an empire that reached greater extents than most of those that preceded it.

At Nippur, a major part of the settlement seems to have been located on the west mound, where Sasanian houses are common. One of the most characteristic elements of these houses is the presence of incantation bowls beneath their floors (Fig. 10.26). The bowls are always placed upside-down so that their openings lie against the ground. The

continued on page 305

INCANTATION BOWLS

Grant Frame

Incantation bowls, also called demon or magic bowls, are wheel-made clay bowls intended to trap demons (e.g., Lilith), ward off illness and the evil eye, and prevent harm to people and property (Fig. 10S5.1). They have been found at many sites in Mesopotamia, but are especially well known from 5th to 8th century CE contexts at Nippur, Babylon, and Cutha. Used by Jews, Christians, Mandeans, and even Manicheans, the bowls were often placed face down under thresholds, in the corners of rooms and courtyards, and in cemeteries. The interior designs of the bowls are often striking: ink inscriptions generally spiral around central images of demons or other creatures. Some demons are shown chained, explicitly indicating what the bowls were meant to do: trap harmful spirits so they could not hurt the inhabitants of the house (Figs. 10S5.2 and 10S5.3). Most of the inscriptions are in the Aramaic language (Jewish Aramaic, Syriac, or Mandaic), but a few are written in Pahlavi and many others in pseudo-scripts (Fig. 10S5.4).

Belief in the protective properties of these bowls was widespread; almost every Sasanian Period house excavated at Nippur had at least one, and some as many as six, buried beneath their floors or under thresholds. Moreover, the use of the bowls expanded beyond the Sasanian era into the early Islamic, as noted by the association of some with Kufic coins of the early Islamic Period (Kufic is the earliest form of Arabic calligraphy).

The inscriptions on the bowls include incantations to bind demons; mention the names of angels, demons, Babylonian and Iranian deities, rabbis, and even Yahweh or Jesus; use legal terminology, especially as drawn from writs of divorce, to expel demons from the house; or cite biblical passages in Hebrew or Aramaic. The name of the individual commissioning a bowl is normally mentioned within the text (Fig. 10S5.5).

The scholar Christa Müller-Kessler translates the text on one incantation bowl (B2945) as follows:

"Again, I, Pabaq son of Kupitay, went with my own might, with my net-like body of iron, my skull of iron, my body of pure fire, and I was clad in a garment of pure and forged steel, and I was strong through the One who had created heaven and earth. (At that time) I went and met with the evil enemies and the rebellious adversaries, and said to them, "If you harm Abuna son of Garibta and Bayba son of Yawitay, I shall put a spell of the sea and a spell of the sea snake Leviathan upon you. If you harm Abuna bar Garibta and his spouse and his children, I shall bend you like a bow and span you like a bowstring. Again, (if) you do some harm to the house of Papaq and his possession and his household, I, Abuna bar Garibta, or Bayba bar Yawita shall put a ban, a decree and an anathema upon you by my own doing, which were (already) put upon Mount Hermon and the sea snake Leviathan, and Sodom and Gomorrah on account of subduing Dews, I, Abuna bar Garibta, and all evil mysteries, and the tongue of the raging Humartas (as well)." (At that time) I went and met with Shedas and Dews, the evil Mabkaltas, male idol-gods and female goddesses, <as> they were getting ready to set themselves up in rank and file…"

Fig. 10S5.1 *Opposite*
This incantation bowl (B16023) may depict a bound Lilith, a dangerous demon of the night in Jewish mythology and one of the demons exorcised in the incantation on the bowl. The incantation also invokes the archangels Gabriel, Michael, and Raphael for protection.

Fig. 10S5.2 *Left*
The image on this incantation bowl (B2965A) depicts a demon whose legs have been chained together. The incantations on these bowls attempt to bind demons and thus prevent them from harming the person or persons named on the bowls.

Fig. 10S5.3 *Right*
This incantation bowl (B2945) depicts two demons, the legs of one of them are shown bound and the arms of the other are fettered. Unusually, the inscription on this bowl continued onto a second bowl.

Fig. 10S5.4 *Right*
Most of the incantation bowls have their inscriptions written in Aramaic square script, but some are written in Mandaic or Syriac script. In addition, some bowls, as in the case of the one (B16002) depicted here, use a meaningless pseudo-script.

Fig. 10S5.5 *Left*
The inscription begins in the center of this incantation bowl (B16108) and spirals outward toward the rim of the bowl in a clockwise direction. Other bowls may begin near the rim and spiral inwards towards the center.

interiors are painted with symbols and script that identify them as mystic emplacements to trap evil spirits.

Incantation bowls were used by people of many different languages and cultures. Some of the first discovered were written in Judeo-Aramaic, which the excavators took to be Hebrew; thus, the type initially became known as the Hebrew or Jewish bowl. The excavators in the earliest expedition to Nippur found so many such bowls that they believed they were excavating an exclusively Jewish quarter of the city. While there were certainly Jewish residents at the site, many other peoples and religions were also represented here.

As in previous periods of its occupation, Nippur was a melting pot during the time of the Sasanian Empire, and many people, languages, and religions were in evidence in the city. Polytheism continued into the Sasanian and early Islamic Periods, though it was on the wane, and though the temple of Inana fell out of use. Christians are known in and around Nippur from at least the 6th century CE; by 900 CE, if not earlier, Nippur was the seat of a Nestorian bishop. A fire temple on the bank of the Shatt en-Nil on Nippur's east mound, just southwest of the temple of Inana, reflects the presence of Zoroastrians. Zoroastrianism was the official religion of the Sasanian Empire and the fire altar appears in stylized form on the reverse of their coins (Fig. 10.27).

The fire temple (Fig. 10.28), uncovered just below the surface in mid-September 1894, was a classic *chahar taq* (Persian "four arches"), with four corner piers that would have supported arches over openings in each side and a dome over the central square. A three-stepped altar set on a base stood in the southeast opening (Fig. 10.29). The altar was plastered with gypsum and the surface of the topmost step was reddened. A block of unbaked brick formed a step 30 centimeters (1 foot) in front of the altar in the central room. A heavy layer of wood ash lay on and around the altar.

Fire temples are commonly part of larger architectural complexes, and the fact that the area outside the Nippur fire temple was also paved with gypsum plaster suggests it was part of such a larger complex. Unfortunately, excavations in the vicinity of the fire temple were limited, and no architectural remains around it were reported.

Early in the 7th century CE, the Sasanians clashed with the Byzantines, fighting an extended war that lasted roughly a quarter century. Sasanian territory had been steadily diminishing, and the administration began overtaxing the populace. Arab raiders, united by the new religion of Islam, began assaulting weakened Sasanian outposts, driving the empire to imminent collapse. Around 651 CE, the region previously under Sasanian rule became an Islamic caliphate.

The end of the Sasanian Period witnessed exactly the opposite of its rise. The complex canal system the Sasanians had set up was so dependent on organized maintenance and oversight at a high level that the Sasanian imperial bureaucracy could no longer keep it functioning when under duress. In addition, population levels decreased substantially in Mesopotamia while the number of urban sites diminished even more markedly.

Fig. 10.27 *Above*
Silver coin (33-62-59) of the Sasanian king Khusrau II (590–628 CE). The obverse shows the head of the king wearing a distinctive headdress, facing right. The reverse shows attendants on each side of a fire altar. Minted in Hamadan.

Fig. 10.28 *Opposite*
Ground plan and section through a Sasanian fire temple excavated in September 1894. Joseph A. Meyer, a graduate student in Architecture at the Massachusetts Institute of Technology, made the plan in 1894 while working at Nippur as a volunteer.

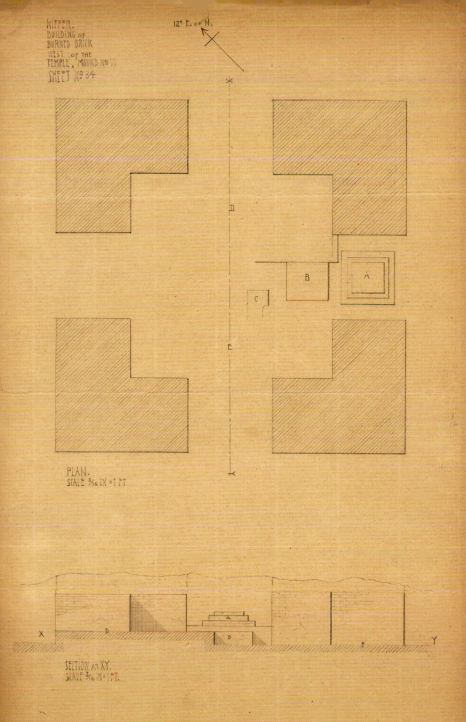

NIPPER.
BUILDING of
BURNED BRICK
WEST of the
TEMPLE, MOUND No VI
SHEET No 34

12° E. of N.

B A

C

D

E

K

PLAN.
SCALE 3/16 IN = 1 FT.

SECTION at XY.
SCALE 3/16 IN = 1 FT.

X D A B B Y

Jos. A. Meyer Jr.
Sept. 26th 1894.

No 345.

Houses of the early Islamic Period at Nippur are found directly above the Sasanian levels, though they do not appear in large numbers and still show many Sasanian characteristics. There was initially no requirement for the inhabitants to convert to Islam, though a tax was levied on non-Muslims. By the time of the Abbasids around 750 CE, however, Islam was prevalent.

By 800 CE, Nippur was no longer occupied as a city. Abbasid (750–1258 CE) inhabitants relocated to a small village near a prominent new canal northeast of Nippur's abandoned and slowly decaying remains. Later, but still minor settlements, Il Khanid (1258–1336 CE) and Jala'irid (1337–1410 CE), arose to the east of Nippur, but the ancient city itself was gradually consigned to the encroaching desert, never to be inhabited again.

Nippur: More than 1,800 Years of History

In the final 1,800 years of Nippur's existence as a city, it passed from the rule of one empire to another, sometimes willingly and sometimes actively resisting or rebelling. Though Nippur was increasingly distant from the center of imperial concerns, it remained important as a producer of grain and wool, for its location between northern and southern Mesopotamia, and for its function as a central node in a network of peoples and trade routes. This is perhaps the most interesting and prominent element of Nippur as a city: its role as a meeting point of diverse peoples including nomads and pastoralists as well as urbanites. As such, Nippur helped to foster the exchange of ideas that continued to move the world. It benefited from the new usage of camels to traverse distant deserts and bring aromatics and other exotic materials to its shops from across the Arabian Peninsula. Its markets became more efficient through the development and widespread use of coins. It saw the exchange of ideas of many different peoples through the many languages spoken and written within its walls, and it witnessed the shift to using an alphabetic script, making writing more accessible to the populace (see Chapter 11S1: Writing and Papermaking Technologies). It moved forward with the times but also kept a link to its past, maintaining many of its old traditions in remembrance of its days as an ancient cultic center.

For Further Reading

Briant, Pierre. 2002. *From Cyrus to Alexander: A History of the Persian Empire*, trans. Peter Daniels. Winona Lake, IN: Eisenbrauns.

Curtis, Vesta S., and Sarah Stewart, eds. 2007. *The Age of the Parthians*. London: I.B. Taurus.

Curtis, Vesta S., and Sarah Stewart. 2008. *The Sassanian Era*. London: I.B. Taurus.

Daryaee, Touraj. 2013. *Sasanian Persia: The Rise and Fall of an Empire*. London: I.B. Taurus.

Joannès, Francis. 2004. *The Age of Empires: Mesopotamia in the First Millennium BC*, trans. Antonia Nevill. Edinburgh: Edinburgh University Press.

Keall, Edward. 2015. Nippur in the Parthian Era. *Canadian Society of Mesopotamian Studies Journal* 9/10:5–15.

Fig. 10.29 *Opposite*

The three-stepped altar of the fire temple discovered at Nippur in 1894. It reflects the importance of Zoroastrianism during the city's Sasanian Period.

11

THE MEDIEVAL AND EARLY MODERN ISLAMIC AND PERSIANATE CITY

Renata Holod

Opposite
Detail of painting showing Layli and Majnun in School from a manuscript (NEP33) of Nizami, *Khamsah* (Quintet) copied and illustrated in Shiraz, 1584 CE.

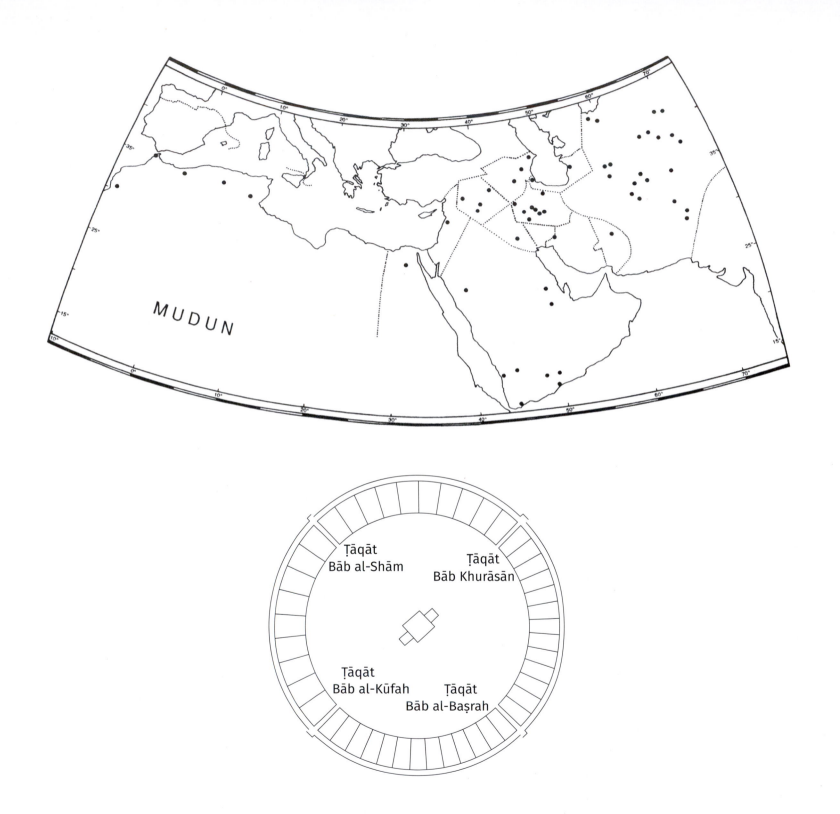

MUDUN

Ṭāqāt
Bāb al-Shām

Ṭāqāt
Bāb Khurāsān

Ṭāqāt
Bāb al-Kūfah

Ṭāqāt
Bāb al-Baṣrah

Locus of Civilization: The City in the Middle East

A rich corpus of geographical literature in Arabic and Persian dates from the 10th through the 14th centuries CE and describes the routes and realms of the Islamic world from the Atlantic to the Hindu Kush and beyond (Fig. 11.1). The geographers responsible for this literature based their accounts on descriptions of the known world from Sasanian way-books as well as the classical (Greek and Latin) tradition. They also drew on actual travelers' accounts, contemporary descriptions, and local histories to supply texture and detail.

The resulting literature offered a vivid "picture of the world" (Arabic: *surat al-'ard*), in addition to presenting an image of individual provinces or regions. Each region, significantly, was understood as centering on its cities (Fig. 11.2). The city, according to the great 14th century CE historian and philosopher, Ibn Khaldun, was the locus of civilization.

Cities in the Middle East, and in Iran specifically, were walled, and typically comprised several parts: the citadel (Arabic: *qala'(h)*, Persian: *kuhandiz* or *arg*); the city proper (Arabic: *madina[h]*, pl. *mudun*, Persian: *shahristan*); and the suburbs (Arabic: *rabad*, Persian: *rustaq*). In order to be recognized as a city, a settlement further had to contain a congregational mosque (Arabic: *masjid al-jami'*, Persian: *masjid-i jami'*) and a dense aggregation of contiguous houses.

In Islamic law, no corporate legal entity such as a municipality existed or could be recognized as a legal person. A city, consequently, was owned by a political and/or military authority or its representatives. This authority guaranteed the safety of the urban population, minted coins, and guarded both city and region. It enforced the rulings of the law courts on inheritance and pious foundations, as well as of the market and market inspectors on trades, prices, buildings, and zoning.

A city's system of communication depended on public streets running from one city gate to another across the urban expanse. These public thoroughfares could not be blocked. With the disappearance of wheeled cart traffic by the 6th to 7th centuries CE in the Middle East, the width of public streets came to be defined as allowing for the adjacent passage of two fully laden camels. The boundaries of streets generally were not vouchsafed, and it was rare for the original plan of any one city to survive the passage of centuries. The street boundaries of inherited cities—cities that existed before the coming of Islam—such as Damascus, Amman, or Merv, thus, were modified significantly over time while the urban plans of newly founded cities such as Kufa or Basra survived only in part.

In 762 CE, a perfect circle was laid out with great ceremony and self-conscious planning by the Caliph al-Mansur (H 136–158/754–775 CE) for the new Abbasid capital in Iraq, Madinat al-Salam, the "city of peace," known popularly as Baghdad (Fig. 11.3). (Regnal dates of rulers throughout this chapter are given in the Hijri year, denoted

continued on page 316

Fig. 11.1 *Overleaf*
Map showing the 11th–12th century CE trade networks in Africa and Eurasia (excerpted from a larger work available here: https://www.easyzoom.com/image/123047). The locations on the map are highlighted due to their strategic importance for travel or commerce (© Martin Jan Månsson).

Fig. 11.2 *Opposite, Top*
Cities (*mudun*) of the Islamic world according to the 10th century CE geographer al-Maqdisi. Figure 5 from Wheatley, P. 2001. *The Places Where Men Pray Together: Cities in Islamic Lands, Seventh Through the Tenth Centuries*. Chicago: University of Chicago Press.

Fig. 11.3 *Opposite, Bottom*
A reconstruction of the round city of Madinat al-Salam ("City of Peace" also known as Baghdad) as a perfect circle. After Lassner 1980, fig. 1, based on both Herzfeld and Creswell. Redrawn by Ardeth Anderson.

11–12th century trade network

Notable locations

Minor locations

— Major routes

— Minor routes

- - - Sea routes

━━━ Named roads

○ Passes

- - - The Spice Route

- - - Muslim Mediterranean routes

- - - Christian Mediterranean routes

━━━ The Silk Road(s)

━━━ European routes

━━━ Russian routes

━━━ South Asian routes

━━━ African routes

━━━ Arabian routes

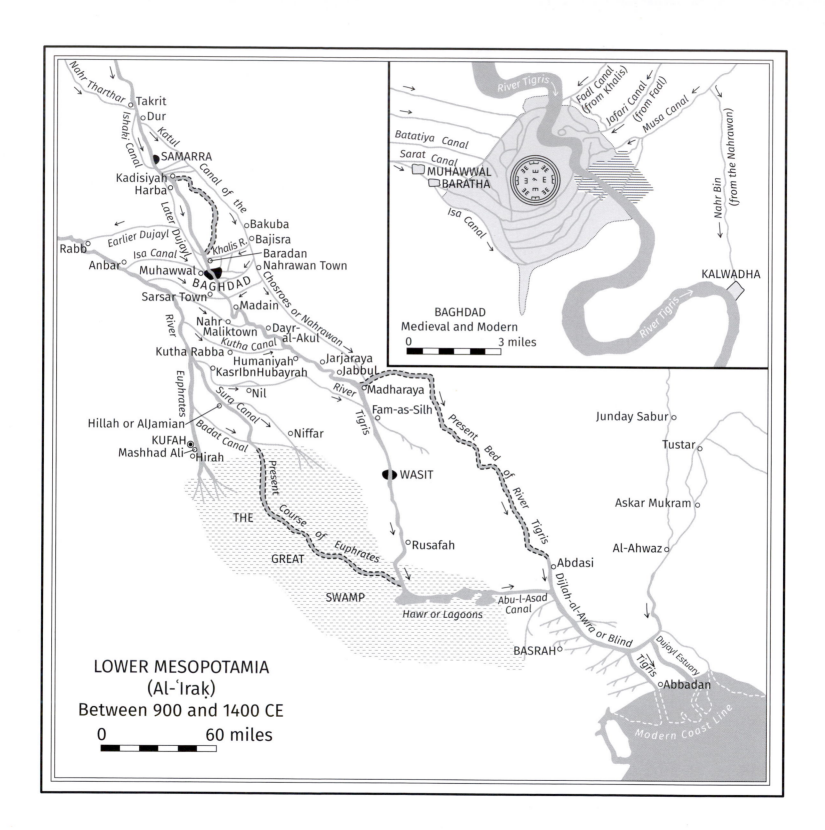

Main map labels

Nahr Tharthar
Takrit
Dur
Ishaki Canal
Katul
Kadisiyah
Harba
Katul Canal of the
SAMARRA
Bakuba
Bajisra
Earlier Dujayl
Later Dujayl
Khalis R.
Baradan
Rabb
Isa Canal
Nahrawan Town
Anbar
Muhawwal
BAGHDAD
Sarsar Town
Madain
Chosroes or Nahrawan
River
Nahr
Maliktown
Dayr-al-Akul
Kutha Canal
Kutha Rabba
Humaniyah
Jarjaraya
Euphrates
KasrIbnHubayrah
Jabbul
River Tigris
Sura Canal
Nil
Madharaya
Hillah or AlJamian
Badat Canal
Niffar
Fam-as-Silh
KUFAH
Present Bed of River Tigris
Mashhad Ali
Hirah
Junday Sabur
WASIT
Tustar
Askar Mukram
THE
Al-Ahwaz
GREAT
Present Course of Euphrates
Rusafah
Abdasi
Dijlah-al-Awra or Blind
SWAMP
Abu-l-Asad Canal
Hawr or Lagoons
BASRAH
Dujayl Estuary
Tigris
Abbadan
Modern Coast Line

LOWER MESOPOTAMIA
(Al-ʿIraḳ)
Between 900 and 1400 CE

0 — 60 miles

Inset map (top right)

River Tigris
Fadl Canal (from Khalis)
Jafari Canal (from Fadl)
Musa Canal
Batatiya Canal
Sarat Canal
MUHAWWAL
BARATHA
Nahr Bin (from the Nahrawan)
Isa Canal
KALWADHA
River Tigris

BAGHDAD
Medieval and Modern

0 — 3 miles

| Properties accessible from thoroughfares | Properties only accessible from cul-du-sacs |

continued on page 325

Fig. 11.4 *Opposite*

Location of Madinat al-Salam (Baghdad) at the narrowest point between the Euphrates and Tigris Rivers in Lower Mesopotamia or al-ʿIraq, ca. 900–1400 CE. After Le Strange [1900] 1983, map 1. Redrawn by Ardeth Anderson.

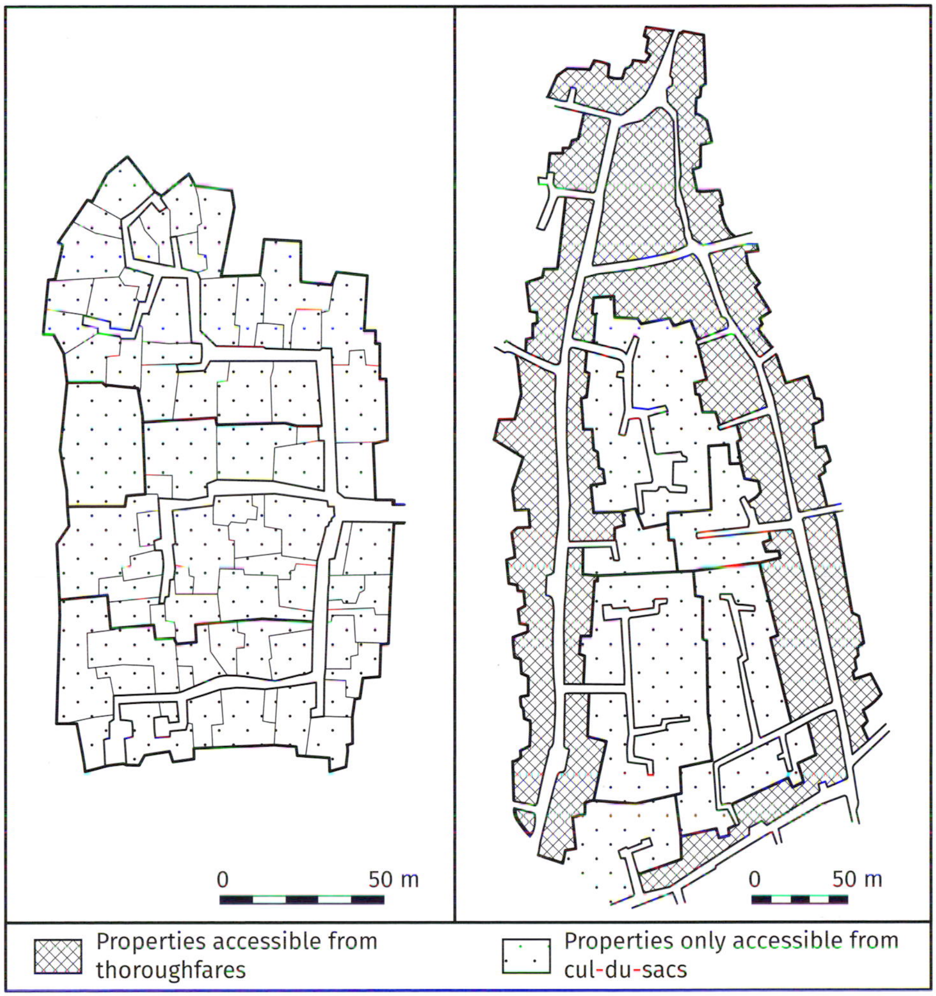

Fig. 11.5 *Right*

Residential "islands" in a densely populated city provide privacy in a large city as seen in Aleppo. After Wirth 1971. Redrawn by Ardeth Anderson.

as H, which follows the Islamic lunar calendar beginning in 622 CE, as well as in the Common Era, denoted as CE). Under the pressure of the city's success, this geometric layout became rapidly effaced. By the beginning decades of the 9th century CE, Baghdad had grown to become the largest urban zone in the world (Fig. 11.4).

In the Islamic city, public streets were the locations of the main markets or bazaars with their shops, storerooms, and hostels or caravanserais. Within this public urban space were also religious and social service buildings such as mosques, churches, synagogues, schools, soup kitchens, public baths, madrasas (legal colleges), hospitals, and Sufi lodges. Public space could also open into squares (Arabic and Persian: *maidan*) or parade avenues (Arabic: *shāriʿa*, Persian: *khiyaban*).

Writing and Papermaking Technologies

Renata Holod

The invention and dissemination of the alphabet changed the ways in which knowledge was stored and transmitted. Early alphabets emerged in the 2nd millennium BCE, starting possibly in Egypt and surely attested in the eastern Mediterranean in the city of Ugarit and in the land of Canaan. Spreading into other areas of the ancient world, the alphabet played a revolutionary role in the transmission of knowledge and the spread of literacy. Unlike the cuneiform writing system of Mesopotamia or the hieroglyphs of Egypt, which required the memorization of hundreds of signs, the alphabet used less than thirty signs and connected each of these to actual sounds: consonants and long vowels. The tasks of

reading and writing were, thus, enormously simplified. Over time, the alphabetic system, whether used for consonants alone, used with long consonants, or fully vowelled, came to be utilized throughout the Middle East for languages including Hebrew, Aramaic, Arabic, Middle and New Persian, Ottoman, Urdu, and finally Baloch.

From the end of the 1st millennium BCE, text was written on parchment, the use of which originated in Asia Minor (modern Turkey). This was a departure from the clay tablets used for cuneiform in Mesopotamia and the papyrus used by the ancient Egyptians. Parchment was made of processed sheepskin or, in the case of vellum (a particularly fine

Fig. 11S1.1 *Left*
Two pages from a Qur'an copy (E16249H), portions from Sura 7 (right page) and Sura 10 (left page), Parchment, datable 11th century CE, copied in Egypt or North Africa (?), collected in Egypt.

parchment), calfskin; texts written on this material were initially stored as scrolls or rolls (Fig. 11S1.1). Only later, by the end of the 5th century CE, did the codex or bound book form come into being. From the 8th century CE onwards, most literature, whether sacred or secular, was written in bound books (Arabic: *kitāb*). Only legal documents continued to be written on parchment scrolls, though later these would also be written on paper (Fig. 11S1.2).

By 650 CE, the Persians started to import Chinese paper made from the bark of the mulberry tree, though this was so rare a commodity that it was only used for important state documents. Papermaking was entrenched within the Middle East by the 8th century CE, and the technology spread rapidly until paper was the primary medium used for the recording of text. While rice straw and mulberry bark were used to produce paper in the Far East, these materials were not easily accessible in the Middle East. Instead, the rags of linen fabrics were processed into paper (Arabic: *waraq*, Persian: *kāghadh*), and their surfaces coated with starch and then polished into writing surfaces suitable for the application of ink. Thick Baghdadi paper (*kāghadh baghdādi*) was used for copying manuscripts and for the correspondence and records of administration. The existence of other types of paper in other places indicates the widespread diffusion of papermaking technology in many urban centers of the Middle East and North Africa.

Towards the end of the 10th or beginning of the 11th century CE, paper entirely replaced papyrus and parchment in Islamic lands. Rag paper books were cheap and effective substitutes for those made of parchment, each of which required the laborious and expensive processing of several sheepskins. The rise of the (comparatively) cheap paper book or codex, in combination with the adoption of the easily learned and reproduced alphabetic script, contributed to an exponential rise in literacy or, at least, semi-literacy in the Middle East between the 11th and 16th centuries CE.

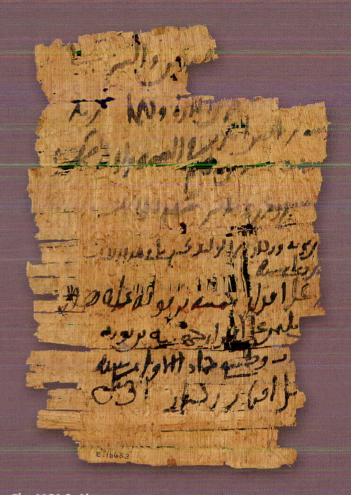

Fig. 11S1.2 *Above*
Lower left side of a deed (E16653) in Arabic of unspecified character, with the signatures of witnesses. Papyrus dated H 227/841 CE, Egypt.

The significance of writing is indirectly indicated through a gorgeous image of a scene from the love story of Layli and Majnun, one of the five stories in the *Khamsa* ("Five Poems") by the 12th century Persian poet Nizami (Figs. 11S1.3 and 11S1.4). This story circulated in various forms for centuries before (and after) its exquisite treatment by Nizami. In Nizami's account, and in the image depicted here, the first meeting between Majnun and his beloved, Layli, is set in school. This is the most frequent image to appear in copies of Nizami's *Khamsa* during the 16th century CE.

Fig. 11S1.3 *Left*

Detail of scene from NEP 33, folio 193A. Layli and Majnun Meet in School. Scene from Layli and Majnun, one of the five stories in Nizami's *Khamsa*, copied and illustrated in Shiraz, late 1582–June 1584. The boy in yellow, seated in an honored position in front of the teacher, practices the alphabet. The child in orange writes a prayer. Layli and Majnun may be represented by either of the girl and boy pairs in the middle ground. The artist has also taken the opportunity to comment on the act of writing, as well as to depict the tools of his profession as bookmaker: the pen, inkwell, scissors, and various writing tablets and volumes. Notice that all the depicted individuals are shown wearing "figured" coats.

Fig. 11S1.4 *Right*

Complete Page from NEP 33, folio 193A, showing all writing. Different types of calligraphy are displayed on this page: the *nasta'liq* style script of the copyist-calligrapher, as well as the children's writing samples. The text on the page translates as follows: "Listen! Among his fellow pupils were girls. Just like the boys, they came from noble families of various tribes. One day a beautiful little girl joined the group—a jewel such as one sees but seldom. She was as slender as a cypress tree. Her eyes, like those of a gazelle, could have pierced a thousand hearts with a single unexpected glance, yes, with one flicker of her eyelashes she could have slain a whole world" (Nizami, trans. Gelpke 1966:16).

Social and Historical Contexts for Islamic Urbanism

Brian Spooner

Cities have been more important in the history of the Middle East than in other parts of the world because, in the arid zone, all occupations, except nomadic pastoralism, require investment, and only urbanization brings together large enough numbers of people to allow the organization of labor, the production of commodities for trade, and the accumulation of wealth for investment. Before engaging in site-specific studies of Islamic and Persianate cities, some discussion of a more general nature is in order.

Persians, Arabs, Turks

There are many ethnic identities in the Middle East. But three are dominant: Persian, Arab, and Turk. The people who brought Islam out of Arabia and designed the first form of Islamic government, the Caliphate, were Arabs. But the area into which they brought it was territory that for over a thousand years had been dominated by Persian empires. Besides Persians (who since 1935 have been known as Iranians) and Arabs, and their languages, Persian and Arabic, there is a third major ethno-linguistic identity in the history and current life of the Middle East and the Islamic world: the Turks. Now known as the population of the modern state of Turkey, the successor nation-state of the Ottoman empire, the Turks are historically related to all the Turkic-speaking populations from Turkey back through Central Asia to Mongolia and northwestern China.

As a result of climate change beginning in the late 10th century CE, the Turks began to move westwards. They became Muslims when they entered the Persianate *ecumene*, or cultural world, that had extended into Central Asia in the 9th century CE, and gradually became politically dominant in most of the historic cities from their homeland in eastern Central Asia to the Mediterranean. Although their language became highly Persianized, especially in its written form, it also became functionally important as a *lingua franca*. While Persian was the *koine*, the common language that provided the standard for public life and writing, Turkish became the *lingua franca*, the common language for informal oral interaction between people with different native languages, and it continues to be an important spoken language in Iran and Afghanistan today, as well as Turkey, and is close to the other Turkic languages of the "-stans" of Central Asia.

Religion and Monotheism

The earliest forms of religion for which documentation has survived were polytheistic. As empires increased in size, the number of gods diminished. The first Persian empire (the Achaemenids, 550–330 BCE), the largest empire up to that time, introduced dualism, based on the revelation of the prophet Zoroaster, according to which there is one good god, Ahura Mazda, who is opposed by the force of evil, personified as Ahriman. The Jews, after the Zoroastrian Persians conquered their Babylonian captors in the 6th century BCE and returned them to Judah (which was the Persian Province of Yahud), advanced the idea of a single good god, but

Fig. 11S2.1 *Right*
This Qur'an (NEP27) in the Museum collection was copied and illuminated in Hamadhan, Iran by Mahmud ibn al-Husayn al-Kirmani, the scribe, in 1164 CE.

downgraded Ahriman to the status of Satan, a rebel against the one god. This model was then spread through the Roman empire by the Roman army as Christianity.

The 1st millennium BCE was the Age of Prophecy, especially the period from 800 to 200 BCE, known now as the Axial Age, when all the basic ideas from which modern religions and modern philosophy have developed were introduced. They were first voiced by Zoroaster (the originator of the major religion of the Persian empires, the Achaemenids, Parthians and Sasanians), Confucius (551–479 BCE), Lao-Tse (604–530 BCE), Gautama Buddha (6th century BCE), and Socrates (470–399 BCE) and other Greek philosophers, and their teachings were written down and became the main philosophical texts and religious scriptures down to the present. Not only the prophets of the Old Testament of the Bible, the originators of Judaism who provided the foundation of Christianity, but also the other major originators of new ways of understanding the world, that have remained important ever since, lived in this period.

Since writing was associated with authority and power, revelation from the Almighty had to be written. Scripture became the basis of Christianity in the early centuries of our Common Era and facilitated the development of the largest social identities in world history, larger than empires. In the 7th century CE, the world of Islam arose, based on a revealed text that was assumed to be "uncreated," i.e., in existence with God from the beginning of time. In the last few centuries before the beginning of our Common Era, the religious texts of Zoroastrianism and Judaism had begun to be written down. Despite the fact that they could not be produced in large numbers (since before the age of paper and printing they had to be written by hand on papyrus, parchment, or vellum), the resulting scripture was a major factor in the historically unprecedented spread of the new religion of Christianity and, later, of Islam.

Islam and the Law

Islam, the third of the three Abrahamic religions, was revealed by the Prophet Muhammad starting in 610 CE in Mecca on the west coast of Arabia. He moved to Medina, some 450 kilometers (280 miles) to the north in 622, and died there in 632 CE. His prophetic pronouncements were collected as the Qur'an ("Reading"), and the teachings of Islam were rationalized in the course of the next two centuries with a focus on the law, the law of family and social organization, and the law of trade. Since Islamic law was understood to have been legitimized by divine revelation, it spread quickly east and west along the inter-urban trade networks of the arid zone from Syria and Mesopotamia to Egypt and North Africa, to Central Asia and northern China, and south into India, producing the largest arena of social interaction and cultural continuity in the world up to that time, which was a major step in the process of globalization that continues today.

Persianate Literacy

The Sasanian court model, which became the primary mode of government in the eastern half of the Islamic world from the 9th to the 19th centuries CE, used Persian as the language of administration, and encouraged poets to eulogize the person in power (the sultan). Persian, now written in the Arabic script, was more cursive than the Aramaic script that had been used by the Sasanians. The technology of paper-making had also been learned from the Chinese in the late 8th century CE, and the city of Samarqand (in present-day Uzbekistan) had become an important center of paper production. This was the beginning of the age of the *munshi*, the writers who formed an elite class of Persian-language administrators in all the cities. Adapted to the new Islamic environment, Persian easily spread beyond the extent of its earlier use. The language carried a culture, and this vast area, from what is now Iraq to China, became the Persianate ecumene. Culturally unified by the use of a single written language, which with paper could now easily be used for remote communication, Persian provided the standard for all public life and everything cultural that came with it, including the genres of literature, especially poetry, Persian art, and Persian cuisine.

Fig. 11S2.2 *Right*

The *Khamsah* by Nizami consists of
five long narrative poems: *Makhzan
al-Asrar* ('Treasury of Secrets'), a
compendium of ethical-philosophical
discourses, composed ca. 1163–1164
CE; *Khosrau and Shirin*, a romance
based on the story of the Sassanian
king Khusraw II Parviz and the
Armenian princess Shirin, completed
ca. 1180 CE; *Layli and Majnun*, a
romance based on the popular Arab
legend of ill-starred lovers, written
in 1188 or 1192 CE; *Haft Paykar*,
an allegorical romance and mirror
for princes, dated 1197 CE; and the
Iskandarnama, ('Book of Alexander'),
in two parts, the *Sharafnama* ('Book
of Honor') and *Iqbalnama* ('Book of
Fortune'), the last work by Nizami
of ca. 1200-1202 CE.

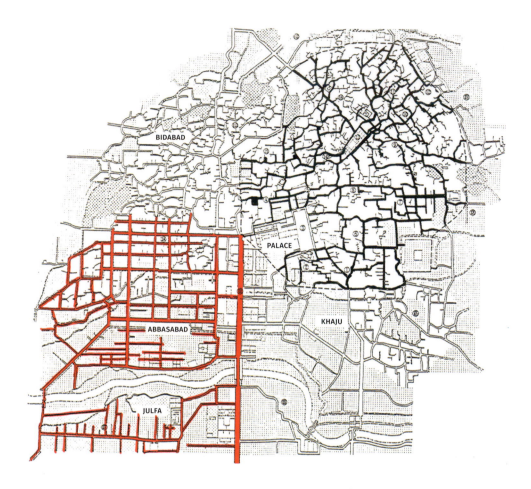

The traffic on the through streets running through the city flowed past urban residential "islands" or quarters (Fig. 11.5), which were accessed by dead-end lanes or cul-de-sacs. The surface of each such access lane was co-owned by all the houses facing on it. Each residential quarter (Arabic and Persian: *mahalleh*) was typically inhabited by a single ethnic, ideological, or confessional group. It usually had its own service centers with local shops, bath, and religious building (Fig. 11.6). In times of internecine or inter-quarter strife, the access lanes to a specific block could even be closed off by internal gates.

Two case studies of Islamic cities in the Middle East, both situated in the region of contemporary Iran, are presented here: one, Rayy, located only a few kilometers from what today is the modern megacity of Tehran, is explored in the Medieval (Early and Middle Islamic) Period through to its fall to Mongol invaders in the second decade of the 13th century CE. The other, Isfahan, the contemporary capital of Isfahan Province in Iran, is examined in its Early Modern incarnation as a new capital of the Safavid Dynasty. Also explored are various technologies that flourished in these and other urban

Fig. 11.7 *Above*
Drachma (33-62-13) of the Parthian king Mithridates I (171–138 BCE). Obverse: Head of king facing left. Reverse: Archer seated holding bow surrounded by inscription.

centers of the Islamic world. These included the introduction of the alphabet and its role in expanding literacy and facilitating the dissemination of knowledge; the making of ceramics, textiles, and paper; the ways in which the layouts and architecture of the cities shaped their inhabitants' interactions with the world and with each other; and the participation of the cities in global networks of trade and interaction.

Rayy: Case Study of a Medieval Islamic City

In *Hudūd al-ʿĀlam* (*The Regions of the World*), an anonymous geographical text in Persian dating from 982 CE, the city of Rayy is described as "a great prosperous town, having many riches, inhabitants and merchants….Water comes from underground canals [*qanat*]. It produces muslin, cloaks, cotton, big glazed plates, and wine. From its districts come good woolen scarves [*taylasān*]."

Rayy is located on the Azdān or Rayy Plain, the best-watered plain on the Iranian Plateau. The region has been the location of human activity from at least the Neolithic Period. It is no surprise, then, that people returned to inhabit this area again and again despite major setbacks until the zone of settlement gave rise to Tehran.

The Penn Museum's excavations on the Rayy Plain, led by archaeologist Erich F. Schmidt in the late 1930s, uncovered materials from many different periods. The main early site on the plain, Cheshmeh ʿAli (the "Spring of Ali") was occupied from the late Neolithic Period through to the Iron Age, approximately the 7th to mid-1st millennium BCE, periods best known from Schmidt's (1934–1936) and later excavations at the site. The more extensive development of Rayy as an urban center came later, during the Parthian Period, from the 2nd century BCE (Fig. 11.7). The new urban structure of the site took the form of a citadel on a spur of a hill and, adjacent to it, a quadrilateral walled city (Persian: *shahristan*). Outside these two units, the later Sasanian Period (ca. 224–651 CE), extended the suburban areas. Numerous rural estates sprang up across the extensive territory of the Rayy Plain. The plain also became the site of a large religious structure at Tepe Mil, likely a Zoroastrian fire temple. Both the district generally and the early city of Rayy specifically saw a rise in population (Fig. 11.8).

During the early Islamic Period (late 7th to early 10th century CE), Rayy came to function as the primary military and administrative center for the eastern provinces of the expanding Islamic Empire, as well as the launching pad for campaigns across the Amu Darya River into Central Asia. The major route connecting the new city of Baghdad to the east also went through Rayy, as did the route coming up from the Persian Gulf, which then ran north along the western coast of the Caspian Sea into the western steppe of Eurasia. The growing significance of Rayy is further indicated by the fact that, after 750 CE, it became common for the heir apparent of the Abbasid caliphate to be appointed as the city's governor.

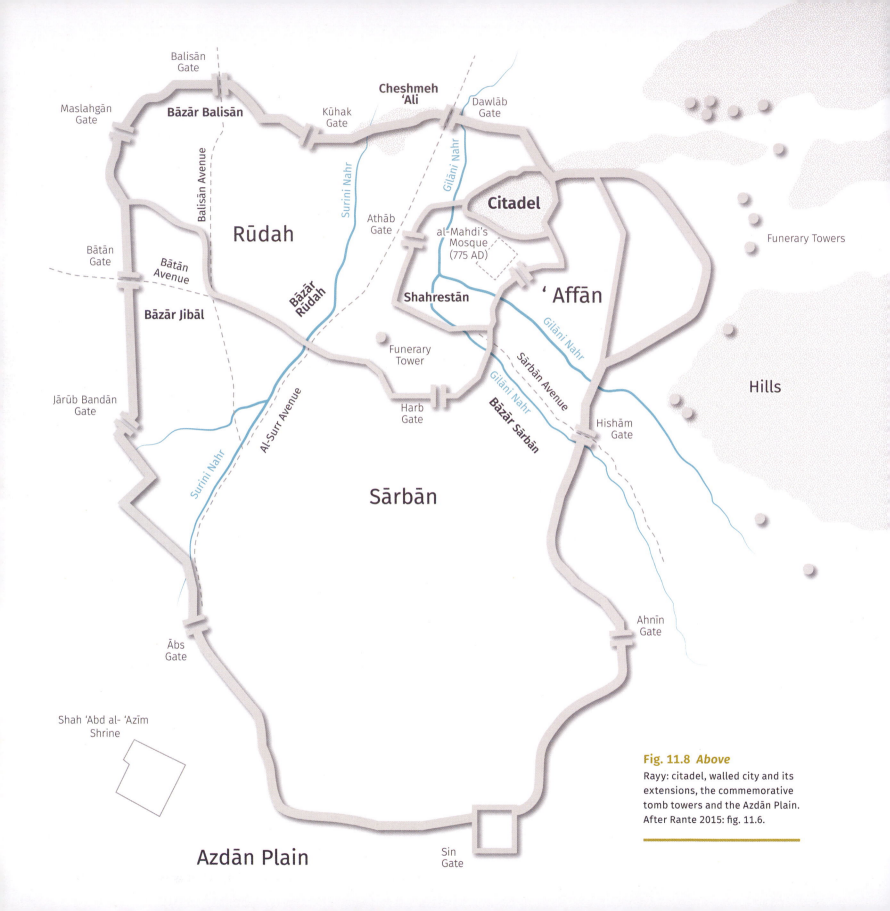

Balisān Gate

Maslahgān Gate

Bāzār Balisān

Kūhak Gate

Cheshmeh 'Ali

Dawlāb Gate

Surini Nahr

Gīlāni Nahr

Citadel

Funerary Towers

Rūdah

Bātān Gate

Bātān Avenue

Athāb Gate

al-Mahdi's Mosque (775 AD)

'Affān

Bāzār Jibāl

Bāzār Rūdah

Shahrestān

Gīlāni Nahr

Jārūb Bandān Gate

Funerary Tower

Sārbān Avenue

Bāzār Sārbān

Gīlāni Nahr

Harb Gate

Hishām Gate

Hills

Surini Nahr

Al-Surr Avenue

Sārbān

Āḃs Gate

Ahnīn Gate

Shah 'Abd al- 'Azīm Shrine

Fig. 11.8 *Above*
Rayy: citadel, walled city and its extensions, the commemorative tomb towers and the Azdān Plain. After Rante 2015: fig. 11.6.

Azdān Plain

Sin Gate

Fig. 11.9 *Above*

Aerial photograph of the Rayy Plain. The 'Tughril Tower,' a commemorative building, appears to the right. Courtesy of the Oriental Institute of the University of Chicago.

Rayy, unlike other cities in the Persianate world such as Merv, Nishapur, Herat, or Isfahan—which moved their loci of power from older centers to newer ones over time—renewed its old nucleus through several iterations. From this base, it also expanded out onto the adjacent plain to the south and southwest. Constant labor was needed to maintain and to strengthen Rayy's fortifications, a point underscored by the results of recent archaeological excavations. Rapid urban development occurred after the 760s and, by the mid-10th century, under the rule of the Buyid Dynasty (H 334–447/945–1055 CE), the city's largest walled extension measured approximately 550 hectares (1,359 acres).

Following a period of instability with factional and sectarian strife in the first half of the 11th century, order and peace returned when the Seljuq Turks made Rayy the capital of their domain. In 1042 CE, Sultan Tughril Beg (H 429–455/1038–1063 CE) made Rayy his residence, ordered the rebuilding of the city walls, and was likely buried there (Fig. 11.9). A large necropolis developed on the eastern slopes while smaller suburban centers spread out along the main roads from the walled city. Bazaars were situated both

continued on page 332

IRRIGATION AND THE QANAT

Brian Spooner

Although dry farming has continued in a few parts of the Middle East, especially in small parts of what are now northern Iraq, northwestern and northeastern Iran and the Caspian littoral, most agriculture in the Middle East depends on irrigation, which requires a significantly greater degree of organization than dry farming, both for investment in construction and for maintenance and management. Adequate organization of labor became possible only as communities became larger, and socially more complex. For this reason, the beginnings of irrigation engineering in the 7th millennium BCE were closely related to the growth of cities in southern Mesopotamia. In the succeeding millennia, there was a similar relationship between irrigation and urbanization on each of the rivers that flow through the arid zone, from the Nile in the west, to the Helmand, Oxus and Jaxartes in Central Asia, and smaller rivers in between, and as far as the Yellow River in China.

Irrigation affords not only the necessary soil moisture for productive agriculture, but the regularity and dependability of agricultural production that facilitates settled life and supports the development of large urban populations. Irrigation greatly increases the productivity and carrying capacity of the land and has played an important role in the history and civilization of the region. However, it also imposes social and economic conditions on the populations that become dependent on it. Until the middle of the 1st millennium BCE it was riverine irrigation that supported cities and was necessary for urban development and the growth of trade. But, after the introduction of *qanat* technology in the 7th century BCE, the profits from inter-urban trade funded investment in the expansion of agriculture by *qanat* irrigation far beyond the rivers.

The *qanat* is an underground channel that brings water by gravity flow from the underground water table at a higher

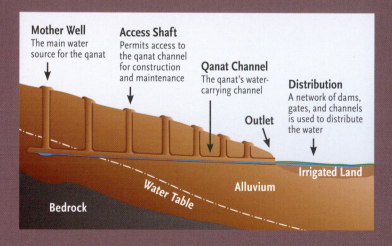

Mother Well
The main water source for the qanat

Access Shaft
Permits access to the qanat channel for construction and maintenance

Qanat Channel
The qanat's water-carrying channel

Outlet

Distribution
A network of dams, gates, and channels is used to distribute the water

Irrigated Land

Water Table

Alluvium

Bedrock

Fig. 11S3.1 *Left*
Diagram showing the various components of a *qanat*.
© Wikimedia Commons/Samuel Bailey.

Fig. 11S3.2 *Opposite*
Aerial view of *qanats* supplying a particular village, and the lines of access shafts from the mother wells to the fields they irrigate. Courtesy of the Oriental Institute of the University of Chicago.

location under the foothills of a nearby mountain range for a varying distance (anything from a few hundred meters to as much as thirty kilometers [18.6 miles] or more) out into a desert plain where there is a deposit of cultivatable soil at a lower altitude far from any surface water. The origin of the technology is unknown. But it was first promoted in the Achaemenid (the first Persian) Empire (550–330 BCE), and spread eastwards through Central Asia as far as northwestern China, westwards through North Africa into Spain, and later with the Spanish to Latin America. In 2016, it was inscribed in UNESCO's World Heritage List (the 22nd Iranian item on the List) as illustrating "a significant stage of human history" with this description:

"The Persian Qanat (Islamic Republic of Iran)—Throughout the arid regions of Iran, agricultural and permanent settlements are supported by the ancient qanat system of tapping alluvial aquifers at the heads of valleys and conducting the water along underground tunnels by gravity, often over many kilometres. The eleven qanats representing this system include rest areas for workers, water reservoirs and watermills. The traditional communal management systems for this type of irrigation are still in place and allow equitable and sustainable water sharing and distribution. The qanats provide exceptional testimony to cultural traditions and civilizations in desert areas with an arid climate." (Source: UNESCO http://whc.unesco.org/en/list/1506/)

The adoption and spread of the qanat through the arid zone had an important effect on the organization of society. Water ownership, in the form of shares in a qanat, became as important a resource as ownership of arable land. Apart from facilitating an enormous expansion of agriculture by providing resources for new clusters of agricultural settlement, it increased the complexity of society.

The most important aspect of qanat technology in this context is that, besides increasing the water supply, it stabilized it, because qanat flow (unlike river flow) is relatively unaffected by seasonal and annual fluctuations in precipitation. This effect of what has been called the "qanat revolution" would, therefore, have made possible an unprecedented growth in settled agricultural life and, consequently, also of cities. Between the qanat revolution and the more recent oil revolution (which generated a completely new source of income), the maintenance of the major qanat systems of the plateau fluctuated in step with other economic variables. In the absence of any significant technological innovation, cities have grown and declined partly because of political decisions (e.g., choice of capital) and resulting changes in patterns of communication and trade, and partly because of migrations onto the plateau and resulting fluctuations in security. The major determining factor in the historical growth and decline of cities derived not so much from changes in the basic availability of water or the occurrence of other environmental problems such as salinity, but from changes in the investment pattern.

The exigencies of irrigation, therefore, help to explain the bias toward urban life in the culture of the arid zone, and especially in Persianate culture, because the exploitation of the countryside depended on the (largely private) financial institutions in the cities, which determined ultimately where and when, and to what extent, satellite agricultural settlements would be developed. A particularly interesting example of historical qanat development is the city of Yazd, a city without a river in the middle of the Iranian plateau, which gets its total water supply from a qanat system. For that reason among others—its traditional houses, bazaars, hammams, mosques, synagogues, Zoroastrian temples, and a historic garden—it is another of the items from Iran that is inscribed on UNESCO's World Heritage List.

Fig. 11.10 *Above*

Aerial photograph from the direction of the citadel toward the excavations of the congregational mosque at Rayy with piers visible. Courtesy of the Oriental Institute of the University of Chicago.

at all the city gates as well as immediately outside these. The entire occupied and built-up area of Rayy would have spanned some 1,000 hectares (2,471 acres) at this time.

The Congregational Mosque

In approximately 775 CE, al-Mahdi (H 158–169/775–785 CE), heir apparent to the Abbasid Empire and governor of the eastern provinces, undertook the construction of a congregational mosque, a place from which the weekly sermon (Arabic: *khutba*) was preached, and the political program and religious policy proclaimed. This mosque was a sizable monument located within the walled city proper (*shahristan*) (Fig. 11.10). The building had a rectangular plan, reconstructed as measuring approximately 60 by 100 meters (197 by 328 feet); its foundation piers were partly uncovered by Schmidt's excavations. Because of the continued economic and political success of Rayy, as well as the increase in conversions to Islam, this monumental mosque may have become

11.12a

11.12b

11.12c

Fig. 11.11 *Above*

A fragmentary grave marker in stone (35-8-302), excavated at Rayy by Erich Schmidt.

Fig. 11.12 *Opposite*

Stucco revetment fragments from the walled city of Rayy. Two fragments (11.12a, 11.12c) are molded and come from the facade of a religious or social service building such as a mosque or hospital. The other (11.12b) is of carved stucco and cut glazed tile from a commemorative building or mausoleum. Philadelphia Museum of Art, Acquired by exchange with the University Museum, 1940, Object Number: 1940-51-1.

Fig. 11.13 *Right*

This iron plaque, recovered from the Rayy Plain, would have been attached in the entry of the tower named the 'Tower of Tughril' (see Figure 11.8 above). Its inscription reads: "The work of 'Abd al-Wahhāb al-Qazvīni ibn Fakhrāvar at the end of Rajab of the year 534 (March 1140 CE)." University of Michigan Museum of Art, Museum Purchase, 1965/1.167.

incapable of containing the entire community of Muslims for Friday prayer by the mid-11th century CE. Likely, an expansion would have been planned, if not completed, by the time the city was destroyed by the Mongol invasion of the 1220s.

City Streets and Parade Avenues

The famous caliph and son of al-Mahdi, Harun al-Rashid (H 170–193/786–809 CE), upon visiting his birthplace of Rayy in 804 and 808 CE, mentioned that the city had a most beautiful avenue, the Sarbān. This great avenue, which was bordered by a watercourse lined with trees, led out from the congregational mosque onto the plain. A similarly notable avenue was the Surr, which linked the city with the citadel. While regular streets, both limited access and thoroughfares, were an expected part of the urban fabric, these grand parade avenues represented entirely different types of public spaces. It was on these thoroughfares that various types of display—military, political, religious, and celebratory—took place within the city. In this, the avenues of Rayy functioned, much as the famous "Street between the Two Palaces" [*Shari'a bain Qasrayn*] of 10th to 12th century Cairo, as sites of panoply and parade.

Cemeteries and Commemorative Buildings

By the 11th century CE, to the east of the fortified city, the western and northern slopes of the nearby Bibi Shahrbanu Hill were covered with cemeteries called the Old Upper Cemetery (Persian: *kohneh gurestān barin*) and the Old Lower Cemetery (Persian: *kohneh gurestān zirin*). These contained numerous ordinary burials, taking the form of pit graves marked by gravestones, such as those excavated in the 1930s (Fig. 11.11). On the slopes to the east stood several commemorative monuments in the form of tomb towers. Each tomb tower would have been decorated with inscriptions in glazed tile and stucco carvings (Fig. 11.12); sometimes the name of the builder or decorator would have been indicated (Fig. 11.13).

continued on page 339

CHAL TARKHAN

Renata Holod

The site of Chal Tarkhan (Fig. 11S4.1) lies some 20 kilometers (12 miles) south of the city of Rayy among an exurban ring of estates that were built up at about the same time as the foundation of Rayy in the first centuries of the 1st millennium CE. The Rayy (Azdān) Plain, the best-watered place on the Iranian plateau, was the ideal location for the development of a garden zone and agricultural hinterland for the new city. Estates such as that found at Chal Tarkhan functioned both as places of continuity for cultural practices and memory as well as bases for innovation in agronomic pursuits. As such, they function effectively as portals into Late Antique and medieval Iranian life on the plain.

What we know about Chal Tarkhan derives from the activities both of looters active at the site in the 1920s and of archaeologists such as Erich Schmidt, who partially excavated the site in 1936 while on a joint expedition of the Penn Museum and the Museum of Fine Arts in Boston (Fig. 11S4.2). The site appears to have flourished from the 7th through the beginning of the 13th centuries CE. Excavations recovered two separate areas at the site, one a square fortified domestic building and the other a vaulted reception hall. Most investment in the buildings and their decorations can be dated to the earlier centuries of the site's existence. Ceramics made of stoneware (Fig. 11S4.3) have been

Fig. 11S4.1 *Left*
Excavations at Chal Tarkhan by Erich Schmidt. Courtesy of the Oriental Institute of the University of Chicago.

Fig. 11S4.2 *Opposite*
Aerial Photo of Chal Tarkhan showing the reception hall and another building, probably a religious site. Courtesy of the Oriental Institute of the University of Chicago.

retrieved from the sites, as have ostraka, potsherds bearing writing, in this case in New Persian (Figs. 11S4.4a–b). The site continued to be inhabited and used through the 12th and into the beginning of the 13th century CE. Like the city of Rayy itself, Chal Tarkhan was abandoned and/or destroyed as a result of the Mongol invasions of the 1220s.

The vaulted reception hall (Fig. 11S4.3), a long rectangular building, was completely decorated with carved and colored stucco reliefs. These reliefs attest to a long-lived tradition of depicting Persian heroes and kings long past the demise of the Sasanian Dynasty in the 7th century CE: King Khusrau II (590, 591–628 CE) and his wife Shirin,

later a famous Persian literary heroine, for example, or King Bahram Gur (420–438 CE) engaged in hunting (Fig. 11S4.5). They also form a bridge to later, 12th to 16th century CE depictions of these same heroes. Whether found on stucco reliefs or on wall paintings, such representations formed part of a visual culture that flowed directly into the later medieval and Early Modern depictions on ceramics or in illuminated manuscripts of the *Shahnameh* ("Book of Kings") by the late 10th to early 11th century Persian poet Ferdowsi, and the *Khamsa* ("Five Poems") by the 12th century Persian poet Nizami (see Chapter 11S1: Writing and Papermaking Technologies).

Fig. 11S4.4 *Above*
This ostrakon (37-33-22) from Chal Tarkhan has a poem written in New Persian (that is in Arabic script).

Fig. 11S4.3 *Above*
This stoneware albarello (37-33-1)—a drug jar made for holding medicinal substances—was excavated at Chal Tarkhan and indicates that this site was still in use until the beginning of the 13th century CE.

Fig. 11S4.5 *Opposite*
Detail of stucco relief from Chal Tarkhan reception hall, likely a depiction of Bahram Gur hunting boar. Courtesy of the Oriental Institute of the University of Chicago.

Fig. 11.14 *Above*
Aerial view of the excavations at
the 12th century CE commemorative
structure, later known as Naqqareh
Khaneh. Courtesy of the Oriental
Institute of the University of Chicago.

The plan and nature of this type of commemorative monument was established by Erich Schmidt's 1936 excavation of a polygonal-based tomb tower containing several chambers at a site then named Naqqareh Khaneh (Fig. 11.14). The monument was interpreted as belonging to an elite family. On the basis of its remaining foundations, and of standing examples at Rayy and elsewhere on the Iranian plateau, a very tall, flanged tower constructed of baked brick was reconstructed (Fig.11.15).

Isfahan: Case Study of an Early Modern City in the Middle East

Safavid Isfahan: "Half the World"

The Early Modern Period city of Isfahan in central Iran began to take shape in 1592 CE when Shah 'Abbas I moved the capital of the Safavid state there. Leaving aside the older, medieval town with its congregational mosque of 10th to 12th century CE foundation, Shah 'Abbas chose to develop the areas adjacent to and stretching along both banks of the Zayandeh River. In this development, he succeeded so well that Isfahan came to be renowned as "half the world."

The remains of an octagonal commemorative structure datable to the second half of the 12th century CE at Rayy. The structure has a rubble masonry core with baked brick revetment. Commemorative buildings for reigning powerholders and religious elites became part of the architectural landscape of Rayy, and the central Islamic world as a whole. Courtesy of the Oriental Institute of the University of Chicago.

Shah 'Abbas's successors, their families, and court officials followed suit; they established palaces, gardens with garden pavilions, legal colleges, Sufi retreats, and commercial buildings. Included also was the suburb of New Julfa for the Armenian trading community, with its far-flung trading network, and the new Qaysariyya Bazaar with its numerous shops, as well as hostels and caravansaries for specialized professions and groups, all made this Early Modern city enormously inviting to merchants. Isfahan became a nexus of global trade. Travelers and traders from Portugal to Holland, from Muscovy to Hindustan, and from Great Britain to Scandinavia and beyond found markets for their goods. In exchange, they took away fabulous Safavid silks and other specialties of the region. The numerous Safavid paintings, memoirs of numerous foreign travelers and missionaries (some 32 European accounts of varying quality are known), and Persian poetry describing events such as the opening of a new bridge over the Zayandeh River all attest to the political will, cultural energy, and economic expansion that characterized Safavid Isfahan during these early decades.

As Isfahan took its place as an imperial capital, representations of the city flourished. Whether appearing on the walls of the Safavid palaces themselves, in Persian or Mughal paintings and drawings, or in prints and drawings in European travelers' accounts, the image (*naqsh*) of the city was replicated. Particularly interesting is a representation of the city as a new type of Early Modern urban space in the Ali Quli Agha complex

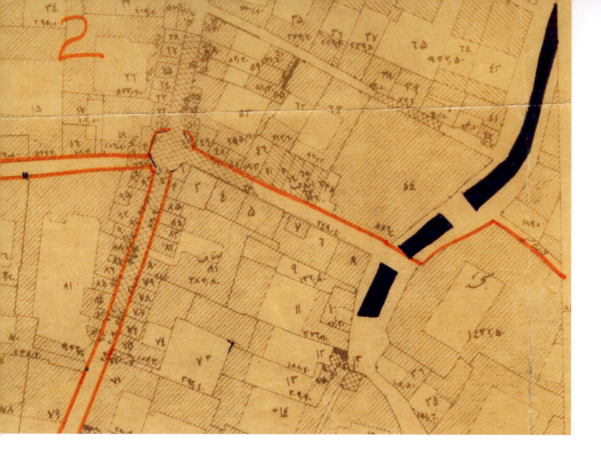

Fig. 11.16 *Left*

The Ali Quli Agha Complex, Baidabad, Isfahan, 1710–1715 CE, showing the crossing of two streets with covered bazaar, a water channel (in blue), with the mosque at bottom right and public double bath above right. Detail from a 1974 cadastral map of Isfahan produced by the Iranian Cartographic Center.

in Isfahan's Baidabad suburb (Fig. 11.16), which dates from the first years of the 18th century CE, only a little more than a century after Isfahan's inauguration as imperial center by Shah 'Abbas. The image was installed in the swimming hall of the complex's large double bath, probably one of the most luxurious baths of its time (Fig. 11.17). Composed from individual tiles the image was made using the *cuerda seca* or "dry cord" technique: different colors of glaze were separated by thin bands of waxed thread that burned off during firing of the tiles but left behind dark lines. The assembled tile image depicts the famous *Khiyaban-i Chahar Bagh*, the great avenue of Isfahan (Fig. 11.18). It is significant that a local ceramic workshop used a printed image as a source. Most likely, the original image had been made for Cornelius Le Bruyn's *Travels into Muscovy, Persia and the Eastern Indies*, which was published in 1737 in London (Fig. 11.19). The volume included an account of the visit to Isfahan of this Dutch painter and indefatigable traveler in the first decade of the 18th century CE.

In the discussion below, the complex in which the image of *Khiyaban-i Chahar Bagh* appears is examined and considered within the larger architectural and social trends evident in 17th and early 18th centuries CE Isfahan. The local knowledge that shaped the design of the Ali Quli Agha complex was, in fact, developed through the design and construction campaign of new Safavid Isfahan: one of the greatest urban designs not

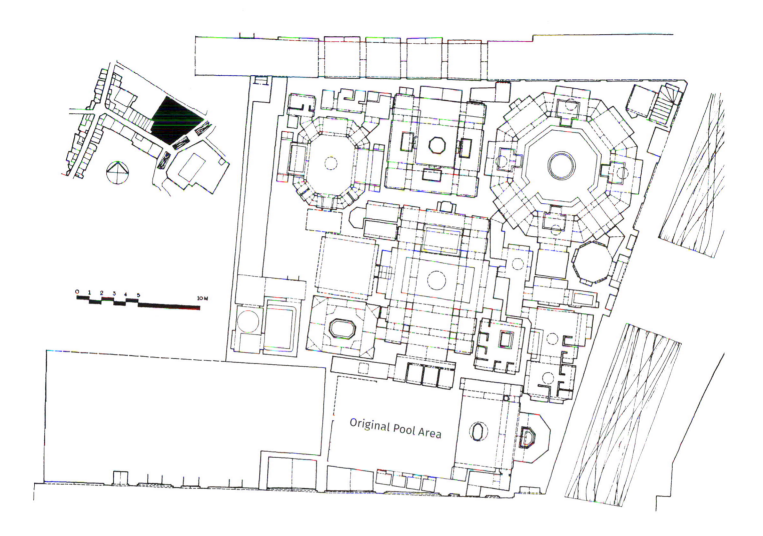

Fig. 11.17 *Above*

Detailed plan of the double bath at Ali Quli Agha Complex (note inset map at top left). The original (swimming) pool area is indicated.

only of Iran but also of the entire Early Modern world. These included the extraordinary and immense *Maidan-i Naqsh-i Jahan*, the "Plaza of the Image of the World," which was surrounded by shops and balconies for viewing activities on the plaza; the new congregational mosque the *Masjid-i Shah*, known today as the Imam Mosque; and the Ali Qapu, the Sublime Porte or Gate, the ceremonial palace gate standing at the threshold between the palace zone with its administrative, reception and residential quarters and the public realm of the plaza. This gate palace included an elaborate viewing platform for members of the court and ambassadors. Opposite the new mosque was the entrance to the commercial zone: the Qaysariyya, the great new covered bazaar with its elaborately painted two-story entrance facade, where traders and missionaries mingled with local inhabitants of the city.

Original Pool Area

In the new imperial capital were the public and private zones of palace pavilions such as Chehel Sutun and Hasht Behesht. Bridges across the Zayandeh River were designed not only for the movement and transport of people and goods but also for socializing and lingering to view the river or elements of the city and suburbs. Of course, the *Khiyaban-i Chahar Bagh* itself, the Avenue of the Four Gardens, a promenade marked by shady groves and fountains was designed both for parade and for leisure. The cognitive and kinesthetic experiences first encountered within these grand new spaces, which were deliberately designed to facilitate social engagement, would be refined into a signature of 17th and early 18th centuries CE architecture and urban spaces in Isfahan. These were then reproduced in digest form in Ali Quli Agha's small, early 18th century CE complex in the newly urbanized neighborhood of Baidabad.

continued on page 350

Fig. 11.18 *Above*
Detail of tile panel in the swimming pool hall in the Ali Quli Agha Complex, Baidabad, Isfahan, 1710–1715 CE, showing an avenue in early modern Isfahan.

Fig. 11.19 *Above*

The Avenue of the Four Gardens ("Khiyaban-i Chahar Bagh"), Isfahan, as depicted in Cornelis Le Bruyn *Travels into Muscovy, Persia, and the Eastern Indies*, London, 1737.

REVOLUTIONS IN CERAMIC PRODUCTION

Renata Holod and Michael Falcetano

Lusterware has a surface that glints with a metallic shine. This technique of ceramic decoration, a closely guarded trade secret, appears to have been produced first in Iraq in the 9th century CE (Fig. 11S5.1). A vessel covered with a tin-opacified white glaze was produced in a first firing. A decorator would then apply a design in a metallic slurry of copper, iron, or, occasionally, silver, and sign the work. A second firing in a reduction kiln drove off the oxygen in the slurry, leaving a shiny design on the surface.

This craft secret of producing shimmering wares appears to have been transferred to ceramic workshops in 10th century CE Egypt, and then to Syria during the following two centuries. In the middle of the 12th century CE, Kashan located on the Iranian plateau some 100 miles south of Rayy, became the key (if not sole) lusterware production center in the Middle East (Fig. 11S5.2).

Lusterware, like *haft rang* (seven colors), another specialty of Kashan potters, was double-fired. Abu'l Qasim, a 14th century CE author and descendant of Kashani masters, describes the process and says that this second firing lasted for 72 hours. A kiln capable of maintaining a consistent firing temperature for this lengthy period of time

Fig. 11S5.1 *Left*
Lusterware bowl (NEP79), inside and from below. This restored bowl is covered with opacified tin glaze and decorated with luster. It was probably made in Basra in the 9th century CE. The inside depicts two bulls and inscriptions in 'Kufic' style Arabic script repeating the formula "Blessing to its owner." From below, the inscription in 'Kufic' style Arabic script reads "Blessing to its owner" "work of ... Abu Shaddād."

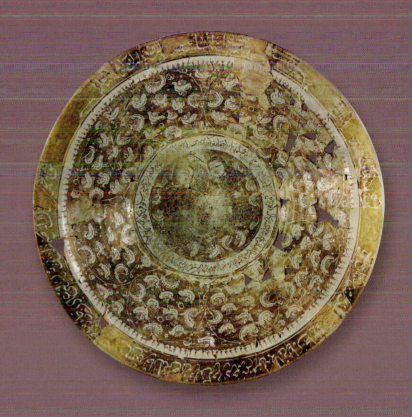

Fig. 11S5.2 *Right*
Lusterware plate (NEP19), from above. Covered with opacified white glaze and decorated with luster, the plate has its date of production inscribed in the central epigraphic ring as H 604/1211 CE; the place of production was Kashan. A plate of this size with a stoneware body would have been very difficult to throw, and is a testament to the potter's skill.

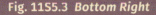

Fig. 11S5.3 *Bottom Right*
Lusterware vase (NEP115). Kashan continued to produce lusterware until the first decades of the 17th century CE.

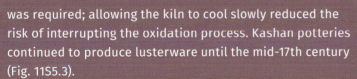

was required; allowing the kiln to cool slowly reduced the risk of interrupting the oxidation process. Kashan potteries continued to produce lusterware until the mid-17th century (Fig. 11S5.3).

By the middle of the 12th century CE, another transformation had also taken place in the production of fine ceramics. Namely, the body was no longer just clay. In fact, it was composed almost entirely of crushed quartz, to which small amounts of white clay and ground-up glaze were added. Known today as stonepaste ware or fritware, this versatile material could be produced as very thin bodies for delicate vessels, or for thicker ones for tiles as part of large-scale architectural ceramics. The similar composition of body and glaze meant that they fused in the kiln.

A Figured 'Cloth of Gold': Isfahan and Global Trade

Renata Holod and Martina Ferrari

The Safavid Period (H 907–1145, 1501–1722 CE) witnessed Iran's incorporation into the global economy of the Early Modern era. Just as Safavid rulers based in the newly built imperial capital of Isfahan sent commercial and diplomatic missions to various Asian and European courts from the late 16th century onwards, so too did they receive traders, merchants, adventurers, and emissaries from foreign polities. Long-distance trade expanded both by land and by sea. Routes across Ottoman territories into central and northern Europe, as well as routes directly north to the Baltic seaboard through the domains of Muscovy or the Polish-Lithuanian Commonwealth, were controlled by the Armenian merchant network based in the Isfahan suburb of New Julfa. Maritime trade also witnessed extraordinary growth during this period with the circumnavigation of Africa due especially to the efforts of the Dutch East India Company (VOC) and the British East India Company (EIC).

The chief commodity exported from Safavid Iran was raw silk produced in the Caspian provinces of Gilan and Mazandaran. This was so sought after that it could be exchanged for its weight in silver. The fact that numerous fine Persian silks from this period are held in museum collections around the world also attests to production of exquisite finished textiles by Safavid manufactories located in Isfahan, Kashan, and Yazd. Many of these finished textiles, indeed, were used for royal or ecclesistical robes. In the Penn Museum collection, there are several fragments of these luxurious and colorful textiles, the most famous of which is the Strawberry and Butterfly Velvet (NEP 6).

This sumptuous silk velvet is among the most resplendent and extravagant of Safavid textiles extant from the first part of the 17th century. Its sophisticated weave structure would have required the use of a complex draw loom and very dense thread counts. The polychrome pattern in a simplified, semi-naturalistic style presents a strawberry plant with a large three-pointed leaf, flowers, and strawberries. The motif is repeated in staggered rows with butterflies (Fig. 11S6.1a). The pattern is spread across a glistening background of brocaded silver-wrapped thread (*fil riant*). A metallic gilded silver strip was wound around a white silk core but left some of the white silk visible, thus providing texture. Today, several areas of the textile are missing the distinctive metal-wrapped thread. If this loss diminishes the former splendor of the velvet, it also exposes the sophistication of the monochrome five-end, warp-faced, satin, double-weave foundation (Fig. 11S6.2).

Technical analysis of this velvet illuminates how Safavid designers and weavers exploited color. The pattern is formed by velvet tufts that enrich the optical, three-dimensional effect of the fabric. It is further outlined with supplementary pile warps in eighteen different colors inserted using the pile-warp substitution technique. This technique, which required cutting selected supplementary warp yarns and replacing them with other colors of yarn, is discernible only on the back of the fabric where the cut warp floats are visible (Figs. 11S6.1b and 11S6.2).

Fig. 11S6.1a *Above*
Front of textile (NEP6).

Fig. 11S6.1b *Above*
Back of textile (NEP6).

WEAVE STRUCTURE

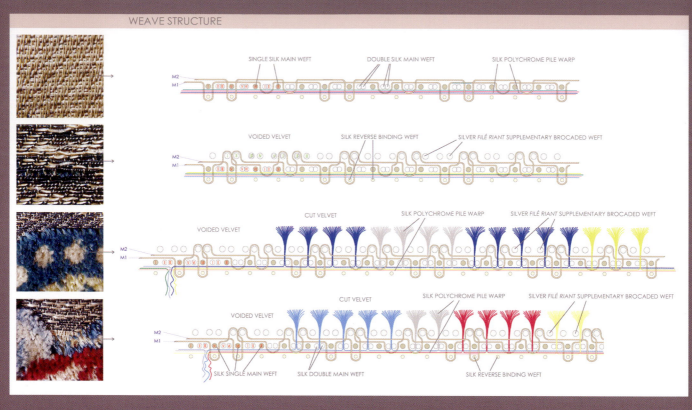

SINGLE SILK MAIN WEFT

DOUBLE SILK MAIN WEFT

SILK POLYCHROME PILE WARP

M2
M1

VOIDED VELVET

SILK REVERSE BINDING WEFT

SILVER *FILÉ RIANT* SUPPLEMENTARY BROCADED WEFT

M2
M1

VOIDED VELVET

CUT VELVET

SILK POLYCHROME PILE WARP

SILVER *FILÉ RIANT* SUPPLEMENTARY BROCADED WEFT

M2
M1

VOIDED VELVET

CUT VELVET

SILK POLYCHROME PILE WARP

SILVER *FILÉ RIANT* SUPPLEMENTARY BROCADED WEFT

M2
M1

SILK SINGLE MAIN WEFT

SILK DOUBLE MAIN WEFT

SILK REVERSE BINDING WEFT

DETAILS

COLOR PALETTE: 18 PILE-WARP SUBSTITUTIONS

WHITE | PINK | YELLOW | BLUE | GREEN | BROWN

KEYS

M1, M2. Silk main warp

Silk single main weft

Silk double main weft

Silver *filé riant* supplementary discontinuous brocaded weft

Silk reverse binding weft

Silk pile warp substitution (18 colors)

Fig. 11S6.2 *Above*
Diagram of colors identified during analysis.

The Ali Quli Agha Complex at Isfahan

In 1709–1710 CE, Ali Quli Agha, who served as an official at the court of the Safavid shahs Suleiman (H 1077–1105/1666–1694 CE) and, later, Sultan Husain (H 1105–1135/1696–1722 CE), signed a registration document (Persian: *vaqfnameh*) establishing a pious foundation to support a social service complex for Baidabad. The complex—nucleus for the new urban neighborhood in Isfahan—provided the necessary religious, social, and commercial services. Its components included, on one side of a preexisting water channel or *madi*, a mosque topped with a legal college, and, on the other, a large double bath, a small covered bazaar (Persian: *bazarcheh*) marked with a monumental covered crossing, and a warehouse. The latter two elements, the bazaar and the warehouse, provided support via rent for the former buildings and for the services housed within them. Unlike the grander areas of the new capital, which were laid out according to a grid, this neighborhood center fitted into existing patterns of land use more typical for garden suburbs. The streets crossing under the bazaar dome, for example, were existing paths rather than newly laid out orthogonally intersecting streets. The mosque's facade, which had shops flanking its entrance, followed the bend of the canal.

The mosque itself, though capacious, also lacked the habitual markers of more monumental structures in Isfahan and elsewhere, such as a tiled dome or even a minaret. Indeed, aside from the tiled portal with its muqarnas-filled niche, and a kiosk atop the portal (Persian: *guldasteh*) for the muezzin, the person who calls to prayer, there is little to signify the structure's function or to endow it with a monumental aspect. A long, vaulted hall behind the four rightmost shops was not connected to the spaces of the mosque; this served as the lecture room for the madrasa (or legal school). A large ablution area was situated behind the leftmost shop of the facade. A vaulted corridor led through into the rectangular space of a large mosque courtyard with a single line of three star vaults in front of the *qibla* wall (the wall indicating the direction of Mecca, faced while praying), mirrored by three vaults opposite it. Five bays, blind niches to the right of the *qibla* wall and shallow bays to the left, measured off the long lateral sides of the open space. The vast emptiness of the court is striking, at least until one recalls that it would have been transformed during the month of Muharram by tenting into a ritual space (*husainiyya*) for the mourning of Hasan and Husain, the Shi'i martyrs. Still, one is left to wonder how the overall mosque space would have been utilized on a weekly rather than yearly basis.

Over the commercial space of the front facade shops of the ground floor were rooms of the madrasa. A small institution, it was never meant to house more than a dozen students and a teacher. Rather than being isolated in the manner of the grander madrasas in the Early Modern city of Isfahan, this madrasa was a homier affair and appears to have been very much integrated into the life of the quarter. Every student room, in fact, incorporated a screened viewing window that provided an outside prospect onto the neighborhood and its water channel. In particular, the main entrance to the double and elaborate bathhouse opposite could be viewed from this vantage point.

The bathhouse entrance from the channel side led into the larger space with a domed octagonal dressing and relaxation/socializing hall and connecting warm and hot rooms. Next to and entered from the octagonal hall stretched a vaulted hall with a swimming pool. A smaller bath complex, located behind the larger one, was entered from a back lane. Alongside this smaller space ran the animal ramp where an ox or donkey hauled water up to a roof cistern.

The overall complex, which is relatively well preserved, appears to have been completed not long before the Afghan invasion of the Safavid Empire (1722–1730 CE) and the subsequent sack of the city of Isfahan. To develop the elements of his complex in the early years of the 18th century CE, Ali Quli Agha called upon his own experience of public architecture in the city to identify spaces in which both the necessities and pleasures of urban life could be fulfilled. The relationship between mosque, madrasa, and double bath is an urban one, and typical of such neighborhood complexes. Here, however, the preexisting water channel, a naturally open element, created a striking space for seeing, gazing, and viewing. This kind of public open space, inviting lingering and prolonged looking was, in fact, characteristic of the grander spaces of the city (introduced above), which had been constructed over the course of the previous century and which would have engendered a "spectatorial" habit among the people of Isfahan. The design of spaces accommodating of this habit on the neighborhood scale, as in the Ali Quli Agha complex, is a natural development, and the process of designing and building the complex should be contextualized as an outgrowth of four to five generations (spanning more than a century) of local experience in developing such spaces.

Conclusion

What makes an Islamic city? The case studies presented here on medieval Rayy and Early Modern Isfahan explore the presence and interaction of many different types of space—private, public, religious, social, commercial—within the city, and consider the ways in which these spaces shaped the lives and experiences of the people who encountered them. Densely concentrated domestic dwellings would have been private, located on dead-end lanes with shared access and responsibility for upkeep. Worship was a private act, and yet the congregational mosque was a fundamental component of the Islamic city. It was, moreover, not merely a communal space for worship but, indeed, intended to accommodate the entirety of the (male) population of a community for the noon prayer on Friday. (Shrines were more typically women's spaces.) The bazaar, a space for commercial services and economic transactions, one in which an enormously diverse range of people might meet and mingle, was also something of a city in miniature, containing not only those shops that supported, via rent, a range of other services and structures, but also hostels, madrasas, bathhouses, and mosques. The great and beautiful avenues described at Rayy represented another type of space within the urban landscape, a public space that accommodated especially the function of parade and display. And, in Safavid Isfahan, to an even greater extent, numerous grand spaces designed for public entertainment, socializing, and leisure encouraged urban inhabitants to linger and engage in prolonged and pleasurable viewing. Such spaces and considerations also seem ultimately to have shaped design and construction on the neighborhood level, as in the case of the Ali Quli Agha complex.

For Further Reading

Golombek, Lisa, Robert H. Mason, Patricia Proctor, and Eileen Reilly. 2014. *Persian Pottery in the First Global Age*. Leiden-Boston-Toronto: Brill-ROM.

Gürsan-Salzmann, Ayse. 2007. *Exploring Iran: The Photography of Erich F. Schmidt, 1930–1940*. Philadelphia: University of Pennsylvania Museum of Archaeology and Anthropology.

Holod, Renata. 2017. Approaching the Mosque: Beginnings and Evolution. In *Mosques: Splendors of Islam*, ed. Jai Imbrey, pp. 14–21. New York: Rizzoli.

Holod, Renata, Salma Jayyusi, Attilio Petruccioli, and André Raymond, eds. 2008. *The City in the Islamic World*. New York-Leiden: Brill.

Lassner, Jacob. 1980. *The Shaping of 'Abbāsid Rule*. Princeton: Princeton University Press.

Le Strange, G. (1900) 1983. *Baghdad during the Abbasid Caliphate*. Oxford: Oxford University Press.

Mackie, Louise W. 2015. *Symbols of Power: Luxury Textiles from Islamic Lands, 7th–21st Century*. New Haven-London: Cleveland Museum of Art and Yale University Press.

Mason, Robert B. 2004. *Shine like the Sun: Lustre-Painted and Associated Pottery from the Medieval Middle East*. Costa Mesa, CA: Mazda.

Rante, Rocco. 2015. *Rayy from Its Origins to the Mongol Invasion: An Archaeological and Historiographical Study*. Leiden: Brill.

Rante, Rocco, and Carmen Di Pasquale. 2016. The Urbanisation of Rayy in the Seljūq Period. *Der Islam* 93(2): 413–432.

Wheatley, Paul. 2001. *The Places Where Men Pray Together*. Chicago: University of Chicago Press.

Wirth, Eugen. 1971. *Syrien: Eine Geographische Landeskunde*. Darmstadt: Wiss. Buchges.

12

THE MODERN CITY

Lauren Ristvet, Ellen Owens, and Jessica Bicknell

Opposite

An ancient map on a tablet (B13885) from Nippur showing waterways important for irrigation and transportation. Beside it is a modern SEPTA (Southeastern Pennsylvania Transportation Authority) transit map.

Introduction

The world's first cities emerged in the ancient Middle East, in the southern plains of Mesopotamia, a little more than five thousand years ago. By 3000 BCE, Uruk, the earliest known city (see Chapter 3: The First Cities), is estimated to have contained perhaps 0.1 percent of the world's population. Some 4,800 years later, in 1800 CE, urbanization would seem to have made little progress: only 3% of the world's total population lived in cities, though urban areas were, of course, more densely clustered in some parts of the world than in others. But the process of urbanization was about to accelerate, and the next two centuries witnessed the rise of cities across the globe. In 2008, for the first time in history, the world's population was evenly split between cities and the countryside. Today, hundreds of millions of people live in megacities, urban agglomerations like Tokyo, Bombay, New York, Shanghai, and Mexico City that have over ten million inhabitants. And, by 2050, projections suggest that more than 70% of the world's population will live in urban areas.

The cities of today are frequently larger and look, at least on initial view, very different from the cities of our ancient past. And yet, ancient and modern cities have a surprising number of features in common. This chapter examines the shared features of cities from their earliest appearance in the ancient Middle East to their modern manifestations in the present day.

The Characteristics of Cities: Ancient and Modern

Anthropologists and sociologists tend to define cities in one of two ways. In 1938, the famous sociologist Louis Wirth emphasized population, arguing that cities were large, permanent settlements characterized by high population density and social diversity, encompassing people of different families, classes, ethnicities, and language groups. Later, geographers, anthropologists, and archaeologists have argued that cities are settlements that have an urban function, e.g., if they house an institution or offer a service, such as a government building, a temple, or a market, that affects people in a wider geographical area.

Cities in the Middle East have usually fit both of the above definitions. By 2400 BCE, Ur was one of the larger cities in southern Mesopotamia and its warren of little streets was lined by densely packed houses inhabited by rich and poor alike; its position as a Persian Gulf entrepôt also made it an economic center (Fig. 12.1) (see Chapter 7: The Ancient Near Eastern City: 2100–500 BCE). In about 1000 CE, the city of Rayy in modern Iran was the capital of Tughirl Beg, the founder of the Seljuq Empire; Rayy's ruins cover an area of some 36 square kilometers (14 square miles), indicating it reached a vast size for a pre-modern (i.e. pre-1800 CE) city (see Chapter 11: The Medieval and Early Modern Islamic and Persianate City).

Fig. 12.1 *Opposite*
Industry and Laws, Then and Now. (Top) Comparing a 16th-century manuscript depicting an arms workshop in Iran to a photo of a modern Campbell's factory line. (Bottom) A close-up view of the laws on the Stele of Hammurabi paired with an image of the U.S. Constitution. Clockwise from top left, photos courtesy of The Metropolitan Museum of Art (Image no. sf1981-473r; Object no. 1981.473), Getty Images/ Bloomberg, National Archives (identifier: 1667751), and the Penn Museum.

Fig. 12.2 *Above*

Markets or gathering places have
been central to cities for millennia.
Reading Terminal Market, Philadelphia
© R. Kennedy for VISIT PHILADELPHIA.
Kennedy for VISIT PHILADEPHIA®.

The characteristics of urban centers on which we have chosen to focus are fundamental
to the definition of the term "city"; they relate to demography, economics, society, politics,
and culture, and they have shaped the lives of city-dwellers and rural residents alike.
Some of these features may seem mundane enough to require little discussion, but it
is precisely these aspects of urban life that are most unique and exciting when they are
considered within the context of the rural ways of life that formed the backdrop for the
rise of the first cities.

The historical cities of the Middle East share a number of features with other ancient
and modern cities. Perhaps most notable among these features is that urban centers do
not just affect the tiny proportion of the world's population who happen to live within
them. They also create new opportunities and risks for those who live outside them.

Here, we will focus on key features that are characteristic of all cities: size and density;
professional specialization; social diversity; political organization; cultural, religious and
economic services; and infrastructure and city services. We will also discuss some of the
ways in which pre-modern cities differed from our modern metropolises, and some of the

unique advantages and disadvantages of each. This comparative analysis is intended to shed new light on both modern and pre-modern cities.

Urban Layout

Modern cities are spatially diverse, containing neighborhoods of tenements and mansions; financial districts where office buildings are concentrated; commercial districts lined with shops; governmental buildings such as a city hall; religious centers like cathedrals, mosques, synagogues, and temples; and cultural and community centers like symphonies, museums, and stadiums. Most contemporary cities are planned, and zoning codes tend to separate (to some degree) the various functions encompassed within them (Fig. 12.2). Often, less densely built up and populated suburbs circle the city, home to people who travel to the city for work or other services.

Different street patterns may exist within a single city, often reflecting the distinctive histories of an old city center and newer satellite neighborhoods. There are four basic "fingerprints" for modern city layouts, which reflect how they are characterized by streets, roads, and block formations, and delineate relationships between cities spanning the globe. Similarities can be found in the layout of cities in opposite parts of the world, such as Washington, D.C. and Paris, France, or Manhattan (New York City) and Campo Grande, Brazil. New York City, the largest city in the United States, features distinctive street patterns within each of its five boroughs that embody each of these fingerprint styles. Differences between contemporary cities are also cast into stark relief: Philadelphia, for example, was organized as a grid by founder William Penn; this design diverged sharply from the more varied layout of his native London.

Patterns of spatial diversity and organization are as evident in many ancient cities as in modern ones. Although none of the Mesopotamian cities were as clearly planned as Philadelphia, they did not grow up entirely by chance. Instead, excavations at sites such as Tell Leilan in Syria have revealed that roads were often set out at the beginning of a neighborhood's history. Similarly, the division of a city into property lots and the persistence of houses in the same place generation after generation in cities like Ur constrained later growth, leading to cities that were at least partly planned.

In Iran during the Seljuq Period (ca. 1040–1196 CE), the long history of the Islamic city of Rayy shaped its urban development. The two centers of the ancient city were the fortified citadel and the *shahristan*, the inner city or government district, both of which dated back to the Parthian Period (ca. 200 BCE). These districts were walled, as were some of the suburbs beyond the city. The gates of the city wall were famous and are described by several contemporaries. Bazaars or markets were located at the gates of the city, which were probably also important gathering points for individual neighborhoods.

Size and Density

Over the last 200 years, cities have grown immensely in both size and density: there are more than 300 cities in the world today with a population of over one million. It is hard to estimate ancient populations, but it seems likely that early cities did not achieve similar populations before the rise of Rome in 100 BCE or, perhaps, even of Baghdad around 800 CE. In 1800, only three cities in the world, all located in East Asia, had populations of a million or more. For most of the roughly 5,000-year history of urbanization, then, there was no consistent trend towards larger size or greater population density. The first city in the world, Uruk in southern Mesopotamia, was, by the late 4th millennium BCE, roughly the size of Philadelphia in 1800, and had perhaps a similar population density. It is notable that Philadelphia with a population of 28,522 in 1800 was the second-most populous city in the United States.

City density is usually defined by measuring the density of urban agglomerations: the city plus its suburban mass, which sprawls adjacent to the boundaries of the city proper. It is an interesting feature of the 20th century that measures of urban density actually plummeted around the world as trains and then cars facilitated commuting, permitting the rapid expansion of less densely settled suburbs. In pre-industrial cities, including both ancient Mesopotamian and later Islamic cities, the primary mode of transportation was by foot; higher urban densities were encouraged by the need to minimize travel time.

If we take into account suburbs in addition to cities proper, we can explore historical rates of urbanization in more comprehensive terms. Archaeological surveys in southern Mesopotamian have shown that between seventy and eighty percent of the population of the region in the mid-3rd millennium BCE lived in urban centers, here defined as places with populations of about 2,000 people. Using a similar definition of urban, the United States did not achieve similar rates of urbanization until the 1960s.

It is worth noting that the characteristic population density of cities has its downsides: if it has facilitated rapid innovation and the development of new technologies, it has also facilitated the rapid spread of diseases including smallpox, measles, and the Black Death. And, if daily life in urban centers entails contact and interaction between strangers and diverse peoples, it also permits anonymity and anonymous crime.

Labor Specialization

If one were to examine in detail the population of any single city block of Philadelphia, one would find people who perform many different types of work including lawyers, teachers, contractors, software developers, homemakers, gas station attendants, doctors, and cab drivers. To a large extent, the story of the development of the city has been the story of labor specialization and diversification.

Among the few types of work that would probably not be represented in a modern city is farming. And yet, before the rise of the city, and even in many of the early cities, farming is how most people made their living. As agriculture became more efficient, it underwrote the development of other professions in Mesopotamia. Over time it became both possible and desirable for farmers to produce more food than they needed to feed themselves and their families. Much of this surplus went to institutions like palaces and temples, which directly employed vast numbers of people and indirectly supported many others. Temples in Mesopotamia, for example, provided rations not only to many different types of religious specialists (e.g., exorcists, professional mourners, and diviners), but also to weavers, metalworkers, and potters. The same was true of palaces. The standard professions list in Mesopotamia, which dates back to the dawn of writing, enumerates a striking range of possible professions from king down to reedworker. Copies of this list are known, albeit with some variations, from the late fourth down to the 1st millennium BCE. At Ur, archaeologists have uncovered both textual and archaeological evidence for the lives and work of different types of professionals; these include artisans like seal-carvers; priests; and princesses. The same is true of later cities in the Middle East and around the globe.

Class and Diversity

Villages are typically relatively homogenous in composition: residents are often similar in social and economic status, in the language they speak, and in ethnicity. In villages, one knows everyone intimately: occupants would often have grown up together, and not only be familiar with the parents, grandparents, siblings, cousins, and children of other residents but are also likely to be related to them through ties of blood or marriage. Village residents, as a result of these circumstances, are situated within a social contract of familiarity.

City populations, in contrast, are characterized by their diversity—social, economic, linguistic, ethnic, occupational, and so forth. In the 3rd millennium BCE city of Ur, for example, residents included people with Sumerian as well as Akkadian names, and foreigners from as far away as the Indus Valley. Residents were already engaged in a range of different occupations and types of labor. Modern cities are characterized by a similar heterogeneity and may, likewise, be sites of trade and labor specialization, as well as offer opportunities for social mobility and economic prosperity. Cities, however, are also characterized by social stratification. They are places where inequality looms

Fig. 12.3 *Left*
Replica of the Stele of Hammurabi.
The original is in the Louvre.

large. Spacious mansions coexist with tiny cottages and disparities in income are far greater than in smaller settlements. The emergence of classes, which possess unequal access to resources, is central to the city, and visible already in the earliest urban centers. In the mid-3rd millennium BCE royal graves at Ur, for example, we can clearly see the disparity in opportunities afforded to Queen Puabi and those afforded to her sacrificed handmaidens (see Chapter 8: The Royal Cemetery of Ur).

Political Organization

Cities, lacking the complex kin systems that provide order in villages, require formal systems for conflict resolution. Laws, courts, judges, property traditions, arbiters, and a complex government structure all perform this important function. Among other things, laws protect and encourage trade and land transactions, provide a tool to handle disputes and prevent violence, and govern the recognition of familial and marital relationships.

In Mesopotamian cities, as in modern ones, a variety of different authorities were involved in making legal decisions and conferring justice. These ranged from assemblies of elders or citizens, who typically heard local disputes in tandem with groups of judges representing leading members of the community, to royal judges appointed by the king, to the king himself. Spaces where legal disputes could be heard were typically public and included temples, the banks of the Euphrates River, the city gates, and,

Fig. 12.5 *Left*
Philadelphia City Hall. © Wikimedia
Commons/Beyond My Ken.

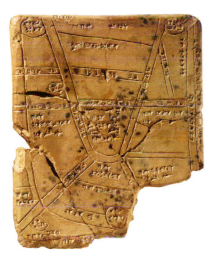

likely, the palace of the king. The concern with justice in the ancient Mesopotamian city is perhaps most clearly apparent in the Law Stele of Hammurabi (famously known as the Law Code of Hammurabi), which is inscribed with an important and instructive collection of legal decisions but not a set of prescriptive laws. These legal decisions emphasize retributive justice, focusing on the punishments of offenders. The punishments outlined, moreover, often embody the principle of *lex talionis*, being proportionate—corresponding in degree and kind—to the offense committed; this principle remains an important element of many contemporary justice systems (Fig. 12.3) and commonly translates to "an eye for an eye."

Cultural, Religious, and Economic Services

Religious functions are critical to many of the cities discussed in this volume—and to the self-definition of these cities. In Mesopotamia, gods were the real owners of the city, and temples were often the geographical and symbolic focal points (Fig. 12.4) (see Chapter 4: Religion and the Gods). Modern cities also tend to contain significant religious and cultural institutions, which function both as meeting places and as a means of safeguarding elements of both tangible and intangible heritage. The interiors and exteriors of these buildings are often critical to public displays of specific values, narratives, and histories adopted or claimed by the city or (at least some of) its inhabitants. They are often long lasting, retaining the same function over centuries, and may ultimately become symbols of the city. This is as true, for instance, of the Citadel at Rayy as it is for City Hall in Philadelphia (Fig. 12.5).

Infrastructure and City Services

Cities also contain spaces that are shared by all of their inhabitants; these include the streets, on which one may encounter friends and strangers alike. They depend on infrastructure such as sewage pipes (Fig. 12.6), irrigation canals, and harbors that need to be maintained by groups larger than an individual or a single family. Southern Mesopotamia, for example, relied on a network of irrigation canals to produce agricultural crops (Fig. 12.7). At their inception, these were relatively simple; they became progressively more elaborate over time until, by the late 1st millennium BCE, some could accommodate ocean-going vessels. Waterways were the cheapest and most efficient means of traveling from one place to the other in the pre-modern world, and the canals of Mesopotamia were vital drivers of economic growth. It is only in the past two centuries that railroads and highways have made overland travel efficient.

Fig. 12.8 *Above Left*
Gaming piece (B16972B).

Fig. 12.9 *Above Right*
Lamp (37-11-997).

City Life: Ancient to Modern

Since their origins in southern Mesopotamia over five thousand years ago, cities have been significant sites of change and innovation. They make possible the interaction of diverse peoples and ideas and accelerate the need for and development and application of new technologies, administrative and otherwise. Public gathering places such as parks, libraries, markets, and schools provide spaces for the cross-pollination of ideas and people. Cultural and religious institutions safeguard tangible and intangible elements of shared history. The earliest city dwellers, too, show many similar interests and concerns to our own. Excavations of early cities in the Middle East have yielded maps, sewer pipes, gaming pieces (Fig. 12.8), and lamps (Fig. 12.9), material testimony to a focus on traveling from place to place, waste management, entertainment, and lighting the night.

Cities are still evolving. What will they look like in the future? High-speed railways and self-driving vehicles may transform the way people commute. Urban farming, green storm water infrastructure, and other environmental practices are becoming ever more prominent as cities grow and sustainability becomes a concern. Even as they develop in remarkable and likely unpredictable ways, the cities of the future, as spaces where diverse peoples live in close quarters and productively interact with each other, will continue to have much in common with the ancient cities of our past.

For Further Reading

Ascher, Kate. 2005. *The Works: Anatomy of a City*. New York: Penguin.

Gates, Charles. 2003. *Ancient Cities: The Archaeology of Urban Life in the Ancient Near East, Egypt, Greece, and Rome*. New York: Routledge.

Gravel, Ryan. 2016. *Where We Want to Live: Reclaiming Infrastructure for a New Generation of Cities*. New York: St. Martin's.

Jacobs, Frank. *How to Fingerprint a City*. Big Think: http://bigthink.com/strange-maps/how-to-fingerprint-a-city. Accessed on December 8, 2017.

Jacobs, Jane. 1961. *The Death and Life of Great American Cities*. New York: Random House.

Kostof, Spiro. 1999. *The City Shaped: Urban Patterns and Meanings through History*. London: Thames & Hudson.

Leick, Gwendolyn. 2001. Mesopotamia: Invention of the City. London: Penguin.

Mumford, Lewis. 1961. The City in History: Its Origins, Its Transformations, and Its Prospects. New York: Harcourt, Inc.

Poon, Linda. Mapping the 'Urban Fingerprints' of Cities. CITYLAB, September 11, 2015. https://www.citylab.com/equity/2015/09/mapping-the-urban-fingerprints-of-cities/404923/. Accessed on December 8, 2017.

Van de Mieroop. 1997. *The Ancient Mesopotamian City*. New York: Oxford University Press.

Wirth, Louis. 1938. Urbanism as a Way of Life. *American Journal of Sociology* 44(1):1–24.

13

Epilogue: The Middle East and Globalization

Brian Spooner

SPANNING THE WORLD

The Middle East is situated on major trade routes running both over land and over water.

With the domestication of the camel around 1000 BCE, the overland routes extended westward from the Sahara Desert to the Atlantic Ocean, and eastward through Central Asia to China.

The sea trade benefitted from monsoon winds, and ultimately connected the east coast of Africa with the Indian subcontinent and China.

By the end of the 1400s, with the circumnavigation of the globe, sea routes became more important and land routes diminished.

CAMELS

Around 800 CE, overland trade employing dromedaries and Bactrian camels expanded to run from the Atlantic to the borders of China. Two camel-loads equaled one cart-load drawn by two oxen.

1 SPOUTED POT
Stonepaste; haft rang
Late 12th–early 13th century CE
Made in Kashan (Iran)

2 CAMEL FIGURINE
Ceramic; modeled
ca. 850 BCE
Ur (Iraq)

SEALS

Seals were used to mark ownership and validate contracts throughout Middle Eastern history. The practice of sealing continued despite the influx of new peoples and customs into the region.

SEALS AND SEALINGS

3 PARTHIAN SEAL
Chalcedony
ca. 1st century CE
Iran or Iraq

4 SASANIAN SEAL
Sard
ca. 3rd–4th century CE
Iran

5 ISLAMIC SEAL
Glass
11th–12th century CE
Excavated at Rayy (Iran)

6 STAMP SEAL
Glass
11th century CE
Excavated at Rayy (Iran)

IMPORTED CERAMICS AT RAYY

Chinese ceramics were extremely popular in the Middle East. The eleventh-century scholar al-Biruni observed "In Rayy a man entertained me in his home. There I saw the bowls, the dishes, the bottles, the plates, the pitchers, the drinking vessels, even the pouring jugs, and the wash-basins, and the ash-boxes, all made of Chinese porcelain. And I was astonished at his desire for luxury."

7 BOWL, SONG DYNASTY
Porcelain
11th–12th century CE
Excavated at Rayy (Iran)

8 BOWL, CHINESE SHAPE
Ceramic; signified to glaze
9th century CE
Made in Basra (Iraq)
Excavated at Rayy (Iran)

9 DISH, CHINESE STYLE
Stonepaste; glazed
12th–13th century CE
Excavated at Rayy (Iran)

WEIGHTS AND THE MARKET

10 BALANCE SCALE (STEELYARD)
Bronze; cast and engraved
13th–14th century CE
Probably (Syria)

11 SUGAR AND WEIGHTS
Brass
19th century CE
Iran

12 TWEEZERS
Brass
10th century CE
Iran

13 TOUCHSTONE
Slate
13th–14th century CE
Rayy (Iran)

Epilogue

In the foregoing chapters, the curatorial team has approached the history, ethnology, and archaeology of the Middle East from a wide range of perspectives in order to illuminate the background of the Middle East Galleries that prompted this volume. During the course of gallery development, which took several years, the team returned time and again to the importance of trade and globalization, and the relationship between them. The following summary reflection is occasioned by the importance of these matters both historically and as drivers for the form the galleries eventually assumed.

An inter-urban trade network began to develop out of the early cities of Mesopotamia by the end of the 4th millennium BCE and continued to grow as more and more settlements grew into cities along each of the rivers of the arid zone. Cities connected because, unlike villages that were self-sufficient communities of food producers, they needed trade for the commodities they produced. The development of the inter-urban trade network from the Middle East through the arid zone to northern China was the beginning of globalization: it brought increasing numbers of people into interaction with each other over larger and larger areas.

The gradual development of this trade network made the Middle East the center and leader of global civilization. The domestication of donkeys and horses as beasts of burden beginning in the 4th millennium BCE, and eventually camels, were important advances. As trade became more important by the end of this millennium, the need to record transactions and send messages led to the adoption of writing—first, again, in Mesopotamia, and spreading gradually west along the trade routes to the Mediterranean and east towards India and China. Trade not only increased human capabilities by facilitating the spread of writing, it changed the natural world by moving cultigens from one ecosystem to another, east to west and west to east. Trade intensified the cultural as well as the economic interaction between west and east Asia (China, India, and Iran). Commodities moved along trade routes—tea and silk; the walnut, peach, apricot, eggplant, spinach, olives, rice, dates, millet, sorghum, and cinnamon; jasmine, henna, indigo; cotton, pepper, and sugar—and so did cultural models, such as the court model of government from the Persian empires, and technologies such as paper, printing, and gunpowder.

Apart from the overland trade network, starting sometime during the Sasanian Period (ca. 224–651 CE), a maritime coastal route began to develop from the port of Siraf in the Persian Gulf to India and southern China. Both of these routes were slow. But in the 1st century BCE the Greeks discovered a much faster way to sail to India, by using the monsoon to cross the Indian Ocean. Nothing faster was found until the 15th century and the beginning of the Age of Discovery, when Europeans developed oceanic sailing, and eventually superseded the Middle East in world leadership during the Colonial Period.

Fig. 13.1 *Opposite*
This animated map in the Middle East Galleries Room 3 shows the development of global trade routes. The picture captures the phase when China becomes connected to Europe via the Middle East during the 17th century CE.

Urbanization is the major engine of globalization. Cities bring more people into interaction with each other. Urban populations reach out for trade with other cities, sharing knowledge, increasing collective learning and stimulating innovation. Urbanization spread from the Middle East throughout the world. Globalization is producing an urban world in which it is not only easy to move from city to city, but remote communication between cities is as routine and easy as face-to-face.

The Middle East has been a major contributor to this globalization process. From the time when the first cities appeared in Mesopotamia in the 4th millennium BCE through the early empires of the ancient world and the growth of Islamic civilization in the 7th century CE onwards the Middle East was a leader in world history. As Chinese cities began to grow and proliferate they were connected to the cities of the Middle East by trade, and the east-west trade networks from China to the Mediterranean formed the largest connected area with the largest connected population in world history up to that time. When writing made it possible to interact remotely and organize the administration of larger territories, the age of empires began. The spread of Islam in the 7th and 8th centuries and the expansion of the Persianate ecumene from the 9th century onwards were major steps in the acceleration of globalization. The Persianate millennium (from the 9th to the 19th centuries) was the most advanced stage of globalization before the modern period, because it produced a culture area, based on a single written language, a koine, from west to east Asia including India and much of China.

Humans have always clustered. They have lived together and interacted in the largest possible numbers. Before the beginning of food production in the Neolithic the numbers were always limited by carrying capacity and the availability of food. Since the beginning of urban life some eight thousand years ago that limitation has almost disappeared. The proportion of the world population living in cities has always grown faster than the world population. It was very slow to begin with, but it has been accelerating, as discussed in the preceding chapter.

The Middle East has been at the center of the expanding arenas of social interaction from the growth of inter-urban trade networks east and west through the arid zone and the beginning of the expansion of empires. It lies at the center of the world's largest landmass and remains the center of Islamic civilization. Since the 19th century, the major drivers of globalization have been in the Western world in the form of new means of

Fig. 13.2 *Above*

Gallery case in Room 3 showing the development of ceramic wares and tiles in Iran during the 12th–18th centuries CE. The imitation Chinese bowl from page 367 is located on the left plinth.

remote interaction, from telegraph, telephone, and wireless to the internet and social media. Although the drivers have changed, the Middle East has experienced similar rates of population growth and migration as the rest of the world and remains as closely connected. Today, although it continues to be united by allegiance to Islamic law, it is divided by the political fragmentation imposed by the colonial powers and, even more significantly, by the pre-Islamic cultural heritage of the tribal Arabian vs. the urban Persian perspective, that was translated into the Sunni vs. the Shi`i division of Islam. As globalization progresses, new global perspectives are likely to replace local divisions.

For Further Reading

Spooner, Brian. 2015. *Globalization: The Crucial Phase.* Philadelphia: University of Pennsylvania Museum of Archaeology and Anthropology.

TIMELINE OF PENN MUSEUM EXCAVATIONS IN IRAQ AND IRAN

Richard L. Zettler

Opposite
View of the Nippur temple excavations
seen from atop the Nippur ziggurat, 1899.

Introduction

The University of Pennsylvania Museum of Archaeology and Anthropology (Penn Museum) has sponsored and supported archaeological research projects in nearly every region of the Middle East. It has been particularly active in the areas that are today Iraq and Iran, and the tens of thousands of artifacts in the Penn Museum's Babylonian and Near East Sections derive largely from its excavations in those areas (Fig. 14.1). *Journey to the City: A Companion to the Middle East Galleries at the Penn Museum* details the histories of the sites Penn Museum archaeologists have investigated over the last one hundred and thirty years and contextualizes the artifacts exhibited in the galleries, both unique discoveries like the "Ram in the Thicket" (see Chapter 8S2: The Goat in a Tree) from the Royal Cemetery of Ur (ca. 2450 BCE) and more mundane objects, such as clay spindle whorls. This timeline of excavations is intended as a brief introduction to the ruin mounds and archaeologists that have been referred to in the main text. It is organized geographically, with sites listed more or less in the order in which they were excavated.

Iraq

Archaeological investigations in the land between the Tigris and Euphrates Rivers in Turkish Arabia (what is today Iraq) began in the early 19th century and large-scale excavations a few decades later, when Paul Émile Botta, a French savant and diplomat, and Austin Henry Layard, a British adventurer, re-discovered the capital cities of the Late (Neo)-Assyrian kings, located near the northern center of Mosul.

Botta excavated the palace of Sargon II (721–705 BCE) at Khorsabad (Dur-Sharukkin), northeast of Mosul. Layard unearthed Nimrud, ancient Kahlu (Biblical Calah), southeast of Mosul, and the so-called Northwest Palace of Ashurnasirpal II (883–859 BCE). The colossal stone bulls with wings and human heads that guarded doorways and thick orthostats with reliefs depicting rituals, hunting and warfare, that lined the walls of the palaces' state ceremonial rooms created a sensation when they were installed in the British Museum and the Louvre.

The European quest for antiquities touched off by Botta and Layard's work spurred Americans, among them John Punnett Peters, an Episcopal clergyman and later Professor of Hebrew at the University of Pennsylvania, to action in the late 19th century. Peters put the proposition on the table at a meeting of the American Oriental Society in New Haven, October 24–25, 1883, "England and France have done a noble work of exploration in Assyria and Babylonia. It is time for America to do her part. Let us send out an American expedition."

William Hayes Ward, Editor of the New York *Independent* and an amateur "orientalist," led an initial exploratory expedition to Turkish Arabia. The Wolfe

Fig. 14.1 *Opposite*

Diggers in Pit X during the 1933–1934 field season at Ur. Excavating in one month, they removed more than 13,160 cubic meters of soil (ca. 17,000 cubic yards) to reach a depth of about 20 meters (ca. 65 feet).

Expedition, named after Catherine Lorillard Wolfe—the New York philanthropist and art collector, who funded it—spent January–April 1885 investigating potential sites for excavations in the area south of Baghdad.

Philadelphians and the University of Pennsylvania initiated the first excavations in Turkish Arabia at Nuffar, ancient Nippur, located near the small tribal market town of Afak, ca. 156 km (97 miles) south of Baghdad, shortly after the return of the Wolfe Expedition. Ward had described Nippur as a mound of "vast extent" that would "richly repay extensive explorations." The Penn Museum was founded contemporaneously with the excavations at Nippur and came to play a prominent role in archaeological research in the modern nation-state of Iraq during the era of big digs in the 1920s and 1930s.

Nuffar (Nippur), 1887–1900 and 1948–1952

A group of affluent Philadelphians, organized as the Babylonian Exploration Fund and affiliated with the University of Pennsylvania, supported three expeditions to Nippur, site of Ekur or "House Mountain," the temple of Enlil, and early Mesopotamia's religious center, in the late 19th century. The first expedition (1888–1889) ended in disaster, when local tribesmen, seeking revenge against one of the Turkish policemen guarding the excavators, burned the camp, forcing them to flee. The disastrous end of the expedition did not deter the Trustees of the Babylonian Exploration Fund, however, and the excavations resumed for another season in 1890. John Punnett Peters (Fig. 14.2) directed the first and second expeditions. A third expedition lasted nearly three years (1893–1895). Peters served as the Scientific Director, but John Henry Haynes, an early archaeological photographer who had been with both Ward and Peters, directed work on site. The Trustees of the Babylonian Exploration Fund dissolved the organization in due course and ceded its resources to the University that, then, funded a fourth campaign of excavations in 1899–1900. Hermann V. Hilprecht, Professor of Assyrian at the University of Pennsylvania, was Scientific Director, but John Henry Haynes again directed the excavations in the field, at least until Hilprecht arrived at Nippur shortly before the end of the expedition.

Critics have characterized the Nippur excavations as mining for cuneiform tablets. The criticism is not unwarranted, since Penn's archaeologists routinely dug tunnels deep into the sides of the ruin mounds, but it is one-sided. Penn's excavators revealed substantial architectural remains including, for example, the stepped temple tower or ziggurat that stood at the heart of Ekur and a large fortress the Parthian inhabitants of Nippur built over it in the 2nd century CE. They unearthed thousands of burials and cataloged an untold number of artifacts, including tens of thousands of cuneiform tablets.

Fig. 14.2 *Opposite*
Osman Hamdi Bey (seated), Director of the Imperial Ottoman Museum, and John P. Peters in the garden of Hamdi Bey's house on the Bosporus, 1889.

Fig. 14.3 *Above*

M. E. L. (Max) Mallowan and Agatha Christie visiting the excavations at Nippur in February 1950. Mallowan is center left (white collar) with Donald E. McCowan, director of the excavations at Nippur. Agatha Christie, carrying a handbag, is on the left side of the photograph while Mohammad Ali Mustafa, Representative of Iraq's Directorate General of Antiquities, is on the right side wearing a beret.

The excavations at Nippur were conducted under the 1884 Ottoman Law of Antiquities that established antiquities as property of the state. The Penn Museum received a substantial share of the finds from the excavations that were, in official parlance, gifts of the Sultan.

The Penn Museum harbored hopes of continuing work at Nippur long after the excavations ended, but fifty years passed before it returned to the site. With the Oriental Institute, the Penn Museum restarted excavations at Nippur in the years following World War II. Thorkild Jacobsen, a Sumerologist, then Director of the Oriental Institute, pressed the case for resuming excavations in the hope of finding more cuneiform tablets. Donald E. McCown, who directed the excavations, opened two operations on the southern tip of Nippur's eastern mound, "Tablet Hill," as it came to be called, where Penn had discovered so many tablets in the 19th century, and recovered substantial numbers of Sumerian literary and lexical texts (Fig. 14.3).

The Penn Museum supported work at Nippur in 1948, 1949–1950, and 1951–1952, but withdrew from the excavations after the third season to focus its resources and efforts on Iran. Carleton S. Coon, the Penn Museum's Curator of Ethnology, participated in the 1948 excavations, while Francis R. Steele represented the Museum for all three field seasons as epigrapher.

Tell al-Muqayyar (Ur), 1922–1934

The British Museum and the Penn Museum joined forces to support excavations at Tell al-Muqayyar, ancient Ur, and several other nearby sites, including Tell al-'Ubaid, in the years following World War I. The Joint Excavations, under C. Leonard (later Sir Leonard) Woolley, were the first archaeological project in the modern nation-state of Iraq. They were begun under a temporary permit and, subsequently, conducted under Iraq's Antiquities Law, approved in 1924, that reserved any artifacts judged to be "needed for the scientific completeness of the Iraq Museum" for the government, but provided for a division of the remaining finds between Iraq and the excavators.

Woolley's excavations initiated an archaeological revival in the region, and arguably constituted the largest field project of the interwar decades. Woolley worked annually for twelve years, 4 or 4½ months a year, with hundreds of local workmen. The architecture he uncovered, in particular the monumental ziggurat that Iraq's Directorate-General of Antiquities restored in the 1960s, stands as a landmark today, and the more than 21,000 artifacts he cataloged, including spectacular finds from the Royal Cemetery, provided the core collections of the newly founded Iraq Museum in Baghdad and substantial additions to the British Museum and the Penn Museum. In his Report to the Board for the year ending June 30, 1934, Penn Museum's Director, Horace H. F. Jayne, observed, "The year

Fig. 14.4 *Left*

The staff working at Ur in 1924–1925:
left to right, J. Linnell, Katharine
Keeling, C. Leonard Woolley, and
Léon Legrain.

also saw the termination of the Joint Expedition to Ur with the British Museum. Probably the most distinguished single project with which the Museum was ever concerned. With its twelve campaigns and their extraordinary results, rich in objects and fundamentally important information, it will be long remembered and referred to."

Woolley worked with a small staff. Katharine Keeling, who initially volunteered as an artist, but later married Woolley, was on site from 1925 to the end of the excavations. M. E. L. "Max" Mallowan, who married Agatha Christie, was Woolley's Assistant from 1925–1926 to 1930–1931. Leon Legrain, Curator of the Penn Museum's Babylonian Section, was epigrapher in 1924–1925 and 1925–1926 (Figs. 14.4 and 14.5).

Tepe Gawra, 1931–1938

Fig. 14.5 *Opposite*

C. Leonard Woolley at Ur with his
foreman Sheikh Hamoudi ibn Ibrahim
from Jerablus in Syria. Hamoudi served
as foreman throughout the excavations
and his three sons were junior foremen
for many of the seasons.

Excavations at Tepe Gawra and Tell Billa (see below) grew out of a survey that Ephraim A. Speiser, Annual Professor of the Baghdad School of the American School of Oriental Research (ASOR), made of archaeological sites in northern Iraq in 1926–1927.

Tepe Gawra ("Great Mound" in Kurdish), located ca. 24 km (15 miles) northeast of Mosul, was a small (1.5 ha/3.7 acres) conical mound, 22 m (72 feet) high, that was occupied from ca. 5000–1500 BCE. Speiser, who was initially drawn to the site by

Fig. 14.6 *Left*

House and staff at Tepe Gawra in 1937–1938. From left to right, Alberto Davico, E. Bartow Müller, Elisabeth Bache, Arthur J. Tobler, and Charles Bache.

surface finds of prehistoric painted pottery, conducted a short exploratory excavation in October 1927. The Penn Museum, ASOR's Baghdad School, and Dropsie College (now Katz Center for Advanced Judaic Studies) supported large-scale excavations from 1931 to 1938. Speiser was appointed Assistant Professor of Semitics at the University of Pennsylvania in 1928 and directed the excavations in 1931, 1931–1932, and 1936–1937; Charles Bache directed work in the other years (Fig. 14.6).

Yorghan Tepe (Nuzi), 1929–1931

Early in 1925, Gertrude Bell, Honorary Director of Antiquities, who founded the Iraq Museum, asked Edward Chiera, Annual Professor of ASOR's Baghdad School in 1924–1925, to undertake excavations at Yorghan Tepe, 13 km (8 miles) southwest of Kirkuk, where cuneiform tablets appearing in the market had reportedly been found. Chiera initiated excavations at the site on behalf of the Iraq Museum in March 1925 and continued work the following month as a joint project of the Iraq Museum and the

THE STAFF OF THE TOLEDO MUSEUM–UNIVERSITY OF MICHIGAN EXPEDITION AT OPIS, MESOPOTAMIA

Fig. 14.7 *Right*

The staff of the Toledo Museum-University of Michigan Expedition at Opis, Mesopotamia. University Museum *Bulletin* 1 (January 1930), pl. VI.

Baghdad School. Gertrude Bell wrote about her visit to the excavations in letters to her father and stepmother, noting that Chiera found a "great quantity of tablets." Harvard University (Fogg Museum and Semitic Museum) and the Baghdad School subsequently continued excavations at the site in the years 1925–1931. Yorghan Tepe's main mound revealed a substantial palace and temple, as well as private houses, dating to the 15th century BCE; surrounding mounds contained large private houses of the same date.

The Penn Museum supported the last two seasons of work at Yorghan Tepe (1929–1930 and 1930–1931), paying the expenses of a field assistant, Charles Bache—who went on to direct excavations at Tepe Gawra and Tell Billa—and contributing to the excavations. In return, the Museum acquired a share of the finds from the excavations including a glazed baked clay statuette of a recumbent lion (31-40-1).

Tell Umar (Seleucia-on-the-Tigris), 1929–1930

The University of Michigan and the Toledo Museum of Art sponsored the excavations at Seleucia 1927–1932 and 1936–1937. The Penn Museum provided modest support for the 1929–1930 excavations, covering the travel expenses of Arthur McCall Mintier, a graduate fellow at the University of Michigan, who represented the Museum, with the remainder of the contribution going toward the excavations (Fig. 14.7).

F-43ㅣ

Tell Billa (Shibaniba), 1930–1933

The Penn Museum and ASOR's Baghdad School excavated Tell Billa, located near the modern town of Bashiqa, ca. 13 km (8 miles) east of Mosul, in 1930–1931, 1931–1932 and 1932–1933, with sporadic work in later years. Ephraim A. Speiser directed the first two seasons of excavations; Charles Bache directed work in 1932–1933.

Tell Billa complemented Tepe Gawra in that its occupation, spanning the 3rd, 2nd, and 1st millennia BCE, began where Tepe Gawra's ended, though Speiser professed to be interested primarily in the site's Middle Assyrian (1392–934 BCE) and Neo-Assyrian (911–609 BCE) phases of occupation.

Fara (Shuruppak), 1931

The excavations at Fara (ancient Shuruppak), ca. 55 km (34 miles) south of Nippur (and the nearby town of Afak), originated from conversations Horace Jayne had with Sydney Smith, Director of Antiquities, when in Baghdad on a trip to the Middle East in March and April 1930, a year after he had become Director of the Penn Museum. Smith apparently told Jayne about illicit excavations in and around Afak and expressed an interest in having a "scientific expedition" in the area with the hope of safeguarding important sites. Smith showed Jayne finds from looting at Fara, an extensive low mound that Hilprecht and Haynes had visited in 1900 and German archaeologists had excavated in 1902–1903. Jayne described what he had seen in his Director's Report for December 1930 as rivaling the best objects from Ur for "their wealth of scientific and artistic importance," and subsequently requested a permit to excavate Fara. Jayne reminded the Penn Museum's Board that Fara might be the last chance to get a permit before the British relinquished the Mandate for Iraq in 1932, but he also envisioned Fara as alternating seasonally with archaeological work he planned to initiate in Iran.

Erich Schmidt, whom Jayne had hired to direct excavations in Iran (see below), worked at Fara mid-February to mid-May 1931, uncovering remains of the late 4th and 3rd millennia BCE center. But, Schmidt was discouraged by winter sandstorms and driving rain, the inaccessibility of potable water, and the extensive German trenches and dumps that covered the site. These factors along with the Penn Museum's lack of funds to support the excavations ended Jayne's plans for a long-term project after just one season (Fig. 14.8).

Fig. 14.8 *Opposite*
The camp at Fara in 1931. The camp was set up in the ruins of the excavation house used by German archaeologists in 1902–1903.

Khafaje and Tell Agrab, 1937–1938

The University of Chicago's Oriental Institute initiated excavations at a number of sites in the lower Diyala River drainage basin, northeast of Baghdad, in 1930–1931. Over the course of seven seasons of excavations the Oriental Institute uncovered impressive architectural remains, including a large oval temple complex of the mid-to-late third millennium BCE at Khafaje, and accumulated a spectacular array of small finds, including sculpture in the round and relief-carved plaques, cylinder seals, etc. dating to earlier 3rd millennium BCE. By 1936, however, the Oriental Institute was facing severe budgetary constraints and was forced to curtail its field projects in Iraq and elsewhere. After discussions with Henri Frankfort, who directed the Oriental Institute's excavations in the Diyala, in mid-December 1936, Ephraim A. Speiser convinced Horace Jayne to provide funding for a short excavation at Khafaje and Tell Agrab. The Oriental Institute had been excavating the sanctuary of a temple at Khafaje—apparently dedicated to Nintu, a mother goddess—in 1936–1937 that some years earlier had yielded late Early Dynastic statuary. Speiser thought the odds good that continuing the work there would yield additional sculptures, potentially giving the Penn Museum objects of a sort that Woolley had not found in his excavations at Ur and helping to raise funds to support future excavations at the site.

The staff of Tell Billa moved to Khafaje in late January 1937 and a month of digging, under the direction of P. P. Delougaz, who had overseen the Oriental Institute's work at the site, proved Speiser's hunch well founded. The excavations revealed, among other important discoveries, a large cache of statues that had been buried beneath the floor of one temple in a sequence of buildings and rebuildings of the Nintu temple.

Jayne found sufficient funds to finance a second season of excavations that lasted from mid-December 1937 to mid-March 1938. Delougaz, with help from the staff of Tepe Gawra, including Charles Bache, continued excavation of the Nintu temple on Khafaje's main mound but also uncovered earlier and later remains, including burials, elsewhere on the mound. When heavy winter rains made work in deeper trenches on the main mound impractical, Delougaz turned his attention to Khafaje's subsidiary mounds, where he uncovered important architectural remains dating to the early second millennium BCE.

The Great Depression made it impossible for the Penn Museum to continue excavations at Khafaje in 1938–1939. While Horace Jayne anticipated having sufficient funds to take up the work again in 1939–1940, World War II brought excavations in Iraq to a halt.

Tell al-Rimah, 1964–1967

Though pre-occupied with excavations at Hasanlu Tepe in Iran since the mid-1950s, the Penn Museum collaborated with the British School of Archaeology in Iraq in excavating Tell al-Rimah, south of the Jebel Sinjar, ca. 80 km (50 miles) west of Mosul, in the mid-to-late 1960s. David Oates, who directed the excavations, had chosen Tell al-Rimah because surface sherds suggested that it had been occupied for the whole of the 2nd millennium BCE. The Penn Museum co-sponsored the excavations in 1964, 1965, and 1966, with Theresa Howard Carter, representing the Museum, serving as Assistant Director. The Museum provided financial support in 1967, but subsequently withdrew from the excavations, leaving the British School to continue for two additional field seasons.

Iran

Archaeological excavations in Persia (Iran) began in 1850, when William Kennett Loftus, a British geologist with the Turco-Persian Frontier Commission, initiated work at Susa (modern Shush) in what is now Khuzestan Province of western Iran. Loftus excavated from 1850 to 1852, but British authorities decided against continuing work at the site. Several decades later French archaeologists initiated a new series of excavations at Susa, and, in 1895 and 1900, Persian authorities signed conventions that gave the French a monopoly over excavations in the country that only a handful of archaeologists were able to break.

Under Reza Shah Pahlavi, a fierce nationalist—who initially came to power in a *coup d'état* in 1921—the Persian government signed a new convention with the French ending the monopoly on excavations and passed an Antiquities Law in November 1930, effectively opening the country to archaeologists of other nationalities. The Antiquities Law, like Iraq's Antiquities Law of 1924, provided for a division of finds between the Persian government and the excavators, but reserved the right of the Persian government to select and appropriate "up to ten items of historical and artistic value" from among the antiquities discovered.

Horace Jayne considered Persia to be "of immense significance to our knowledge of the history of civilization." When he got word from several well-informed sources that Persia would soon open to foreign archaeologists of all nationalities, he dispatched Frederick R. Wulsin, an archaeologist (and old friend) from Harvard's Peabody Museum to Tehran to represent the interests of the Penn Museum. Wulsin kept Jayne appraised of developments in Iran and submitted requests for permission to excavate several sites, including Damghan (see below), shortly after the Assembly (*Majlis*) had approved the Antiquities Law.

Tureng Tepe, 1931

Though Jayne had not sent Wulsin to Iran to excavate, Wulsin nevertheless proposed excavations in the area of Asterabad (Gorgon) in northeastern Iran to Jayne in January 1931. Jayne turned to his colleague Langdon Warner (Fogg Museum, Harvard University) to help secure funding for the project. Warner, an adviser on Asian art to the Trustees of the William Rockhill Nelson Trust, then purchasing "objects of fine art" for what was to be the William Rockhill Nelson Memorial Art Gallery (later, the Nelson-Atkins Museum of Art), convinced the Trustees to risk the investment with the hope of securing exhibition-quality objects from the excavations. Wulsin and his wife worked at Tureng Tepe in June and October 1931, but the Trustees were disappointed with the finds. As per an unwritten understanding, Jayne took the excavator's share of the finds from Tureng Tepe, providing the Trustees with objects from Penn Museum's collections, including jewelry and other artifacts from Woolley's 1929–1930 excavations of the Royal Cemetery of Ur.

Damghan and Tepe Hissar, 1931–1932 and 1976

The Penn Museum and the Philadelphia Museum of Art joined forces to excavate Damghan, ca. 315 km (196 miles) east of Tehran—erroneously thought to the Parthian capital city, Hecatompylos—and other sites in its vicinity. Jayne hired Erich Schmidt, a young German archaeologist with a PhD from Columbia University, who had worked in the American Southwest and later in central Turkey, to direct the Museum's excavations in Iran. After closing the excavations at Fara, Schmidt traveled over land from Baghdad to Tehran and began work on Damghan's citadel in June 1931. When his excavations revealed no pre-Islamic remains, Schmidt re-focused his efforts on Tepe Hissar, a Chalcolithic and Early Bronze Age site, ca. 2 km (1.2 miles) southeast of Damghan, and a nearby unnamed Sasanian mound. Schmidt worked at Tepe Hissar until November; spent the winter in Tehran; and, completed the excavations in May to November 1932, with critical financial support from Mrs. William Boyce Thompson, whom he had met while working in Arizona (Fig. 14.9).

In a postscript, the Penn Museum, the University of Turin, and the Iranian Center for Archaeological Research, undertook a joint venture to restudy Tepe Hissar in 1976. Their work, under the overall direction of Robert H. Dyson, Jr., focused on categories

Fig. 14.9 Above
Erich Schmidt, back to the camera, and
Iranian government officials at Tepe Hissar.

of finds that Schmidt had been unable to study closely with the technologies of his day, such as plant and animal remains and metallic slag, but also included a detailed survey of Parthian and Sasanian settlements in the area around Damghan.

Rayy (Rhages), 1934–1936

Buoyed by Mrs. William Boyce Thompson's pledges of support for Schmidt's work in tough financial times, the Penn Museum sponsored his excavations throughout the 1930s. From 1934 to 1936, the Penn Museum joined with Boston's Museum of Fine Arts in excavations at Rayy, on the southern outskirts of Tehran. Rayy was a large concession, covering 14 square kilometers (5.4 square miles), with multiple sites. Over the course of the excavations Schmidt uncovered Neolithic and Chalcolithic, as well as Parthian, occupation levels at Cheshmeh 'Ali; late Sasanian-early Islamic (Umayyad) buildings with decorative stuccos at Chal Tarkhan; and, Early Islamic remains at Rayy, occupied until the Mongol invasions.

Persepolis, 1937–1939

In 1931, the Oriental Institute initiated excavations and restoration work at Persepolis, the Achaemenid Persian royal capital, near Shiraz in Fars Province, under Ernst Herzfeld, but dismissed Herzfeld and hired Erich Schmidt to direct excavations at the site, simultaneously with Rayy, in 1935 and 1936. As noted above, by 1936, the Oriental Institute was facing severe financial problems and the excavations at Rayy were drawing to a close. With Schmidt's encouragement, the Oriental Institute, the Penn Museum, and Boston's Museum of Fine Arts signed a cooperative agreement to pool their resources and continue work at Persepolis and other sites in its immediate vicinity, including Tall-Bakun, with its pre- and proto-historic occupations, Naqsh-i Rustam, burial site of the Achaemenid kings, and Istakhr, the Sasanian capital city. The Museum of Fine Arts withdrew after two seasons, and the Penn Museum and the Oriental Institute funded one last year of excavations in 1939.

Luristan, 1935 and 1938

In sponsoring Rayy and Persepolis, the Penn Museum (and Boston's Museum of Fine Arts) facilitated Schmidt's survey and excavations in the central Zagros Mountains (Luristan) during October and November 1935, funded in large part by Mrs. Christian

Fig. 14.10 *Above*
Excavation camp and airplane at Chigha Sabz in Luristan, November 1935.

R. Holmes's donation to the American Institute for Persian Art and Archaeology. The Penn Museum (and the Oriental Institute) contributed to his second season of work in Luristan in May and June 1938. The Penn Museum's support also facilitated Schmidt's aerial surveys of archaeological sites in Iran, carried out during his years at Rayy and Persepolis, which appeared in his book *Flights over Ancient Cities of Iran* (Fig 14.10).

Prehistoric Cave Archaeology, 1949 and 1951

World War II brought archaeological excavations in Iran to an end, but the Penn Museum resumed work shortly after it ended. Carleton Coon, Curator of Ethnology, initiated survey and excavations at four widely scattered cave sites in Iran in June–November 1949, looking for the remains of Paleolithic and Neolithic occupations. The sites included Bisitun Cave near Kermanshah; Tamtama Cave in eastern Azerbaijan, overlooking Lake Urmia; Belt Cave in Mazandaran, on the southern shore of the Caspian Sea; and, Khunik shelter in Khorasan. Coon returned to Iran to continue work at Belt Cave and initiated excavations at nearby Hotu Cave in February, March and April 1951.

Hasanlu, 1956–1977

In 1956, Robert H. Dyson, Jr. initiated excavations at Hasanlu Tepe, in the Gadar River (or Ushnu-Solduz) Valley, south of Lake Urmia in western Azerbaijan, sponsored and supported by the Penn Museum, the Metropolitan Museum of Art, and the Archaeological Service of Iran. Dyson conducted fourteen seasons of excavations at Hasanlu and nearby sites, with the last excavations in 1977. Hasanlu has a long sequence of occupation, but it is arguably best known for its burned Early Iron Age (Hasanlu IVB) remains that preserved the evidence of the violent destruction of the site's citadel and surrounding lower town ca. 800 BCE (Fig. 14.11).

One of Dyson's aims in initiating a long-term field project in northwestern Iran was to reconstruct the cultural history of the Ushnu-Solduz Valley. In addition to working at Hasanlu, the largest site in the valley, he also conducted excavations at other sites nearby in order to get larger exposures of the remains of various eras that he could not readily reach at Hasanlu itself. These sites included Pisdeli Tepe and Dalma Tepe (1961); Hajji Firuz Tepe (1961 and 1968); Agrab Tepe and Ziwiye (1964); and Se Girdan and Dinkha Tepe (1966 and 1968).

Tall-i Malyan (Anshan), 1971–1978

While Dyson was working in northwestern Iran, the Penn Museum also sponsored, in association with Ohio State University, William M. Sumner's excavations at Tall-i Malyan, located ca. 46 km (28 miles) north of Shiraz in the Zagros Mountains of Fars Province. Sumner worked at Malyan through the 1970s, with field seasons in 1971, 1972,

1974, 1976, and 1978. Malyan was occupied already in the mid-6th millennium BCE, but seemingly flourished in the Banesh (ca. 3500–2800 BCE), the Kaftari (2200–1600 BCE), and the Middle Elamite (1300–1000 BCE) Periods.

Fig. 14.11 *Above*

Robert H. Dyson, Jr. and Taghi Assefi, Iranian Archaeological Inspector, looking at the gold bowl with repoussé decoration found in excavations at Hasanlu in 1958 before it was consigned to a bank vault for safekeeping.

Qabr Sheykheyn, 1970–1971

The Penn Museum also sponsored and supported, along with the National Science Foundation, the PhD dissertation field research of Harvey Weiss, a graduate student in the University of Pennsylvania's Department of Oriental Studies, at Qabr Sheykheyn, located in Khuzestan, ca. 30 km (19 miles) southeast of Dizful and 20 km (12 miles) northwest of Shushtar, in 1970–1971.

References

Adams, Robert McC. 1960. *The Evolution of Urban Society*. Chicago: University of Chicago Press.

Adelson, Howard L. 1962. *Medieval Commerce*. Princeton: D. Van Nostrand Company, Inc.

Allan, James W. 1973. *Abūl-Qāsim's Treatise on Ceramics*. Iran 11:111–120.

Alvarez-Mon, Javier, Gian Pietro Basello, and Yasmina Wicks, eds. 2018. *The Elamite World*. New York: Routledge.

Anonymous. Jan. 12, 1959. The Secrets of a Golden Bowl: Unknown Culture is Unearthed. *Life Magazine* pp. 50–60.

Anthony, David W. 2007. *The Horse, the Wheel, and Language: How Bronze-Age Riders from the Eurasian Steppes Shaped the Modern World*. Princeton: Princeton University Press.

Aruz, Joan, ed., with Ronald Wallenfels. 2003. *Art of the First Cities: The Third Millennium B.C. from the Mediterranean to the Indus*. New York, New Haven: Metropolitan Museum of Art, Yale University Press.

Ascher, Kate. 2005. *The Works: Anatomy of a City*. New York: Penguin.

Baadsgaard, Aubrey. 2008. Trends, Traditions, and Transformations: Fashions in Dress in Early Dynastic Mesopotamia. Ph.D. Dissertation in Anthropology, University of Pennsylvania.

Baadsgaard, Aubrey, Janet Monge, Samantha Cox, and Richard Zettler. 2011. Human Sacrifice and Intentional Corpse Preservation in the Royal Cemetery of Ur. *Antiquity* 85:27–42.

Baadsgaard, Aubrey, Janet Monge, and Richard Zettler. 2012. Bludgeoned, Burned, and Beautified: Reevaluating Mortuary Practices in the Royal Cemetery of Ur. In *Sacred Killing: The Archaeology of Sacrifice in the Ancient World*, ed. Anne Porter and Glenn M. Schwartz, pp. 125–158. Winona Lake: Eisenbrauns.

Baadsgaard, Aubrey and Richard Zettler. 2014. Royal Funerals and Ruling Elites at Early Dynastic Ur. In *Contextualizing Grave Inventories in the Ancient Near East: Proceedings of a Workshop at the London 7th ICAANE in April 2010 and an International Symposium in Tübingen in November 2010, both Organised by the Tübingen Post-Graduate School "Symbols of the Dead*, ed. Peter Pfälzner, Herbert Niehr, Ernst Pernicka, Sarah Lange and Tina Köster, pp. 105–122. Wiesbaden: Harrassowitz Verlag.

Baker, Heather D. 2009. A Waste of Space? Unbuilt Land in the Babylonian Cities of the First Millennium BC. *Iraq* 71:89–98.

Barth, F. 1961. *Nomads of South Persia*. Boston: Little, Brown & Company.

Beckwith, Christopher I. 2009. *Empires of the Silk Road: A History of Central Eurasia from the Bronze Age to the Present*. Princeton: Princeton University Press.

Benati, Giacomo. 2015. Re-modeling Political Economy in Early 3rd Millennium BC Mesopotamia: Patterns of Socio-Economic Organization in Archaic Ur (Tell al-Muqayyar Iraq). *Cuneiform Digital Library Journal* 2015/2:1–37.

Benati, Giacomo and Camille Lecompte. 2017. Nonadministrative Documents from Archaic Ur and from Early Dynastic I–II Mesopotamia: A New Textual and Archaeological Analysis. *Journal of Cuneiform Studies* 69:3–31.

Black, Jeremy, and Anthony Green. 1992. *Gods, Demons, and Symbols of Ancient Mesopotamia: An Illustrated Dictionary*. Austin: University of Texas Press.

Black, Jeremy, Graham Cunningham, Eleanor Robson, and Gabor Zolyomi (eds.). 2006. *The Literature of Ancient Sumer*. Oxford: Oxford University Press.

Bloom, Jonathan M. 2001. *Paper Before Print: The History and Impact of Paper in the Islamic World*. New Haven: Yale University Press.

Briant, Pierre. 2002. *From Cyrus to Alexander: A History of the Persian Empire*, trans. Peter Daniels. Winona Lake, IN: Eisenbrauns.

Brusasco, Paolo. 2004. Theory and Practice in the Study of Mesopotamian Domestic Space. *Antiquity* 78:142–157.

Buchanan, Briggs. 1954. The Date of the So-Called Second Dynasty Graves of the Royal Cemetery at Ur. *Journal of the American Oriental Society* 74.3:147–153.

Burney, Charles, and David Lang. 2001. *The Peoples of the Hills: Ancient Ararat and Caucasus*. Phoenix Press.

Burrows, Eric. 1935. *Ur Excavations Texts, Volume II: Archaic Texts*. London: Trustees of the Two Museums.

Charpin, Dominique. 1986. *Le clergé d'Ur au siècle d'Hammurabi (XIXe–XVIIIe siècles av J.-C.)*. Geneva: Librairie Droz.

Charpin, Dominique. 1989. Un quartier de Nippur et le problème des écoles a l'époque paléobabylonienne. *Revue d'Assyriologie* 83:97–112.

Charvát, Petr. 2002. *Mesopotamia Before History*. London: Routledge.

Childe, V. Gordon. 1950. The Urban Revolution. *Town Planning Review* 21:3–17.

Ciuk, Krzysztof. 1999. Pottery from Parthian, Sasanian, and Early Islamic Levels at Nippur, Iraq 1st–9th century AD. *The Canadian Society for Mesopotamian Studies Bulletin* 34:57–79.

Clayden, Tim. 2014. Kassite Housing at Ur: The Dates of the EM, YC, XNCF, AH and KPS Houses. *Iraq* 86:19–64.

Cline, Eric. 2014. *1177: The Year Civilization Collapsed*. Princeton: Princeton University Press.

Cole, Steven W. 1996. *Nippur in Late Assyrian Times*. Helsinki: The Neo-Assyrian Text Corpus Project.

Crawford, Harriet. 1991. *Sumer and the Sumerians*. Cambridge: Cambridge University Press.

Crawford, Harriet, ed. 2013. *The Sumerian World*. New York: Routledge.

Cribb, Roger. 1991. *Nomads in Archaeology*. Cambridge: Cambridge University Press.

Curtis, Vesta S., and Sarah Stewart, eds. 2007. *The Age of the Parthians*. London: I.B. Taurus.

Curtis, Vesta S., and Sarah Stewart. 2008. *The Sassanian Era*. London: I.B. Taurus.

Danti, Michael. 2014. Hasanlu (Iran) Gold Bowl in Context: All that Glitters. *Antiquity* 88(341):791–804.

Daryaee, Touraj. 2013. *Sasanian Persia: The Rise and Fall of an Empire.* London: I.B. Taurus.

Delnero, Paul. 2010. Sumerian Extract Tablets and Scribal Education. *Journal of Cuneiform Studies* 62:53–69.

Drews, Robert. 1993. *The End of the Bronze Age: Changes in Warfare and the Catastrophe ca. 1200 B.C.* Princeton: Princeton University Press.

Dyson, Robert, Jr., and Mary Voigt, eds. 1989. East of Assyria: The Highland Settlement of Hasanlu. *Expedition* 31(2–3).

Finkelstein, Jacob J. 1968/1969. The Laws of Ur-Nammu. *Journal of Cuneiform Studies* 22:66–82.

Fisher, Clarence. 1904. The Mycenean Palace at Nippur. *American Journal of Archaeology* 8:403–432.

Floor, Willem. 2005. PAPER ii. Paper and Papermaking. *Encyclopædia Iranica,* online edition, available at http://www.iranicaonline.org/articles/paper-and-papermaking.

Foster, Benjamin R. 1995. *From Distant Days: Myths, Tales, and Poetry of Ancient Mesopotamia.* Potomac, MD: CDL Press.

Fox, Richard G. 1977. U*rban Anthropology: Cities in their Cultural Settings.* Englewood Cliffs: Prentice-Hall.

Frahm, Eckart, ed. 2017. *A Companion to Assyria.* Hoboken, NJ: Wiley Blackwell.

Gates, Charles. 2003. *Ancient Cities: The Archaeology of Urban Life in the Ancient Near East, Egypt, Greece, and Rome.* New York: Routledge.

Gelpe, Rudolf, trans. and ed. 1966. *Nizami. The Story of Layla and Majnun.* Oxford: Cassirer.

Gibson, McGuire. 1974. Coins as a Tool in Archaeological Surface Survey. In *Near Eastern Numismatics. Iconography, Epigraphy and History. Studies in Honor of George C. Miles,* ed. Dickran K. Kouymjian, pp. 9–13. Beirut: American University of Beirut.

Gibson, McGuire. 1992. Patterns of Occupation at Nippur. In *Nippur at the Centennial.* Papers Read at the 35e Rencontre Assyriologique Internationale, Philadelphia 1988, ed. Maria deJong Ellis, pp. 33–54. Philadelphia: University Museum.

Gibson, McGuire. 1993. Nippur, Sacred City of Enlil, Supreme God of Sumer and Akkad. *Al-Rafidan* 14:1–18.

Gockel Wolfgang. 1982. D*ie Stratigraphie und Chronologie der Ausgrabungen des Diyala-Gebietes unter der Stadt Ur in der Zeit von Uruk/Eanna IV bis zur Dynastie von Akkad.* Rome: Giorgio Brettschneider.

Godley, Alfred D., trans. 1972. *Herodotus.* Cambridge: Harvard University Press.

Golombek, Lisa, Robert H. Mason, Patricia Proctor and Eileen Reilly. 2014. *Persian Pottery in the First Global Age.* Leiden-Boston-Toronto: Brill-ROM.

Gravel, Ryan. 2016. *Where We Want to Live: Reclaiming Infrastructure for a New Generation of Cities.* New York: St. Martin's.

Gürsan-Salzmann, Ayse. 2007. *Exploring Iran: The Photography of Erich F. Schmidt, 1930–1940.* Philadelphia: University of Pennsylvania Museum of Archaeology and Anthropology.

Hafford, William B. 2005. Mesopotamian Mensuration: Balance Pan Weights from Nippur. *Journal of the Economic and Social History of the Orient* 48:345–387.

Harper, Prudence, Joan Aruz, and Françoise Tallon, eds. 1992. *The Royal City of Susa: Ancient Near Eastern Treasures in the Louvre.* New York: Metropolitan Museum of Art.

Heinrich, Ernst. 1984. *Paläste im alten Mesopotamien.* Berlin: Verlag Walter de Gruyter.

Hilprecht, Hermann, with I. Benzinger, Fritz, Hommel, Peter Christian Albrecht Jensen, and Georg Steindorff. 1903. *Explorations in Bible Lands During the 19th Century.* Philadelphia: A.J. Holman and Company.

Hole, Frank, ed. 1987. *The Archaeology of Western Iran: Settlements and Society from Prehistory to the Islamic Conquest.* Smithsonian Series in Archaeological Inquiry. Washington, DC.

Hole, Frank. 1990. Cemetery or Mass Grave? Reflections on Susa I, pp. 1–14. In *Contribution a l'histoire de l'Iran: Mélanges offerts à Jean Perrot,* edited by Françoise Vallat. Paris: Editions Recherche sur les Civilisations.

Holod, Renata. 2017. Approaching the Mosque: Beginnings and Evolution. In *Mosques: Speldors of Islam,* ed. Jai Imbrey, pp. 14–21. New York: Rizzoli.

Holod, Renata, Salma Jayyusi, Attilio Petruccioli, and André Raymond, eds. 2008. *The City in the Islamic World.* New York-Leiden: Brill.

Horsnell, Malcolm J. A. 1999. The Year-Names of the First Dynasty of Babylon, Vol. 2: *The Year-Names Reconstructed and Critically Annotated in Light of Their Exemplars.* Hamilton: McMaster University Press.

Jacobs, Frank. How to Fingerprint a City. Big Think: http://bigthink.com/strange-maps/how-to-fingerprint-a-city. Accessed on December 8, 2017.

Jacobsen, Thorkild. 1960. The Waters of Ur. *Iraq* 22:174–185.

Jayyusi, Salma K., Renata Holod, Attilio Petruccioli, and André Raymond, eds. 2008. *The City in the Islamic World,* 2 vols. Leiden: Brill.

Joannès, Francis. 2004. *The Age of Empires: Mesopotamia in the First Millennium BC,* trans. Antonia Nevill. Edinburgh: Edinburgh University Press.

Kahle, Paul. 1956. Chinese Porcelain in the Lands of Islam. *Opera Minora.* Leiden: Brill.

Karstens, Karsten. 1994. Die erste Dynastie von Ur. Überlegungen zur relativen Datierung. In *Beiträge zur altorientalischen Archäologie und Altertumskunde: Festschrift für Barthel Hrouda zum 65. Geburtstag,* ed. Peter Calmeyer, Karl Hecker, Liane Jakob-Rost, and Christopher B. F. Walker, pp. 133–142. Wiesbaden: Harrassowitz Verlag.

Keall, Edward. 1970. The Significance of Late Parthian Nippur. PhD Dissertation, University of Michigan.

Keall, Edward. 1975. Parthian Nippur and Vologases' Southern Strategy: A Hypothesis. Journal of the American Oriental Society 95(4):620–632.

Keall, Edward. 2015. Nippur in the Parthian Era. *Canadian Society of Mesopotamian Studies Journal* 9/10:5–15.

Kennedy, Hugh. 2002. *An Historical Atlas of Islam.* Leiden: Brill.

Khazanov, Anatoly. 1994. *Nomads and the Outside World.* Madison: University of Wisconsin Press.

Knudstad, James. 1966. Excavations at Nippur. *Sumer* 22:111–115.

Knudstad, James. 1968. A Preliminary Report on the 1966–67 Excavations at Nippur. *Sumer* 24:95–106.

Koldewey, Robert. 1914. *The Excavations at Babylon*, trans. Agnes S. Johns. London: Macmillan and Co.

Kostof, Spiro. 1999. *The City Shaped: Urban Patterns and Meanings through History*. London: Thames & Hudson.

Kuhrt, Amélie. 1995. *The Ancient Near East c. 3000–330 BC, Vol. 1*. London: Routledge.

Lassner, Jacob. 1980. *The Shaping of 'Abbāsid Rule*. Princeton: Princeton University Press.

Laursen, Steffen and Piotr Steinkeller. 2017. *Babylonia, the Gulf Region, and the Indus: Archaeological and Textual Evidence for Contact in the Third and Early Second Millennia B.C.* Winona Lake: Eisenbrauns.

Leemans, Wilhelmus François. 1950. *The Old-Babylonian Merchant; His Business and His Social Position*, vol. 3. Studia et Documenta ad Iura Orientis Antiqui Pertinentia. Leiden: E.J. Brill.

Legrain, Leon. 1936. *Ur Excavations Texts, Volume III: Archaic Seal Impressions*. Philadelphia: Trustees of the Two Museums.

Leick, Gwendolyn. 2001. *Mesopotamia: Invention of the City*. London: Penguin.

Leskov, A. 2008. *The Maikop Treasure*. Philadelphia: University of Pennsylvania Museum of Archaeology and Anthropology.

Le Strange, G. (1900) 1983. *Baghdad during the Abbasid Caliphate*. Oxford: Oxford University Press.

Lloyd, Seton and Fuad Safar. 1947. Eridu: Preliminary Report on the First Season's Excavations. *Sumer* 3:84–111.

Loding, Darlene. 1981. Lapidaries in the Ur III Period. *Expedition* 23:6–14.

Mackie, Louise W. 2015. *Symbols of Power: Luxury Textiles from Islamic Lands, 7th–21st Century*. New Haven-London: Cleveland Museum of Art and Yale University Press.

Magee, Peter, 2008. Deconstructing the Destruction of Hasanlu: Archaeology, Imperialism, and the Chronology of the Iranian Iron Age. *Iranica Antiqua* XLIII:89–106.

Malko, Helen. 2014. Investigation into the Impacts of Foreign Ruling Elites in Traditional State Societies: The Case of the Kassite State in Babylonia (Iraq). Ph.D. Dissertation in Anthropology, SUNY Stony Brook.

Marchesi, Gianni. 2004. Who Was Buried in the Royal Tombs at Ur? *Orientalia* 73:153–97.

Mason, Robert B. 2004. *Shine Like the Sun: Lustre-Painted and Associated Pottery from the Medieval Middle East*. Costa Mesa, CA: Mazda Publishers.

Medvedskaya, Inna, 1988. Who Destroyed Hasanlu IV? *Iran* 26:1–15.

Miller, Naomi F. 1990. Palm Trees in Paradise: Victorian Views of the Ancient Near Eastern Landscape. *Expedition* 32(2):53–60.

Miller, Naomi F. 2001. Down the Garden Path: How Plant and Animal Husbandry Came Together in the Ancient Near East. *Near Eastern Archaeology* 64.1/2 (March–June):4–7.

Miller, Naomi F. 2002. *Drawing on the Past: An Archaeologist's Sketchbook*. Philadelphia: University of Pennsylvania Museum.

Miller, Naomi F. 2013. Agropastoralism and Archaeobiology: Connecting Plants, Animals and People in West and Central Asia. *Environmental Archaeology* 18:247–256.

Above

Lion plaque (53-11-95) from Nippur.

Miller, Naomi F., and Willma Wetterstrom. 2000. The Beginnings of Agriculture: The Ancient Near East and North Africa. In *The Cambridge World History of Food*, eds. K.F. Kiple and K.C. Ornelas, vol. 2, pp. 1123–1139. Cambridge: Cambridge University Press.

Molleson, Theya and Dawn Hodgson. 2003. The Human Remains from Woolley's Excavations at Ur. *Iraq* 65:91–129.

Moorey, Peter R. S. 1977. What Do We Know About the People Buried in the Royal Cemetery? *Expedition* 1977:24–40.

Moorey, Peter R. S. 1984. Where Did They Bury the Kings of the IIIrd Dynasty of Ur? *Iraq* 46:1–18.

Moorey, Peter R. S. 1991. The Decorated Ironwork of the Early Iron Age Attributed to Luristan in Western Iran. *Iran* 29:1–12.

Moorey, Roger. 1974. *Ancient Bronzes from Luristan*. London: British Museum.

Moortgat, Anton. 1949. *Tammuz: Der Unsterblichkeitsglaube in der altorientalischen Bildkunst*. Berlin: Verlag Walter de Gruyter.

Morony, Michael. 1984. *Iraq after the Muslim Conquest*. Princeton: Princeton University Press.

Muscarella, Oscar White. 2013. *Archaeology, Artifacts and Antiquities of the Ancient Near East: Sites, Cultures, and Proveniences*. Leiden: Brill.

Nissen, Hans. 1966. *Zur Datierung des Königsfriedhofes von Ur*. Bonn: Rudolph Habelt Verlag.

Oates, Joan. 1979. *Babylon*. London: Thames and Hudson.

Oates, Joan. 1986. *Babylon*. Revised ed. London: Thames and Hudson.

Peters, John P. 1895. University of Pennsylvania Expedition to Babylonia III. The Court of Columns at Nippur. *American Journal of Archaeology* 10:439–468.

Peters, John P. 1899. *Nippur, or, Explorations and Adventures on the Euphrates. The Narrative of the University of Pennsylvania Expedition to Babylonia in the Years 1888–1890*. Vol. 1: First Campaign. New York: G. P. Putnam's Sons.

Piotrovsky, Boris. 1969. *The Ancient Civilization of Urartu*. Spokane, WA: Cowles Book Co.

Podany, Amanda H. 2013. *The Ancient Near East: A Very Short Introduction*. Oxford: Oxford University Press.

Pollock, Susan M. 1985. Chronology of the Ur Royal Cemetery. *Iraq* 47:129–185.

Pollock, Susan M. 1991. Of Priestesses, Princes and Poor Relations: The Dead in the Royal Cemetery of Ur. *Cambridge Archaeological Journal* 1:171–189.

Pollock, Susan M. 2007. The Royal Cemetery of Ur: Ritual, Tradition, and the Creation of Subjects. In *Representations of Political Power: Case Histories from Times of Change and Dissolving Order in the Ancient Near East*, ed. Marlies Heinz and Marian H. Feldman, pp. 89–110. Winona Lake: Eisenbrauns.

Poon, Linda. Mapping the 'Urban Fingerprints' of Cities. CITYLAB, September 11, 2015. https://www.citylab.com/equity/2015/09/mapping-the-urban-fingerprints-of-cities/404923/. Accessed on December 8, 2017.

Postgate, J. Nicholas. 1992. *Early Mesopotamia: Society and Economy at the Dawn of History*. London: Routledge.

Potts, Daniel T., ed. 2013. *The Oxford Handbook of Ancient Iran*. Oxford: Oxford University Press.

Potts, Daniel T. 2015. *The Archaeology of Elam: Formation and Transformation of the Iranian State*. 2nd edition. Cambridge: Cambridge University Press.

Radner, Karen. 2015. *Assyria: A Very Short Introduction*. Oxford: Oxford University Press.

Rante, Rocco. 2007. Topography of Rayy During Early Islamic Period. *Iran* 45:161–180.

Rante, Rocco. 2008. Iranian City of Rayy: Urban Model and Military Architecture. *Iran* 46:189–211.

Rante, Rocco. 2009. *Rayy: Développement De L'urbanisme Et Culture Matérielle (VIIe-XIe Siècles)*. PhD diss. Aix Marseille.

Rante, Rocco. 2015. *Rayy from Its Origins to the Mongol Invasion: An Archaeological and Historiographical Study*. Leiden: Brill.

Rante, Rocco, and Carmen Di Pasquale. 2016. The Urbanisation of Rayy in the Seljūq Period. *Der Islam* 93(2):413–432.

Reade, Julian. 1982. Tell Taya. In *Fifty Years of Mesopotamian Discovery*, ed. John Curtis, pp. 72–78. London: The British School of Archaeology in Iraq.

Reade, Julian. 2001. Assyrian King-Lists, the Royal Tombs of Ur, and Indus Origins. *Journal of Near Eastern Studies* 60:1–29.

Richter, Christina Heike. 2011. *Parthische Pantoffelsarkophage: Untersuchungen zu einer Sargform Mesopotamiens im Vergleich mit Tonsärgen von Ägypten über den Mittelmeerraum bis Zentralasien*. Münster: Ugarit-Verlag.

Roaf, Michael. 1990. *Cultural Atlas of Mesopotamia and the Ancient Near East*. New York: Facts on File.

Robson, Eleanor. 2001. The Tablet House: A Scribal School in Old Babylonian Nippur. *Revue d'Assyriologie et d'Archéologie Orientale* 95:39–66.

Roux, Georges. 1964. *Ancient Iraq*. London: George Allen & Unwin, Ltd.

Rowton, Michael B. 1974. Enclosed Nomadism. *Journal of the Economic and Social History of the Orient* 17:1–30.

Sallaberger, Walther, and Ingo Schrakamp, eds. 2015. *History and Philology. Associated Regional Chronologies for the Ancient Near East and the Eastern Mediterranean*. Turnhout, Belgium: Brepols.

Salvini, Mirjo. 2011. An Overview of Urartian History. In *Urartu: Transformations in the East*, ed. K. Koroglu and E. Konyar, pp. 74–101. Istanbul: YKY.

Schuol, Monica. 2000. *Die Charakene: Ein mesopotamisches Königreich in hellenistisch-parthischer Zeit*. Stuttgart: Franz Steiner Verlag.

Selinsky, Page. 2009. Death, a Necessary end: Perspectives on Paleodemography and Aging from Hasanlu, Iran. PhD diss. University of Pennsylvania, Department of Anthropology. Philadelphia.

Smith, A., and R. Heilbroner. 1986. *The Essential Adam Smith*. New York: W.W. Norton & Co.

Spooner, Brian. 2015. *Globalization: The Crucial Phase*. Philadelphia: University of Pennsylvania Museum of Archaeology and Anthropology.

Steinkeller, Piotr. 2003. An Ur III Manuscript of the Sumerian King List. In *Literatur, Politic und Recht in Mesopotamien: Festschrift für Claus Wilcke*, ed. Walther Sallaberger, Konrad Volk, and Annette Zgoll, pp. 267–292. Orientalia Biblica et Christiana 14. Wiesbaden: Harrassowitz.

Stolper, Matthew W. 1985. *Entrepeneurs and Empire: The Murašû Archive, the Murašû Firm, and Persian Rule in Babylonia*. Leiden: Nederlands Instituut voor het Nabije Oosten.

Stone, Elizabeth C. 1977. The Economic and Social Upheaval in Old Babylonian Nippur. In *Mountains and Lowlands: Essays in the Archaeology of Greater Mesopotamia*, ed. T. Cuyler Young, Jr. and Louis D. Levine, pp. 267–289. Malibu: Undena Publications.

Stone, Elizabeth C. 1987. *Nippur Neighborhoods*. Studies in Ancient Oriental Civilization 44. Chicago: Oriental Institute Press.

Stone, Elizabeth C. and Paul Zimansky. 2016. Archaeology Returns to Ur: A New Dialog with Old Houses. *Near Eastern Archaeology* 79:246–259.

Stone, Elizabeth C., Paul Zimansky, Piotr Steinkeller, and Vincent Pigott. 2004. *The Anatomy of a Mesopotamian City: Survey and Soundings at Mashkan-shapir*. Winona Lake: Eisenbrauns.

Sürenhagen, Dietrich. 2002. Death in Mesopotamia: The 'Royal Tombs' of Ur Revisited. In *Of Pots and Plans: Papers on the Archaeology and History of Mesopotamia and Syria Presented to David Oates in Honour of His 75th Birthday*, ed. Lamia al-Gailani Werr, John Curtis, Harriet Martin, Augusta McMahon, Joan Oates, and Julian Reade, pp. 324–338. London: NABU Publications.

Suter, Claudia E. 2014. Human, Divine or Both? The Uruk Vase and the Problem of Ambiguity in Early Mesopotamian Visual Arts. In *Critical Approaches to Ancient Near Eastern Art*, ed. Marian Feldman and Brian Brown, pp. 545–568. Berlin: Walter de Gruyter.

Thornton, Christopher, and Vincent Pigott. 2011. Blade Type Weaponry of Hasanlu Period IVB. In *People and Crafts at Hasanlu, Iran*, ed. M. De Schauensee, pp. 135–182. Philadelphia: University of Pennsylvania Museum of Archaeology and Anthropology.

Tinney, Steve. 1998. Texts, Tablets, and Teaching: Scribal Education in Nippur and Ur. *Expedition* 40:40–50.

Ur, Jason. 2014. Households and the Emergence of Cities in Ancient Mesopotamia. *Cambridge Archaeological Journal*, 24(2):249–268.

Van De Mieroop, Marc. 1992. *Society and Enterprise in Old Babylonian Ur.* Berlin: Dietrich Reimer Verlag.

Van De Mieroop, Marc. 1997. *The Ancient Mesopotamian City.* New York: Oxford University Press.

Van de Mieroop, Marc. 2015. *History of the Ancient Near East.* 3rd edition. Oxford: Blackwell.

Watson, Oliver. 2004. *Ceramics from Islamic Lands.* London: Thames and Hudson.

Wheatley, Paul. 2001. *The Places Where Men Pray Together: Cities in Islamic Lands, Seventh Through the Tenth Centuries.* Chicago: University of Chicago Press.

Widell, Magnus. 2008. The Ur III Metal Loans from Ur. In *The Growth of an Early State in Mesopotamia: Studies in Ur III Administration. Proceedings of the First and Second Ur III Workshops at the 49th and 51st Rencontre Assyriologique Internationale, London July 10, 2003 and Chicago July 19, 2005*, ed. Stephen J. Garfinkle and J. Cale Johnson, pp. 207–23. Biblioteca del próximo oriente antiguo 5. Madrid: Consejo Superior de Investigaciones Científicas.

Wirth, Eugen. 1971. *Syrien: eine geographische Landeskunde.* Darmstadt: Wissenschaftliche Buchgesellschaft.

Wirth, Louis. 1938. Urbanism as a Way of Life. *American Journal of Sociology* 44(1):1–24.

Wiseman, Donald J. 1960. The Goddess Lama at Ur. *Iraq* 22:166–171.

Woolley, C. Leonard. 1927. Excavations at Ur, 1926–7. *Antiquaries Journal* 7:385–423.

Woolley, C. Leonard. 1928. Excavations at Ur, 1927–28. *Antiquaries Journal* 8:415–448.

Woolley, C. Leonard. 1929. *Ur of the Chaldees: A Record of Seven Years of Excavation.* London: E. Benn Limited.

Woolley, C. Leonard. 1930. Excavations at Ur, 1929–30. *Antiquaries Journal* 10:315–343.

Woolley, C. Leonard. 1931. Excavations at Ur, 1930–1. *Antiquaries Journal* 11:343–381.

Woolley, C. Leonard. 1934a. *Ur Excavations Volume II: The Royal Cemetery.* London: Trustees of the Two Museums.

Woolley, C. Leonard. 1934b. The Excavations at Ur, 1933–34. *Antiquaries Journal* 14:355–378.

Woolley, C. Leonard. 1939. *Ur Excavations V: The Ziggurat and Its Surroundings.* Philadelphia: Trustees of the Two Museums.

Woolley, C. Leonard. 1955. *Ur Excavations IV: The Early Periods.* Philadelphia: Trustees of the Two Museums.

Woolley, C. Leonard. 1965. *Ur Excavations VIII: The Kassite Period and the Period of the Assyrian Kings.* London: Trustees of the Two Museums.

Woolley, C. Leonard. 1974. *Ur Excavations VI: The Buildings of the Third Dynasty.* Philadelphia: Trustees of the Two Museums.

Woolley, C. Leonard and Max E. L. Mallowan. 1962. *Ur Excavations IX: The Neo-Babylonian and Persian Periods.* London: Trustees of the Two Museums.

Woolley, C. Leonard and Max E. L. Mallowan. 1976. *Ur Excavations VII: The Old Babylonian Period*, ed. Terrence Mitchell. London: Trustees of the Two Museums.

Wright, Henry. 1981. The Southern Margins of Sumer: Archaeological Survey of the Area of Eridu and Ur. Appendix to *Heartland of Cities: Surveys of Ancient Settlement and Land Use on the Central Floodplain of the Euphrates*, Robert McC. Adams, pp. 295–345. Chicago: University of Chicago Press.

Zettler, Richard L. 1987. Enlil's City, Nippur, at the End of the Late Third Millennium B.C. *Bulletin of the Society for Mesopotamian Studies* 14:7–19.

Zettler, Richard L. 1991. Nippur Under the Third Dynasty of Ur: Area TB. In *Velles Paraules: Ancient Near Eastern Studies in Honor of Miguel Civil*, ed. Piotr Michalowski, Piotr Steinkeller, Elizabeth C. Stone, and Richard L. Zettler, pp. 251–281. Barcelona: Editorial Ausa.

Zettler, Richard L. 1992. *The Ur III Temple of Inanna at Nippur: The Operation and Organization of Urban Religious Institutions in Mesopotamia in the Late Third Millennium B.C.* Berlin: D. Reimer.

Zettler, Richard L. 1993. *Nippur III: Kassite Buildings in Area WC-1.* Chicago: The Oriental Institute.

Zettler, Richard. 1994. *The Ur III Inanna Temple at Nippur. Berliner Beiträge zum Vorderen Orient 11.* Berlin: Dietrich Reimer Verlag.

Zettler, Richard. 1998a. The Royal Cemetery of Ur. In *Treasures from the Royal Tombs of Ur*, ed. Richard Zettler and Lee Horne, pp. 21–25. Philadelphia: University of Pennsylvania Museum of Archaeology and Anthropology.

Zettler, Richard. 1998b. The Burials of a King and Queen. In *Treasures from the Royal Tombs of Ur*, ed. Richard Zettler and Lee Horne, pp. 33–38. Philadelphia: University of Pennsylvania Museum of Archaeology and Anthropology.

Zettler, Richard L. and William B. Hafford. 2015. Ur B: *Archäologisch. Reallexikon der Assyriologie und Vorderasiatischen Archäologie* 14 5/6:367–385.

Zettler, Richard L., and Lee Horne, eds. 1998. *Treasures of the Royal Tombs of Ur.* Philadelphia: University of Pennsylvania Museum of Archaeology and Anthropology.

Zimmerman, Paul. 1998. Two Tombs or Three? In *Treasures from the Royal Tombs of Ur*, ed. Richard Zettler and Lee Horne, p. 39. Philadelphia: University of Pennsylvania Museum of Archaeology and Anthropology.

Zohary, Michael. 1973. *Geobotanical Foundations of the Middle East.* Stuttgart: Gustav Fischer Verlag.

Right

Stamp seal (38-10-118) from Khafaje.

Author Biographies

Note: Unless otherwise stated, all contributors and exhibitions mentioned below are affiliated with the Penn Museum.

Jessica Bicknell is the Interpretive Planning Manager at the Penn Museum. She leads the visitor-focused aspects of exhibition development, including editing label text and carrying out audience research. Bicknell has over 15 years of experience in creating engaging exhibitions at urban institutions of varying collections—from art museums to botanic gardens. A former board member of the National Association for Museum Exhibition, she has taught classes related to interpretation and informal science education at the University of Pennsylvania and Rutgers University.

Michael Falcetano received his B.A. in Art History and Modern Middle Eastern Studies from the University of Pennsylvania in 2012 and is currently pursuing an M.A. in Art History at the University of Texas at Austin. He specializes in Islamic art from the Seljuq Period and has been a research assistant at the Penn Museum where he worked on excavated material from Rayy, Iran. He also worked as a research assistant at the Metropolitan Museum of Art for the catalogue on the exhibition *Court and Cosmos: The Great Age of the Seljuqs* (2016), for which he contributed essays on Seljuq textiles. Most recently he was an editorial consultant for the book *Mosques: Splendors of Islam* (2017).

Martina Ferrari is the Andrew Mellon Fellow in Costume and Textiles Conservation at the Philadelphia Museum of Art. She completed her M.A. in Textiles Conservation in 2014 at the Conservation and Restoration Center "La Venaria Reale," University of Turin. She also holds a B.A. in Art History from the University of Parma.

Grant Frame, Ph.D., Associate Curator, Babylonian Section, is Associate Professor of Assyriology in Penn's Department of Near Eastern Languages and Civilizations and Director of the Center for Ancient Studies. He specializes in the Akkadian language and the history and culture of Mesopotamia in the 1st millennium BCE, and he is director of the NEH-funded Royal Inscriptions of the Neo-Assyrian Period project. He was co-curator of *Magic in the Ancient World* (2016–2017). His focus in the Middle East Galleries is on the history, culture, and economy of Babylonia and Assyria.

William B. Hafford, Ph.D., Dyson Post-Doctoral Fellow, Near East Section, has been researching and teaching at Penn for nearly 20 years. His research interests involve ancient economics and cross-cultural trade as well as the early development of weights and measures for standardized evaluation. Currently he is excavating at the site of Ur in Iraq, and he has excavated in many other countries including Syria, Egypt, and Greece. Much of his field research involves examining the development of cities and the exchange between them. His focus in the Galleries has therefore been on trade and currency through time as well as daily life in ancient cities and empires.

Renata Holod, Ph.D., Curator, Near East Section, is College of Women Class of 1963 Term Professor in the Humanities in Penn's History of Art Department. An art and architectural historian and archaeologist of the Islamic world, she has carried out archaeological and architectural fieldwork in Syria, Iran, Morocco, Turkey, Central Asia, Tunisia, and Ukraine. She was Convener, Steering Committee Member, and Chair, Master Jury for the Aga Khan Award for Architecture. She was also co-curator of *Archaeologists and Travelers in Ottoman Lands* (2010–2011); co-curator Line and Letter: Studying a 16th Century Shirazi Manuscript (Van Pelt Library, University of Pennsylvania, 2005); and guest curator *'From the Two Pens': Line and Color in Islamic Art* (Williams College Museum of Art, 2002).

Philip Jones, Ph.D., Associate Curator and Keeper, Babylonian Section, is an Assyriologist who has worked on the Museum's Pennsylvania Sumerian Dictionary Project since 1996. A co-curator of *Sacred Writings: Extraordinary Texts of the Biblical World* (2015), he is also co-curator of the upcoming Writing Gallery at the Museum. Besides Sumerian lexicography, his scholarly interests focus on the history of religious and political ideas in ancient Mesopotamia and the impact of scribal literacy on that civilization.

Naomi F. Miller, Ph.D., Consulting Scholar, is a Near Eastern archaeologist who specializes in the analysis of archaeological plant remains, mostly from West and Central Asia. She was the first archaeologist to recognize that many charred seeds from Middle Eastern sites originated in animal dung burned as fuel; this insight has informed her studies of ancient environment and land use. She has analyzed materials from a number

of Penn Museum excavations, including Malyan (Iran), Anau (Turkmenistan), Gordion (Turkey), and Sweyhat (Syria). Her interest in plant symbolism led to the identification of date palm and apple representations in some of the jewelry from the Royal Tombs of Ur.

Katherine M. Moore, Ph.D., Mainwaring Teaching Specialist, Center for the Analysis of Archaeological Materials (CAAM), is Practice Professor and the Undergraduate Chair in Penn's Department of Anthropology. Her research interests include cultural ecology of animal production, pastoralists and hunter-gatherers, and craft production in animal materials. She teaches courses on zooarchaeology and the archaeology of food and environment. Her work in the Middle East involves the relation of pastoral economies with agriculture peoples in Turkmenistan (Gonur depe, Anau depe). She also works on the prehistory of herding peoples in Peru and Bolivia in South America.

Ellen Owens is the Director of Learning Programs at the Penn Museum and has extensive experience managing education and public programs. Her work at the Museum includes having overseen the significant expansion of free K–12 programs to Title I schools. Prior to joining the Penn Museum in 2014, Owens served as Executive Director of Philadelphia's Magic Gardens for five years, where she established vibrant core programs. Owens is also an adjunct professor in the Museum Studies graduate program at University of the Arts. She holds an M.A. in Museum Education from the University of the Arts and a certificate in museum leadership from the Getty Leadership Institute.

Holly Pittman, Ph.D., Curator, Near East Section, is the Bok Family Professor in the Humanities and Professor in Penn's History of Art Department. She was co-curator, with Richard Zettler, of the traveling Penn Museum exhibition *Treasures from the Royal Tombs of Ur*. She studies the art and culture of Mesopotamia and Iran, focusing on cultural interaction through iconographic and stylistic evidence, and has participated in excavations in Cyprus, Iran, Syria, Turkey, and Iraq. Before coming to Penn, she was a curator in the department of Ancient Near Eastern Art at the Metropolitan Museum in New York City for 14 years.

Lauren Ristvet, Ph.D., Dyson Associate Curator, Near East Section, is Associate Professor in Penn's Department of Anthropology. She is also the associate director of excavations at Tell Leilan, Syria, and co-director of the Naxcivan Archaeological Project in Azerbaijan. She is co-lead curator of *Cultures in the Crossfire: Stories from Syria and Iraq* (through November 2018) and curated *Sex: A History in 30 Objects* (2015–2016). Her research interests include complex societies, political transformation, imperialism, and human response to environmental change in the Middle East, Caucasus, and Central Asia, with an emphasis on the formation and collapse of archaic states, landscape archaeology, and ancient imperialism.

Karen Sonik, Ph.D., is Assistant Professor in the Department of Art and Art History at Auburn University. She earned her PhD at the University of Pennsylvania in the Art and Archaeology of the Mediterranean World and has since been an American Council for Learned Societies New Faculty Fellow in the Department of Art at the University of California, Los Angeles; a postdoctoral fellow in Egyptology and Ancient Western Asian Studies at Brown University; and a Visiting Research Scholar at the Institute for the Study of the Ancient World, New York University. Her research focuses on Mesopotamia's visual arts and literature, with an emphasis on the materiality and agency of divine and other religious imagery; pictorial and written treatments of out-groups and Others (including feminine Others); and theoretical approaches to non-Western arts and aesthetics.

Brian Spooner, D.Phil., Curator, Near East Section, is Professor in Penn's Department of Anthropology. He has done ethnographic research in Afghanistan, Iran, and Pakistan, as well as research in China, India, Kazakhstan, Tajikistan, Turkmenistan, and Uzbekistan. His research interests include globalization, social organization, religion, ecology, and non-industrial economies in the Middle East and South and Central Asia.

Steve Tinney, Ph.D., Coordinating Curator of the Middle East Galleries, is Associate Curator-in-Charge of the Babylonian Section and the Clark Research Associate Professor in Assyriology in Penn's Department of Near Eastern Languages and Civilizations. His research focuses on the Sumerian language and the cultural and intellectual history of ancient Mesopotamia, particularly ancient education and scholarship, and he directs the Pennsylvania Sumerian Dictionary Project. He has worked with cuneiform tablets for more than 30 years, 20 of those in the Babylonian Section. He was co-curator of *Sacred Writings: Extraordinary Texts of the Biblical World*, presented in honor of the 2015 Philadelphia visit of Pope Francis.

Richard L. Zettler, Ph.D., Associate Curator-in-Charge, Near East Section, is Associate Professor in Penn's Department of Near Eastern Languages and Civilizations. He has curated or co-curated several exhibitions which focused on the Penn Museum/British Museum excavations at the Royal Tombs of Ur. He has excavated at Nippur and Umm al-Hafriyat in southern Iraq and Uç Tepe in the Hamrin Dam Salvage Project. He directed excavations at Tell es-Sweyhat, an Early Bronze Age site in Syria, and is currently involved in excavations focused on the early Iron Age in the area of Rowanduz-Soran in northern Iraq (Kurdistan). His research focuses broadly on the 3rd and early 2nd millennia BCE, with particular interests including urbanism and the socioeconomic organization of complex societies.

Above
Wall tile (37-11-152) from Rayy.

Opposite
Priest statue (37-15-28) from Khafaje.

Figure Credits

front cover - string of beads (30-12-567) PM image 295642, cuneiform tablet (B10000) PM image 296349, painted bowl (33-21-116) PM image 295615, bearded bull's head and shell plaque from a lyre (B17694A-B) PM image 250852, gold ostrich egg (B16692) PM image 295553, silver drachma (33-62-31) PM image 296137, wine jar (69-12-15) PM image 295805, and glazed tile (2001-15-45) PM image 250789

p. i - frieze of bulls (B15880) PM image 296793

p. ii - brick with human footprint (B16460) PM image 295549

p. iii - Queen Puabi's headdress wreath detail (B17710) PM image 296229 [detail] and foundation figure (B16216) PM image 295526

p. x - PM image 139776

p. xii - bearded bull's head from a lyre (B17694B) PM image 295562

p. xiii - obsidian bowl (35-10-287) PM image 152756

p. xiv - lusterware plate (NEP19) PM image 296534

p. 1 - wine jar (69-12-15) PM image 295805

p. 3 - Penn Museum (gallery shot)

p. 6 - Penn Museum (gallery shot)

p. 7 - Penn Museum (gallery shot)

p. 9 - Penn Museum (gallery shot)

p. 11 - Penn Museum (gallery shot)

p. 13 - Penn Museum (gallery shot)

p. 16 - Assyrian relief (29-21-1) PM image 152774 [detail]

p. 17 - clay tablet (B13885) PM image 150398

p. 19 - map courtesy of Haley Sharpe Design (HSD) and adapted by Matt Todd

p. 21 - after map 5: Rain Map of the Middle East from Zohary, Michael. 1973. *Geobotanical Foundations of the Middle East.* Stuttgart: Gustav Fischer Verlag

p. 22 - after map 7: Geobotanical Outline Map of the Middle East from Zohary, Michael. 1973. *Geobotanical Foundations of the Middle East.* Stuttgart: Gustav Fischer Verlag. Adapted by N. F. Miller and M. A. Pouls. Redrawn by Ardeth Anderson.

p. 24 - drawing by Naomi Miller

p. 25 - photo by Katherine Burge

p. 27 - photo by Naomi Miller

p. 28 – photo by Naomi Miller

p. 29 – photo by Katherine Burge

p. 30 – photo by Donald Hansen/al-Hiba Archive

p. 31 – courtesy of the Oriental Institute of the University of Chicago

p. 33 – © Ninara (flickr)/Kaisu Raasakka

p. 34 – photo by Naomi Miller

p. 35 – photo by Naomi Miller

p. 37 – obsidian core (33-3-163) PM image 295437

p. 38 – photo by Naomi Miller

p. 39 – plate (NEP74) PM image 296687

p. 40 – tablet (B3293) PM image 296652

p. 41 – lion's head (B17064) PM image 152055

p. 42 – photo by Naomi Miller

p. 44 – stag and gazelle pendants (B16684) PM images 152242 and 152264

p. 45 – stone tablet (B10000) PM image 296349

p. 47 – map courtesy of Haley Sharpe Design (HSD) and adapted by Matt Todd

p. 48 – clay sealing (B11158) PM image 296660

p. 49 – © Nik Wheeler

p. 50 – after city map of Uruk on page 60 of Roaf, Michael. 1990. *Cultural Atlas of Mesopotamia and the Ancient Near East.* New York: Facts on File. Redrawn by Ardeth Anderson.

p. 51 – part (d) of figure 2 from Ur, J. 2014. Households and the Emergence of Cities in Ancient Mesopotamia. *Cambridge Archaeological Journal*, 24(2), 249-268. © The McDonald Institute for Archaeological Research 2014, published by Cambridge University Press.

p. 52 – after figure 3 in Lloyd, S. and F. Safar. 1947. Eridu: Preliminary Report on the First Season's Excavations. *Sumer* 3:84–111. Redrawn by Ardeth Anderson.

p. 53 – © Erich Lessing/Art Resource, NY

p. 54 – cone decoration (B17981) PM image 225838

p. 55 – © Foto Marburg/Art Resource, NY

p. 56 – after figure 1 in Suter, C. E. 2014. Human, Divine or Both? The Uruk Vase and the Problem of Ambiguity in Early Mesopotamian Visual Arts. In *Critical Approaches to Ancient Near Eastern Art*, ed. Marian Feldman and Brian Brown. Berlin: Walter de Gruyter, pp. 545–568. Redrawn by Ardeth Anderson.

p. 56 – photo by Naomi Miller

p. 57 - Ur-Namma Stele (B16676) PM image 8881. Photo adapted by Matt Todd.

p. 59 - © RMN-Grand Palais/Art Resource, NY

p. 61 - stamp seal (37-16-357) PM image 295477

p. 62 - round stamp (36-6-306) PM image 296468

p. 63 - cylinder seal (B16727) PM images 296096 [seal] and 296097 [impression]

p. 64 - cylinder seal (B16747) PM images 296100 [seal] and 296102 [impression]

p. 65 - © The Trustees of the British Museum (Object no. BM 89110)

p. 65 - © The Trustees of the British Museum (Object no. BM 89767)

p. 65 - cylinder seal (B15592) PM image 29905

p. 66 - seal (33-35-293) PM image 296593

p. 67 - cylinder seal (31-17-16) PM images 296005 [seal] and 296006 [impression]

p. 72 - amulet (B16685) PM image 295815

p. 73 - choker (30-12-706) PM image 152138

p. 74 - ostrich egg shell (B16692) PM image 295553

p. 75 - alabaster statuette (37-15-31) PM image 296626

p. 77 - © The Trustees of the British Museum (Object no. BM 89767)

p. 77 - tablet (B10673) PM image 296500

p. 80 - tablet (B8383) PM image 296774

p. 81 - vase (B9305+B9601) PM image 296424

p. 82 - tablet fragment (B14220) PM image 225841

p. 83 - © The Trustees of the British Museum (Object no. BM 114308)

p. 86 - clay tablet (B4561) PM image 296346

p. 87 - plaque (32-22-3) PM image 295787

p. 89 - diorite head (B16664) PM image 225832

p. 91 - copper statue (31-17-8) PM images 295661 [front] and 295662 [back]

p. 93 - stele fragment (B16676.14) PM image 152349

p. 94 - after plate 10 of Canby, J. V. 2001. *The "Ur-Nammu" Stela.* Philadelphia: University of Pennsylvania Museum of Archaeology and Anthropology. Adapted by Matt Todd.

p. 95 - Ur-Namma stele (B16676) PM image 297004

p. 95 - drawn by HSD/John Pearson

p. 97 - brick (B16461) PM image 234258A

p. 99 - large tablet (B13972) PM image 296512

p. 101 - gold mouflon head ornament (33-22-177) PM image 295676

p. 103 - map courtesy of Haley Sharpe Design (HSD) and adapted by Matt Todd

p. 105 - © Ninara (flickr)/Kaisu Raasakka

P. 107 - © The Trustees of the British Museum (Object no. BM 89137)

p. 108 - plaque (B15606) PM image 225826

p. 109 - clay tablet (29-13-209) PM image 296433

p. 110 - © The Trustees of the British Museum (Object no. BM 89763)

p. 110 - plaque (B15192) PM image 299910

p. 111 - raw lapis (B17102) PM image 299906

p. 112 - string of carnelian and lapis beads (30-12-627) PM image 299907

p. 113 - map courtesy of Haley Sharpe Design (HSD) and adapted by Matt Todd

p. 114 - necklace (B16799) PM image 296526

p. 114 - mace head (B14933) PM image 234252A

p. 115 - necklace B16794 PM image 295746

p. 116 - buff pottery (L-2018-3-3 and L-2018-3-4 on loan from the Louvre) PM images 295958 and 295959

p. 117 - grey ware pottery (33-21-853, 32-41-32, and 32-41-12) PM images 295862, 295788, and 295843

p. 119 - pouring vessels (33-15-722 and 32-41-31) PM images 296443 and 296251

p. 120 - horned animal head (33-22-177) PM image 295676

p. 121 - copper slag (33-22-343) PM image 297029

p. 122 - spearhead (33-22-107) PM image 296450

p. 122 - copper animal figures (33-15-586 and 33-22-136) PM images 299911 and 299912)

p. 123 - alabaster objects (33-15-720, 33-22-186, 33-22-70, and 33-15-512) PM images 296264, 299909, 296275, and 299908

p. 126 - chlorite vessel (30-12-81) PM image 251011

p. 126 - chlorite vessels (B17168 and B16226) PM images 152198 and 234247A

p. 127 - Maikop shroud (30-33-1) PM image 295988 [detail]

p. 129 - ceramic rider on horseback (B15473) PM image 250784

p. 132 - incense burner (32-20-413) PM image 296864

p. 133 - gold bracelet (53-31-6) PM image 295588

p. 134 - silver rhyton (53-31-1) PM image 152845

p. 135 - gold leaf (53-31-2A) PM image 295722

p. 136 - courtesy of the Oriental Institute of the University of Chicago

p. 137 - crouching lion (31-40-1) PM image 150838

p. 138 - "stone spirit" (92-4-1) PM image 296754

p. 139 - tablet (B3446) PM image 296767

p. 140 - tablet map (B10434) PM image 296780

p. 142 - map courtesy of Haley Sharpe Design (HSD) and adapted by Ardeth Anderson after Lauren Ristvet

p. 143 - Nuzi ware (32-20-400) PM image 299913

p. 143 - Kassite glass bottle (31-43-231) PM image 296707

p. 144 - after figure 1 from Drews, Robert. 1993. *The End of the Bronze Age: Changes in Warfare and the Catastrophe ca. 1200 BC*. Princeton: Princeton University Press. Redrawn by Ardeth Anderson.

p. 145 - cheekpiece depicting horses (30-38-11) PM image 184894

p. 146 - horse gear collar (73-5-555) PM image 150232

p. 147 - sword (66-22-36) PM image 296942

p. 148 - disc wand (41-21-5) PM image 296907

p. 150 - bronze axe head (43-29-1) PM image 295488

p. 150 - pendant (43-29-55) PM image 295492

p. 151 - gold inlay (30-33-1) PM image 295988

p. 153 - kylix (30-33-130) PM image 173759

p. 154 - golden panther (30-33-2a) PM image 173617

p. 155 - brick (B16458) PM image 296806

p. 157 - PM image 6005

p. 159 and p. 160 - brick (84-26-14) PM image 296753

p. 161 - PM image 191884

p. 163 - PM image 190915

p. 164 - after a map from the Penn Museum Archives (PM image 181205). Redrawn by Ardeth Anderson.

p. 165 - PM image 190211

p. 166 - PM image 150421

p. 167 - Enheduanna disk (B16665) PM image 295918

p. 168 - Enannatumma statue (B16229) PM image 291638

p. 168 - Enannatumma brick (B16543A) PM image 296808

p. 169 - plaque (L-29-300) PM image 296828. Loaned by the Philadelphia Museum of Art.

p. 171 - courtesy of the British Museum

p. 172 - PM image 181204

p. 174 - PM image 149979. Adapted by Matt Todd.

p. 175 - cylinder seal (31-17-19) PM images 296007 [seal] and 296009 [impression]

p. 176 - courtesy of the British Museum

p. 176 - plaque (31-43-577) PM image 149013

p. 177 - PM image 191813

p. 178 - awl (B17463) PM image 297002

p. 179 - seal (31-43-75) PM images 296017 [seal] and 296018 [impression]

p. 180 - monkey (B15724) PM image 295523

p. 181 - standardized weight (B17101) PM image 295969

p. 182 - duck weight (B6210) PM image 295965

p. 182 - pieces of silver (38-10-82) PM image 295923

p. 183 - weight (B12468) PM image 296503

p. 185 - tablet (B6043) PM image 150616

p. 186 - tablet (B14156) PM image 296509

p. 188 - tablet (B7866) PM image 296657

p. 188 - tablet (B7051) PM image 150212

p. 188 - tablet (B7847+29-15-472) PM image 150016

p. 189 - plaque (31-43-577) PM image 149013 [detail]

p. 192 - foundation cylinder (L-652-1) PM image 299914. Loaned by Frederick and Ronald Clark.

p. 193 - PM image 191813

p. 195 - Penn Museum (gallery shot)

p. 197 - after a plan from the Penn Museum Archives (PM image 149989). Redrawn by Ardeth Anderson.

p. 200 - PM images 151271, 151275, and 151273

p. 201 - PM image 191208

p. 203 - PM image 191606

p. 205 - bull's head and shell plaque (B17694A and B17694B) PM image 250852

p. 206 - shell plaque (B17694A) PM image 295565

p. 207 - "Ram in the Thicket" (30-12-702) PM image 250851

p. 208 - PM image 191216

p. 208 - © bpk Bildagentur/Vorderasiatisches Museum, Staatliche Museen, Berlin, Germany/Olaf M. Tessmer/Art Resource, NY

p. 211 - © Illustrated London News Ltd/Mary Evans

p. 212 - reconstruction by William B. Hafford

p. 213 - PM image 297042

p. 214 - PM image 191051

p. 214 - © Illustrated London News Ltd/Mary Evans

p. 216 - © PENN ORSA (Open Research Scan Archive)

p. 217 and p. 218 - cylinder seal (30-12-2) PM images 295992 [seal] and 295994 [impression]

p. 220 - PM image 299823

p. 220 - drawn by HSD/John Pearson

p. 221 - drawn by HSD/John Pearson

p. 222 - PM image 191960

p. 223 - after a plan from the Penn Museum Archives (PM image 149980). Redrawn by Ardeth Anderson.

p. 225 - helmet (29-22-2) PM image 234272

p. 227 - PM image 141592

p. 228 - PM image 191259

p. 228 - necklace and gold diadem (30-12-567 and 30-12-600) PM images 295642 and 295648

p. 229 - cylinder seal (30-12-38) PM images 296001 [seal] and 296002 [impression]

p. 230 - PM image 190956

p. 230 - courtesy of the British Museum PM image 192327

p. 234 - box lid, dish, and tweezers (B16744A, B16710, and B16714) PM images 296521, 295820, and 295822

p. 235 - map courtesy of Haley Sharpe Design (HSD) and adapted by Matt Todd

p. 237 - after Kimberly Leaman Insua's 2009 plan on p. xxviii of de Schauensee, Maude. 2011. *Peoples and Crafts in Period IVB at Hasanlu, Iran.* University of Pennsylvania Museum of Archaeology and Anthropology (Philadelphia). Redrawn by Ardeth Anderson.

p. 238 - arrowheads (73-5-90) PM image 299915

p. 239 - PM image 301112

p. 241 - spouted bowl and tripod stand (60-20-71A and 60-20-71B) PM images 296919 and 296738

p. 242 - PM image 302229

p. 244 - iron sword (30-38-18) PM image 295834

p. 244 - saw (63-5-172) PM image 295507

p. 245 - inlaid eyes (65-31-339 and 61-5-205) PM images 296336 and 296334

p. 245 - wooden throne foot (65-31-611) PM image 299916

p. 245 - garment pin (56-20-1) PM image 295889

p. 246 - beads (65-31-728) PM image 296940

p. 247 - ivory lion (65-31-353) PM image 296427

p. 247 - glass goblet (65-31-403) PM image 296939

p. 248 - PM image 139776

p. 248 - cast copper stand (59-4-116) PM image 296735

Right

Human figurine (32-41-68) from Tureng.

Left

Bearded bull pendant (B16726) from Puabi's tomb, PG 800.

Wirth, Eugen. 1971. *Syrien: eine geographische Landeskunde. Wissenschaftliche Buchgesellschaft*. Redrawn by Ardeth Anderson.

p. 317 - pages of Qur'an (E16249H) PM image 249545

p. 318 - deed (E16653) PM image 250020

p. 319 - scene (NEP33) PM image 226234 [detail]

p. 320 - page (NEP33) PM image 226234 [whole page]

p. 322 - Qur'an (NEP27) PM image 239144

p. 324 - manuscript (NEP33) PM image 226459

p. 325 - after Kennedy, H. 2002. An Historical Atlas of Islam. Leiden: Brill.

p. 326 - drachma (33-62-13) PM images 299921 [obverse] and 299922 [reverse]

p. 327 - after figure 11.6 from Rante, R. 2015. *Rayy from Its Origins to the Mongol Invasion: An Archaeological and Historiographical Study*. Leiden: Brill. Adapted by HSD.

p. 328 - courtesy of the Oriental Institute of the University of Chicago

p. 329 - © Wikimedia Commons/Samuel Bailey

p. 330 - courtesy of the Oriental Institute of the University of Chicago

p. 332 - courtesy of the Oriental Institute of the University of Chicago

p. 333 - Philadelphia Museum of Art, Acquired by exchange with the University Museum, 1940, Object Number: 1940-51-1. 11.11a: The partial inscription in Arabic ('amara) reading: "he ordered," is set into a tile-like design, and gives the beginning of a well-known formula that recorded the patron/commissioner of a building. Datable to the 12th to early 13th century CE. [PMA 1940-51-1_RG 8135] 11.11b: The cut glazed tile shaped the letter 'ha' ending a noun in Arabic as part of an inscription of blessings and good wishes. Datable to the 12th to early 13th century CE. [PMA 1940-51-1_RCH1728-4] 11.11c: The inscription in squared Arabic (Kufic) script on a blue-colored background would have been part of the formula of blessings and good wishes typically found on public buildings. Datable to the 11th to 12th century CE. [PMA 1940-51-1_RGQ8637]

p. 334 - grave marker (35-8-302) PM image 299923

p. 334 - University of Michigan Museum of Art, Museum Purchase, 1965/1.167

p. 335 - courtesy of the Oriental Institute of the University of Chicago

p. 336 - courtesy of the Oriental Institute of the University of Chicago

p. 337 - stoneware albarello (37-33-1) PM image 297033

p. 337 - ostrakon (37-33-22) PM image 297036

p. 338 - courtesy of the Oriental Institute of the University of Chicago

p. 339 - courtesy of the Oriental Institute of the University of Chicago

p. 340 - courtesy of the Oriental Institute of the University of Chicago

p. 341 - detail from a 1974 cadastral map of Isfahan produced by the Iranian Cartographic Center

p. 342 - plan by C. Breede courtesy of the Isfahan City Study Project, co-directed by R. Holod, 1974–1976

p. 343 - photo courtesy of Renata Holod

p. 344 - The Avenue of the Four Gardens ("Khiyaban-I Chahar Bagh"), Isfahan, as depicted in Cornelis Le Bruyn *Travels into Muscovy, Persia, and the Eastern Indies*, London, 1737.

p. 345 - lusterware bowl (NEP79) PM images 299924 [top view] and 299925 [bottom view]

p. 346 - lusterware plate (NEP19) PM image 296534

p. 346 - lusterware vase (NEP115) PM image 296854

p. 348 - textile front (NEP6) PM image 151018

p. 348 - textile back (NEP6) PM image 299926

p. 349 - diagram courtesy of Martina Ferrari

p. 353 - Penn Museum (gallery shot)

p. 355 - photos courtesy of: (a) The Metropolitan Museum of Art (Image no. sf1981-473r; Object no. 1981.473); (b) GettyImages / Bloomberg; (c) National Archives (identifier: 1667751); and (d) PM image 297043 [detail].

p. 357 - © R. Kennedy for VISIT PHILADEPHIA®

p. 361 - replica stele of Hammurabi (B1999) PM image 297043

p. 362 - © Wikimedia Commons/Tla2006

p. 363 - © Wikimedia Commons/Beyond My Ken

p. 364 - sewer pipe (B2292A) PM images 296343 and 296344

p. 364 - canal map (B13885) PM image 150398

p. 365 - gaming dice (B16972B) PM image 295529

p. 365 - lamp (37-11-997) PM image 296295

p. 367 - bowl (33-15-800) PM image 295945

p. 369 - Penn Museum (gallery shot)

p. 372 - Penn Museum (gallery shot)

p. 373 - PM image 139049

p. 375 - PM image 192290

p. 378 - PM image 19194

p. 379 - PM image 49024

p. 381 - PM image 141571

p. 382 - PM image 191953

p. 383 - PM image 44945

p. 384 - PM image 299808

p. 385 - PM image 101285A

p. 390 - PM image 85206

p. 392 - PM image 299820

p. 394 - PM image 67897

p. 395 - ceramic vessel (35-8-7) PM image 295693

p. 398 - lion plaque (53-11-95) PM image 296324

p. 400 - stamp seal (38-10-118) PM image 296050

p. 401 - human figurine (32-41-25) PM image 295845

p. 403 - priest statue (37-15-28) PM image 251022

p. 404 - wall tile (37-11-152) PM image 295582

p. 405 - grey ware pot (32-41-32) PM image 295788

p. 408 - human figurine (32-41-68) PM image 295852

p. 409 - pendant (B16726) PM image 251035

p. 410 - animal figurine (33-15-523) PM image 296255

back cover - plaque of boy with pipe (L-29-301 on loan from the Philadelphia Museum of Art) PM image 296685, portrait tile (NEP20) PM image 297013, string of gold and carnelian beads (30-12-562) PM image 295639, and mosaic panel (NEP58) PM image 255700

Right

Animal figurine (33-15-523) from Tepe Hissar.